Fitness *for* Living

third edition

Bill Hyman, Ph.D.
Sam Houston State University

Gary Oden, Ph.D.
Sam Houston State University

David Bacharach, Ph.D.
St. Cloud State University

Tim Sebesta, M.A.
Cy-Fair College

KENDALL/HUNT PUBLISHING COMPANY
4050 Westmark Drive Dubuque, Iowa 52002

Cover photo courtesy of Digital Stock.
Title page photos © Jupiter Images Corporation.

Copyright © 1999, 2000, 2006 by Kendall/Hunt Publishing Company

ISBN 13: 978-0-7575-3046-3
ISBN 10: 0-7575-3046-X

Printed in the United States of America
10 9 8 7 6 5 4 3 2 1

Contents

Chapter 11

HIV/AIDS and Sexually Transmitted Diseases   215

Chapter 12

Your Personal Program   225

Preface

The young adult years are a critical time of transition for many people as long-term relationships are being formed, career choices are being considered, and adult lifestyles are being developed. As a college student, you are faced with expectations and opportunities like never before, and the choices you make are some of the most important of your life. *Fitness for Living, Third Edition,* is designed to assist and encourage you to make lifestyle choices regarding fitness and wellness that can provide lasting benefits. You will be introduced to the latest research that clearly points to the lifelong benefits of healthy dietary habits, regular physical activity, maintenance of healthy weight, disease risk reduction, and stress management.

The topics covered in *Fitness for Living, Third Edition,* are designed to educate you on the topics of health promotion and disease prevention. Like the first edition, key terms and specific objectives are included for each chapter, helping you to understand the most important concepts. However, this new edition contains additional self-assessments designed to help identify your personal strengths and weaknesses and to formulate plans for healthy choices. A personal health profile and behavior change plan included in chapter one challenges you to take the opportunity to make this course the one in which you get on the lifelong path to better health. Also, additional charts display new norms allowing you to compare your performance to peers, and to more clearly indicate health parameters needing improvement. Finally, we hope the information is presented in a way that will motivate you to take self-responsibility and personal action accordingly. This is a course designed strictly for you, so we challenge you to take it seriously.

Sincere gratitude is extended to the staff of Kendall/Hunt Publishing Company for their encouragement and support in the development of this book.

Bill Hyman
Gary Oden
David Bacharach
Tim Sebesta

© 2006 JUPITER IMAGES CORPORATION.

1 The Importance of Fitness and Wellness

Key Terms

diseases of lifestyle
physical fitness
motor fitness
physical wellness
cardiorespiratory endurance
muscular strength
muscular endurance
flexibility

body composition
resting pulse
maximum oxygen
   consumption
blood pressure
cholesterol
caloric intake
caloric expenditure

Specific Objectives

1. List the pathological and behavioral causes of death of Americans.

2. Explain the concept of "diseases of lifestyle" and the four determinants of health.

3. Name the major benefits of physical fitness.

4. Define and contrast physical fitness and total wellness.

5. List and describe the five components of physical fitness.

6. Differentiate between physical fitness for health and motor fitness.

7. Identify positive and negative personal health behaviors and formulate a personal plan for health enhancement.

HEALTH STATUS OF AMERICANS

Lester Breslow once stated, "It's what you do hour by hour, day by day, that largely determines the state of your health; whether you get sick, what you get sick with, and perhaps when you die." The causes of death in America tend to remain the same from year to year, and most are highly preventable. Chronic diseases caused by unhealthy behavior dominate the causes of death in the United States (see Figure 1.1). Every year, chronic diseases cause over 1.6 million deaths, claiming almost seven of every ten lives lost. In fact, almost two-thirds of the deaths in the U.S. each year are caused by only five diseases: heart disease, cancer, stroke, chronic respiratory disease, and diabetes (Health, United States, 2005). In contrast, the leading causes of death in the United States 100 years ago were quite different. In 1900, the leading cause of death in the U.S. was pneumonia and influenza, followed by tuberculosis, then diarrhea (Box 1.1). The average life expectancy was only 47.3 years (National Center for Health Statistics, 2000). Many people did not live long enough for the effects of chronic diseases like heart disease and cancer to take their toll on health. Today, with an average life expectancy of 77.3 years, the chronic lifestyle diseases dominate the health charts (Health, United States, 2005).

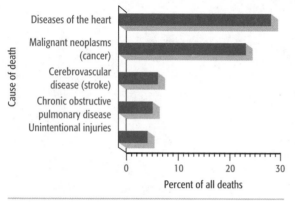

Figure 1.1 ☉ *Leading causes of death in the United States in 2003.*

Although our national health statistics reveal the leading patho-physiological causes of death, it is important to note that the underlying contributors to these deaths are often controllable lifestyle factors. Heart disease, cancer, and stroke, as well as other chronic diseases, are almost exclusively caused by smoking and other tobacco use, poor diet and physical inactivity (and accompanying obesity), alcohol consumption, and other poor lifestyle choices (see Figure 1.2). Most Americans die from what are referred to as diseases of lifestyle.

Health compromising behaviors are abundant in our society, and either directly or indirectly, we all pay the price for poor health. These behaviors and their consequential diseases result in the premature loss of family and friends, mental and emotional burdens that accompany illness, physical pain and suffering, lifelong disabilities, and tremendous stresses on the economy as a result of the high cost of health care. Health care spending in the U.S. reached an all-time high of 1.7 trillion

Box 1.1

Leading Causes of Death in the United States in 1900

1. Pneumonia and influenza
2. Tuberculosis
3. Diarrhea, enteritis, and ulceration of the intestines
4. Disease of the heart
5. Intracranial lesions of vascular origin

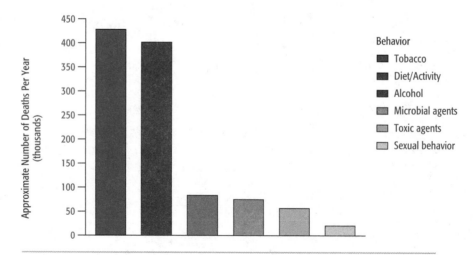

Figure 1.2 ☉ *Leading behavioral causes of death.*

dollars in 2003, representing over 15 percent of the Gross Domestic Product. From 2002 to 2003, total national health expenditures increased by 7.7 percent—4 times the rate of inflation (National Coalition on Health Care, 2004). But the most tragic realization is that many of these costly diseases are preventable. The self-exploration opportunities provided throughout this text are designed to create a greater awareness about prevention. Knowledge about nutrition, physical fitness, stress management, disease risk reduction, and risk assessments provide opportunities for you to set goals and develop strategies for change. The first opportunity for self-assessment provides an overview of personal health behaviors, and is found in Laboratory 1.1. Laboratory 1.2 then offers a guide for establishing a personal behavior change plan to begin your journey toward a healthier lifestyle.

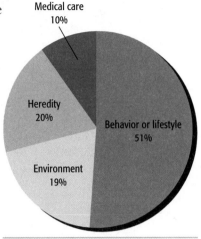

Figure 1.3 ⊙ *The four determinants of health status.*

INDIVIDUAL CONTROL

While some uncontrollable life events will undoubtedly occur, most of what happens to us is the result of factors within our control. There are four major factors which determine an individual's health at any given time. Those factors, shown in Figure 1.3, are lifestyle, heredity, our environment, and health care services. Note that the number one determinant is one's behavior or lifestyle, accounting for over half of health status. The remaining three determinants combined do not match the impact of our behaviors. Clearly, those individuals who do not believe that their actions will make any difference in their health status have misdirected their quest for well-being. They attempt to blame or rely on other people, the medical care system, their environment, and even their parents for their health status. Individuals should recognize personal control over their well-being, and take active and deliberate action toward a higher quality of life.

The extent to which an individual believes they have control over their own health status is known as their Locus of Control. Some believe that their choices and actions are the primary factors that determine health outcomes, while others believe that what they do has little effect on their health status. The belief that one controls their own destiny, including their health status, through their own personal actions is known as an Internal Locus of Control. People with this view are much more likely to develop a personal plan of action to attain high level wellness. An External Locus of Control is the belief that factors outside of one's control determine health status. Those factors include powerful others like doctors, hospitals, the government, the health care system, friends and family members, and even chance, luck, and fate. Individuals with an External Locus of Control, since they do not believe that their actions make a difference, are less likely to take personal actions that can lead to good health.

Another important factor that should be considered when determining our ability and willingness to take positive actions toward good health is our degree of self-efficacy. Self-efficacy is the belief in one's capabilities to organize and execute the course of action required to manage prospective

situations (Bandura, 1995). It influences the choices we make, the effort we put forth, and how long we persist when we confront obstacles. In relation to health pursuits, a high degree of self-efficacy will serve as a motivating factor. When one feels capable of making a health behavior change or maintaining good health habits, the likelihood of implementing and continuing healthy lifestyles is enhanced.

BENEFITS OF PHYSICAL FITNESS

As volumes of research continue to pour in about the benefits of healthy lifestyles, perhaps none is more significant and to the point than the Surgeon General's Report on Physical Activity and Health (Appendix A). The scientific data cited in this historic report point toward physical fitness as the most powerful factor in general well-being. Regular physical activity improves health in the following ways:

⊙ Reduces the risk of dying prematurely
⊙ Reduces the risk of dying from heart disease
⊙ Reduces the risk of developing diabetes
⊙ Reduces the risk of developing high blood pressure
⊙ Helps reduce blood pressure in people who already have high blood pressure
⊙ Reduces the risk of developing colon cancer
⊙ Reduces feelings of depression and anxiety
⊙ Helps control weight
⊙ Helps build and maintain healthy bones, muscles, and joints
⊙ Helps older adults become stronger and better able to move without falling
⊙ Promotes psychological well-being

The report also targets physical inactivity as a primary contributor to the degenerative diseases of hypertension, obesity, cancer, diabetes, and osteoporosis, all of which are discussed in this text.

TOTAL WELLNESS

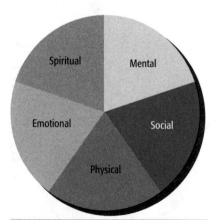

Total wellness encompasses more than physical fitness. In fact, it is quite possible for an individual to possess a high level of physical fitness, yet experience low levels of health in other areas of life. Total wellness includes the spiritual, social, mental, and emotional domains as well as the physical. It is readily acknowledged that problems in one area often have a negative impact in other areas. Therefore, individuals should strive to maintain balance in all areas. Figure 1.4 shows the need for overall balance.

Figure 1.4 ⊙ *Components of wellness.*

PHYSICAL FITNESS FOR HEALTH

The physical component of wellness is highly instrumental in determining one's overall health status. Physical wellness means that the organ systems of the human body (primarily the heart and lungs and their systems as well as muscles and bones) are disease free and capable of functioning at a high level of efficiency. This enables a person to engage in daily tasks and participate in leisure activities at an enthusiastic and vigorous level, thereby deriving more pleasure from life. Health-related physical fitness involves the development and maintenance of five primary components. They are:

© 2006 JUPITER IMAGES CORPORATION.

1. **Cardiorespiratory Endurance.** This important component of physical fitness is also known by other names, including aerobic capacity, aerobic fitness, cardiovascular fitness, and stamina. It is the ability of the heart, circulatory system, lungs, and respiratory system to transport and deliver blood and oxygen to the cells of the body, primarily the working muscles. As muscles are provided with oxygenated blood, they are capable of working more efficiently and sustaining work and activity for longer periods of time. This should be the primary goal of any fitness program, since it provides significant protection against certain chronic diseases, specifically heart disease. Another desirable effect of cardiorespiratory endurance training is that it provides residual benefits for improving the remaining four components of fitness.

2. **Body Composition.** The percentage of a person's total body weight that is made up of adipose (fat) tissue as opposed to lean body tissue is known as their body composition. Disease risk is closely related to body composition. Lean individuals carry lower risk for a number of diseases than those who carry excess fat.

3. **Flexibility.** Defined as the capacity of a joint to move through a full range of motion, this component of fitness provides freedom of movement that enables a person to stretch, bend, twist, and perform other physical tasks with a minimal risk of injury to the muscles and connective tissues.

4. **Muscular Endurance.** This term refers to the ability of a muscle or muscle group to sustain the exertion of force over a period of time without fatiguing. Certain daily living tasks and a number of recreational endeavors demand that work be continued for a sustained time period. Muscular endurance allows effective participation in these activities.

5. **Muscular Strength.** This is the ability of a muscle or muscle group to exert a maximum force against a resistance. While similar to muscular endurance, muscular strength involves a one-time exertion as opposed to sustained muscular activity. Applying heavy force or lifting heavy objects demands muscular strength.

MOTOR FITNESS

Motor fitness, as opposed to health fitness, refers to skill-related components, and is linked more to physical performance than health and wellness. While it does not directly improve a person's health status, it can indirectly enhance physical fitness. These components include:

1. **Balance.** The ability to maintain equilibrium while static (stationary) or dynamic (moving) is important in recreational endeavors, but it is also an important characteristic for health maintenance for certain populations, such as the elderly, who are at greater risk of falling.

2. **Agility.** This is the ability to change direction while moving and is influenced by body coordination and quickness. It is beneficial in many sports activities.

3. **Coordination.** This neuromuscular skill of using the senses and multiple body movements in unison is fundamental to daily functioning, as well as sports and other physical activity performance. The synchronization of hand-eye movement in racquet sports is an example of coordination.

4. **Quickness.** Also known as reaction time, quickness is the ability to produce a rapid and efficient response to a stimulus. Reacting promptly to hit a moving object such as a baseball or a tennis ball are examples of quickness.

5. **Speed.** The time required to move from one location to another reflects a person's capacity for speed, and is probably the greatest skill-related asset for most sports endeavors. Speed may also refer to the performance of a rapid movement, such as generating bat speed while swinging at a ball.

6. **Power.** This is the combination of strength and speed, and is a primary skill-related component in many sports.

Most of the components of motor fitness are largely inherited, while the components of physical fitness are generally attainable by most individuals. However, participation in activities requiring motor fitness can work toward the development of physical fitness. Performance in sports and recreational activities is a great motivator to be active. After all, who doesn't like performing well in a competition or setting personal performance goals and attaining them? Motor fitness skills certainly have a place in the pursuit of wellness. Nevertheless, optimal physical fitness can be developed by anyone simply by focusing on the health-related components discussed earlier, and ultimately the pursuit of health holds greater benefits than the pursuit of athletic performance.

FITNESS EDUCATION AND ASSESSMENT

A number of positive changes occur to the human body as a result of physical activity. Despite the benefits described earlier, most Americans still do not engage in enough exercise to produce good health. Sadly, only about 23 percent of adults exercise sufficiently to experience those results (Healthy People–2010). Hopefully, you will take control of your own health by adopting a lifestyle that includes beneficial activity. The chapters of this text will describe the benefits of various activities, identify proper performance guidelines, provide assessment opportunities to determine your current level of fitness, and help you set goals. It is an opportunity for self-discovery and self-improvement. Important indicators of health status which may be assessed include:

1. **Resting Pulse.** A low resting pulse rate is a valid indicator of cardiac output, the product of heart rate and stroke volume (amount of blood pumped per beat). Generally, the lower the resting heart rate, the greater the level of cardiovascular fitness.

2. **Body Composition.** A healthy body fat percentage helps protect against back pain, heart disease, stroke, Type 2 diabetes, and several other diseases and disorders. A good percentage of body fat is approximately 15 percent for men and 23 percent for women. While some variation is acceptable, a body fat percentage of 25 or above for men and 33 or above for women is too high for good health (Nieman, 2003).

3. **Maximum Oxygen Consumption.** This measurement reflects the fitness level of the cardiovascular and respiratory systems. A good score reflects an energy level that can add greatly to a person's quality of life. Measured in milliliters of oxygen per kilogram of body weight per minute, an oxygen consumption level of about 43 ml/kg/min for young men and about 36 ml/kg/min for young women would place a person in the upper 50th percentile, and is a worthy goal.

4. **Blood Pressure.** Proper blood pressure reduces wear and tear on the heart, correlating with longevity and reducing the chances for cardiovascular disease. The standard maximum normal blood pressure is 140/90, and the ideal is near 120/80.

5. **Cholesterol.** An excessive amount of this natural waxy substance in the blood is linked to heart and circulatory diseases. The level that indicates increased risk is 180 milligrams per deciliter of blood in young adults, and 200 milligrams per deciliter of blood in older individuals. Additionally, a ratio of good cholesterol, known as HDL, to total cholesterol of at least one to four and one-half is desirable for heart health.

6. **Flexibility and Abdominal Strength.** High scores on strength and flexibility lower the chances of low-back pain and other joint ailments.

7. **Risk for Cancer, Diabetes, and Osteoporosis.** Internal and external factors contribute to the incidence of these three diseases, and risk assessments found in the text present the opportunity to identify and modify factors which increase one's chances of disease.

8. **Caloric Intake and Expenditure.** Appropriate nutritional balance of carbohydrates, fat, and protein is an important measure of health, and an aerobic expenditure of approximately 1000–2000 calories per week promotes proficient cardiorespiratory endurance and increased longevity (McArdle, Katch, and Katch, 2001). The high carbohydrate, low fat diet provides numerous health benefits, and Chapter 6 provides opportunity to identify dietary deficiencies.

9. **Stress Status.** The stressful impact of life events, the value of your social support connections, and even the impact of your outlook and personality will be assessed to help you understand and identify common stressors and the way they impact health. Coping and control strategies are offered.

TAKING ACTION

The following "Personal Health Profile" will help identify any behaviors that are causing your health to be compromised. Complete the profile and calculate your total health score. Hopefully, the results will affirm the positive things you do and help you establish goals to enhance your health status. The "Personal Behavior Change Plan" provides a framework for making those adjustments.

References

Bandura, A. ed. (1995). *Self-efficacy in changing societies.* New York: Cambridge University Press.

Breslow, Lester. Vision and reality in state health care: Medi-Cal and other public programs, 1946–1975: An interview conducted by Gabrielle Morris in 1984. Berkeley, Calif.: Regional Oral History Office, Brancroft Library, University of California, Government History Documentation Project, Ronald Reagan Gubernatorial Era, 1985.

Centers for Disease Control and Prevention. (2005). *The burden of chronic diseases as causes of death, United States: National and state perspectives, 2004.* www.cdc.gov/nccdphhhhp/burdenbook2004/Section01/tables

Centers for Disease Control and Prevention. (2004). *Leading causes of death, 1900–1998.* www.cdc.gov/nchs/statab/lead1900_1998.pdf

Centers for Disease Control and Prevention. (1999). *Physical Activity and Health: A Report of the Surgeon General.* Washington, D.C.: U.S. Government Printing Office.

McArdle, W.D., Katch, F.I., & Katch, V.L. (2001). *Exercise physiology: Energy, nutrition, and human performance, 5th edition.* Baltimore: Lippincott, Williams, and Wilkins.

Mokdad, A.H., Marks, J.S., Stroup, D.F., & Gergerding, J.L. (2004). Actual causes of death in the United States, 2000. *Journal of the American Medical Association,* 291 (10).

National Center for Health Statistics. (2000). *Health, United States, 2005.* Hyattsville, MD: U.S. Government Printing Office.

Nieman, D.C. (2003). *Exercise testing and prescription: A health-related approach. 5th edition.* New York: McGraw-Hill.

chapter 1
LABORATORY (1)

Personal Health Profile

Think about your overall health status and specific health behaviors and respond to each item below:

	Column A *Yes*	Column B *No*
1. Engage in vigorous exercise (running, swimming, brisk walking, aerobics, a related activity) for 20–30 minutes 3 to 5 days per week.	_____	_____
2. Perform resistance exercises to strengthen my bones and muscles.	_____	_____
3. Always warm-up and cool-down before and after exercise.	_____	_____
4. Get 7–8 hours of sleep each night.	_____	_____
5. Know the warning signs for cancer, heart attack, and stroke.	_____	_____
6. See my doctor regularly for checkups.	_____	_____
7. Know the appropriate self-examinations and perform them regularly.	_____	_____
8. Body weight is within the recommended healthy range.	_____	_____
9. Consistently choose low-fat, high fiber foods.	_____	_____
10. Consume salt and sugar in moderation.	_____	_____
11. Eat lots of fruits and vegetables.	_____	_____
12. Have never used tobacco.	_____	_____
13. Socialize with close friends weekly.	_____	_____
14. Always wear my seatbelt.	_____	_____
15. Drive carefully, within the speed limit, and take no unnecessary risks while driving.	_____	_____
16. Abstain from alcohol or drink lightly (no more than 1 drink per day for women, no more than 2 drinks per day for men).	_____	_____
17. Never drink and drive or ride with a driver who has been drinking.	_____	_____
18. Have several stress management and coping strategies that I use successfully.	_____	_____
19. Know my blood pressure and it is within the desirable range.	_____	_____
20. Know my cholesterol level and it is within the desirable range.	_____	_____
21. Have good study habits.	_____	_____
22. Have several leisure time activities which I enjoy.	_____	_____

	Column A	**Column B**
	No	*Yes*

23. Get tired easily. _____ _____

24. Get very little or no exercise. _____ _____

25. Eat out often. _____ _____

26. Diet consists of lots of high-fat, high cholesterol foods. _____ _____

27. Smoke cigarettes. _____ _____

28. Use other forms of tobacco. _____ _____

29. Waste time watching television, sleeping too much, or being idle. _____ _____

30. Drink to intoxication. _____ _____

31. Life is highly stressful. _____ _____

32. Frequently feel overwhelmed with too many tasks and expectations. _____ _____

33. Don't eat breakfast or skip other meals regularly. _____ _____

34. Do not limit the time that I am exposed to the sun and rarely wear sunscreen. _____ _____

Add up every check mark made in column A and multiply by 3. Determine your relative risk by identifying your health behavior score in one of the categories below:

Your Score	**Grade**	**Comment**
90–100	A	Overall excellent health practices. Few risky behaviors. Nice work.
80–89	B	Good health behaviors. Where could improvements be made?
70–79	C	OK in most areas, but can definitely improve in others.
60–69	D	Need some help in reducing health risks.
Below 60	F	Have few healthy behaviors. Immediate action is needed.

chapter 1
LABORATORY ②

Personal Behavior Change Plan

Using the Personal Health Profile, identify at least one area of health behavior that you would like to change. Take a couple of days to consider where you would like to be with that health behavior at the end of the semester. Use the Behavior Change Plan below to generate a strategy for reaching your healthy goal by the end of the course.

1. What is the primary identifiable health behavior that I want to change?

2. When I make this behavior change, I will enjoy the following benefits:

3. What could happen if I do not make this behavior change?

4. The specific date that I am committed to change by is

   _____ .

5. The support system that I will notify about my goal and enlist help in attaining it includes:

6. Three possible steps that I must take in order to make this change are:

   Step I—

   Step II—

   Step III—

7. People, places, and situations that I must avoid to make this change are:

8. Role models or people who might positively influence me through this endeavor are:

9. I will know that I am working successfully toward my behavior change when:

10. The signs that I need to regroup and develop an alternative strategy are:

11. When my behavior change is accomplished, I will enjoy the following rewards:
    Internal rewards—

    External rewards—

12. I, _____ , commit to work toward
    completing the above behavior change by _____ ,
    and I will acknowledge success when _____ .

_____   _____
Signature   Signature of witness

_____   _____
Date   Date

Behavior Change Follow Up

(to be completed on target change date)

I did/did not attain my goal for changing to a healthier behavior.

The reasons I did/did not attain my goal were:

From this behavior change experience, I learned that:

2 Cardiorespiratory Endurance

Key Terms

cardiorespiratory endurance
stroke volume
cardiac output
metabolism
adenosine triphosphate
aerobic activity

maximal oxygen
    consumption
target heart rate
maximal heart rate
cross training

Specific Objectives

1. Explain why fitness experts view cardiorespiratory endurance as the most important component of physical fitness.

2. List the important functions of the cardiorespiratory system.

3. Describe the function of the heart, blood vessels and lungs in oxygen transport.

4. Explain the relationship of heart rate, stroke volume, cardiac output and oxygen consumption.

5. Identify the three energy systems involved in metabolism and the production of adenosine triphosphate (ATP) for muscle action.

6. Distinguish between anaerobic and aerobic activity.

7. Define maximal oxygen consumption.

8. List and explain at least five major benefits of cardiorespiratory endurance.

9. Explain acute and chronic changes that take place in the circulatory, respiratory, and muscular systems as a result of aerobic activity.

10. Identify the components of an exercise prescription and subsequent energy use.

11. Describe in detail at least three methods used to assess cardiorespiratory endurance.

12. Design a personal program for developing and maintaining a healthy level of cardiorespiratory endurance.

OVERVIEW

If we were to rank the chapter topics in this book in order of importance, cardio-respiratory endurance would be at the top of the list. Moreover, cardiorespiratory endurance receives universal recognition among fitness experts as the primary component of physical fitness, attaining a superior status to strength, muscular endurance, flexibility and body composition. The beauty of cardiorespiratory endurance is its contribution to greater development or improvement in the other four components. That claim can only be made for the cardiorespiratory endurance component.

Commonly used interchangeably with such terms as aerobic capacity, aerobic fitness, cardiovascular endurance and stamina, the cardiorespiratory endurance term more accurately describes what is essentially our energy output, the physical parameter that potentially enhances our quality of life more than any other. Furthermore, a proficient cardiorespiratory system promotes an increased lifespan. For these reasons alone, it is easy to understand why many people think of aerobic fitness as synonymous with physical fitness.

FUNCTION OF THE CARDIORESPIRATORY SYSTEM

Cardiorespiratory endurance is the ability to extract oxygen from the air, which we breath, and supply this oxygen to working muscles in order to sustain body movement over an extended period of time. As the definition implies, two vital organs necessary for survival are involved: the heart and lungs. The cardiorespiratory system combines the cardiovascular and the respiratory systems into one functional unit. While the respiratory system provides a means of exchanging oxygen and carbon dioxide via the lungs, the cardiovascular system pumps oxygen-rich blood to the body's active tissues and returns waste products of normal metabolic function to be exchanged again in the lungs.

Function of the Cardiorespiratory System in Oxygen Transport

This system of transport has four components: the heart, blood vessels, blood and the lungs (Figure 2.1). The heart works as a pump with the right side of the heart pumping deoxygenated blood to the lungs and the left side of the heart pumping oxygen rich blood to the entire body. The latter function demands more attention with respect to health and fitness. Blood vessels include the arteries, veins and capillaries. Arteries take fuel-rich blood away from the heart, delivering oxygen and other nutrients to the tissues via the capillaries (small vessels). The capillaries in turn connect to veins that transport waste from the tissues back to the heart and ultimately the lungs for elimination.

REGULATION OF THE CARDIORESPIRATORY SYSTEM

Under normal resting conditions for the average adult, the heart pumps about five liters of blood each minute through the cardiorespiratory system. The amount of blood pumped out of the heart per minute is called cardiac output. Cardiac output is the product of heart rate and stroke volume. Heart rate is simply the number of times the heart beats per minute while stroke volume is the amount of blood pumped out of the heart each beat.

$$\text{Cardiac Output} = \text{Heart Rate} \times \text{Stroke Volume}$$

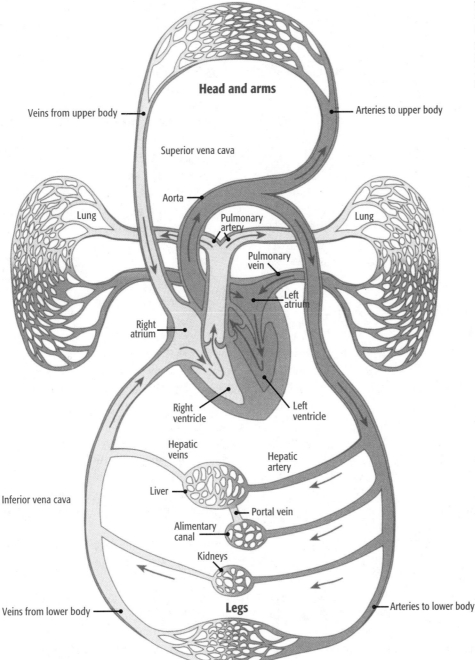

Figure 2.1 ⊙
Cardiorespiratory system.

From *Essentials of Exercise Physiology* by McArdle, Katch and Katch. Copyright © 1994 by Williams & Wilkins. Reprinted by permission.

During exercise, cardiac output can be increased by speeding up the heart rate or by increasing the stoke volume. Stroke volume increases along with heart rate up to about 40 percent of maximum heart rate (about 100 beats/minute) (Figure 2.2). At maximal levels, the heart pumps 20–25 liters of blood per minute. That represents a four- to five-fold increase from resting conditions. With aerobic training, the heart becomes more efficient by increasing stroke volume. In this case, cardiac output increases even though the heart rate is reduced.

Increased Stroke Volume × Decreased Heart Rate = Cardiac Output

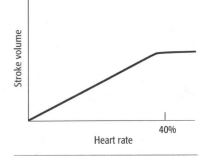

Figure 2.2 ⊙ *Relationship of stroke volume to heart rate.*

From *Fitness for Life* by Prentice, W. et al. Copyright © 1995. Reprinted by permission of The McGraw-Hill Companies.

Maximal cardiac output is also influenced by age. After approximately 20 years of age, maximal heart rate declines. The standard formula for estimating maximal heart rate is as follows:

$$\text{Maximal Heart Rate} = 220 - \text{age (year)}$$

Using this formula, the average college-age student (20 years) has a maximal heart rate of 200 beats/minute, and a 50-year-old professor has a maximal heart rate of 170 beats/minute.

Pressure inside the blood vessels is what moves blood through the system. When the heart contracts, arterial blood pressure reaches its highest level (systolic pressure). Blood pressure declines slightly when the heart relaxes between beats (diastolic pressure). This change in pressure can be felt as a pulse. Resting blood pressure varies among individuals; however, a systolic pressure above 140 mmHg and/or a diastolic pressure above 90 mmHg are the borderline pressures for hypertension (high blood pressure).

ENERGY SYSTEMS

All living organisms must perform several functions to remain alive. Each cellular function is dependent upon energy. The process by which we break down and build up our bodies is called metabolism. The single most important energy molecule for metabolism is adenosine triphosphate (ATP). As outlined in Table 2.1, there are three main sources or means to generate ATP: the ATP-PC system or phoscreatine, a very fast way to access ATP, but is very limited in capacity (one-six seconds); the anaerobic system, also fast, but still limited in capacity (ten seconds-three minutes); and the relatively slow aerobic system, which is unlimited in ATP capacity (more than three minutes).

In most physical activities, a combination of anaerobic and aerobic energy production occurs. A person's maximal level of energy production is often translated from a measurement of maximal oxygen consumption (VO_2 max). This is the body's ability to transport and use oxygen while removing carbon dioxide. As one increases the workload of a task, more oxygen is consumed. The fairly linear relationship of workload to oxygen consumption remains consistent until a person reaches a maximal level of oxygen consumption. Thus, maximal oxygen consumption represents the physiological limit or full capacity of one's cardiorespiratory system for transporting and utilizing oxygen. This maximal value can be measured with precision in a laboratory setting or easily estimated via field tests involving standards of workload and time.

TABLE 2.1	Energy Systems for Generating ATP		
	Energy System	*Duration*	*Activity*
	ATP-PC system	1–10 seconds	Sprint, jump, throw, etc.
	Anaerobic System	10 seconds–3 minutes	Medium sprint, hockey, baseball, softball, etc.
	Aerobic System	> 3 minutes	Distance runs, walking, cycling, swimming, etc.

PHYSIOLOGICAL BENEFITS OF CARDIORESPIRATORY ENDURANCE

The physiological benefits of cardiorespiratory endurance are innumerable; however, here are a few major ones to consider.

1. **Greater cardiac output.** Remember that cardiac output is the product of heart rate and stroke volume. During a strenuous effort, a person possessing good cardiorespiratory endurance is able to deliver far greater quantities of blood to the tissues than an individual who exhibits subpar conditioning of the cardiorespiratory system.

2. **Longevity.** Research by Paffenbarger (1986, 1978) was the first to confirm the link between cardiorespiratory proficiency and greater life expectancy. Nearly 17,000 Harvard alumni were investigated to determine the effects of physical activity on longevity. Individuals expending 2,000 or more calories during exercise per week, as opposed to the rates of less active participants, extended their life expectancy by more than two years.

3. **Improved maximum oxygen consumption.** By increasing the ability to deliver and process oxygen, an individual enhances his/her capacity to produce more ATP, the universal energy source. It is interesting to note that the world record for maximum oxygen consumption is in the mid-90s for an adult male and high-70s for an adult female, about double the current capacity of the average American college male and female, respectively, suggesting that most adults demonstrate significant room for improvement.

4. **Lowered blood pressure (if high prior to chronic exercise).** Both diastolic (pressure between heartbeats) and systolic (pressure during heartbeat) pressure tend to go down in hypertensive individuals when they engage in long-term aerobic activity. The end result is less strain on the heart.

5. **Reduced body fat content.** Vigorous activity causes a greater hypertrophy in the working muscle groups, plus long bouts of submaximal exercise promote the type of calorie burning that is conducive to reducing body fat percentage. A body fat standard that promotes good health in male adults is about 20 percent or less, and roughly 25 percent or less for female adults.

6. **Increased metabolism.** The body simulates a finely tuned engine when the rate of calorie expenditure is high. While it is common knowledge that even two or three hours of weekly aerobic exercise necessitates huge calorie expenditures, it is uncommonly known that the metabolic rate remains elevated for several hours during each recovery period. Since the average person's metabolism slows a few percentage points every decade of life, this particular cardiorespiratory endurance benefit helps combat the tendency to gain weight as one gets older.

7. **Increased HDL cholesterol and lowered LDL cholesterol levels.** The cholesterol level, measured as the number of milligrams per deciliter (100 milliliters) of blood, includes HDL and LDL types. The HDL, sometimes labeled "good" cholesterol, is coupled with the LDL or "bad" cholesterol to derive a total cholesterol reading. Staying aerobically active is a factor in a person's ability to keep the total cholesterol amount under 200, considered the red flag figure because diseases and other ailments stemming from circulatory problems tend to escalate for persons surpassing the 200 figure.

Persons possessing greater cardiorespiratory endurance levels also benefit from higher amounts of "good" cholesterol in their blood. The LDL amount, the cholesterol culprit in the bloodstream, is lowered by aerobic exercise, resulting in a healthy ratio for the two types of cholesterol. The proper ratio is kept in check by the HDL's ability to extract portions of the LDL via the liver.

8. **Less bone mineral loss.** Strengthened by cardiorespiratory endurance activity at any age, the bones better retain their capacity to make the body more functional and mobile. Females receive particular benefit in this area as their calcium intake is insufficient to provide adequate protection for the bones. In other words, a lifetime of participation in aerobic activities significantly retards the onset of debilities such as osteoporosis.

9. **Curbing of appetite.** This is a powerful benefit that is hard for some people to believe. Obviously, as greater energy is expended in aerobic activities, the exerciser requires larger amounts of food to compensate for the extra caloric expenditure. However, aerobically active people, when compared to inactive persons of comparable weight, tend to eat proportionally less than their counterparts.

COLLECTIVE RESULT OF PARTICIPATION IN AEROBIC ACTIVITY

Each time a person exercises, the body adapts to the stress of the activity. Some of the adaptations are acute (short-lived) while others are chronic (long-term). Acute changes include an increase in metabolism (energy consumption) as well as increased cardiac output, systolic blood pressure and ventilation to match the demands of the activity. Working muscles also enlarge because an increased amount of blood is flowing to them. Blood is therefore shunted away from the internal organs, resulting in the slowing of digestion and/or absorption. Each of these adaptations is quick to return to pre-exercise levels after the activity ends.

Chronic adaptations, on the other hand, do not return to pre-exercise levels. Such chronic changes include increased metabolism primarily due to an increase in lean body mass, lowered resting heart rate, increased stroke volume, increased aerobic activity at the cellular level (enzyme activity, mitochondrial density, lipid or fat fuel utilization), increased capillarization of muscle tissue, and improved oxygen utilization. How long do these adaptations last? Chronic changes last as long as the body feels a need to meet the exercise stress that is used to produce the adaptations. For example, a person exercises for ten weeks and achieves a 30 percent improvement in his/her aerobic capacity. Then the person stops exercising. In only five weeks the body will lose the aerobic adaptations it took ten weeks to develop. And, the body will revert back to its starting point in all areas within another five weeks. What does this really mean? Simply but impressionistic, it means that a person wanting to possess a strong aerobic capacity must engage in some form of aerobic activity over the entire lifespan to maintain the benefits derived from the training.

COMPONENTS OF AEROBIC EXERCISE PRESCRIPTION

An exercise prescription is much like any medical prescription. There are things to consider before beginning an activity program. Current evidence suggests that cardiorespiratory endurance can be improved and maintained with as little as an accumulation of 30 minutes of physical activity per day.

Mode

This term identifies the type of exercise being performed. The key here is that the activity should involve large muscles of the body in a slow rhythmical fashion and preferably be weight-bearing in nature. There are several factors to consider when selecting a mode of exercise. First and foremost, it must be enjoyable. A second important element is convenience. If the activity requires too much preparation or is lacking in accessibility, then chances of sticking to the activity are reduced. A third very important factor is the risk of injury. Common sense should prevail. If you are an injury-prone individual, choose low-impact, low-intensity activities until you have a solid foundation of activity without injury. If you rarely get injured, feel free to try higher impact activities. Using a variety of activities (cross training) with a mixture of low and high impact and intensity can be a good way of keeping your exercise program interesting and fun. Remember that mode of activity is only one part of a well-rounded exercise prescription.

Frequency

Frequency of activity is a second aspect of an exercise prescription. Current epidemiological research suggests that a person can simply accumulate 30 minutes of physical activity each day and reduce his/her risk of cardiovascular disease. The American College of Sports Medicine endorses the concept of cumulative activity, as well as the general claim that engagement in aerobic activity three–five times per week produces gains in cardiorespiratory fitness. Do not be misled by the old misconception that if a little activity is good, more must be better. Maximum benefits from aerobic activity can be attained by using a frequency of five days per week without substantially increasing risk of injury. Six or seven days per week is excessive because the body has little time to recover, and overuse injuries are virtually guaranteed. One can see from Figure 2.3 that the risk of injury increases dramatically in individuals whose exercise regimen exceeds five days weekly. Also, little or no additional aerobic benefits are acquired by adding the sixth or seventh day.

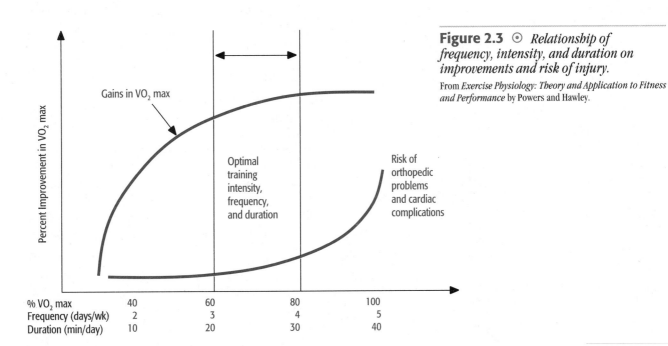

Figure 2.3 ⊙ *Relationship of frequency, intensity, and duration on improvements and risk of injury.*

From *Exercise Physiology: Theory and Application to Fitness and Performance* by Powers and Hawley.

Taking the rest heart rate.

CORBIS

Intensity

Intensity is another important component of a good exercise prescription. Improvement in cardiorespiratory endurance occurs when intensity is about equal to or greater than 50 percent of one's maximal aerobic capacity. Since oxygen consumption is closely related to changes in heart rate during activity, it is quite simple to estimate exercise intensity by monitoring heart rate. However, there is about a 10–15 percent difference between oxygen consumption and heart rate at a given submaximal effort. If a 50 percent intensity for oxygen consumption is required, a training heart rate level should then be about 60–65 percent of maximum heart rate. Optimal range for improving cardiorespiratory endurance is 50–85 percent of oxygen consumption. That relates to a heart rate range of 60–95 percent of maximal heart rate. By knowing how to calculate maximal heart rate, you can quickly find the heart rate training zone for appropriate intensity. For example, a 20-year-old person has a maximal heart rate of 200 beats/minute (maximal heart rate = 220 – age). At 60 percent, the low end of the training heart rate range is 120 beats/minute, and at the 95 percent end, training heart rate is 190 beats/minute. As you can see, this is a wide range and explains why most experts suggest intensities between 70–90 percent maximal heart rate. Intensity is also related to frequency and duration. The greater the frequency or the longer the duration, the lower the intensity can be. For athletes, the greater improvements in cardiorespiratory endurance come with high intensities, between 80 and 90 percent of maximal heart rate. This would suggest that as a person becomes more fit, intensity must increase to continue gains in cardiorespiratory endurance. For most college age individuals an intensity between 70 and 90 percent of maximal heart rate is a good rule of thumb; however, keep in mind that activity of lower intensity still has cardiorespiratory benefits.

A second method to determine the heart rate training zone or target heart rate (THR), is to use the Karvonen formula. The Karvonen formula calculates the training heart rate using a percentage of the heart rate reserve, which is the difference between the maximum heart rate and the resting heart rate. The Karvonen formula is as follows:

$$THR = [(MHR - RHR) \times I] + RHR$$

THR = target or training heart rate
MHR = maximum heart rate
RHR = resting heart rate
I = intensity (60 to 90 percent)

In order to use Karvonen a person will need to know their resting heart rate. Resting heart rate can be measured during rest by counting the heart rate at either the radial or carotid artery. Using Karvonen, a 20-year-old person with a resting heart rate of 70, who wished to exercise at an intensity of 65 percent, would have a training heart rate of 148.

$$THR = [(200 - 70)60\%] + 70$$
$$THR = 148$$

Perceived Exertion

A subjective method for measuring exercise intensity is called perceived exertion. Following the scale in Table 2.2, the exerciser estimates his/her level of exertion (RPE) when asked by a tester in a laboratory situation. The subjective rating becomes more objective once an individual learns to exercise at an RPE level that corresponds well to the aforementioned objective measures of exercise intensity.

Each number on the Borg scale (Table 2.2) multiplied by ten approximates heart rate. For example, number 19 on the scale is close to a maximum heart rate. Ratings from "fairly light" to "hard" constitute an appropriate heart rate training zone.

Duration

Duration at a training intensity should be between 20–60 minutes. As stated before, accumulation of 30 minutes of activity daily produces an adequate level of cardiorespiratory endurance and is a significant factor in reducing the chance of cardiovascular disease. Duration is best determined by two factors: individual goals for cardiorespiratory improvement; and, amount of exercise time available in a daily schedule. Generally speaking, you must exercise for longer durations to achieve higher levels of cardiorespiratory endurance. However, remember our earlier discussion that aerobic energy expenditure beyond 2,000 calories weekly yields minimal additional cardiorespiratory gains while increasing the risk of overuse injuries. We know from all the wonderful benefits the body derives from participation in aerobic activity that nature clearly intends for it to be part of a universal health prescription. The second part of nature's prescription is that moderate intensity and duration suffice for the development and maintenance of proper cardiorespiratory health.

TABLE 2.2	
Rating of Perceived Exertion	
Scale	*Verbal Rating*
6	
7	Very, very light
8	
9	Very light
10	
11	Fairly light
12	
13	Somewhat hard
14	
15	Hard
16	
17	Very hard
18	
19	Very, very hard
20	

From *Med Sci Sports Exercise*, 15:523–528, 1983.

MEDICAL CLEARANCE

Perhaps the most important decision you must make before engaging in activity is whether or not it is safe to do so. Research is conclusive that aerobic activity is safe for the majority of people. To insure safe entry into an aerobic activity, use the Physical Activity Readiness Questionnaire (PAR-Q) found in Appendix B as a screening tool. Endorsed by the American College of Sports Medicine, the PAR-Q is a useful method for clearing people for participation in exercise programs. One "yes" answer on the questionnaire is all that it takes to warrant medical clearance before proceeding to engage in activity. As a precaution, people over 45 years of age should receive medical clearance regardless of the responses to the questionnaire. We all must remember that for a small number of people, physical activity can be inappropriate.

DESIGNING YOUR OWN PROGRAM

Both specific short- and long-term goals should be addressed when initiating an exercise program. Other issues include concerns for safety, warm-up, type of activity, cool-down, progression, and possible cross-training options.

Safety

Common sense should prevail when questions arise concerning exercise. Proper attire is important. If you plan to walk or run, pay close attention to your shoes. Quality shoes can circumvent many unpleasant injuries of the feet, ankles and leg muscles. You probably should spend a little extra on a pair of shoes. Wear them around in the store for at least 10–15 minutes. It is worth the extra time to help you determine if they are truly a good fit. Common sense must also supersede your desire to exercise when you are not feeling well. A day off with rest may allow you to return to your regimen both sooner and stronger. Furthermore, the occurrence of pain during activity is a clear sign that something is wrong. Address that pain immediately. Where is it coming from? What could be the cause? Try to answer these questions before you continue with your activity. The old adage of "no pain, no gain" is totally inappropriate, and you need to make sure that your activity program is directed toward reducing health problems instead of creating them.

Warm-up

Every workout should begin with a short warm-up which prepares the body for the upcoming stress of activity. Blood is shunted away from internal organs and delivered to the muscles. Muscles are contracted and stretched, causing an increase in their metabolic activity, plus sensory input from joints are activated. A good warm-up might include a few minutes of walking, stretching and light calisthenics. During the warm-up session, impulses are sent to the brain, helping to prepare a person psychologically for exercise. Thus, warm-up has both a physiological and psychological influence on the exerciser.

Activity

To improve cardiorespiratory endurance, one must use large muscles of the body. Typically, this means the hips and legs. Components of activity previously described should be addressed, but remember that any activity that involves a large muscle mass can be used to benefit your endurance. Choose activities that are enjoyable and vary the activity (cross-training) from time to time to prevent boredom. Variety in exercise may be the "spice" you need to maintain an activity program for life.

Cool-down

After any vigorous activity, you should always try to slow things down gradually. Five minutes of slow walking, light movements, or stretching of the muscles just used aids in the prevention of muscle cramps and even cardiac arrhythmia (abnormal heartbeat) in some extreme cases. Once your body has reached a steady state during exercise, it takes a few minutes for it to return to pre-exercise conditions. Without a proper cool-down, blood tends to pool in the working muscles (the legs in most instances) and slows your rate of recovery. Some type of mild movement enhances recovery and makes the exercise experience more enjoyable.

Progression

There is no set pattern of exercise progression for everyone, but some general guidelines should be followed to help you increase your aerobic capacity to a de-

Guidelines for Continuous Training				TABLE 2.3
Training Level	Frequency (Sessions per Week)	Duration (Minutes)	Intensity of Exercise (% of VO$_2$ max or HRR)	
Beginner	3	20	40%–50%	
Intermediate	4–5	30–45	50%–75%	
Advanced	5–6	45–60	75%–85%	

From *Fitness for Life* by Prentice, W. et al. Copyright © 1997. Reprinted by permission of The McGraw-Hill Companies.

sired level. Table 2.3 outlines a progression for an aerobic activity program based on initial levels of fitness. As this information indicates, progression is modified first by frequency, next by duration, and finally by intensity. This is a good rule of thumb for individuals interested in planning a personal progression.

ASSESSING CARDIORESPIRATORY ENDURANCE

The best measurement of cardiorespiratory fitness is the direct measurement of oxygen consumption (VO$_2$) during maximal exercise. The exercise is performed using either a treadmill or a stationary bicycle. The amount of oxygen consumed during the exercise test is measured using a computerized metabolic cart. Maximal oxygen consumption (VO$_2$ max) is the highest rate at which oxygen can be consumed during this test and is our best measurement of cardiorespiratory fitness. The higher a persons VO$_2$ max, the higher their cardiorespiratory fitness level. Other, non laboratory or field tests have been developed for testing large groups of individuals. These tests are practical, inexpensive, less time-consuming, and easier to administer than laboratory tests. At the end of this chapter are three field

Equivalent Performances for Various Distances					TABLE 2.4
VO$_2$ max (ml.kg$_{-1}$.min$_{-1}$)	Performance Time for Various Distances (hours:minutes:seconds)				
	1.5 km	1 mile	5 km	10 km	42.2 km
28	13:30	14:46	56:49	2:39:14	31:41:25
31.5	11:27	12:29	47:04	2:02:00	16:35:05
35	9:56	10:49	40:10	1:38:53	11:13:52
38.5	8:46	9:33	35:02	1:23:08	8:29:26
42	7:51	8:33	31:04	1:11:43	6:49:30
45.5	7:07	7:44	27:54	1:03:03	5:42:21
49	6:30	7:03	25:20	0:56:15	4:54:07
52.5	5:59	6:29	23:11	0:50:47	4:17:48
56	5:32	6:01	21:23	0:46:17	3:49:28
59.5	5:09	5:36	19:50	0:42:30	3:26:44
63	4:50	5:14	18:30	0:39:33	3:08:06
66.5	4:32	4:55	17:20	0:36:33	2:52:34
70	4:17	4:38	16:18	0:34:10	2:39:23
73.5	4:03	4:23	15:23	0:32:12	2:28:05
77	3:50	4:09	14:34	0:30:12	2:18:16
80.5	3:39	3:57	13:50	0:28:33	2:09:41
84	3:29	3:46	13:10	0:27:04	2:02:06
87.5	3:20	3:36	12:34	0:25:44	1:55:21

From *J Sports Med* 27:401–409, 1987.

TABLE 2.5

Norms for the 1.5-Mile Run Test
(for People between the Ages of 17 and 35)

Fitness Category	Time: Ages 17–25	Time: Ages 26–35
Superior		
Males	< 8:30	< 9:30
Females	< 10:30	< 11:30
Excellent		
Males	8:30–9:29	9:30–10:29
Females	10:30–11:49	11:30–12:49
Good		
Males	9:30–10:29	10:30–11:29
Females	11:50–13:09	12:50–14:09
Moderate		
Males	10:30–11:29	11:30–12:29
Females	13:10–14:29	14:10–15:29
Fair		
Males	11:30–12:29	12:30–13:29
Females	14:30–15:49	15:30–16:49
Poor		
Males	> 12:20	> 13:29
Females	> 15:49	>16:49

Note: Before taking this running test, it is highly recommended that the student or individual be "moderately fit." Sedentary people should first start an exercise program and slowly build up to 20 minutes of running, 3 days per week, before taking this test.

From JOPERD by DO Draper and GL Jones, American Alliance for Health, Physical Education, Recreation and Dance.

tests for assessing cardiorespiratory endurance. These tests are intended to provide meaningful estimates for students interested in their level of cardiorespiratory fitness. When completing one of these tests, do your best so the results will give you an accurate picture of your current level of cardiorespiratory condition.

SUMMARY

1. Cardiorespiratory endurance is the ability to supply oxygen to working muscles for extended periods of body movement.

2. Fitness experts recognize cardiorespiratory endurance as the primary component of physical fitness because its improvement enhances energy output, promotes longer life, and positively influences the development of strength, muscular endurance, flexibility and body composition.

3. The heart, blood vessels, blood and the lungs enable oxygen transport in the body.

4. Blood vessels include the arteries, veins and capillaries.

5. The combination of an increased stroke volume and decreased heart rate improves cardiac output.

6. Maximal heart rate is estimated by subtracting yearly age from 220.

7. A systolic (pressure during heart contraction) blood pressure above 140 mmHg and/or a diastolic (resting blood pressure) pressure above 90 mmHg are the borderline indicators for hypertension or high blood pressure.

8. Adenosine triphosphate (ATP), the universal energy source, is accessed by the systems of ATP-PC (one-six seconds), anaerobic (ten seconds-three minutes), and aerobic (more than three minutes).

9. An exercise prescription includes recommendations for mode, frequency and intensity. Performance in one or a variety of aerobic activities at least 30 minutes daily at moderate intensity is a safe and effective prescription for developing and maintaining a cardiorespiratory endurance level that leads to a long and healthy life. The exerciser benefits from 30 minutes of cumulative aerobic movement as well as continuous.

10. Perceived exertion is a subjective method for measuring exercise intensity.

11. Due to the numerous positive changes the body experiences when cardiorespiratory endurance is improved, it is clear that nature intends for the human body to be active.

12. Warm-up activities enable the body to receive physiological and psychological preparation for movement.

13. Cross-training in aerobic activities allays boredom in the exercise routine.

14. Proper cool-down hastens recovery from strenuous exercise.

References

Allsen, P.E., Harrison, J.M., & Vance, B. (1997). *Fitness for Life: An Individualized Approach* (6th ed.). Madison, WI: Brown & Benchmark Publishers.

Collins, D.R., Hodges, P.B., & Kelly, J.M. (1999). *Practical Aerobic Conditioning* (3rd ed.). Bloomington, IN: Tichenor Publishing.

Corbin, C.B., & Lindsey, R. (1997). *Concepts of Physical Fitness* (9th ed.). Madison, WI: Brown & Benchmark Publishers.

Hoeger, W.K., & Hoeger, S.A. (1997). *Principles and Labs for Fitness and Wellness* (4th ed.). Englewood, CO: Morton Publishing Company.

McArdle, W.D., Katch, F.I., & Katch, V.L. (1994). *Essentials of Exercise Physiology.* Philadelphia: Lea & Febiger.

Paffenbarger, R.S., Jr., et al. (1986). Physical activity, all cause mortality and longevity of college alumni. *New England Journal of Medicine,* 314:606–613.

Paffenbarger, R.S., Jr., et al. (1978). Physical activity as an index of heart attack risk in college alumni. *American Journal of Epidemiology,* 108:161–175.

Plowman, S.A., & Smith, D.L. (1997). *Exercise Physiology for Health, Fitness, and Performance.* Needham Heights, MA: Allyn & Bacon.

Powers, S.K., & Dodd, S.L. (1996). *Total Fitness: Exercise, Nutrition and Wellness.* Needham Heights, MA: Allyn & Bacon.

Prentice, W.E. (1997). *Fitness for College and Life* (5th ed.). St. Louis: Mosby-Year Book, Inc.

chapter 2
LABORATORY (1)

Cooper's 12-Minute Walking/Running Test

Purpose
To determine the level of cardiorespiratory endurance of college students during a 12-minute running or walking activity.

Equipment
1. Measured running course, preferably a track.
2. Stopwatch

Procedure
1. During a 12-minute period the subject attempts to cover as much distance as possible by either running or walking.

Treatment of Data
1. Distance covered should be rounded off to the nearest ⅛ mile.
2. Consult table below. Locate the distance covered for either men or women under the appropriate age classification, and determine the level of fitness.

12-Minute Walking/Running Test Distance (Miles) Covered in 12 Minutes							
		Distance by Age (Years)					
Fitness Category		**13–19**	**20–29**	**30–39**	**40–49**	**50–59**	**60+**
Superior	(males)	>1.87	>1.77	>1.70	>1.66	>1.59	>1.56
	(females)	>1.52	>1.46	>1.40	>1.35	>1.31	>1.19
Excellent	(males)	1.73–1.86	1.65–1.76	1.57–1.69	1.54–1.65	1.45–1.58	1.33–1.55
	(females)	1.44–1.51	1.35–1.45	1.30–1.39	1.25–1.34	1.19–1.30	1.10–1.18
Good	(males)	1.57–1.72	1.50–1.64	1.46–1.56	1.40–1.53	1.31–1.44	1.21–1.32
	(females)	1.30–1.43	1.23–1.34	1.19–1.29	1.12–1.24	1.06–1.18	.99–1.09
Fair	(males)	1.38–1.56	1.32–1.49	1.31–1.45	1.25–1.39	1.17–1.30	1.03–1.20
	(females)	1.19–1.29	1.12–1.22	1.06–1.18	.99–1.11	.94–1.05	.87–.98
Poor	(males)	1.30–1.37	1.22–1.31	1.18–1.30	1.14–1.24	1.03–1.16	.87–1.02
	(females)	1.00–1.18	.96–1.11	.95–1.05	.88–.98	.84–.93	.78–.86
Very Poor	(males)	<1.30	<1.22	<1.18	<1.14	<1.03	<.87
	(females)	<1.0	<.96	<.94	<.88	<.84	<.78

chapter 2
LABORATORY ②

1.0 Mile Walk Test

Purpose
To determine the level of cardiorespiratory endurance of individuals unable to run because of injury or poor fitness. This test is recommended for unconditioned people, men over age 40 and women over age 50. One must merely be able to walk briskly while generating a heart rate (HR) ?120 bpm by the completion of the test.

Equipment
Measured one mile course, preferably a track.
Scale to determine body weight prior to the walk and a stop watch.

Procedures
1. Walk the measured 1.0 mile course as fast as possible.
2. Record your walking time and immediately take your pulse for 10 sec.
3. Multiply your pulse by 6 to obtain your exercise HR (bpm).
4. Convert your time from minutes and seconds to minutes and fractions of minutes by dividing the seconds by 60 (i.e., if walking time is 13:30, then 30 sec. divided by 60 sec. = .5 minutes, yielding a total of 13.5 min.).
5. Use the following formula to estimate your Maximal Oxygen Consumption in relative terms as VO_2 max in ml/kg/min.

VO_2 max = 88.768 − (0.0957 ∞ Wt) + (8.892 ∞ G) − (1.4537 ∞ Tt) − (0.1194 ∞ HR)

Where: Wt = body weight (lbs), G = gender (0 = female, 1 = male), Tt = total time to walk one mile, and HR = heart rate at the end of the test.

6. Then find and circle your level of fitness based on gender and age using the Fitness Chart.

Example:

20 yr old female weighing 150 lbs completes the one mile walk in 13:30 with an ending HR of 144 bpm. The predicted VO_2 max would be: 37.6 ml/kg/min (Average Fitness Level)

Information needed:

Wt = 150 lbs, gender = 0, Tt = 13 min + (30 sec/60 sec) = 13.5 min, HR = 144 bpm.

VO_2 max = 88.768 − (0.0957 ∞ 150) + (8.892 ∞ 0) − (1.4537 ∞ 13.5) − (0.1194 ∞ 144)

= 88.768 − 14.355 + 0 − 19.62 − 17.19

= 37.6 ml/kg/min

Source: "Validation of the Rockport Fitness Walking Test in College Males and Females," by F. A. Dolgener, L. D. Hensley, J. J. Marsh, and J. K. Fjelstul, *Research Quarterly for Exercise and Sport, 65* (1994), 152–158.

Fitness Chart—Women

Age	Low	Fair	Avg.	Good	High
20–29	<24	24–30	31–37	38–48	49+
30–39	<20	20–27	28–33	34–44	45+
40–49	<17	17–23	24–30	31–42	42+
50–59	<15	15–20	21–27	28–37	38+
60–69	<13	13–17	18–23	24–34	35+

Fitness Chart—Men

Age	Low	Fair	Avg.	Good	High
20–29	<25	25–33	34–42	43–52	53+
30–39	<23	23–30	31–38	39–48	49+
40–49	<20	20–26	27–35	36–44	45+
50–59	<18	18–24	25–33	34–42	43+
60–69	<16	16–22	23–30	31–41	41+

chapter 2
LABORATORY ③

1.5 Mile Run Test

Purpose
To determine the level of cardiorespiratory endurance of healthy, well conditioned individuals that have been cleared for exercise. This test is *NOT* recommended for unconditioned people, men over age 40, women over age 50 without proper medical approval, or people with known risk factors of heart disease.

Equipment
Measured running course, preferably a track.
Stop watch.

Procedures
1. Complete a warm-up that includes some walking, light jogging, some stretches and perhaps a few calisthenics.
2. Complete the measured 1.5 mile course as fast as possible.
3. Cool down by jogging/walking slowly for another 4–6 minutes. Do NOT sit or lie down immediately after finishing the test.
4. Consult the Estimated Maximal Oxygen Consumption Table below to find and circle your relative VO_2 max in ml/kg/min. Then find and circle your level of fitness based on gender and age using the Fitness Chart (p. 30).

Time	VO_2	Time	VO_2	Time	VO_2	Time	VO_2	Time	VO_2
6:10	80.0	8:50	59.1	11:30	44.4	14:10	35.5	16:40	29.5
6:20	79.0	9:00	58.1	11:40	43.7	14:20	35.1	16:50	29.1
6:30	77.9	9:10	56.9	11:50	43.2	14:30	34.7	17:00	28.9
6:40	76.7	9:20	55.9	12:00	42.3	14:40	34.3	17:10	28.5
6:50	75.5	9:30	54.7	12:10	41.7	14:50	34.0	17:20	28.3
7:00	74.0	9:40	53.5	12:20	41.0	15:00	33.6	17:30	28.0
7:10	72.6	9:50	52.3	12:30	40.4	15:10	33.1	17:40	27.7
7:20	71.3	10:00	51.1	12:40	39.8	15:20	32.7	17:50	27.4
7:30	69.9	10:10	50.4	12:50	39.2	15:30	32.2	18:00	27.1
7:40	68.3	10:20	49.5	13:00	38.6	15:40	31.8	18:10	26.8
7:50	66.8	10:30	48.6	13:10	38.1	15:50	31.4	18:20	26.6
8:00	65.2	10:40	48.0	13:20	37.8	16:00	30.9	18:30	26.3
8:10	63.9	10:50	47.4	13:30	37.2	16:10	30.5	18:40	26.0
8:20	62.5	11:00	46.0	13:40	36.8	16:20	30.2	18:50	25.7
8:30	61.2	11:10	45.8	13:50	36.3	16:30	29.8	19:00	25.4
8:40	60.2	11:20	45.1	14:00	35.9				

Source: Adapted from "A Means of Assessing Maximal Oxygen Intake," by K. H. Cooper, in *Journal of the American Medical Association*, 203 (1968), 201–204; *Health and Fitness Through Physical Activity,* by M. L. Pollock, J. H. Wilmore and S. M. Fox III (New York: John Wiley & Sons, 1978); and *Training for Sport and Activity,* by J. H. Wilmore and D. L. Costill (Dubuque, IA: Wm C. Brown Publishers, 1988).

3 Body Composition

Key Terms

essential fat
storage fat
lean mass
overfat
overweight
body composition
hydrostatic weighing

skinfold calipers
bioelectrical impedance
    analysis
body mass index
waist-to-hip ratio
ideal body weight

Specific Objectives

1. Differentiate between various types of body fat and their physiological functions.

2. Differentiate between the terms overweight, overfat, and obese.

3. Explain the importance of a desirable ratio of lean to fat body tissue.

4. List the problems which accompany an overweight condition.

5. Describe the various methods available for the assessment of body composition.

6. Understand the relationship of fat distribution to health.

7. Determine your body composition, body mass index, and waist-to-hip ratio.

8. Calculate your ideal body weight.

OVERVIEW

Bodies come in all shapes and sizes, and while no perfect body exists, there does seem to be a point at which certain shapes and sizes of bodies begin to present health risks to their inhabitants. What our bodies are made up of is significant because certain tissues, such as muscles and bones, are highly functional, while fatty tissue beyond a certain level has negative consequences on health and well-being. Americans seem to be carrying with them more and more of this fatty tissue which can compromise health. In fact, the Centers for Disease Control and Prevention (2005) report that nearly two-thirds of adults in the United States are overweight, and 30.5 percent are obese, and that the annual cost of overweight and obesity to our nation is $117 billion.

Relationships between high levels of fat and certain chronic diseases and other unwanted conditions have become more evident over recent years as body weights have increased. For these reasons, the composition of our bodies is a critical issue in the pursuit of overall health.

Body composition refers to the fat versus the non-fat makeup of the human body. Everyone carries a certain amount of adipose, or fat, tissue. This tissue is referred to as fat mass. Everything which is not adipose tissue is referred to as fat-free mass or lean mass. This lean mass includes muscles, bones, blood, organs, and other tissues, or in other words, everything except the fat mass.

Fat mass consists of the fat found just beneath the surface of the skin, called subcutaneous fat, as well as fat distributed in other parts of the body, specifically that surrounding vital organs. About half of the fat in the body is subcutaneous, where it provides cushion and helps regulate body temperature. It is also the fat which sometimes causes dissatisfaction when one looks into the mirror. While some of this fat is necessary, many individuals carry with them considerably more than is needed. The fat which is necessary for good health is called essential fat. The body cannot function normally without a certain amount of fat in the heart, brain, liver, lungs, nerves, and a few other body parts. About three percent of the total weight in men and about twelve percent of the total weight in women is considered essential body fat. It is important for females to have more essential body fat because some of it is sex-specific. This extra essential fat is found primarily in the breasts and the uterus and is attributed to the energy requirements of pregnancy and lactation. Table 3.1 shows the typical body composition of male and female young adults.

TABLE 3.1		
Typical Body Composition of Male and Female Young Adults		
	Men	*Women*
Muscle	45%	36%
Essential fat	3%	12%
Non-essential fat	12%	15%
Bone	15%	12%
Other	25%	25%

Adapted from: Fahey, T.D., Insel, P.M., and Roth, W.T. (1997). *Fit & Well* (2nd ed.). Mountain View, CA: Mayfield Publishing Company, p. 132.

Fat in excess of essential fat is called, as you might guess, non-essential fat. It is also referred to as storage fat. The amount of storage fat varies a great deal from person to person and is determined by factors such as heredity, age, and metabolism, but is primarily influenced by diet and activity level. This variation in the amount of storage fat carried by individuals sometimes results in the potentially dangerous conditions known as overweight, overfat, and obese. While these terms are sometimes used interchangeably, there are distinct differences among them.

OVERFAT VS. OVERWEIGHT

The term overweight takes into consideration only a person's total body weight in relationship to height and frame size. It does not take into account the relationship of fat mass to lean mass. Height-weight charts are used for this assessment, and are sometimes used to determine health status, but they are actually a very poor measure of health because there is so much variation in body makeup from person to person. For example, a very muscular and athletic individual may measure their height, then step on the scales, and, according to a height-weight chart, determine that they need to lose weight. This is probably not the case because the weight comes from the accumulation of muscle tissue, which is very functional and useful, and not detrimental to health. Other persons may step on the scales and determine, again according to a height-weight chart, that their weight is appropriate for their height and receive a false sense of security about their health status, while actually carrying extra body fat which places them at risk. It is very possible to be within a suggested weight range for one's height, yet still be overfat. Since muscle tissue is denser and heavier than fat, these two scenarios are highly possible. A height-weight chart is shown in Table 3.2 for comparison purposes.

The term overfat refers to the actual percentage of body mass made up of adipose tissue. When the percentage of fat reaches a level that compromises health, a person is referred to as overfat. Fatness is a much more meaningful indicator of health status, and cannot be measured with a height-weight chart. As stated earlier, this relationship of fat to lean tissue is called body composition, and there are several assessment tools which can be used to determine this important component of fitness. When the percent of body fat reaches a level that causes the health risks to become critical, the person is obese. Obesity is usually considered as ten percent above the optimal fat percentage. Since the optimal fat percentage for men is 15 percent or less, obesity for men is 25 percent body fat and higher. The optimal fat percentage for women is 22 percent or less, so obesity in women is 32 percent body fat and higher (Neiman, 2003). Table 3.3 shows desirable and undesirable body fat percentages for men and for women.

TABLE 3.2

Metropolitan Height-Weight Tables (In Pounds by Height and Frame in Indoor Clothing, Men—5 lbs, 1-inch Heel; Women—3 lbs, 1-inch Heel)

Men				Women			
Height (inches)	small	medium	large	Height (inches)	small	medium	large
	Frame				Frame		
62	128–134	131–141	138–150	58	102–111	109–121	118–131
63	130–136	133–143	140–153	59	103–113	111–123	120–134
64	132–138	135–145	142–156	60	104–115	113–126	122–137
65	134–140	137–148	144–160	61	106–118	115–129	125–140
66	136–142	139–151	146–164	62	108–121	118–132	128–143
67	138–145	142–154	149–168	63	111–124	121–135	131–147
68	140–148	145–157	152–172	64	114–127	124–138	135–151
69	142–151	148–160	155–176	65	117–130	127–141	137–155
70	144–154	151–163	158–180	66	120–133	130–144	140–159
71	146–157	154–166	161–184	67	123–136	133–147	143–163
72	149–160	157–170	164–188	68	126–139	136–150	146–167
73	152–164	160–174	168–192	69	129–142	139–153	149–170
74	155–168	164–178	172–197	70	132–145	142–156	152–173
75	158–172	167–182	176–202	71	135–148	145–159	155–176
76	162–176	171–187	181–207	72	138–151	148–162	158–179

Source: Metropolitan Life Insurance Company, New York.

| **TABLE 3.3** | **Percent Body Fat Classifications** |

Classification	Male	Female
Unhealthy range	5% and below	8% and below
Acceptable range (lower end)	6–15%	9–23%
Acceptable range (higher end)	16–24%	24–31%
Unhealthy range	25% and above	32% and above

Source: Neiman, D.C. (2003). *Exercise Testing and Prescription: A Health Related Approach* (5th ed.). New York: McGraw Hill.

PROBLEMS WITH OVERWEIGHT AND OBESITY

The health risks of obesity and being overfat are well documented. The National Institutes of Health (2004) includes heart disease, hypertension and stroke, renal disease, gallbladder disease, diabetes mellitus, pulmonary diseases, osteoarthritis and gout, and breast and endometrial cancer, among others, as the health problems associated with obesity. Several of the negative health consequences of obesity are discussed more thoroughly in the chapter on weight control.

Not only does the overfat or obese person compromise their health, but additional problems result. Overfat individuals are likely to have problems sustaining any type of regular exercise, activity, or recreation program. In addition to missing the health benefits of regular recreational pursuits, the overfat person also misses out on the social interaction and pure enjoyment of participation and, in some cases, the enjoyment of competition.

Daily physical demands of a job or physical activities may also create a problem. Jobs which require a great deal of walking or other type of physical movement, which on one hand could be very beneficial for the overfat person, on the other hand might be perceived as exceptionally challenging. Walking a flight of stairs without feeling exhausted or a walking tour of a park, zoo, or other attraction may be a burden for the overfat. Trekking across a college campus may even be difficult for some.

Also, self-image and self-esteem may be low in the overfat person. Being overfat in a society which still places an emphasis on thinness may lead to dissatisfaction with self. Unfortunately, this dissatisfaction may in turn lead to distress or depression, and may be manifested in unhealthy behaviors including eating disorders, as discussed in the chapter on weight control.

ASSESSSING BODY COMPOSITION

The determination of body composition can be a valuable tool in developing an overall plan for good health, and there are several methods available for the measurement of body composition. While some of these measures are more accurate than others, each has certain advantages and is considerably more valuable than the use of total body weight or height-weight charts. Each of the measures described here are considered indirect measures of body composition. Direct measurement would consist of actually dissecting a cadaver, separating the fat and lean tissue, weighing both, and calculating the ratio of lean tissue to fat tissue.

Hydrostatic Weighing

Hydrostatic weighing is considered the most accurate of the indirect methods for the measurement of body composition. This method, also called underwater weighing, is the standard against which other current methods are validated. It involves total submersion of an individual in a specially designed water tank and the use of a scale to measure the person's weight in the water (shown in Figure 3.1).

Muscle tissue has a higher density than water and tends to sink. Fat tissue has a lower density than water and tends to float. Therefore, the heavier the weight of the person in the water, the more muscle and less fat they possess. To perform this measurement accurately, not only does there need to be access to the special tank and scale apparatus, the subject must be quite cooperative as well. Accurate measurements are possible only when the subject can forcefully exhale as much air from the lungs as possible, then sit very still while completely submerged so the technician can gather an accurate reading from the scales. Several trials are required to gain an accurate measure of water weight. This submersion is not an easy task, and can contribute to error in the test. A trained and experienced technician is also a must for accuracy. Finally, measurement of residual air volume is needed to determine how much air the subject leaves in their lungs following the forceful exhalation. When all measures have been made, a computer program uses the factors of dry weight, water weight, water density, and residual volume to determine body density. Since few settings have the technical equipment, trained technicians, and time needed to perform this test, it is

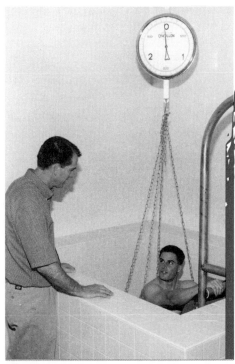

Figure 3.1 ⊙ *Body composition measurement using hydrostatic weighing tank.*

found only in specialized settings. Sports medicine laboratories, university exercise physiology programs, and some medical settings may have this method of measurement available.

Skinfold Measurements

A more practical and widely used approach for measuring fat mass is called the skinfold measure. This assessment uses a special tool called a skinfold caliper to measure the thickness of the layer of fat just beneath the surface of the skin (the subcutaneous fat) at several sites on the body. Knowing that approximately half of the body's fat is subcutaneous fat, and knowing what sites on the body typically hold that fat, researchers have been able to generate equations which predict the percentage of body fat based on these measurements. Skinfold measurements have a very high correlation with hydrostatic weighing, and are considerably more accurate than other measures which utilize only weight, height, or circumference measures of the body.

Calipers are relatively inexpensive and simple to use, but great care must be taken in order to attain accurate results. Calipers should be durable and of good quality, and must be properly calibrated. Inexpensive plastic calipers may at times give accurate results, but are less reliable than metal calipers. Various types of calipers are shown in Figure 3.2. Technicians should be trained in a professional setting, and as with any

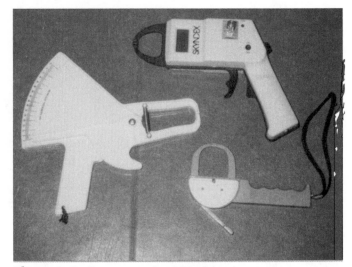

Figure 3.2 ⊙ *Various skinfold calipers.*

laboratory skill, the more experience they have gained, the more capable they will be. Even an experienced technician should take several measures at each recommended site to reduce the error of the test. Location of the skinfold is also important, as a slight deviation in the area of the pinch of skin taken can produce erroneous readings. Less experienced technicians may even prefer to measure and mark the location on the subject's body. Good lab technicians who know how to locate the site, pinch the skin, place the calipers, and measure properly, can attain very accurate results.

Various sites may be used in a skinfold measurement, but the most common test uses three locations on the body. Those locations are the chest, abdomen and thigh for men and the triceps, suprailium and thigh for women (see Figure 3.3). The total of the three skinfolds is then located on the appropriate chart which has been developed using tested prediction equations. That chart can be found along with instructions for a skinfold measurement in Laboratory 3.1.

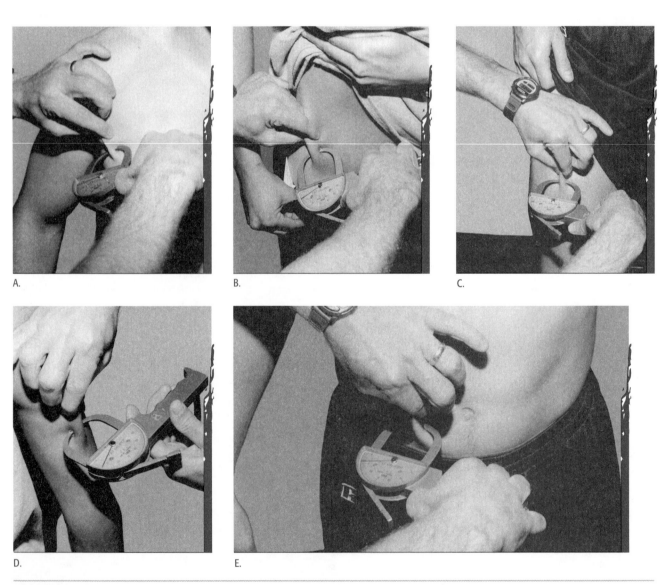

A.

B.

C.

D.

E.

Figure 3.3 ⊙ *Anatomical sites for skinfold measures. A. Chest skinfold, B. Suprailium skinfold, C. Thigh skinfold, D. Tricep skinfold, E. Abdominal skinfold.*

Chapter 3

Bioelectrical Impedance Analysis

Another method for the assessment of body composition is called bioelectrical impedance analysis, or BIA. A specialized piece of equipment is needed to conduct this test. Several different BIA devices are available, but all work on the same principle. For this procedure, small electrodes are positioned to measure an undetectable electrical current as it passes through the body. Since muscle tissue contains a considerable amount of water and fat tissue contains little water, and since water is a good conductor of electricity, the leaner individual will more readily conduct the electrical current. The more fat tissue the person has, the more impedance, or resistance there is to the electrical current.

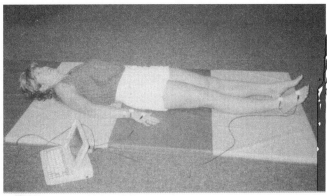

Figure 3.4 ⊙ *Body composition measurement using bioelectrical impedance analysis.*

This technique has the advantages of being portable and non-invasive, plus it takes very little time compared to hydrostatic weighing. The test is also very easy to administer, so the possibility of technician error is greatly reduced. While the accuracy of this method probably needs some further research, it does seem to hold promise as a safe and convenient assessment of body composition. Its major limitation is revealed when used for very lean or obese individuals. It tends to overestimate body fat in very lean individuals and underestimate body fat in the obese (American College of Sports Medicine, 2005).

Other Methods of Measuring Body Composition

The use of air displacement plethysmography (ADP) is gaining popularity as a method for measuring body composition in some settings. It works on a similar principle to underwater weighing, but instead of measuring water displacement, it measures air displacement. The BOD POD is a fiberglass unit designed to measure changes in pressure within the closed chamber of the unit (see Figure 3.5). It measures the subject's mass and volume, and calculates whole body density. From these measures, body composition is determined. This measure is non-invasive and there is little technical expertise needed to attain accurate results. Research studies have validated the accuracy of ADP (Maddalozzo, et al., 2002; Frisard, et al., 2005). The expense of the equipment makes it a method which is not yet widely available.

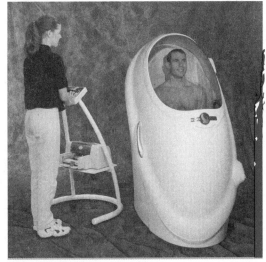

Figure 3.5 ⊙ *The BodPod®—Air Displacement Plethysmography, is another product that measures body composition.*

Photo courtesy of Life Measurement, Inc. Photography by Park Design Group.

The Dual Energy X-Ray Absorptiometry (DEXA) technology is another relatively new method for assessing body composition. It measures body fat, muscle, and bone using x-ray energies. It is considered to be a highly accurate measure of assessing body composition (Maddalozzo, et al., 2002), but again, is a costly procedure, so it is not yet widely available.

Body Mass Index

Another technique useful for measuring body mass, although not specifically a measure of body composition, is called body mass index, or BMI. Like height-weight

TABLE 3.4

Body Mass Index

= Underweight;

= Desirable;

= Increased health risks;

= Obese;

= Extremely obese

From American College of Sports Medicine, 2003, ACSM Fitness Book, 3rd ed., page 81. © 2003 by American College of Sports Medicine. Reprinted with permission of Human Kinetics (Champaign, IL). Based on values published by the Panel on Energy, Obesity and Body Weight Standards, 1987, American Journal of Clinical Nutrition, 15, p. 1035.

12
x5
60
goal ~233 weight.
im 71 inches

Height (in.)	49	51	53	55	57	59	61	63	65	67	69	71	73	75	77	79	81	83
Weight (lb.)																		
66	19	18	16	15	14	13	12	12	11	10	10	9	9	8	8	8	7	7
70	20	19	18	16	15	14	13	13	12	11	10	10	9	9	8	8	8	7
75	22	20	19	17	16	15	14	13	12	12	11	10	10	9	9	9	8	8
79	23	21	20	18	17	16	15	14	13	12	12	11	11	10	9	9	9	8
84	24	22	21	19	18	17	16	15	14	13	12	12	11	11	10	10	9	9
88	26	24	22	20	19	18	17	16	15	14	13	12	12	11	11	10	10	9
92	27	25	23	21	20	19	17	16	15	15	14	13	12	12	11	11	10	10
97	28	26	24	22	21	20	18	17	16	15	14	14	13	12	12	11	10	10
101	29	27	25	23	22	20	19	18	17	16	15	14	13	13	12	12	11	10
106	31	28	26	24	23	21	20	19	18	17	16	15	14	13	13	12	11	11
110	32	30	27	26	24	22	21	20	18	17	16	15	15	14	13	13	11	11
114	33	31	29	27	25	23	22	20	19	18	17	16	15	14	14	13	12	12
119	35	32	30	28	26	24	22	21	20	19	18	17	16	15	14	14	13	12
123	36	33	31	29	27	25	23	22	21	19	18	17	16	16	15	14	13	13
128	37	34	32	30	28	26	24	23	21	20	19	18	17	16	15	15	14	13
132	38	36	33	31	29	27	25	23	22	21	20	19	18	17	16	15	14	14
136	40	37	34	32	29	28	26	24	23	21	20	19	18	17	16	16	15	14
141	41	38	35	33	30	28	27	25	24	22	21	20	19	18	17	16	15	15
145	42	39	36	34	31	29	27	26	24	23	22	20	19	18	17	17	16	15
150	44	40	37	35	32	30	28	27	25	24	22	21	20	19	18	17	16	15
154	45	41	38	36	33	31	29	27	26	24	23	22	20	19	18	18	17	16
158	46	43	40	37	34	32	30	28	26	25	24	22	21	20	19	18	17	16
163	47	44	41	38	35	33	31	29	27	26	24	23	22	20	19	19	18	17
167	49	45	42	39	36	34	32	30	28	26	25	23	22	21	20	19	18	17
172	50	46	43	40	37	35	32	30	29	27	25	24	23	22	21	20	19	18
176	51	47	44	41	38	36	33	31	29	28	26	25	23	22	21	20	19	18
180	52	49	45	42	39	36	34	32	30	28	27	25	24	23	22	21	20	19
185	54	50	46	43	40	37	35	33	31	29	27	26	25	23	22	21	20	19
189	55	51	47	44	41	38	36	34	32	30	28	27	25	24	23	22	20	20
194	56	52	48	45	42	39	37	34	32	30	29	27	26	24	23	22	21	20
198	58	53	49	46	43	40	37	35	33	31	29	28	26	25	24	23	21	20
202	59	54	50	47	44	41	38	36	34	32	30	28	27	25	24	23	22	21
207	60	56	52	48	45	42	39	37	35	33	31	29	27	26	25	24	22	21
211	61	57	53	49	46	43	40	38	35	33	31	30	28	27	25	24	23	22
216	63	58	54	50	47	44	41	38	36	34	32	30	29	27	26	25	23	22
220	64	59	55	51	48	44	42	39	37	35	33	31	29	28	26	25	24	23
224	65	60	56	52	49	45	42	40	37	35	33	31	30	28	27	26	24	23
229	67	62	57	53	49	46	43	41	38	36	34	32	30	29	27	26	25	24
233	68	63	58	54	50	47	44	41	39	37	35	33	31	29	28	27	25	24
238	69	64	59	55	51	48	45	42	40	37	35	33	32	30	28	27	26	24
242	70	65	60	56	52	49	46	43	40	38	36	34	32	30	29	28	26	25
246	72	66	61	57	53	50	47	44	41	39	37	35	33	31	29	28	27	25
251	73	67	63	58	54	51	47	45	42	39	37	35	33	32	30	29	27	26
255	74	69	64	59	55	52	48	45	43	40	38	36	34	32	31	29	28	26
260	76	70	65	60	56	52	49	46	43	41	39	36	34	33	31	30	28	27
264	77	71	66	61	57	53	50	47	44	42	39	37	35	33	32	30	29	27
268	78	72	67	62	58	54	51	48	45	42	40	38	36	34	32	31	29	28
273	79	73	68	63	59	55	52	48	46	43	40	38	36	34	33	31	30	28
277	81	75	69	64	60	56	52	49	46	44	41	39	37	35	33	32	30	29
282	82	76	70	65	61	57	53	50	47	44	42	40	37	35	34	32	30	29
286	83	77	71	66	62	58	54	51	48	45	42	40	38	36	34	33	31	29
290	84	78	72	67	63	59	55	52	48	46	43	41	39	37	35	33	31	30
295	86	79	74	68	64	60	56	52	49	46	44	41	39	37	35	34	32	30
299	87	80	75	69	65	60	57	53	50	47	44	42	40	38	36	34	32	31
304	88	82	76	70	66	61	57	54	51	48	45	43	40	38	36	35	33	31
308	90	83	77	71	67	62	58	55	51	48	46	43	41	39	37	35	33	32
312	91	84	78	72	68	63	59	55	52	49	46	44	41	39	37	36	34	32

charts, BMI uses only the measures of height and weight. However, BMI is superior to the use of a height-weight chart in that it calculates a ratio of weight to height, and then compares this to a desired ratio based on population studies of mortality rates. While the body mass index does not indicate the percent of body fat a person carries, it will project their disease risk based on relative mortality rates from these studies. Research indicates that a high body mass index carries an increased risk of hypertension, high cholesterol, and cardiovascular disease (Anspaugh, Hamrick, and Rosato, 1994). This method has a good correlation with hydrostatic weighing for most people (Revick and Israel, 1986), but like height-weight charts, may be misleading for people with exceptionally high or low amounts of muscle tissue. Heavily muscled individuals may be incorrectly classified into a high disease risk category, while those with little muscle may inaccurately reflect a low disease risk.

Body mass index is determined by dividing body weight (in kilograms) by height in meters squared. Therefore, BMI = wt(kg)/ht (m)^2. Divide body weight in pounds by 2.2 to convert to kilograms. Height in inches can be converted to meters by multiplying by 0.0254. For example, if a person weighs 180 pounds and stands six feet tall, his/her BMI would be calculated as shown:

1-2 pounds a week.

$$weight = 82 \text{ kg } (180/2.2)$$
$$height = 1.83 \text{ meters}$$
$$(72 \text{ inches} \times .0254)$$
$$BMI = 82/1.832^2 = 82/3.35 = 24.47$$

Age and other factors determine the best BMI for an individual, but the American College of Sports Medicine recommends a BMI of 21 to 23 for women and 22 to 24 for men as desirable ranges (ACSM, 2005). Laboratory 3.2 for the determination of BMI is found at the conclusion of this chapter. Table 3.4 provides a simple chart to identify BMI as well as a guide to determine the various categories of disease risk according to the results.

Waist-to-Hip Ratio

In addition to how much body fat a person carries, the location of that fat is an important factor in its effect on health. In fact, some research indicates that waist-to-hip ratio is a stronger predictor of diabetes, coronary artery disease, and overall death risk than body weight, body mass index, or percent body fat (Brownell, 1987; Folsom, 1993). Individuals have a tendency to carry body fat in different locations, with the major difference in location of stored fat being between men and women. Men generally store fat in the upper half of their body, specifically in the abdominal area. This is called the android form of obesity, and has been referred to as the apple-shaped body. Women generally store fat in the lower half of their body, specifically in the hips and thighs. This is called the gynoid form of obesity and has been referred to as the pear-shaped body. A third type of obesity is found in individuals who carry fat in both the upper and lower body, and is known as intermediate obesity. All three forms of obesity can be found in both sexes.

The location of the fat storage is very important from a health perspective. Android obesity, or body fat stored in the upper body and abdominal area, clearly is the type of fat storage which creates the most significant health risk. Individuals with upper body and abdominal fat show higher incidence of diabetes, hypertension, elevated cholesterol, and heart disease than do individuals who store their fat in the lower body (Van Itallie, 1988). Additionally, those with high levels of visceral

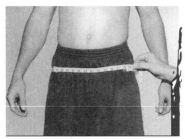

A.

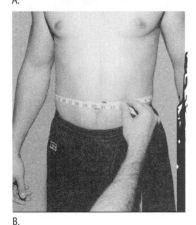

B.

Figure 3.6 ⊙ *Anatomical locations for circumference measures. A. Hip circumference, B. Waist circumference.*

fat, or fat found on and around internal organs, are at greater risk than those with mostly subcutaneous fat, or fat just beneath the surface of the skin.

Since the location of the stored fat is a health concern, measures which help to identify the primary site of fat storage can be valuable. Many researchers prefer the ratio of the waist-to-hip circumference as an assessment for this identification. Measurement of waist-to-hip ratio (WHR) is quite simple, and very informative as to fat location.

Measurement of the waist is taken with a soft, flexible tape measure at the point of smallest circumference between the bottom of the rib cage and the umbilicus. Measurement of the hip is taken at the point of greatest circumference of the hip area. Both measures should be taken while the subject is in a relaxed, standing position, with the tape positioned on a horizontal plane around the measurement site. Clothing around the site should be minimal so it does not interfere with an accurate reading (Figure 3.6).

When waist circumference is divided by hip circumference, the WHR is the result. For example, if a person has a 34-inch waist circumference and a 36-inch hip circumference, their WHR would be .94 (34 divided by 36). The average WHR in males between the ages of 17–39 is .90, and in females of this same age group, the average WHR is .80. Increased disease risks accompany greater WHR measurements for both sexes (Stamford, 1991). Table 3.5 shows the relative disease risk for waist-to-hip ratio. Use Laboratory 3.3 to determine your WHR.

IDEAL BODY WEIGHT

Once a body composition assessment reveals the percentage of body fat an individual possesses, that person's ideal body weight can be determined. If the percent of body fat is already within a desirable range, no changes would be recommended in body weight. If, however, as with many Americans, excessive body fat is present, a new body weight can be recommended. This recommendation is made with the assumption that the individual will pursue the weight loss in the correct way, that is by exercising and following a prudent eating plan as discussed in the chapter on nutrition. This will result in the maintenance of the lean body mass, with the weight loss coming from the reduction in fat tissue.

A target percent of body fat should be identified using Table 3.3 found earlier in this chapter. Remember that everyone does not have to attain the ideal category, and that moderate reductions in body fat can provide great health benefits. Con-

TABLE 3.5	Relative Disease Risk for Waist-to-Hip Ratio			
	Men		**Women**	
	Age 20–39	*40 and over*	*Age 20–39*	*40 and over*
Very high risk	>.95	>1.0	>.85	>.85
High risk	.9–.95	.95–1.0	.79–.85	.8–.85
Moderate risk	.85–.9	.9–.95	.72–.79	.75–.8
Low risk	<.85	<.9	<.72	<.75

Adapted from: Bray, G.A. and Gray, D.S. (1988). Obesity: Part I–Pathogenesis, *Western Journal of Medicine*, 149:429–441 and American College of Sports Medicine. (1995). *Guidelines for Testing and Exercise Prescription*. Baltimore: Williams & Wilkins, p. 59.

Chapter 3

sultation with your physician may help you decide what your target body fat should be. Once you have determined what your goal is, the following formula can assist you in determining what that means in terms of body weight.

1. Identify your fat weight (FW). This is done by multiplying your total body weight (BW) by the percent body fat (%F) from your skinfold or hydrostatic weighing test. The equation is:

$$FW = BW \times \%F$$

2. Identify how much lean weight (LW) you have by subtracting your fat weight (FW) from your total body weight (BW).

$$LW = BW - FW$$

3. Identify your target fat percentage that you desire to attain using Table 3.3. Using your target fat percentage (TFP), calculate your ideal body weight (IBW) using the following formula:

$$IBW = LW / (1 - TFP)$$

Once target weight is determined, proper weight loss techniques are critically important. Unfortunately, many people turn to fraudulent, ineffective, and sometimes dangerous attempts to lose weight. It is important to stick to the basics and remember:

1. Safe and effective weight loss is not a rapid process. It is recommended that the target weight loss be set at a maximum of two pounds per week.
2. It takes a combination of caloric reduction and increase in caloric expenditure through exercise to attain healthy weight loss.
3. While heredity is a factor in a person's body shape and weight, everyone can improve their health status through the attainment of a more desirable body composition.

Example

A skinfold measurement for Sam finds that he has 23 percent body fat. He weighs 200 pounds and is 25-years-old. He decides that he wants to set a target goal of 18 percent body fat. Therefore, his determination of ideal body weight would be as follows:

1. $FW = BW \times \%F$
   $FW = 200 \times .23$
   $FW = 46$ Sam has 46 pounds of fat.

2. $LW = BW - FW$
   $LW = 200 - 46$
   $LW = 154$ Sam has 154 pounds of lean mass.

3. $IBW = LW/(1 - TFP)$
   $IBW = 154/(1 - .18)$
   $IBW = 154/.82$
   $IBW = 189$ If Sam uses proper reduction techniques to reduce to 18 percent body fat, his target weight is 189 pounds.

4. P[...] reassessment of body composition is recommended. Body composition [...] with the normal aging process. As we age, fat accumulates and we lose [...] [m]ass. In fact, there is a 15–30 percent reduction in lean mass by the age [...] [Ro]gers and Evans, 1993). In addition, lifestyle changes such as eating or [...] habits will also result in body composition changes. Remember, the scales are not a good way to assess health status. Have your body composition measured periodically to keep up with your ratio of fat mass to lean body mass.

References

American College of Sports Medicine. (2005). *Guidelines for Exercise Testing and Prescription, 7th edition*. Baltimore: Lippincott,Williams & Wilkins.

Anspaugh, D.J., Hamrick, M.H., & Rosato, F.D. (2006). *Wellness: Concepts and Applications* (6th ed.). New York: McGraw Hill.

Brownell, K.D., Steen, S.N., & Wilmore, J.H. (1987). Weight regulation practices in athletics: Analysis of metabolic and health effects. *Medicine and Science in Sports and Exercise*. 19(6).

Fahey, T.D., Insel, M.I., & Roth, W.T. (2005). *Fit & Well: Core Concepts and Labs in Physical Fitness and Wellness, 6th edition*. New York: McGraw Hill.

Folsom, A.R., Kaye, S.A., Sellers, T.A., Hong, C.P., Cerhan, J.R., Potter, J.D., & Prineas, R.J. (1993). Body fat distribution and five year risk of death in older women. *Journal of the American Medical Association*. 269(4).

Frisard, M.I., Greenway, F.L., & Delaney, J.P. (2005). Comparison of methods to assess body composition changes during a period of weight loss. *Obesity Research* 13(5).

Hoeger, W.K., & Hoeger, S.A. (2003). *Lifetime Physical Fitness and Wellness, 7th edition*. Belmont, CA: Wadsworth.

Maddalozzo, G.F., Cardinal, B.J., & Snow, C.A. (2002). Current validity of the BOD POD and dual energy x-ray absorptiometry techniques for assessing body composition in young women. *Journal of the American Dietetic Association*. 102(11).

National Institutes of Health. (2005). Statistics related to overweight and obesity. Win.niddk. nih.gov/statistics/index.htm

Neiman, D.C. (2003). *Exercise testing and prescription: a health-related approach*. New York: McGraw Hill.

Plowman, S.A., & Smith, D.L. (2003). *Exercise physiology for health, fitness, and performance, 2nd edition*. Boston: Pearson Addison-Wesley.

Revick, D.A., & Israel, R.G. (1986). Relationship between body mass indices and measures of body adiposity. *American Journal of Public Health*, 76:992–997.

Rogers, M.A., & Evans, W.Y. (1993). Changes in skeletal muscle with aging: Effects of exercise training. *Exercise and Sports Science Reviews*, 21:65–102.

Stamford, B. (1991). Apples and pears: Where you wear your fat can affect your health. *The Physician and Sportsmedicine*, 19:123–124.

United States Department of Health and Human Services. (2005). *Overweight and obesity: Health consequences*. www.surgeongeneral.gov/topics/obesity/calltoaction/fact_consequences.htm

Van Itallie, T.B. (1988). Topography of body fat: Relationship to risk of cardiovascular and other diseases. In: Anthropometric standardization reference manual. Edited by T.G. Lohman, A.F. Roche, and R. Martorelli. Champaign, IL: Human Kinetics Publishers, Inc.

chapter 3
LABORATORY ①

Skinfold Lab and Worksheet

In preparation for this assessment, the subject should wear clothing which will allow the technician access to the appropriate sites. A quiet room which promotes modesty and is free from distractions is best. Subjects should be standing for the test, and all skinfolds should be taken on the right side of the body.

Step I
The technician locates the proper anatomical sites for the three-site skinfold assessment. The sites for men are the chest, abdomen, and thigh. The sites for women are the triceps, suprailium, and thigh. It is important that the sites for the skinfold be accurate. Figure 3.3 assists you in locating the correct sites. The technician may choose to mark them as follows:

Thigh—Use a vertical fold in the front of the thigh halfway between the knee and the hip.

Suprailium—Use a diagonal fold just above the crest of the ilium or hipbone.

Tricep—Use a vertical fold on the back of the upper arm halfway between the shoulder and the elbow.

Abdomen—Use a vertical fold one inch to the right of the umbilicus or navel.

Chest—Use a diagonal skinfold halfway between the shoulder crease and the nipple.

Step II
The technician will grasp the site with their index finger and thumb. Lightly pinch the skin and adipose tissue, but do not grasp muscle. Do not pinch too hard or you may compress the fat and get an inaccurate reading. Take a vertical or diagonal measurement (depending on the site) about one-quarter of an inch from the fingertips. After allowing the tips of the calipers to settle, read the dial to the nearest half millimeter. Take at least two measures at each site to ensure consistency. If the two readings are not the same, conduct further tests until consistent readings are attained. Be sure the skin is released and re-grasped between readings. If tests are going to be repeated at a later date for comparison purposes, conduct them at the same time of day. Also, do not conduct this test soon after exercise, as normal skinfold size will be inflated due to body fluid shifting to the skin.

Step III
Have someone record the three readings on the chart below.

Women		Men	
Thigh	_____	Thigh	_____
Suprailium	_____	Abdomen	_____
Triceps	_____	Chest	_____

Step IV

Add the measurements of the three skinfolds. Refer to the skinfold charts found with this lab exercise to determine your percent body fat.

Sum of three skinfolds = _____

Percent body fat = _____

Refer back to Table 3.3 to determine your health classification according to your sum of skinfolds.

> *Example*
>
> Eddie is a 22-year-old male whose skinfold measurements yield the following readings:
>
> Thigh = 15 mm
> Chest = 8 mm
> Abdomen = 21 mm
> Sum of skinfolds = 44 mm
> Percent of body fat = 12.5
> Fitness category according to body fat = Optimal

Percent Fat Estimates for Women Calculated from Triceps, Suprailium, and Thigh Skinfold Thickness

Sum of 3 Skinfolds	Under 22	23 to 27	28 to 32	33 to 37	38 to 42	43 to 47	48 to 52	53 to 57	Over 58
23–25	9.7	9.9	10.2	10.4	10.7	10.9	11.2	11.4	11.7
26–28	11.0	11.2	11.5	11.7	12.0	12.3	12.5	12.7	13.0
29–31	12.3	12.5	12.8	13.0	13.3	13.5	13.8	14.0	14.3
32–34	13.6	13.8	14.0	14.3	14.5	14.8	15.0	15.3	15.5
35–37	14.8	15.0	15.3	15.5	15.8	16.0	16.3	16.5	16.8
38–40	16.0	16.3	16.5	16.7	17.0	17.2	17.5	17.7	18.0
41–43	17.2	17.4	17.7	17.9	18.2	18.4	18.7	18.9	19.2
44–46	18.3	18.6	18.8	19.1	19.3	19.6	19.8	20.1	20.3
47–49	19.5	19.7	20.0	20.2	20.5	20.7	21.0	21.2	21.5
50–52	20.6	20.8	21.1	21.3	21.6	21.8	22.1	22.3	22.6
53–55	21.7	21.9	22.1	22.4	22.6	22.9	23.1	23.4	23.6
56–58	22.7	23.0	23.2	23.4	23.7	23.9	24.2	24.4	24.7
59–61	23.7	24.0	24.2	24.5	24.7	25.0	25.2	25.5	25.7
62–64	24.7	25.0	25.2	25.5	25.7	26.0	26.2	26.4	26.7
65–67	25.7	25.9	26.2	26.4	26.7	26.9	27.2	27.4	27.7
68–70	26.6	26.9	27.1	27.4	27.6	27.9	28.1	28.4	28.6
71–73	27.5	27.8	28.0	28.3	28.5	28.8	29.0	29.3	29.5
74–76	28.4	28.7	28.9	29.2	29.4	29.7	29.9	30.2	30.4
77–79	29.3	29.5	29.8	30.0	30.3	30.5	30.8	31.0	31.3
80–82	30.1	30.4	30.6	30.9	31.1	31.4	31.6	31.9	32.1
83–85	30.9	31.2	31.4	31.7	31.9	32.2	32.4	32.7	32.9
86–88	31.7	32.0	32.2	32.5	32.7	32.9	33.2	33.4	33.7
89–91	32.5	32.7	33.0	33.2	33.5	33.7	33.9	34.2	34.4
92–94	33.2	33.4	33.7	33.9	34.2	34.4	34.7	34.9	35.2
95–97	33.9	34.1	34.4	34.6	34.9	35.1	35.4	35.6	35.9
98–100	34.6	34.8	35.1	35.3	35.5	35.8	36.0	36.3	36.5
101–103	35.2	35.4	35.7	35.9	36.2	36.4	36.7	36.9	37.2
104–106	35.8	36.1	36.3	36.6	36.8	37.1	37.3	37.5	37.8
107–109	36.4	36.7	36.9	37.1	37.4	37.6	37.9	38.1	38.4
110–112	37.0	37.2	37.5	37.7	38.0	38.2	38.5	38.7	38.9
113–115	37.5	37.8	38.0	38.2	38.5	38.7	39.0	39.2	39.5
116–118	38.0	38.3	38.5	38.8	39.0	39.3	39.5	39.7	40.0
119–121	38.5	38.7	39.0	39.2	39.5	39.7	40.0	40.2	40.5
122–124	39.0	39.2	39.4	39.7	39.9	40.2	40.4	40.7	40.9
125–127	39.4	39.6	39.9	40.1	40.4	40.6	40.9	41.1	41.4
128–130	39.8	40.0	40.3	40.5	40.8	41.0	41.3	41.5	41.8

Body density is calculated based on the generalized equation for predicting body density of women developed by A. S. Jackson, M. L. Pollock, and A. Ward. *Medicine and Science in Sports and Exercise* 12, (1980), 175–182. Percent body fat is determined from the calculated body density using the Siri formula.

Source: *Lifetime Physical Fitness and Wellness: A Personalized Program* (4th ed.) W. Hoeger & S. Hoeger–Morton Publishing Co.

Percent Fat Estimates for Men Under Age 40 Calculated from Chest, Abdomen, and Thigh Skinfold Thickness

Sum of 3 Skinfolds	Age to the Last Year							
	Under 19	20 to 22	23 to 25	26 to 28	29 to 31	32 to 34	35 to 37	38 to 40
8–10	.9	1.3	1.6	2.0	2.3	2.7	3.0	3.3
11–13	1.9	2.3	2.6	3.0	3.3	3.7	4.0	4.3
14–16	2.9	3.3	3.6	3.9	4.3	4.6	5.0	5.3
17–19	3.9	4.2	4.6	4.9	5.3	5.6	6.0	6.3
20–22	4.8	5.2	5.5	5.9	6.2	6.6	6.9	7.3
23–25	5.8	6.2	6.5	6.8	7.2	7.5	7.9	8.2
26-28	6.8	7.1	7.5	7.8	8.1	8.5	8.8	9.2
29–31	7.7	8.0	8.4	8.7	9.1	9.4	9.8	10.1
32–34	8.6	9.0	9.3	9.7	10.0	10.4	10.7	11.1
35–37	9.5	9.9	10.2	10.6	10.9	11.3	11.6	12.0
38–40	10.5	10.8	11.2	11.5	11.8	12.2	12.5	12.9
41–43	11.4	11.7	12.1	12.4	12.7	13.1	13.4	13.8
44–46	12.2	12.6	12.9	13.3	13.6	14.0	14.3	14.7
47–49	13.1	13.5	13.8	14.2	14.5	14.9	15.2	15.5
50–52	14.0	14.3	14.7	15.0	15.4	15.7	16.1	16.4
53–55	14.8	15.2	15.5	15.9	16.2	16.6	16.9	17.3
56–58	15.7	16.0	16.4	16.7	17.1	17.4	17.8	18.1
59–61	16.5	16.9	17.2	17.6	17.9	18.3	18.6	19.0
62–64	17.4	17.7	18.1	18.4	18.8	19.1	19.4	19.8
65–67	18.2	18.5	18.9	19.2	19.6	19.9	20.3	20.6
68–70	19.0	19.3	19.7	20.0	20.4	20.7	21.1	21.4
71–73	19.8	20.1	20.5	20.8	21.2	21.5	21.9	22.2
74–76	20.6	20.9	21.3	21.6	22.0	22.2	22.7	23.0
77–79	21.4	21.7	22.1	22.4	22.8	23.1	23.4	23.8
80–82	22.1	22.5	22.8	23.2	23.5	23.9	24.2	24.6
83–85	22.9	23.2	23.6	23.9	24.3	24.6	25.0	25.3
86–88	23.6	24.0	24.3	24.7	25.0	25.4	25.7	26.1
89–91	24.4	24.7	25.1	25.4	25.8	26.1	26.5	26.8
92–94	25.1	25.5	25.8	26.2	26.5	26.9	27.2	27.5
95–97	25.8	26.2	26.5	26.9	27.2	27.6	27.9	28.3
98–100	26.6	26.9	27.3	27.6	27.9	28.3	28.6	29.0
101–103	27.3	27.6	28.0	28.3	28.6	29.0	29.3	29.7
104–106	27.9	28.3	28.6	29.0	29.3	29.7	30.0	30.4
107–109	28.6	29.0	29.3	29.7	30.0	30.4	30.7	31.1
110–112	29.3	29.6	30.0	30.3	30.7	31.0	31.4	31.7
113–115	30.0	30.3	30.7	31.0	31.3	31.7	32.0	32.4
116–118	30.6	31.0	31.3	31.6	32.0	32.3	32.7	33.0
119–121	31.3	31.6	32.0	32.3	32.6	33.0	33.3	33.7
122–124	31.9	32.2	32.6	32.9	33.3	33.6	34.0	34.3
125–127	32.5	32.9	33.2	33.5	33.9	34.2	34.6	34.9
128–130	33.1	33.5	33.8	34.2	34.5	34.9	35.2	35.5

Body density is calculated based on the generalized equation for predicting body density of men developed by A. S. Jackson and M. L. Pollock. *British Journal of Nutrition* 40, (1978) 497–504. Percent body fat is determined from the calculated body density using the Siri formula.

Percent Fat Estimates for Men Over Age 40 Calculated from Chest, Abdomen, and Thigh Skinfold Thickness

Sum of 3 Skinfolds	Age to the Last Year							
	41 to 43	44 to 46	47 to 49	50 to 52	53 to 55	56 to 58	59 to 61	Over 63
8–10	3.7	4.0	4.4	4.7	5.1	5.4	5.8	6.1
11–13	4.7	5.0	5.4	5.7	6.1	6.4	6.8	7.1
14–16	5.7	6.0	6.4	6.7	7.1	7.4	7.8	8.1
17–19	6.7	7.0	7.4	7.7	8.1	8.4	8.7	9.1
20–22	7.6	8.0	8.3	8.7	9.0	9.4	9.7	10.1
23–25	8.6	8.9	9.3	9.6	10.0	10.3	10.7	11.0
26–28	9.5	9.9	10.2	10.6	10.9	11.3	11.6	12.0
29–31	10.5	10.8	11.2	11.5	11.9	12.2	12.6	12.9
32–34	11.4	11.8	12.1	12.4	12.8	13.1	13.5	13.8
35–37	12.3	12.7	13.0	13.4	13.7	14.1	14.4	14.8
38–40	13.2	13.6	13.9	14.3	14.6	15.0	15.3	15.7
41–43	14.1	14.5	14.8	15.2	15.5	15.9	16.2	16.6
44–46	15.0	15.4	15.7	16.1	16.4	16.8	17.1	17.5
47–49	15.9	16.2	16.6	16.9	17.3	17.6	18.0	18.3
50–52	16.8	17.1	17.5	17.8	18.2	18.5	18.8	19.2
53–55	17.6	18.0	18.3	18.7	19.0	19.4	19.7	20.1
56–58	18.5	18.8	19.2	19.5	19.9	20.2	20.6	20.9
59–61	19.3	19.7	20.0	20.4	20.7	21.0	21.4	21.7
62–64	20.1	20.5	20.8	21.2	21.5	21.9	22.2	22.6
65–67	21.0	21.3	21.7	22.0	22.4	22.7	23.0	23.4
68–70	21.8	22.1	22.5	22.8	23.2	23.5	23.9	24.2
71–73	22.6	22.9	23.3	23.6	24.0	24.3	24.7	25.0
74–76	23.4	23.7	24.1	24.4	24.8	25.1	25.4	25.8
77–79	24.1	24.5	24.8	25.2	25.5	25.9	26.2	26.6
80–82	24.9	25.3	25.6	26.0	26.3	26.6	27.0	27.3
83–85	25.7	26.0	26.4	26.7	27.1	27.4	27.8	28.1
86–88	26.4	26.8	27.1	27.5	27.8	28.2	28.5	28.9
89–91	27.2	27.5	27.9	28.2	28.6	28.9	29.2	29.6
92–94	27.9	28.2	28.6	28.9	29.3	29.6	30.0	30.3
95–97	28.6	29.0	29.3	29.7	30.0	30.4	30.7	31.1
98–100	29.3	29.7	30.0	30.4	30.7	31.1	31.4	31.8
101–103	30.0	30.4	30.7	31.1	31.4	31.8	32.1	32.5
104–106	30.7	31.1	31.4	31.8	32.1	32.5	32.8	33.2
107–109	31.4	31.8	32.1	32.4	32.8	33.1	33.5	33.8
110–112	32.1	32.4	32.8	33.1	33.5	33.8	34.2	34.5
113–115	32.7	33.1	33.4	33.8	34.1	34.5	34.8	35.2
116–118	33.4	33.7	34.1	34.4	34.8	35.1	35.5	35.8
119–121	34.0	34.4	34.7	35.1	35.4	35.8	36.1	36.5
122–124	34.7	35.0	35.4	35.7	36.1	36.4	36.7	37.1
125–127	35.3	35.6	36.0	36.3	36.7	37.0	37.4	37.7
128–130	35.9	36.2	36.6	36.9	37.3	37.6	38.0	38.5

Body density is calculated based on the generalized equation for predicting body density of men developed by A. S. Jackson and M. L. Pollock, *British Journal of Nutrition* 40 (1978), 497–504. Percent body fat is determined from the calculated body density using the Siri formula.

chapter 3
LABORATORY ②

Body Mass Index Lab and Worksheet

Step I
Attain an accurate measure of your height and weight. A properly calibrated physician's scale is preferred.

Step II
Record height and weight and make the following conversions:

A. Convert weight from pounds to kilograms:

Weight in pounds _____ /2.2 = _____ weight in kilograms.

B. Convert height from inches to meters and square that result:

Height in inches _____ × .0254 = _____ height in meters.

C. Square this result for height in meters squared

Height in meters _____ × height in meters _____ = _____
height in meters squared.

Step III
Use those values in the following formula:

BMI = wt(kg) / ht(m)^2

Your Body Mass Index = _____

Step IV
Using the chart found with Table 3.4, identify your health category according to BMI.

Your health category is _____ .

chapter 3
LABORATORY ③

Waist-to-Hip Ratio Lab and Worksheet

Step I
Using a flexible tape measure, measure hip circumference at the largest point and waist circumference at the smallest point.

Step II
Determine the ratio of those measures using the following:

Waist circumference _____ / Hip circumference _____ = _____
Waist-to-hip ratio.

Step III
Using Table 3.5, compare your waist-to-hip ratio to your relative disease risk.

Your relative waist-to-hip disease risk ratio is _____ .

chapter 3
LABORATORY (4)

Ideal Body Weight Lab and Worksheet

Step I
After having your percent body fat accurately measured using skinfold calipers or hydrostatic weighing, and after weighing on a physician's scale, calculate your fat weight:

Body weight _____ × percent body fat _____ = _____ fat weight.

Step II
Identify how much lean weight you possess:

Body Weight _____ – fat weight _____ = _____ lean weight.

Step III
Select a target fat percentage which you would desire to attain through proper combination of exercise and healthy diet. Use that target fat percentage to determine ideal body weight:

Lean weight _____ / (1 – _____ selected fat percentage) = _____ ideal body weight.

Step IV
Calculate your weight loss goal by subtracting your ideal body weight from your current body weight:

Body weight _____ – ideal body weight _____ = _____ weight loss goal.

In order to attain your ideal body weight, your goal will be to lose _____ pounds of adipose tissue.

4 Flexibility

Key Terms

flexibility

mobility

static

dynamic

ballistic

proprioceptive neuromuscular

active isolated stretching

facilitation

sit-and-reach

trunk extension

plastic elongation

elastic elongation

Specific Objectives

1. Define flexibility and its importance as a component of health related physical fitness.

2. List the important factors affecting flexibility including plastic and elastic elongation.

3. Describe the relationship between abdominal, back, hip and thigh muscles for reducing low back pain.

4. Describe the benefits of having activity appropriate flexibility.

5. Identify howbalistic, static, PNF and AIS methods are used to develop and maintain flexibility.

6. Determine your flexibility via modified sit-and-reach, trunk extension, body rotation and shoulder flexibility tests.

7. Identify several strategies for improving/maintaining flexibility.

8. Discuss pilates and yoga as ways of maintaining a healthy level of flexibility.

OVERVIEW

Flexibility may be best defined as the range of motion (ROM) possible of a joint, or the ability to move through a ROM that is controlled by the musculotendinous structures of the joint(s). There are essentially two types of flexibility: (1) static, and (2) dynamic. Static flexibility addresses ROM without regard to how rapidly the ROM can be achieved. Dynamic flexibility, on the other hand, is the resistance to motion that affects how easily a joint can move through its ROM. In daily living, we often must make rapid, strenuous movements which may cause injury if a joint cannot move through its full ROM. According to the President's Council on Physical Fitness and Sports (Plowman, 1993), 80 percent of all low-back problems in the United States result from improper alignment of the spine and pelvic girdle due to inflexibility and weak abdominal muscles. The Bureau of National Affairs (1988) estimates over one billion dollars are lost annually by businesses with employees who suffer from low-back problems. Although flexibility varies from person to person because of body structure, it is important to understand that having adequate flexibility is an acquired state and various forms of stretching are the mechanisms by which we can achieve an appropriate level of flexibility. Without attention being paid to maintaining flexibility, ROM decreases and although there is little research to document this most experts feel the potential for musculotendinous injury increases.

WHY FLEXIBILITY IS IMPORTANT FOR HEALTH AND FITNESS

There are several reasons why medical personnel endorse stretching exercises to attain a desirable level of flexibility. Of primary importance is the need to maintain a balanced relationship in the muscles crossing the hips or pelvis. On the front or anterior side of the body, the abdominal muscles and the hip flexors act to stabilize the pelvis. On the back or posterior side of the body, your buttocks, back muscles and hamstrings (posterior thigh) work together to stabilize the pelvis. When combined, these muscle groups control how much or how little the pelvis can tilt. Tilting of the pelvis directly affects the lower lumbar vertebrae of the spinal column. If the abdominal muscles are weak, the hip flexors often pull hard enough to cause a person's back to curve inward too much. This places undue pressure on the vertebral discs of the lower back and places the affected person at greater risk of a low-back injury. Conversely, if the hamstring muscles are too tight, they may tilt the pelvis in the opposite direction resulting in little or no curve of the lower back. This too can place undue stress on vertebral discs and put the person at greater risk of injury to his/her lower back. Figure 4.1 illustrates the desired relationship in these muscle groups. One must visualize "long/strong" muscles controlling the pelvis. With this image in mind, it is easy to appreciate good postural alignment for the back.

Concerns for flexibility are not confined to the lower back and/or pelvis, however. Many older adults get caught in a vicious cycle of inactivity and declining health and lose flexibility. If a person loses flexibility, he/she can no longer participate in certain physical activities. Worse yet is when a person's daily activities are limited by his/her inability to bend, turn, or reach. Oftentimes, pain becomes associated

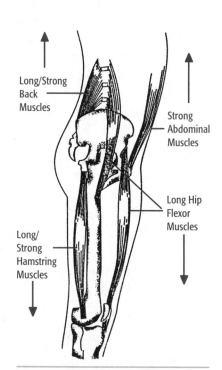

Long/Strong Back Muscles

Strong Abdominal Muscles

Long Hip Flexor Muscles

Long/ Strong Hamstring Muscles

Figure 4.1 ⊙ *"Long/Strong" muscles for maintaining proper posture and low-back stability.*

From *Fitness and Wellness Strategies*, 2nd edition by Seiger, L. et al. Copyright © 1998 by McGraw-Hill Companies, Inc. Reprinted by permission of The McGraw-Hill Companies.

with activity and the person further reduces activity, thereby worsening the situation. A simple stretching routine can help those individuals regain their lost ROM and oftentimes return to an active lifestyle. A commitment of five minutes per day for those people with a normal ROM can most often prevent this dilemma.

FACTORS AFFECTING FLEXIBILITY

A number of major structural factors contribute to the limits of movement: bone, cartilage, ligaments, muscles, tendons, and connective tissue, which make up the joint capsule. Since bones have a fixed shape, they cannot be changed. Nor do we care to alter the state of cartilage, which cushions the bone ends, or ligaments which connect bone to bone and maintain the integrity of the joint itself. With this in mind it is easy to understand how ROM about a joint is highly specific to the individual, and that it can vary from one joint to another.

Excluding bones, cartilage and most ligaments, that leaves muscles, tendons, and the joint capsule tissue as the primary components to target with stretching for improving flexibility. The combination of the three can account for 98 percent of the resistance to flexibility. Of these three, tendons and joint capsule tissue are nonelastic. Even though they are nonelastic, they can undergo plastic elongation (permanent lengthening of soft tissue).

There has been a resurgence of interest in optimizing ROM through various methods of stretching. If one recalls that types of stretches can fall into one of two categories, either static or dynamic, we can then address each method and determine which method might yield optimal results for a given individual. At the peak of this debate is research that has shown slow static stretching prior to competition may be detrimental to athletic performance. Without getting into an in-depth narrative on this topic, it can be summarized by suggesting slow static stretching alters the muscle's active length. When subjects were tested on vertical jump after slow static stretching, they actually lost jump height. This phenomenon can be explained by the leg muscles being ever so slightly longer after stretching can go through a greater ROM before they want to contract and return to their resting length. This small change in muscle length has a large influence on the mechanical characteristics of the muscle reducing the force it produces thereby reducing vertical jump performance. Although not everyone is an athlete, this same reaction takes place in almost every movement we perform. So, does this mean we should not stretch? No, but it could mean we should not use slow static stretching prior to competitive activities if we are concerned with explosive muscle power needed for jumping and/or running.

So when is it important to stretch? Most experts would agree that stretching is best done after an active warm-up or exercise where the muscles planning to be stretched have good blood flow and are physically warmer because of it. The type of stretch can then vary from slow, sustained stretches to mild dynamic stretches. The key to improving ROM is changing the tendons, and connective tissue that link the muscles to the bones without injuring the bones, ligaments or joints themselves. For a more comprehensive review of the research on stretching and sports injury risk, one should read Thacker et al. (2004).

There are really two forms of stretching or elongation that the muscle experiences. Elastic elongation or temporary lengthening describes the changes muscle tissue undergoes during stretching. Muscle actively resists elongation and has intrinsic neural properties that actually cause it to contract in response to being overstretched. This principle is the same one that is represented by a simple reflex or tendon tap (knee jerk) test. The muscle is stretched beyond a point of comfort and the spinal cord signals the muscle to contract, enabling it to regain its normal resting length. Taking advantage of this same response is what allows athletes to develop greater power for jumping and running. But when the interest is in improving ROM, it makes good sense then to address stretching in such a manner as to not involve the activation of the stretch reflex. Three good options for this are using slow, static stretching where only mild tension is applied to the muscles crossing the joint being stretched, or active isolated stretching where opposing muscles are contracted to reduce the reflexive action and proprioceptive neuromuscular facilitation where the muscle being stretched is activated and then relaxed just prior to stretching. Each of these techniques is discussed in further detail later in this chapter.

BENEFITS OF FLEXIBILITY

The many benefits of appropriate flexibility include:

1. maintaining normal joint motion,
2. greater resistance to lower back and spinal column problems,
3. maintenance of good posture,
4. improved personal appearance/self image,
5. maintenance of motor skills, allowing one to remain active throughout life,
6. reduced muscle tension and/or stress,
7. improvement of spinal mobility in older adults,
8. reduced muscle spasm and soreness,
9. reduction or prevention of muscle trigger points that may produce muscle stiffness, and localized or referred pain, plus
10. prevention or reduction of some cases of dysmenorrhea (painful menstruation) in women.

COMMON METHODS OF STRETCHING

To maintain flexibility, a person simply moves the desired joint through its full ROM. Improving flexibility requires a stretching of the muscles and soft tissue crossing the joint. Four fairly common methods are effective for improving flexibility: ballistic (rapid) stretching, static (slow, sustained) stretching, active isolated stretching (AIS) and proprioceptive neuromuscular facilitation (PNF), a combination of contracting and relaxing muscles crossing the joint(s) and being manipulated.

Ballistic

Ballistic actions promoting increased ROM are effective and often used in specific sports training, but they invariably induce muscle damage and delayed muscle soreness. Ballistic stretching of tissue can also loosen ligaments which increases the risk of partial or full joint dislocation. Certain forms of plyometric training can be considered ballistic stretching as well. Box or depth jumps, bounding drills, and platform shoes used by many basketball programs, are good examples of ballistic stretching. For the purpose of improving overall ROM, however, ballistic stretching is not recommended. Faster, safer methods include static, AIS or PNF stretching.

Static (Slow, Sustained)

With a slow, sustained stretching technique, muscles and joint tissue are gradually lengthened and held in their final position for a short time, and then slowly returned to the muscle's resting length. There is, however, considerable variation as to the ideal technique and time allotted to each step in this action. The most current literature on effective stretching suggests that ROM of each stretching exercise should be determined near the point whereby a sensation of tightness, but not discomfort, is developed. The optimal time to hold a stretch is unknown; however, most research suggests that the exerciser should hold it to the point of tightness for 15–30 seconds. Each stretching exercise should be repeated two to four times at a frequency of three times per week.

Active Isolated Stretching (AIS)

Active isolated stretching has been presented best by Jim and Phil Wharton in their book "*The Wharton's Stretch Book.*" The principles of this method are simple with the following steps as a guide: (1) The person should prepare to stretch one isolated muscle or muscle group. (2) Actively contract the muscle opposite the muscle being stretched. (3) Stretch the targeted muscle gently and quickly holding for no more than two seconds. (4) Release the stretch before the muscle reacts to being stretched. (5) Repeat 2–3 times. For some stretches assistance from a partner is helpful; however, a rope or flexible tubing can be used for most muscles. The Whartons also propose that AIS should be part of a warm-up routine and if done correctly will not diminish the reflex reaction of the muscle that may often occur with slow static stretching.

Proprioceptive Neuromuscular Facilitation (PNF)

The concept of alternating the contraction and stretching of a relaxed muscle is not new, but along with AIS it has gained renewed popularity in recent years. Traditionally done with a partner, some pieces of exercise equipment are now being sold for the expressed use of assisting a person in PNF stretching. No matter how it is accomplished, the basis remains the same. Using a partner, a person is assisted in obtaining a moderate stretch in the muscle. At that point, the partner braces the limb to prevent movement, and the person isometrically (no movement) contracts the stretched muscle for four to five seconds. After contracting, the person once again relaxes, and the partner assists by increasing the stretch to a greater angle. The isometric contraction is repeated again, followed by relaxed and assisted stretching. This sequence continues four to five times with the final stretched position being held several seconds.

A modified version of PNF stretching, whereby an active contraction of opposing muscles occurs, has recently become popularized by several professional athletes. Essentially, it includes one additional step in the standard PNF sequence previously described. In a normal PNF stretch, the person stretching relaxes all muscles and passively allows his/her partner to move the limb through a progressively greater ROM. In this modified PNF stretch, the person stretching actively contracts muscles that assist his/her partner in moving the limb to a greater angle. It is also thought that an active contraction of opposing muscles causes the central nervous system to send inhibitory signals to the muscle being stretched, thereby further enhancing the stretching process. This technique has been supported anecdotally and may hold merit for the future, but as of yet, its value has not been verified by research.

ALTERNATIVE METHODS OF STRETCHING

Three recently popular activities have surfaced that integrate some elements of stretching into their philosophies of mind-body control. They are pilates, yoga and tai chi.

Pilates

Pilates gets its name from its inventor Joseph Pilates, a German-born innovator that combined pieces of yoga, martial arts and calesthenics to produce an activity that he claimed helped him and his fellow internees resist an influenza epidemic when he was in England during the First World War. Also during that time he engineered a way to rig springs on hospital beds to offer light resistance exercises to bedridden patients, thereby enhancing their recoveries. His combined muscle control, coordination and stretching activities by where efficiency of movement is paramount is still evident in the more modern day variations of his original pilates routine. Some of the movements devised from hospital beds are still evident today in the use of pilates machines that resemble a bed and use springs or shock cords to offer mild resistance to whole body movements.

Yoga

Originating in India over 6,000 years ago, yoga has been practiced by many adhering to the basic philosophy that most illness is associated with poor posture, diet and mental attitude. People practicing various forms of yoga often report reduced stress, improved self control over poor habits such as overeating and smoking and overall enhanced well-being. Yoga's main premise is to unite the mind and body. This is accomplished by using various body positions to improve body alignment and breathing techniques to optimize blood flow and energy to body tissues. Research has demonstrated reduced blood pressure and heart rate while releasing more endorphins (body's own morphine-like pain killer) with deep controlled breathing practiced during a yoga session. Caution should be executed in some cases where extreme yoga positions may be contraindicated for some individuals.

Tai Chi

Tai Chi is a form of martial art involving slow flowing movements. The person most people acknowledge as the founder of modern Tai Chi was a monk named Chang San-feng. Some debate has surfaced as to his actual existence versus a literary construct while other research and records from the Ming dynasty seem to indicate that he lived in the period from 1391 to 1459 AD.

Chapter 4

Regardless of real or construct Tai Chi exercises stress suppleness and elasticity as opposed to hardness and force demonstrated by other martial art forms. San-feng is credited with creating the fundamental "Thirteen Postures" of Tai Chi corresponding to the eight basic trigrams of the I-Ching and the five elements. The eight "postures" are: ward-off, rollback, press, push, pull, split, elbow strike and shoulder strike and the five "attitudes" are: advance, retreat, look left, gaze right, and central equilibrium. Research on the effects of Tai Chi has been shown to increase strength, improve balance and restore ROM using these basic postures and attitudes. The fundamental philosophy of Tai Chi can be summed up in the following verse:

> Yield and overcome;
> Bend and be straight.
> And,
> He who stands of tiptoe is not steady.
> He who strides cannot maintain the pace.

DETERMINING YOUR FLEXIBILITY

An important step in establishing optimal flexibility is completing an assessment of one's current ROM of major joints and muscles. Most flexibility tests developed over the years are sport-specific and offer little insight into health- or fitness-related status for the average person. There are, however, several simple tests that apply to all people. One must first realize that flexibility is joint-specific. This means that the presence of one flexible joint does not indicate the same for all joints in the body. Therefore, several tests are needed to measure flexibility of the major joints. The three tests that follow are the modified sit-and-reach, total body rotation, and shoulder flexibility.

Modified Sit-and-Reach

This test is helpful in assessing ROM of the hamstrings and, to some degree, muscles of the lower back. To perform the modified sit-and-reach, one simply needs a box about 12 inches (30 cm) square and a yard or meter stick. The steps are as follows:

1. Warm up properly before beginning (brisk walk, light calisthenics, static stretches, etc.).
2. Remove your shoes and sit on the floor with your back, shoulders and head touching a vertical wall; extend your legs with your feet touching the box.
3. Place one hand on top of the other and extend your arms forward toward the box without removing your head or back from the wall behind you. Your shoulders may move away slightly as you reach as far as possible. A partner or assistant should then match the yard or meter stick to the tip of your longest finger.
4. Gradually reach forward as far as possible, allowing your head, shoulders and back to flex forward as you stretch. Repeat this action three times, making sure the back of your knees do not come off the floor.
5. Record the maximum distance reached, either in inches to the nearest half inch or to the nearest centimeter.

TABLE 4.1

Percentile Ranks for Modified Sit-and-Reach Test

	Rank	≤18	19–35	36–49	≥50		Rank	≤18	19–35	36–49	≥50	
			Age Category						Age Category			
			MEN						WOMEN			
4 pts.	99	20.8	20.1	18.9	16.2	High fitness standard	99	22.6	21.0	19.8	17.2	4 pts.
	95	19.6	18.9	18.2	15.8		95	19.5	19.3	19.2	15.7	
	90	18.2	17.2	16.1	15.0		90	18.7	17.9	17.4	15.0	
	80	17.8	17.0	14.6	13.3		80	17.8	16.7	16.2	14.2	
	70	16.0	15.8	13.9	12.3		70	16.5	16.2	15.2	13.6	
3 pts.	60	15.2	15.0	13.4	11.5	Health fitness standard	60	16.0	15.8	14.5	12.3	3 pts.
	50	14.5	14.4	12.6	10.2		50	15.2	14.8	13.5	11.1	
2 pts.	40	14.0	13.5	11.6	9.7		40	14.5	14.5	12.8	10.1	2 pts.
	30	13.4	13.0	10.8	9.3		30	13.7	13.7	12.2	9.2	
1 pt.	20	11.8	11.6	9.9	8.8		20	12.6	12.6	11.0	8.3	1 pt.
	10	9.5	9.2	8.3	7.8		10	11.4	10.1	9.7	7.5	
	05	8.4	7.9	7.0	7.2		05	9.4	8.1	8.5	3.7	
	01	7.2	7.0	5.1	4.0		01	6.5	2.6	2.0	1.5	

Copied from: *Lifetime Physical Fitness & Wellness* (4th ed.) by W. Hoeger & S. Hoeger 1995. Morton Publishing Co.

Health fitness standards for men and women are shown in Table 4.1. An age-specific range of 11.5–15 inches (29–38.5 cm) for males and 12–16 inches (31–40.5 cm) for females is necessary for a person to meet the health fitness standards for adequate trunk flexibility. Ranges for the 99th percentile are: 16–20 inches (41–53 cm) for males and 17–22.5 inches (43.5–57.5 cm) for females. Conversely, the lowest one percent range for males is 4–7 inches (10–18 cm), and for females 1.5–6.5 inches (4–16.5 cm).

Total Body Rotation

Three lines are required for this test: a vertical line on a wall six feet from the floor, a three-foot line on the floor perpendicular to the vertical line, and a yard or meter stick for measuring rotation. The steps are as follows:

1. Stand arms length from the wall with toes of both feet touching the line on the floor.

2. Tape a yardstick to the wall at shoulder height so that one can measure 15" in either direction from the vertical line on the wall.

3. Rotate the body so the arm and shoulder farthest from the wall moves backward while keeping the shoulders horizontal. Reaching with the outside arm, rotate as far as possible. Keep the fingers and wrist straight, reaching as far for the yardstick as possible.

4. Repeat the rotation in the other direction and record the highest score in either inches or centimeters.

Health fitness standards for total body rotation in women and men are found in Tables 4.2a and 4.2b, respectively. For basic health fitness standards to be

TABLE 4.2A

Female Percentile Ranks for Total Body Rotation Test

	Percentile Rank	Left Rotation						Right Rotation			
		≤18	19–35	36–49	≥50			≤18	19–35	36–49	≥50
4 pts.	99	29.3	28.6	27.1	23.0	High fitness standard		29.6	29.4	27.1	21.7
	95	26.8	24.8	25.3	21.4			27.6	25.3	25.9	19.7
	90	25.5	23.0	23.4	20.5			25.8	23.0	21.3	19.0
	80	23.8	21.5	20.2	19.1			23.7	20.8	19.6	17.9
	70	21.8	20.5	18.6	17.3			22.0	19.3	17.3	16.8
3 pts.	60	20.5	19.3	17.7	16.0	Health fitness standard		20.8	18.0	16.5	15.6
	50	19.5	18.0	16.4	14.8			19.5	17.3	14.6	14.0
2 pts.	40	18.5	17.2	14.8	13.7			18.3	16.0	13.1	12.8
	30	17.1	15.7	13.6	10.0			16.3	15.2	11.7	8.5
1 pt.	20	16.0	15.2	11.6	6.3			14.5	14.0	9.8	3.9
	10	12.8	13.6	8.5	3.0			12.4	11.1	6.1	2.2
	05	11.1	7.3	6.8	0.7			10.2	8.8	4.0	1.1
	01	8.9	5.3	4.3	0.0			8.9	3.2	2.8	0.0

Copied from: *Lifetime Physical Fitness & Wellness* (4th ed.) by W. Hoeger & S. Hoeger 1995. Morton Publishing Co.

TABLE 4.2B

Male Percentile Ranks for Total Body Rotation Test

	Percentile Rank	Left Rotation						Right Rotation			
		≤18	19–35	36–49	≥50			≤18	19–35	36–49	≥50
4 pts.	99	29.1	28.0	26.6	21.0	High fitness standard		28.2	27.8	25.2	22.2
	95	26.6	24.8	24.5	20.0			25.5	25.6	23.8	20.7
	90	25.0	23.6	23.0	17.7			24.3	24.1	22.5	19.3
	80	22.0	22.0	21.2	15.5			22.7	22.3	21.0	16.3
	70	20.9	20.3	20.4	14.7			21.3	20.7	18.7	15.7
3 pts.	60	19.9	19.3	18.7	13.9	Health fitness standard		19.8	19.0	17.3	14.7
	50	18.6	18.0	16.7	12.7			19.0	17.2	16.3	12.3
2 pts.	40	17.0	16.8	15.3	11.7			17.3	16.3	14.7	11.5
	30	14.9	15.0	14.8	10.3			15.1	15.0	13.3	10.7
1 pt.	20	13.8	13.3	13.7	9.5			12.9	13.3	11.2	8.7
	10	10.8	10.5	10.8	4.3			10.8	11.3	8.0	2.7
	05	8.5	8.9	8.8	0.3			8.1	8.3	5.5	0.3
	01	3.4	1.7	5.1	0.0			6.6	2.9	2.0	0.0

Copied from: *Lifetime Physical Fitness & Wellness* (4th ed.) by W. Hoeger & S. Hoeger 1995. Morton Publishing Co.

achieved, a specific range of 15.5–21 inches (39.5–53 cm) is necessary for females with 14–20 inches (35–50.5 cm) needed for males. For the 99th percentile, the female range is 21.5–29.5 inches (55–75 cm), while the male range is 21–29 inches (53–74 cm). Conversely, the lowest one percent range for females is 0–9 inches (0–23 cm), and for males 0–3.5 inches (0–8.5 cm).

TABLE 4.3

	Shoulder Flexibility Fitness Level		
Percent Rank	**Distance**	**Fitness Level**	**Points**
≥90	+3" (7.5 cm)	Excellent	5
70–89	1–2" (2.5–5 cm)	Good	4
50–69	0" (2.5 cm)	Average	3
30–49	–1" (–2.5 cm)	Fair	2
<30	>–1" (>–2.5 cm)	Need Work	1

From E. Fox, T. Kirby and A. Fox, *Bases of Fitness*. Copyright © 1987 by Allyn & Bacon. Reprinted by permission.

Shoulder Flexibility

No specific equipment is needed to conduct this test. Steps are as follows:

1. While standing, raise your left arm and reach down your back as far as possible.
2. Move your right arm behind your back and upward as high as possible.
3. Try to overlap your fingers and/or hands as much as possible. Estimate the overlap of fingers in inches or centimeters.
4. Repeat with the right arm up and left arm down.

Scores for this test apply to men and women alike. If you cannot touch your hands together, your shoulder flexibility is poor. A score of +1 inches (2.5 cm) is average while a score of +3 inches (7.5 cm) is excellent.

How Do You Rate?

For a global estimate of flexibility, first derive a point total for each test. For the sit-and-reach test, three (3) points are awarded for meeting the minimum health fitness score. The same is true for the body rotation test. If you exceeded the minimum, give yourself four (4) points. If you were barely under the minimum score, two (2) points should be given. One point is the proper score if you are not very close to the minimum health fitness score, regardless of the distance away. Now, add your points from the sit-and-reach test, the total body rotation test, and the shoulder flexibility test (see Table 4.3) for a grand total. Use Table 4.4 to establish your current overall flexibility category.

It is not uncommon for all people, active and inactive to be classified as average or even below average for any of these tests. Research has shown that only people that routinely engage in stretching exercises are likely to score above average in these tests. However, that does not excuse any of us from setting a goal of achieving an average to above average level in all of these tests.

TABLE 4.4	
Overall Flexibility Score	
Total Score	Category
13	Superior
10–12	
7–9	Typical
4–6	
3	Room for Improvement

Adapted from "Overall Flexibility Score," *Lifetime Physical Fitness & Wellness*, W. Hoeger & S. Hoeger.

CONTRAINDICATED EXERCISES

A discussion of flexibility is not complete without including some information about contraindicated stretches. As the name implies, contraindicated stretches are not recommended because they require certain body parts to be placed in positions that greatly increase the chance of injury. Unfortunately, a number of these type stretches still persist in today's society, despite much research and published information advising against their use.

Chapter 4

The following stretch exercises should head a list of contraindicated stretches. They are serious violations of the principles of proper stretching.

Figure 4.2 A–F ⊙

WRONG

RIGHT

A. Plow—Pressure on the cervical vertebrae can cause paralysis.

AVOID

B1. Bridge—Causes undue stress on the lower lumbar vertebrae.

WRONG

RIGHT

B2. Double Leg Lift—Causes undue stress on the lower lumbar vertebrae.

WRONG

RIGHT

B3. Fire Hydrant—Causes undue stress on the lower lumbar vertebrae.

C. Deep Knee Bend—Bending knees beyond 90 degrees endangers the ligaments and cartilage of the knees.

D1. Hurdler's Stretch—Makes the inside or medial area of the knee vulnerable to ligament and cartilage damage.

D2. Hero Stretch—Makes the inside or medial area of the knee vulnerable to ligament and cartilage damage.

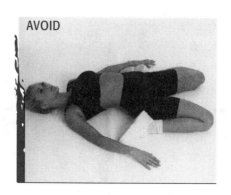

E. *Quadriceps Stretch—Hyperflexing the knee 120 degrees or more increases the possibility of injury to the cartilage and/or ligaments.*

F. *Ballistic Bar Stretch— Hyperextension of the knee predisposes the knee to ligament damage, sciatica and pyriformis syndrome.*

References

Alter, M.J. (1996). *The Science of Stretching.* Champaign, IL: Human Kinetics Publishers, Inc.

Back Injuries: Cost, Causes, Cases, and Prevention. (1988). Washington, D.C.: Bureau of National Affairs.

Corbin, C.B., & Lindsey, R. (1997). *Concepts of Physical Fitness* (9th ed.). Madison, WI: Brown & Benchmark Publishers.

Hoeger, W.K., & Hoeger, S.A. (1997). *Principles and Labs for Fitness and Wellness* (5th ed.). Englewood, CO: Morton Publishing Company.

Hoeger, W.K., & Hopkins, D.R. (1990). Assessing muscular flexibility. *Fitness Management,* 6:34–36.

Kokkonen, J., & Lauritzen, S. (1995). Isotonic strength and endurance gains through PNF stretching. *Medicine and Science in Sports and Exercise,* 27:127.

Majka, C. *The history of Tai Chi Chuan.* (2006). http://www.chebucto.ns.ca/Philosophy/Taichi/history.html, Empty Mirror Press, Inc.

Pilates, J. (2006). *History of pilates.* http://www.pilatesinsight.com/pilates/pilates-history.aspx

Plowman, S.A. (1993). Physical Fitness and Low Back Function. *President's Council on Physical Fitness and Sports: Physical Activity and Fitness Research Digest.* Series 1, 3:3.

Plowman, S.A., & Smith, D.L. (1997). *Exercise Physiology for Health, Fitness, and Performance.* Needham Heights, MA: Allyn & Bacon.

Powers, S.K., & Dodd, S.L. (1996). *Total Fitness: Exercise, Nutrition and Wellness.* Needham Heights, MA: Allyn & Bacon.

Prentice, W.E. (2004). *Get Fit, Stay Fit* (4th ed.). Boston: McGraw Hill, Inc.

Seiger, L., Kanipe, D., Vanderpool, K., & Barnes, D. (1998). *Fitness and Wellness Strategies* (2nd ed.). Boston: WCB/McGraw-Hill.

Sullivan, M.K., DeJulia, J.J., & Worrell, T.W. (1992). Effect of pelvic position and stretching method on hamstring muscle flexibility. *Medicine and Science in Sports and Exercise,* 24:1383–1389.

Thacker, S.B. et al. (2004). The impact of stretching on sports injury risk: A systematic review of the literature. *Medicine and Science in Sports and Exercise,* 36(3):371–378.

Wharton, J., & Wharton, P. (1996). *The Wharton's stretch book.* New York: Three Rivers Press, Random House Inc.

Chapter 4

chapter 4
LABORATORY (1)

Flexibility Lab and Worksheet

Step I

For the modified sit-and-reach, use the procedures found in Chapter 4 and record the maximum distance achieved in the "Actual Value" column on the next page. To determine whether you meet the health standard, refer to Table 4.1.

Step II

For the total body rotation, use the procedures found in Chapter 4 and record the greatest distance achieved in the "Actual Value" column below. To determine whether you meet the health standard, refer to Table 4.2.

Step III

For shoulder flexibility, use the procedures found in Chapter 4 and record the greatest distance achieved in the "Actual Value" column below. To meet the health standard, you must be above the 30 percent rank (Table 4.3) which is a minimum distance of a negative one inch (-1"). You can also record points earned for this test using Table 4.3 as well.

Step IV

Your overall flexibility score can be calculated by giving yourself:

From sit-and-reach and total body rotations tests

4 points	Exceed the health standard
3 points	Meet the standard
2 points	Barely under minimum standard
1 point	Not very close to minimum standard

Be sure to use the proper age category!

Add those points from the shoulder flexibility test (Table 4.3) to those received for the sit-and-reach and total body rotation. Table 4.4 can be used to rate your overall flexibility.

Test	Actual Value	Meet Health Standard? (Y/N)	Points
Modified Sit-and-Reach			
Total Body Rotation			+
Shoulder Flexibility		($\geq -1" =$ minimum standard)	+
		Overall Flexibility Score	=

Question:
1. Can a person be flexible in some joints and not in others? Why/why not?

_____

_____

_____

_____

_____

_____

© 2006 JUPITER IMAGES CORPORATION.

5 Muscular Strength and Endurance

Key Terms

muscular strength
muscular endurance
muscular power
hypertrophy
atrophy

fast/slow twitch fibers
specificity of training
lean body mass
metabolism
overload principle

Specific Objectives

1. Name the functions of the musculoskeletal system.

2. Understand the role strength plays in maintenance of good health.

3. Explain how muscular strength, endurance and muscle power are related.

4. Identify muscle fiber types and factors affecting strength/endurance.

5. Identify what is responsible for strength differences between sexes.

6. Understand the overload principle for strength development.

7. Identify the components of a sound strength training program.

8. Identify methods for assessing muscular strength/endurance.

9. Demonstrate a method to assess muscular strength/endurance.

10. Design your own program to develop and maintain a healthy level of muscular strength/endurance.

OVERVIEW

The development and maintenance of muscular strength is an essential component of anyone's activity program. Strength is simply a measure of force generated by a person's muscles. Strength for the most part is something one obtains through daily living. From the day an individual is born, he/she gains strength through movement and growth. As people reach mature stature, however, they only alter strength levels through movement. In essence, individual levels of strength are reflected by the lifestyle each of us has. How important is developing or maintaining strength? Very important! A certain level of muscular strength is necessary for daily activities such as sitting, standing, walking, lifting, carrying, and it appears that muscular strength is the most important factor of physical fitness for elderly populations. While heart disease is the number one killer of adults in the United States, it is the loss of strength that compromises independent living for most elderly. Over more than a decade, Wayne Wescott and colleagues, have demonstrated elderly people, both men and women benefit greatly by strength training. The most dramatic demonstration of this fact was a study where older individuals, resigned to full care nursing facilities were able to return to an unassisted living arrangement after 6–12 months of basic strength training. Strength training is also important for kids and Faigenbaum et al. (2003) showed many strength training benefits for healthy children. What is important however, is to clearly define strength training. By definition, strength training is any activity aimed at increasing the muscle's ability to generate force against a resistance. That resistance can be body weight as in push-ups, picking rocks from a garden, painting a house or lifting dumbbells in a gym. Regardless of the method of strength training, current literature suggests people of all ages benefit from increasing or maintaining their muscular strength. That makes the following phrase appropriate for everyone:

We lose what we do not use, but we can regain what is lost at a simple cost:
Strength train.

So, how much strength does a person really need? That is a difficult question to answer. First, let's address some basic fundamentals regarding muscles, how they work, and how they adapt. Then this question will be revisited for a possible clear answer.

FUNCTIONS OF MUSCULOSKELETAL SYSTEM

Muscle makes up a fairly large portion of our bodies. On average, there are 600 different muscles that make up some 40 percent of our total body weight. Beyond the most obvious role of movement, muscle performs several key functions. Muscles work constantly to maintain posture and to generate heat needed to stabilize body temperature. Contracting muscle also helps return blood to the heart during lower intensity activity. Another important role muscle has, albeit indirect, is its relationship to metabolism. Metabolism is a measure of energy expended (calories) to maintain normal cellular function (life).

ROLE OF STRENGTH IN GOOD HEALTH

Strength is rarely an issue for children and young adults since they are usually quite active, and that activity is enough to maintain functional strength. However, it is well documented that substantial declines in strength occur in both males and females, starting somewhere between 25–40 years of age and continuing to old age. The rate of this decline is quite varied (25–40 percent reduction) and is dependent on several factors: (1) loss of muscle mass, (2) changes in the muscle fiber, and (3) reduced nerve activation to the muscles.

Declines in muscle size and weight alter the muscle's ability to contract with the same force. This may be the largest contributor to the decline in strength. The size of muscle fibers also declines with age and this too contributes to the inability of the same muscle to exert force. Finally, the motor nerves that activate the muscles reduce the frequency in which they stimulate the muscles. This reduction in the rate of signaling the muscles results in physiological changes in the muscles that make them smaller, which further reduces mass.

Of greater concern is not so much the exact amount of strength we lose, but how that strength loss affects our lifestyle and/or health. Reduced strength is a direct result of weakened muscles. Weak muscles can lead to instability of joints. Unstable joints can lead to musculoskeletal injuries that may limit activity for life. Weak muscles often reduce one's ability to regain balance once lost. Fear of a fall by the elderly is a very real problem which often leads to less movement and even more dependence on others for activities of daily living. Poor respiratory muscle function will reduce ability for aerobic activity. The loss in aerobic capacity leads to less activity, further reducing strength. Insufficient strength can make daily tasks such as rising from a chair, carrying packages, or opening jars, a real challenge. This is the path that many adults are on and it leads right to a nursing home. Activities of daily living become tasks that depend upon others. Thus, muscular strength is important for maintaining a healthy life. Aging of any tissue, including muscle, cannot be prevented; however, muscle is special in that it can and will respond to exercise training in the same way at any adult age; it gets stronger. Simply put, strong muscles produce more force and allow people of all ages to do more.

MUSCULAR STRENGTH, ENDURANCE, AND POWER

As indicated earlier, muscular strength is defined as a muscle's ability to exert effort against a resistance. It is clear that maintenance of at least a minimum level of strength is important. Muscular endurance, although closely related to strength, is a measure of sustained muscle activity. Usually, if one's maximal effort is high, then a sustained submaximal effort will also be good. Dynamic endurance for repeated activities such as raking or shoveling is one form of muscular endurance. More static activities such as postural control or even digestion time through the intestine is dependent more on a muscle's endurance than a percentage of a muscle's absolute maximal strength. In fact, adequate abdominal muscle endurance, for example, is important to control the pelvis and subsequent lower back stability. Abdominal endurance can also maintain regular digestive rates which reduce the time carcinogenic agents are exposed to the intestinal lining, thereby reducing one's risk of certain forms of colon cancer. All things considered to this point, it appears that for most people muscular endurance is of greater interest than strength since it has a stronger influence on one's health. But, one must remember that muscular strength and endurance are closely linked. No matter how we name them, good working muscles are essential pieces of good health and fitness.

Comparatively, muscular power is a combination of strength and speed. Most experts would place power in a skill-related category of fitness because it is a measure of the amount of force being exerted over a given period of time. As soon as speed becomes an issue, genetics plays a larger role. On the other hand, power is related to strength and strength is clearly a health-related category of fitness. Garnica (1986), studying muscle power in young women, suggested that humans operate most effectively for daily tasks when using optimal muscle power. Optimal muscle power is thought to be produced when force and speed are about one-third of their respective greatest efforts.

In sports, power is probably the most important factor for performance. The stronger person is not always the more powerful person. Since power is a function of force and time, it becomes specific to the task requirements. Namely, if time is of the essence, the resistance to be overcome must be relatively low. In order to throw a ball very fast, the ball must be relatively light (i.e., a baseball versus a shot-put). Whereas in the shot-put, time is not critical, only distance is important. So, with a heavier resistance to overcome, the task is performed at a slower speed. Power type activities have been shown to positively influence muscular strength and endurance. Power training that emphasizes speed tends to positively affect muscular endurance more so than strength. Conversely, power training that emphasizes heavy resistance and slower speeds has a greater positive influence on muscular strength. Knowing the desired task can help determine what type of training can best be utilized to enhance performance. This same concept holds true for all activities, so keep this in mind as we address specific issues regarding muscle tissue itself.

MUSCLE FIBER TYPES

Although there are more than three distinct muscle fiber types, for simplicity we can separate fibers into three types: (1) fast-twitch fibers, (2) intermediate fibers, and (3) slow-twitch fibers. Each fiber type has specific characteristics that make it more suitable for certain tasks than the other two. Table 5.1 outlines the properties of each fiber type. All humans have a mixture of each, but people do vary as to the amount of each type they possess. Most people have near equal portions of fast-, intermediate, and slow-twitch fibers; however, some successful athletes have been shown to have a greater portion of fibers most appropriate for their sport.

Sprinters have more fast-twitch fibers, while marathoners have many more slow-twitch fibers. A simple way to estimate your own fiber type is to assess your ability for sprinting/jumping and/or endurance type events. If you excel in neither, then you are like most people, somewhere in the middle with a similar number of each fiber type. This notion of fiber type has given rise to the comment that elite international athletes are not trained, but are born.

This may be true; however, it does not prevent any of us from enjoying activity while getting the most out of the body we own. What is important to remem-

TABLE 5.1	Properties of Human Skeletal Muscle		
		Fiber Type	
Property	Slow-Twitch	Intermediate	Fast-Twitch
Speed of contraction	Slow	Intermediate	Fast
Fatigability	High	Intermediate	Low
Energy demands	Aerobic	Aerobic-anaerobic	Anaerobic
Force capacity	Low	Intermediate	High

From S. Powers & S. Dodds, *Total Fitness: Exercise, Nutrition and Wellness.* Copyright © 1994 by Allyn & Bacon. Reprinted with permission.

Chapter 5

ber about muscle and fiber types is that muscles are activated by the demands of the task. Walking, for example, may require 25–30 percent of the muscles in a person's legs. When looking at Table 5.1, one can see that an individual typically uses slow-twitch fibers for walking. That is great exercise for slow-twitch fibers, but what about the other fiber types? If you do not use those fibers, they will decrease in size (atrophy) and total muscular strength will decrease. This suggests that walking, although great for general fitness, would not be enough to sustain muscle mass. A person needs to engage in other physically demanding tasks throughout the day that require muscular strength, endurance and/or power.

GENDER DIFFERENCES IN STRENGTH

Strength development in humans is clear from birth to maturity. Boys and girls from age 3–12 exhibit nearly identical patterns of strength. Upon puberty, overall strength in boys continues to increase, while overall strength in girls begins to plateau (Figure 5.1). Male and female hormones, testosterone and estrogen, respectively, are primarily responsible for this difference. Even though the quality of the muscle between

© 2006 JUPITER IMAGES CORPORATION.

males and females is identical, hormone-wise, they are very different. The notion that a female engaging in strength training will develop large bulging muscles is a misconception. Some female body builders are able to give this appearance during a contest via specific training that creates an acute muscle hypertrophy or "pumped up" look that lasts for a few hours.

Under normal resting conditions, however, a woman's muscles will not appear the same as a man's. There are of course alternative means of generating muscle mass, namely anabolic steroids. Anabolic steroids add to or take the place of existing testosterone. The action is the same since it stimulates the development of the muscle. For women who have little endogenous testosterone, adding additional "artificial" testosterone can have significant effects. Hoeger and Hoeger (1997) re-

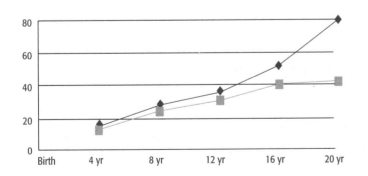

Figure 5.1 ⊙ *Strength development in males and females.*

port that about 80 percent of female body builders use steroids, and perhaps as many as 95 percent of female track and field athletes around the world have used steroids to remain internationally competitive.

Even without modifying substances, females can achieve the same relative strength as males. Pound for pound, female athletes are as strong as male athletes. Many top level female gymnasts are considered to be some of the strongest athletes in the world.

OVERLOAD PRINCIPLE FOR STRENGTH DEVELOPMENT

Strength gains are generally achieved in one of two ways: (1) more muscle fibers are stimulated at any given point in time, or (2) each muscle fiber increases the force it can generate. In order for strength gains to be made, one has to place such demands on the muscles. These demands are more commonly referred to as overload, hence the overload principle. By providing a systematic overloading of the muscle, it responds first by changing the nerves that stimulate the muscle and then physically changing the muscle structure.

Not only is the systematic and progressive increase in overload a necessity for optimal changes in strength, training specificity is important. Specificity of training means that a given increase in muscular strength and/or endurance is achieved through training specific to the desired outcome.

COMPONENTS OF SOUND STRENGTH TRAINING PROGRAM

Many professional groups such as the National Strength and Conditioning Association (NSCA) or the American College of Sports Medicine (ACSM) have dedicated journal issues to strength training or established position papers outlining what they believe to be sound components of a strength training program. Each of these groups agree that the specifics of strength training are addressed by mode, volume of resistance, and frequency. That however is where the agreement ends. In a lengthy paper by Carpinelli et al. (2004), the authors critically examine the ACSM's position stand and argue that much of the recommendations are unsubstantiated. Alternatively, Carpinelli et al. suggest simple, low-volume, time-efficient, resistance training is just as effective as complex, high-volume, time consuming protocols. This is great news for most of us that are only interested in generating a healthy level of strength and then maintaining that level as we age. Therefore, the three pieces of the strength training puzzle include mode, volume and frequency.

Mode

Mode is the type of activity used to strengthen the muscle. Static muscle contractions involve little or no movement and dynamic muscle contractions involve a full range of motion. Dynamic activities make up the bulk of training options; however, some simple static muscle contractions such as those used for neck and/or abdominal strengthening can be equally effective.

Volume

Volume of resistance refers to the number of repetitions and sets of a given exercise that are used to overload the muscle. Resistance in strength training is analogous to intensity for cardiorespiratory training. Here again, a level of 50–60 percent of a single maximal effort, also known as a one-repetition maximum (1RM), is a good place to start. Much has been written about multi sets versus single sets and changes in percent load, but data from Carpinelli et al. would suggest keeping it simple. If it's maintenance or muscle tone you are after, then one set of 8–12 reps may be sufficient to meet your needs.

Frequency

Frequency of strength training is very important in proper muscle development. To achieve a total body workout, a training schedule of two to three bouts per week is recommended, while alternating days of training with days of rest. People who want to train more often may choose to split the body into halves, working the upper body one day and the lower body the next. To obtain marked strength improvement, one needs to train a minimum of eight consecutive weeks. Once a desired level of strength is achieved, training once each week is usually enough to maintain the newly established strength level. Table 5.2 outlines particular achievement objectives using various strength training routines. These guidelines constitute a basis for establishing the foundation of a sound program. Once the goals of the program are set, selection of exercises for specific muscle groups can be made.

FUNCTIONAL STRENGTH TRAINING

As stated previously, not only are the systematic and progressive increases in overload a necessity for optimal changes in strength, specificity is important. Functional strength training attempts to address the specificity to an even greater extent than modification of mode, volume and frequency. Using stability balls, medicine balls, foam pads, soft discs and balance boards, it tries to combine neuromuscular control with strength development. These exercises put a premium on balance and require the person to control movement in all three planes. This same idea is the rationale of many people to train with free weights versus machines. Machines stress a muscle or muscle group, but do not require the person to balance the resistance as it is moving. Free weights on the other hand require the person to control the load while moving it through a full range of motion. Functional strength training adds yet an additional dimension forcing the lifter to not only balance the resistance, but control his/her body while completing the movement. An additional benefit to functional strength training is the enhancement of core strength. Core strength has become a popular term that basically implies one's strength to control the trunk and how much each limb is allowed to move during activity.

ASSESSING STRENGTH AND ENDURANCE

Although muscular strength and endurance are related, they are assessed with different procedures. Muscular strength is determined by a person's ability to complete

Outline for Strength Training Based on Program Goals				TABLE 5.2
Program Goal	**Resistance**	**Reps**	**Sets**	**Frequency**
Muscle Tone	60–70% 1RM	8–12	1–3	2–3x's/wk
Strength	65–90% 1RM	1–8	3–8	3x's/wk
Endurance	50–65% 1RM	10–20	3–5	3–6x's/wk

TABLE 5.3

Percent Body Weights Used to Assess Combined Strength and Endurance Utilizing Free Weights or a Multi-Station Machine

| | Percent of Body Weight | |
Lift	Males	Females
Leg Extension	65% BW	50% BW
Leg Curl	32% BW	25% BW
Bench Press	75% BW	45% BW
Lat Pull-down	70% BW	45% BW
Arm Curl	35% BW	18% BW

one repetition at his or her maximal resistance (1RM). However, finding a true 1RM is problematic since it requires the person to perform several single repetitions to determine the amount of weight that he/she can actually lift. Add the factors of learning, technique and endurance, and the tester has a difficult task at hand.

Endurance is typically measured by the number of completed repetitions of a submaximal resistance, and is much easier to assess. With either strength or endurance it is important to assess several different muscle groups. More than two tests are needed to properly assess strength since strength tends to be very specific. Five basic lifts are effective for assessing most large muscles of the body. As outlined by Hoeger and Hoeger (1997), Table 5.3 shows the five lifts and the percent body weights used for determining a combined muscular strength and endurance ranking.

Finally a simple test called the "plank" for core strength is presented. Stuart McGill (2002) has several additional assessments for core strength that he uses in his laboratory in Canada to assess back pain problems in his patients. He has found that by re-establishing a minimal level of core strength in his patients, they can delay and/or even prevent expensive and often less effective surgeries.

Muscular Strength and Endurance Assessment

On the following page are two examples on how to determine the resistance (weight) for each lift. Using the appropriate percentage of weight complete as many repetitions of each lift as possible and record the number of repetitions. Table 5.4 outlines a healthy standard for the repetitions completed on each lift. Any level above these standards places a person in a high fitness category. Values below the healthy standards suggest a need for improvement.

Several simple field tests exist for measuring upper and lower body muscular endurance. Abdominal crunches, modified push-ups and/or traditional push-ups, as well as modified dips, work well for assessing trunk and upper body muscle endurance. A one-minute bench jump with the use of a bleacher step or a 16¼ inch box is an excellent test of lower body muscular endurance. Specific instructions to complete each of these assessments are provided in the section below.

Four muscular endurance tests are used for men and three for women. Each test should be done with a partner. The proper procedure for each test is as follows:

Bench Jump (both males and females). Using a bench or box that is 16¼ inches high, jump up and down with a two-foot jump as many times as possible in one minute. One repetition is counted every time both feet touch the floor.

Push-ups (modified push-ups may be done by females). Lie face down on the floor while placing the hands by the shoulders and pointing the fingers forward.

Example 1

Female, weighing 130 lbs.

Lift	% of BW	Amount to lift
Leg Extension	.50 × 130 =	(65) 65 lbs.
Leg Curl	.25 × 130 =	(32.5) 30 lbs.
Bench Press	.45 × 130 =	(58.5) 60 lbs.
Lat Pull-down	.45 × 130 =	(58.5) 60 lbs.
Arm Curl	.18 × 130 =	(23.4) 25 lbs.

Example 2

Male, weighing 180 lbs.

Lift	% of BW	Amount to lift
Leg Extension	.65 × 180 =	(117) 120 lbs.
Leg Curl	.32 × 180 =	(57.6) 60 lbs.
Bench Press	.75 × 180 =	(135) 135 lbs.
Lat Pull-down	.70 × 180 =	(126) 125 lbs.
Arm Curl	.35 × 180 =	(63) 65 lbs.

The arms must fully extend and support the body on the hands and feet. Lower the body toward the floor and allow only the chest to touch it. Each chest touch counts as one repetition. A modified push-up allows females to support the lower body by the knees instead of the feet. Employing a two-second, down-up cadence, complete as many continuous repetitions as possible. Stop counting when repetitions fail to be performed while adhering to the aforementioned cadence.

Abdominal Crunch (both males and females). Although the abdominal crunch has come under scrutiny for administrative feasibility (Hall, et al., 1992; Knudson & Johnston, 1995), it still remains the safest test to assess muscular endurance of the trunk. A modified crunch test developed at St. Cloud State University (Figure 5.2) is a way to assess initial strength prior to completing the standard crunch test. Start at level four and move up or down to reach the highest level possible. If a level of four or greater is achieved, then the crunch test can be completed. If a level of three or less is achieved, then repetitions at the level of modified crunches achieved should be done on a routine basis until a level of four can be reached.

Upon reaching a level of four or more, one can complete the crunch test. While lying in a supine position, cross the arms over the chest. Bend the knees at a near right angle, with legs slightly apart and soles of the feet on the floor. The feet are not held during the test and the starting position begins when the head is held slightly off the floor. Then, using a two-second cadence, curl up until the shoulders are clearly off the floor and return to the starting position. Count the number of repetitions completed without losing the correct cadence, or until 100 repetitions are completed.

Healthy Standards for Combined Muscular Strength/Endurance					**TABLE 5.4**
	Number of Repetitions to Meet Healthy Standards				
Gender	Leg Ext.	Leg Curl	Bench Press	Lat-Pull	Arm Curl
Females	9–10	6–7	10–11	10–11	10–12
Males	12–13	10–11	10–11	10–11	9–10

Figure 5.2 ⊙

Abdominal Strength

Lie down flat on back and bend knees at a 60° angle. Heels must remain on floor at all times. Start with #4: If completed, go on to #5; if unable to complete, go back to #3.

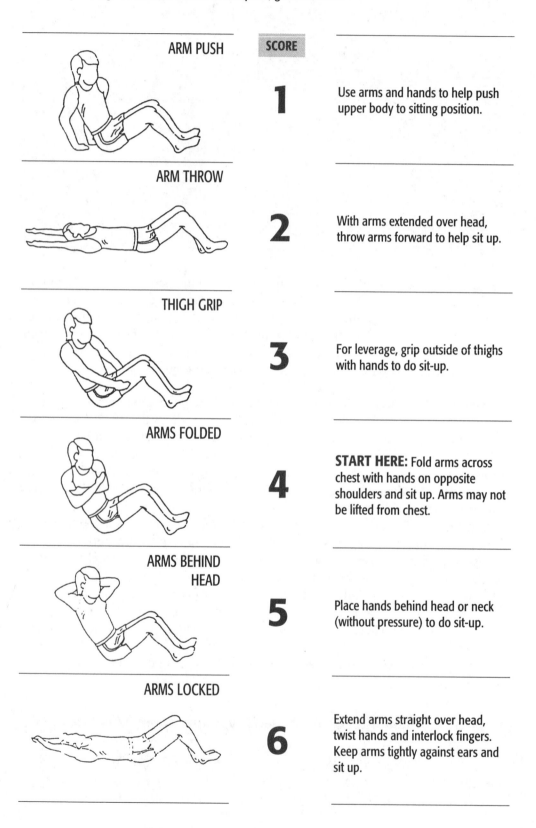

ARM PUSH

SCORE

1 Use arms and hands to help push upper body to sitting position.

ARM THROW

2 With arms extended over head, throw arms forward to help sit up.

THIGH GRIP

3 For leverage, grip outside of thighs with hands to do sit-up.

ARMS FOLDED

4 **START HERE:** Fold arms across chest with hands on opposite shoulders and sit up. Arms may not be lifted from chest.

ARMS BEHIND HEAD

5 Place hands behind head or neck (without pressure) to do sit-up.

ARMS LOCKED

6 Extend arms straight over head, twist hands and interlock fingers. Keep arms tightly against ears and sit up.

Modified Dip (men only). Using a bench or bleacher step and a box or three chairs, place the hands on the bench or each hand on a chair; the fingers should be forward and the feet up on the box or the third chair. The starting position calls for the arms to be extended, and the trunk bent at the hips approximately 90 degrees. Lower the body so you achieve a 90-degree angle at the elbow (upper arm should be about parallel to the floor). Using a two-second cadence, complete as many repetitions as possible.

Table 5.5 shows the number of repetitions needed to achieve a normal health-related fitness standard for each of these muscular endurance tests.

Core Strength Assessment—The Plank

Although the standard abdominal crunch is in part a measure of core strength, the plank will give you a true test of overall core strength that involves almost all of your trunk muscles. The test starts in a modified push-up position hence its name "the plank." Similar to the up position of a push-up the plank starts with a straight body supporting your weight on your toes and your forearms. Your elbows should be beneath your shoulders and your hands should be under your forehead. Your arms should look like two sides of a triangle coming together at your hands. Start the test by holding this position for 30 seconds. After 30 seconds, try to lift your left arm straight out in the air balancing your body on your other 3 limbs. After 15 seconds, put your left hand down and your right hand up. After another 15 seconds put your right hand down and lift your left leg up. Then after 15 more seconds, put the left leg down and lift the right leg up. This next part is tricky. Pick your left hand up and your right leg up. Now hold this for 15 seconds. Switch to your right hand and left leg for 15 seconds. Lastly come back to the original plank position and hold it for 30 more seconds. If you can complete this test, you have a very strong core. If any part of your body touches the ground other than the specified limbs the test is over. As you get stronger you will be able to go longer making this test a great gauge for marking improvement. As a side note, as you are able to stay in the plank longer, your forearms might benefit by the use of a mat or something soft underneath them. Good luck and have fun!

DESIGNING YOUR OWN STRENGTH PROGRAM

When planning your own program, give consideration to several issues. Of primary importance is the establishment of specific strength goals. Next are the types of equipment available to you. First and foremost, however, is safety. In order to set up a safe weight training regimen, these simple guidelines are recommended:

1. Warm-up properly before engaging in any lifting and/or strenuous calisthenics. A 5–15 minute aerobic warm-up that combines walking, light jogging or cycling, plus slow arm swings combined with a few dynamic stretches would suffice.

Number of Repetitions to Meet Healthy Standards					TABLE 5.5
Gender	Bench Jumps	Push-ups	Modified Push-ups	Crunches	Modified Dips
Females	39–42	N/A	30–33	31–34	N/A
Males	54–56	30–33	N/A	33–38	25–27

2. Remain conscious of your breathing. Do not hold your breath while lifting weights. A recommended pattern is to exhale while lifting the weight and inhale while returning the weight. Additionally, a few controlled, deep breaths in through the nose and out the mouth can be used to enhance recovery between sets and lifts.

3. Start with a weight or an exercise that you feel confident in completing. Starting too aggressively may lead to failure or increase risk of injury.

4. If free weights are used, have a spotter at all times and personally inspect the weight you are about to lift, making sure it is the proper weight and the collars holding the weights are secure.

5. Cool-down properly by repeating 5–15 minutes of aerobic activity and stretching. This period is the most important for maintaining and/or gaining flexibility. As you may recall from Chapter 4, it is during this time that connective tissue of a joint can be modified best since the elastic muscle tissue offers less resistance in post-exercise.

6. If delayed muscle soreness develops, stretching the muscles that are sore and repeating the same activities with a lower intensity, will relieve much of the discomfort. Uniqueness of any activity causes some micro-damage to the involved muscles, which is thought to produce this delayed soreness phenomenon.

Because muscular strength/endurance and core stability are daily requirements, a program should include all aspects when desired. In agreement with Carpinelli et al. (2004) and the ACSM (1990) the following recommendation for strength training to establishing a healthy level of muscular strength/endurance include: (1) one set of 8–12 repetitions using a resistance allowing the completion of that set to end nearing muscle failure; (2) complete 8–10 exercises that incorporate each major muscle group of the body; and (3) repeat this one set of exercises two or three times each week.

SUMMARY

Some people are fortunate enough (or unfortunate, depending on how one looks at it) to have jobs that provide the daily physical demands needed to maintain muscle mass. But reality suggests that the future will offer less and less need for manual labor or even physical activity of any kind. In much of society, the need to even physically move about is being lost. Elevators, escalators, home shopping networks, video games, e-mail, cell phones and computer-based work stations at home (eliminating the need to commute to a job site), are all examples of how our daily lives are becoming less active.

On the surface this may appear harmless and it most likely would be if we adapted appropriately. Fewer physical demands mean less activity. Less activity means less need for muscle and less need for food. Will we match our dietary intake to our daily physical requirements? That remains to be seen; however, if current generations are any indication of how our society has adapted, the experts would reply with a resounding NO! Quite simply, we are not adjusting to the lack of daily activity and we are getting fatter as a result of it. So, how much strength do you need and how do you get it? It is simple. Be active!

On a daily basis, you need to do some:

1. Aerobic activity that will stimulate the large muscles of the legs. Occasionally, add a little greater stress to those same muscles in order to recruit all the fiber types into the activity. If that requires weight training, so be it.
2. Activity where there is a demand for muscular strength of the upper body. Daily chores or simple calisthenics work equally well.
3. Abdominal crunches and/or "the plank" to maintain a sound level of muscular endurance for the trunk.

The rewards are not only medicinal but aesthetic as well. There is no equal to having adequate strength for activities of daily living. We lose what we fail to use and if we want it later, we have to use it now, every day.

References

American College of Sports Medicine. (1990). The recommended quantity and quality of exercise for developing cardiorespiratory and muscular fitness in healthy adults. *Medicine and Science in Sport and Exercise*, 22:265–274.

Campbell, W.W., Crim, M.C., Young, V.R., & Evans, W.J. (1994). Increased energy requirements and changes in body composition with resistance training in older adults. *American Journal of Clinical Nutrition*, 60:167–175.

Carpinelli, R.N., Otto, R., & Winett, R.A. (2004). A critical analysis of the ACSM position stand on resistance training: Insufficient evidence to support recommended training protocols. *Journal of Exercise Physiology online.* 7(3): June 1–60.

Faigenbaum, A., Milliken, L.A. & Westcott, W.L. (2003). Maximal strength training in healthy children. *Journal of Strength Conditioning Research*, 17(1):162–166.

Garnica, R.A. (1986). Muscle power in young women after slow and fast isokinetic training. *Journal of Orthopedics and Sports Physical Therapy*, 8:1.

Hall, G.L., Hetzler, R.K., Perrin, D., & Weltman, A. (1992). Relationship of timed sit-up tests to isokinetic abdominal strength. *Research Quarterly for Exercise and Sport*, 63:80–84.

Hesson, J.L. (1995). *Weight Training for Life*. Englewood, CO: Morton Publishers.

Hoeger, W.K., & Hoeger, S.A. (1997). *Principles and Labs for Fitness and Wellness* (5th ed.). Englewood, CO: Morton Publishing Company.

Knudson, D., & Johnston, D. (1995). Validity and reliability of a trunk bench curl-up test of abdominal endurance. *Journal of Strength and Conditioning Research*, 9:165–169.

McGill, S. (2002). *Low-Back Disorders: Evidence-Based Prevention and Rehabilitation.*, Leeds, UK: Human Kinetics Publishing.

Wescott, W., & Baechle, T. (1998). *Strength training past 50*. Champaign, IL: Human Kinetics Publishers.

chapter 5
LABORATORY ①

Muscular Strength/Endurance Lab and Worksheet

Instructions: Complete either Part A, Part B or both if you wish.

Part A
For assessing strength and endurance, use the procedures found in Chapter 5. Complete each test with a partner. No special equipment is required. Record the number of repetitions in the "Actual Value" column below.

To determine whether you meet the health standard for each test, refer to Table 5.5.

Males—complete all four tests: bench jumps, push-ups, crunches, and modified dips.

Females—complete the three appropriate tests: bench jumps, either modified push-ups or standard push-ups, and crunches. If you are an athlete that requires considerable upper body strength, feel free to try the modified dip test. A realistic minimum number would be 20 repetitions.

Your overall score can be calculated by giving yourself points for all tests as follows:

4 points   Exceed the health standard
3 points   Meet the standard
2 points   Barely under minimum standard
1 point   Not very close to minimum standard

Test	Actual Value	Meet Health Standard? (Y/N)	Points
Bench Jumps			
Push-ups/Modified Push-ups			+
Crunches			+
Modified Dips (males only)			+
		Overall Score	=

If your overall strength score is ≥ 8 for females and ≥ 10 for males, you've met the health standards with reasonable success. Review the areas that perhaps need improvement and think about how you might be able to do that.

Part B

If you have access to free weights and/or machines and you have received some general instruction or experience using such weights, you can complete the combined total body strength and endurance test described in Chapter 5. This could be used in place of the above described tests or done in addition to the above tests.

Use the percents shown in Table 5.3 for each specific lift. An example is provided for you on the top of page 81. Use Table 5.4 to determine if you meet and/or exceed the healthy standards for combined strength and endurance. Give yourself points using the same scale as used in Part A.

Test	# of Reps	Meet Health Standard? (Y/N)	Points
Leg Extension			
Leg Curl			+
Bench Press			+
Lat-pulls			+
Arm Curls			+
		Overall Score	=

If your strength/endurance score is ≥ 13 for females or males, you have met the health standards with reasonable success. Review the areas that perhaps need improvement and think about how you might be able to do that.

Questions: Name six fundamental safety issues for safe weight training.

1. _____

2. _____

3. _____

4. _____

5. _____

6. _____

© 2006 JUPITER IMAGES CORPORATION.

6 Nutrition

Key Terms

Dietary Guidelines for
   Americans
essential nutrients
kilocalories (calories)
nutrient-dense foods
non-nutrient-dense foods
fats (saturated,
   polyunsaturated, and
   monounsaturated)
proteins

carbohydrates
vitamins (fat-soluble and
   water-soluble)
minerals
amino acids
cholesterol
antioxidants
phytochemicals
Food Pyramid
vegetarianism

Specific Objectives

1. List and explain the Dietary Guidelines for Americans.

2. Design a diet which conforms to the Food Guide Pyramid.

3. List and explain the role of the various nutrients needed by the body.

4. Comprehend the various types of dietary fats and the role they play in cardiovascular health.

5. Identify the role of important vitamins and minerals in the human body.

6. Present specific suggestions for reducing sodium, sugar, fat, saturated fat and cholesterol in your diet.

7. Describe vegetarianism and nutritional supplementation, and explain important considerations about the practices.

8. Explain the pros and cons of dietary supplements.

9. Plan for healthy eating in fast food and other restaurants.

10. Incorporate information from food labels into dietary decisions.

11. Analyze your diet and make plans for improvement.

ost people know that eating right is a critical factor in how we look and feel, and that we may even be able to reduce our risks of certain health problems by following sound dietary principles. We know that proper nutrition is important, yet we remain trapped in old eating patterns that are not conducive to positive health. Many individuals feel as though their current diet is so bad that it would be futile to attempt to attain prudent eating habits. Some realize that minor adjustments could provide benefits, but lack the knowledge of basic nutritional principles. Still others know what needs to be done, yet mistakenly believe that it would be very costly and inconvenient for them to pursue a healthy diet, and still others are misled by the abundance of unscientific and misleading nutrition information that is being disseminated.

None of these situations needs to be the case. Healthful and enjoyable eating habits have been attained by millions of Americans, and are certainly attainable by anyone, including college students. Most diets need only minor adjustments to provide the benefits of good health, and with some study and explanation provided in this chapter, good eating habits can be adopted for lifelong health. Unfortunately, there is a great deal of misinformation and misrepresentation in the area of nutrition which is very misleading to the average consumer. Nutrition information can be presented in a very simple format, or it can be made to appear quite complicated, and while certain individuals may desire to study the science of nutrition in detail, most people simply want to know the basic guidelines in order to make easy lifestyle application of good nutrition principles. For this reason, several government agencies have published documents which provide excellent information to help the general public sort through the vast array of information, both good and bad, to make decisions. Although some of the specific information in those documents has been debated, a proper diet is virtually assured if one follows the general recommendations provided.

The 2005 Dietary Guidelines for Americans from the United States Department of Agriculture provide several key recommendations for achieving optimal nutrition. Since these Guidelines provide an excellent framework for a healthy diet, they will serve as the center of our discussion. The following pages contain an explanation of the importance of the Guidelines as well as practical suggestions for incorporating them into your daily eating plan. Specific application for various population groups are included under each recommendation for a complete understanding of how these guidelines influence healthy eating through the lifespan.

DIETARY GUIDELINES FOR AMERICANS

1. Adequate Nutrients within Calorie Needs

Key Recommendations

⊙ Consume a variety of nutrient-dense foods and beverages within and among the basic food groups while choosing foods that limit the intake of saturated and *trans* fats, cholesterol, added sugars, salt, and alcohol.

⊙ Meet recommended intakes within energy needs by adopting a balanced eating pattern, such as the USDA Food Guide Pyramid or the DASH Eating Plan.

Key Recommendations for Specific Population Groups

⊙ **People over age 50.** Consume vitamin B_{12} in its crystalline form (i.e., fortified foods or supplements).

- **Women of childbearing age who may become pregnant.** Eat foods high in heme-iron and/or consume iron-rich plant foods or iron-fortified foods with an enhancer of iron absorption, such as vitamin C-rich foods.

- **Women of childbearing age who may become pregnant and those in the first trimester of pregnancy.** Consume adequate synthetic folic acid daily (from fortified foods or supplements) in addition to food forms of folate from a varied diet.

- **Older adults, people with dark skin, and people exposed to insufficient ultraviolet band radiation (i.e., sunlight).** Consume extra vitamin D from vitamin D-fortified foods and/or supplements.

© 2006 JUPITER IMAGES CORPORATION.

2. Weight Management

Key Recommendations

- To maintain body weight in a healthy range, balance calories from foods and beverages with calories expended.

- To prevent gradual weight gain over time, make small decreases in food and beverage calories and increase physical activity.

Key Recommendations for Specific Population Groups

- **Those who need to lose weight.** Aim for a slow, steady weight loss by decreasing calorie intake while maintaining an adequate nutrient intake and increasing physical activity.

- **Overweight children.** Reduce the rate of body weight gain while allowing growth and development. Consult a healthcare provider before placing a child on a weight-reduction diet.

- **Pregnant women.** Ensure appropriate weight gain as specified by a healthcare provider.

- **Breastfeeding women.** Moderate weight reduction is safe and does not compromise weight gain of the nursing infant.

- **Overweight adults and overweight children with chronic diseases and/or on medication.** Consult a healthcare provider about weight loss strategies prior to starting a weight-reduction program to ensure appropriate management of other health conditions.

3. Physical Activity

Key Recommendations

- Engage in regular physical activity and reduce sedentary activities to promote health, psychological well-being, and a healthy body weight.

  - To reduce the risk of chronic disease in adulthood: Engage in at least 30 minutes of moderate-intensity physical activity, above usual activity, at work or home on most days of the week.

- For most people, greater health benefits can be obtained by engaging in physical activity of more vigorous intensity or longer duration.
- To help manage body weight and prevent gradual, unhealthy body weight gain in adulthood: Engage in approximately 60 minutes of moderate- to vigorous-intensity activity on most days of the week while not exceeding caloric intake requirements.
- To sustain weight loss in adulthood: Participate in at least 60 to 90 minutes of daily moderate-intensity physical activity while not exceeding caloric intake requirements. Some people may need to consult with a healthcare provider before participating in this level of activity.

- Achieve physical fitness by including cardiovascular conditioning, stretching exercises for flexibility, and resistance exercises or calisthenics for muscle strength and endurance.

Key Recommendations for Specific Population Groups

- **Children and adolescents.** Engage in at least 60 minutes of physical activity on most, preferably all, days of the week.
- **Pregnant women.** In the absence of medical or obstetric complications, incorporate 30 minutes or more of moderate-intensity physical activity on most, if not all, days of the week. Avoid activities with a high risk of falling or abdominal trauma.
- **Breastfeeding women.** Be aware that neither acute nor regular exercise adversely affects the mother's ability to successfully breastfeed.
- **Older adults.** Participate in regular physical activity to reduce functional declines associated with aging and to achieve the other benefits of physical activity identified for all adults.

4. Food Groups to Encourage

Key Recommendations

- Consume a sufficient amount of fruits and vegetables while staying within energy needs. Two cups of fruit and 2½ cups of vegetables per day are recommended for a reference 2,000-calorie intake, with higher or lower amounts depending on the calorie level.

Chapter 6

© 2006 JUPITER IMAGES CORPORATION.

© 2006 JUPITER IMAGES CORPORATION.

⊙ Choose a variety of fruits and vegetables each day. In particular, select from all five vegetable subgroups (dark green, orange, legumes, starchy vegetables, and other vegetables) several times a week.

⊙ Consume 3 or more ounce-equivalents of whole-grain products per day, with the rest of the recommended grains coming from enriched or whole-grain products. In general, at least half the grains should come from whole grains.

⊙ Consume 3 cups per day of fat-free or low-fat milk or equivalent milk products.

Key Recommendations for Specific Population Groups

⊙ **Children and adolescents.** Consume whole-grain products often; at least half the grains should be whole grains. Children 2 to 8 years should consume 2 cups per day of fat-free or low-fat milk or equivalent milk products. Children 9 years of age and older should consume 3 cups per day of fat-free or low-fat milk or equivalent milk products.

5. Fats

Key Recommendations

⊙ Consume less than 10 percent of calories from saturated fatty acids and less than 300 mg/day of cholesterol, and keep *trans* fatty acid consumption as low as possible.

⊙ Keep total fat intake between 20 to 35 percent of calories, with most fats coming from sources of polyunsaturated and monounsaturated fatty acids, such as fish, nuts, and vegetable oils.

⊙ When selecting and preparing meat, poultry, dry beans, and milk or milk products, make choices that are lean, low-fat, or fat-free.

⊙ Limit intake of fats and oils high in saturated and/or *trans* fatty acids, and choose products low in such fats and oils.

Key Recommendations for Specific Population Groups

⊙ **Children and adolescents.** Keep total fat intake between 30 to 35 percent of calories for children 2 to 3 years of age and between 25 to 35 percent of calories for children and adolescents 4 to 18 years of age, with most fats coming from sources of polyunsaturated and monounsaturated fatty acids, such as fish, nuts, and vegetable oils.

6. Carbohydrates

Key Recommendations

⊙ Choose fiber-rich fruits, vegetables, and whole grains often.

⊙ Choose and prepare foods and beverages with little added sugars or caloric sweeteners, such as amounts suggested by the USDA Food Guide and the DASH Eating Plan.

⊙ Reduce the incidence of dental caries by practicing good oral hygiene and consuming sugar- and starch-containing foods and beverages less frequently.

7. Sodium and Potassium

Key Recommendations

⊙ Consume less than 2,300 mg (approximately 1 tsp of salt) of sodium per day.

⊙ Choose and prepare foods with little salt. At the same time, consume potassium-rich foods, such as fruits and vegetables.

Key Recommendations for Specific Population Groups

⊙ **Individuals with hypertension, blacks, and middle-aged and older adults.** Aim to consume no more than 1,500 mg of sodium per day, and meet the potassium recommendation (4,700 mg/day) with food.

8. Alcoholic Beverages

Key Recommendations

⊙ Those who choose to drink alcoholic beverages should do so sensibly and in moderation—defined as the consumption of up to one drink per day for women and up to two drinks per day for men.

⊙ Alcoholic beverages should not be consumed by some individuals, including those who cannot restrict their alcohol intake, women of childbearing age who may become pregnant, pregnant and lactating women, children and adolescents, individuals taking medications that can interact with alcohol, and those with specific medical conditions.

⊙ Alcoholic beverages should be avoided by individuals engaging in activities that require attention, skill, or coordination, such as driving or operating machinery.

9. Food Safety

Key Recommendations

⊙ To avoid microbial foodborne illness:

  ○ Clean hands, food contact surfaces, and fruits and vegetables. Meat and poultry should not be washed or rinsed.

- Separate raw, cooked, and ready-to-eat foods while shopping, preparing, or storing foods.
- Cook foods to a safe temperature to kill microorganisms.
- Chill (refrigerate) perishable food promptly and defrost foods properly.
- Avoid raw (unpasteurized) milk or any products made from unpasteurized milk, raw or partially cooked eggs or foods containing raw eggs, raw or undercooked meat and poultry, unpasteurized juices, and raw sprouts.

Key Recommendations for Specific Population Groups

⊙ **Infants and young children, pregnant women, older adults, and those who are immunocompromised.** Do not eat or drink raw (unpasteurized) milk or any products made from unpasteurized milk, raw or partially cooked eggs or foods containing raw eggs, raw or undercooked meat and poultry, raw or undercooked fish or shellfish, unpasteurized juices, and raw sprouts.

⊙ **Pregnant women, older adults, and those who are immunocompromised.** Only eat certain deli meats and frankfurters that have been reheated to steaming hot.

U.S. Department of Health and Human Services.

THE DASH EATING PLAN

The DASH Eating Plan, referred to in the Dietary Guidelines, stands for Dietary Approaches to Stop Hypertension. Research studies show that diet affects hypertension (high blood pressure), and that blood pressure can be lowered by following a particular eating plan. The DASH plan is low in saturated fat, total fat, and cholesterol, and emphasizes consumption of fruits, vegetables, and low fat dairy products. It includes whole grains, fish, poultry, and nuts, and is reduced in red meats, sweets, and sugar sweetened beverages. It is consistent with the Dietary Guidelines and the Food Pyramid which provide the basis for nutrition information in this chapter. The DASH plan can be viewed in its entirety at the following website:

www.nhlbi.nih.gov/health/public/heart/hbp/dash/new_dash.pdf

THE FOOD PYRAMID

The Food Pyramid (USDA, 2005) is another helpful guide to good eating. It is important to note that the Dietary Guidelines for Americans and the Food Pyramid are consistent with and compliment each other. They support the same basic nutrition information. The pyramid plan also places emphasis on regular physical activity. The plan, called the MyPyramid Plan, is an individualized approach to building a healthy diet. As shown in Figure 6.1 each vertical piece of the pyramid represents a different food group, and the width of the section represents the amount to be consumed in a healthy diet. With all nutrients, the amount needed by an individual varies depending on age, gender, and activity level, and more specific and detailed information on how to personalize the pyramid for optimal results can be found at the USDA website highlighted below:

www.mypyramid.gov

GRAINS	VEGETABLES	FRUITS	MILK	MEATS & BEANS

GRAINS	VEGETABLES	FRUITS	MILK	MEATS & BEANS
Make half your grains whole	Vary your veggies	Focus on fruits	Get your calcium-rich foods	Go lean with protein
Eat at least 3 oz. of whole-grain cereals, breads, crackers, rice, or pasta every day 1 oz. is about 1 slice of bread, about 1 cup of breakfast cereal, or 1/2 cup of cooked rice, cereal, or pasta	Eat more dark-green veggies like broccoli, spinach, and other dark leafy greens Eat more orange vegetables like carrots and sweet-potatoes Eat more dry beans and peas like pinto beans, kidney beans, and lentils	Eat a variety of fruit Choose fresh, frozen, canned, or dried fruit Go easy on fruit juices	Go low-fat or fat-free when you choose milk, yogurt, and other milk products If you don't or can't consume milk, choose lactose-free products or other calcium sources such as fortified foods and beverages	Choose low-fat or lean meats and poultry Bake it, broil it, or grill it Vary your protein routine—choose more fish, beans, peas, nuts, and seeds

For a 2,000-calorie diet, you need the amounts below from each food group. To find the amounts that are right for you, go to MyPyramid.gov

Eat 6 oz. every day	Eat 2½ cups every day	Eat 2 cups every day	Get 3 cups every day; for kids aged 2 to 8, it's 2	Eat 5½ oz. every day

Find your balance between food and physical activity

- Be sure to stay within your daily calorie needs.
- Be physically active for at least 30 minutes most days of the week.
- About 60 minutes a day of physical activity may be needed to prevent weight gain.
- For sustaining weight loss, at least 60 to 90 minutes a day of physical activity may be required.
- Children and teenagers should be physically active for 60 minutes every day, or most days

Know the limits on fats, sugars, and salt (sodium)

- Make most of your fat sources from fish, nuts, and vegetable oils.
- Limit solid fats like butter, stick margarine, shortening, and lard, as well as foods that contain these.
- Check the Nutrition Facts label to keep saturated fats, *trans* fats, and sodium low.
- Choose food and beverages low in added sugars. Added sugars contribute calories with few, if any, nutrients.

Figure 6.1 ⊙ *MyPyramid guidelines.*

Source: U.S. Department of Agriculture.

The first section of the pyramid represents the grain group. Foods from this group are excellent sources of complex carbohydrates, fiber, iron, niacin, and vitamin B_1, among other nutrients. Everyone needs to consume 3–4 ounces of whole grain bread, cereal, crackers, rice, or pasta daily. One ounce equals one slice of bread, one cup of ready to eat cereal, or one-half cup of cooked rice, pasta, or cereal. The second section of the pyramid is made up of the vegetable group. Everyone should strive to eat more dark green vegetables, orange vegetables, and dry beans and peas. Two to three cups each day are recommended, and a one cup serving is considered as one cup of raw or cooked vegetables or two cups of leafy green vegetables. The third section of the pyramid is the fruit group. A variety of fruits (fresh, frozen, canned, or dried) should be consumed. The recommended amount is one and one-half to two cups daily, and a cup is considered as one cup of fruit juice, one-half cup of dried fruit, or one cup of cut fruit. Go easy on the fruit juice, since it adds calories to the diet without significantly contributing to a feeling of fullness. Fruits and vegetables are also carbohydrate rich foods, and provide fiber, vitamins C, B_6, A, and E as well as folic acid. The next part of the pyramid, represented by the thinnest of the vertical sections, is the oils group. Many foods from this group contain little nutritional value, but provide empty calories. Most oils should be chosen from fish, nuts, and vegetable oils, with a limitation of fats like butter, stick margarine, shortening, and lard. Instead of a recommended amount of this food group, it is represented as a daily allowance, with the allowance being five to seven tablespoons. The amount of oils varies greatly from product to product, so it is recommended that consumers refer to the USDA website for guidance. The fifth vertical pyramid section is the milk, yogurt, and cheese group. Dairy foods provide calcium, protein, vitamin B_{12}, and other nutrients. It is recommended that low fat dairy choices be made, and the recommended daily amount is three cups. One cup is a cup of milk or yogurt, one and one-half ounces of natural cheese, or two ounces of processed cheese. The last part of the pyramid is the meat and beans group, which provide protein, niacin, iron, and vitamin B_1, as well as other important nutrients. Low fat choices of lean meats and poultry should be chosen, with meats being baked, broiled, or grilled. For variety, include fish, beans, peas, nuts, and seeds to provide the valuable nutrients from this group. Five to six ounces a day is recommended, and one ounce is a one ounce serving of meat, fish, or poultry, one-fourth cup of cooked dry beans, one egg, one tablespoon of peanut butter, or one-half ounce of nuts or seeds. The pyramid plan emphasizes that one size does not fit all, so again, a visit to the USDA website can be of great assistance in formulating a prudent eating plan.

THE NUTRIENTS AND MACRONUTRIENTS

There are six categories of nutrients needed by the human body. The macronutrients are the energy (calorie) providing nutrients—fats, carbohydrates, and protein. The micronutrients vitamins, minerals, and water do not provide energy (calories). Figure 6.2 illustrates the percentages of the macronutrients recommended for a balanced diet, compared to the percentages in the current American diet.

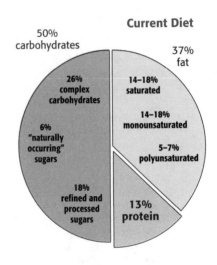

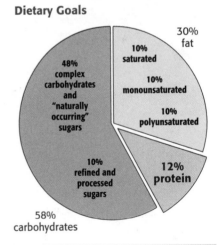

Figure 6.2 ⊙ *Percent of calories from different nutrients in the current American diet and in an ideal diet.*

Source: Based in part from *Dietary Goals for the United States*, 1977; prepared by the Senate Committee on Nutrition and Human Needs.

Copied from: *Health Decisions* by C.E. Bruess and G.E. Richardson. Brown & Benchmark, 1994.

TABLE 6.1
Your Fat Budget

Fat Budget for Men

Age	Weight	Fat Budget	Based on Average Caloric Need of:
19–24	140–160	90 g	2700
	160–180	105 g	3150
	180–200	115 g	3450
25–50	140–160	85 g	2550
	160–180	95 g	2850
	180–200	105 g	3150
over 50	140–160	70 g	2100
	160–180	75 g	2250
	180–200	85 g	2550

Fat Budget for Women

Age	Weight	Fat Budget	Based on Average Caloric Need of:
19–24	110–130	70 g	2100
	130–160	80 g	2400
	150–170	90 g	2700
25–50	110–130	65 g	1950
	130–160	75 g	2250
	150–170	85 g	2550
over 50	110–130	55 g	1650
	130–150	65 g	1950
	150–170	75 g	2250

*If you believe you do not have the same average caloric needs for your sex, age, and weight, you can calculate your own fat budget with the following equation:

$$\text{FAT BUDGET (in grams)} = (\text{CALORIC NEEDS} \times .3)/9$$

For example, if you determine that you consume approximately 2000 calories per day, your fat budget would be calculated as follows:

$$FB = (2000 \times .3)/9$$
$$FB = 600/9$$
$$FB = 67 \text{ grams per day}$$

Fats

Dietary fat has been vilified, but we all need some fat in our diet. Fats provide an avenue for the transportation and storage of fat soluble vitamins (A, D, E, and K) and is important in the regulation of certain body functions. They help form cell membranes and hormones. They add flavor to food and provide satiety, or that satisfied feeling of fullness which we like to experience after a meal. Many foods containing fat are good sources of high quality protein. Fats also provide energy at a rate of nine calories per gram, making them the most concentrated form of energy for the body. Yet while an excellent source of concentrated energy, this also makes fat the fattening nutrient, and anyone interested in losing weight will certainly need to watch their fat intake. The amount of fat actually needed is significantly less than most people's current intake. A good goal for fat intake is between 25–30 percent of total calories. A helpful guide called determining your fat budget is shown in Table 6.1.

While some dietary fat is needed, the high fat diet has been identified as a contributor to poor health. A diet high in fat, saturated fat and cholesterol contributes significantly to one's risk for the number one killer of Americans, heart disease. Table 6.2 compares the fat, saturated fat, cholesterol and calories from selected foods. Excessive dietary cholesterol cause increases in serum cholesterol (cholesterol in the bloodstream) levels. For this reason, it is important to include fewer high cholesterol products in our diet. Numerous products are attempting to capitalize on the health-conscious consumer by touting their low-cholesterol or cholesterol-free qualities. It is important to note that although these are certainly good qualities, knowing that a product is low in cholesterol or cholesterol free is not enough. Some foods contain no cholesterol, yet are high in saturated fats or trans fats. As a rule, food products which come from plant sources never contain cholesterol. Cholesterol is present only in foods of animal origin.

Even more important than cholesterol is the role that saturated fat plays in serum cholesterol levels. Saturated fat in the diet raises the levels of low-density lipoproteins in the blood. Low-density lipoproteins are the type of cholesterol molecules that adhere to the inside walls of the arteries, causing a condition known as atherosclerosis, or the buildup of fatty deposits on artery walls. This interferes with the flow of oxygenated blood through those arteries. Because of this quality, low-density lipoprotein, or LDL, is often referred to as bad cholesterol. Foods high in saturated fat are the type of foods most likely to be converted into LDL, so it is very important to limit their consumption, preferably to less than ten percent of caloric intake. Saturated fats are usually solid at room temperature and include foods like whole dairy products, fatty meats such as bacon, lunch meats, sausage, and heavily marbled steaks and roasts, fried and breaded foods, many desserts, sauces, gravies

Comparison of Calories, Fat, Saturated Fat and Cholesterol Content of Selected Foods

TABLE 6.2

Food	Calories	Fat	Saturated Fat	Cholesterol
Dairy products				
1 cup whole milk	150	8	5	33
1 cup 2% milk	120	5	3	22
1 cup skim milk	86	trace	trace	4
1 cup ice cream	269	14	8	59
1 cup sherbet	270	4	2	113
1 oz cheddar cheese	114	9	6	30
1 oz part skim mozzarella cheese	80	5	3	1
Beef, fish, pork, and chicken				
3 oz water packed tuna	135	1	trace	48
7 medium fried shrimp	200	10	2.5	168
3.5 oz boiled shrimp	109	1.5	trace	147
3 oz baked salmon	140	5	1	60
3 oz ground beef patty	240	17	6.5	75
2.5 oz broiled sirloin steak (fat trimmed)	150	6	2.5	64
3 medium bacon slices	109	9	3	16
3 oz roasted ham (fat trimmed)	133	5	1.5	47
3 oz fried chicken w/skin	154	8.5	2.5	52
3 oz roasted chicken w/out skin	85	3	.5	45
Snack foods, sauces, condiments				
1 tbsp butter	100	11.5	7	247
1 tbsp margarine	100	11.5	2	0
1 egg	79	5.5	1.5	274
1 egg white	16	0	0	0
1 tbsp corn oil	125	14	2	0
1 tbsp mayonnaise	100	11	2	8
1 avocado	305	30	5	0
4 chocolate chip cookies	185	9	3.5	8
1 slice pecan pie	583	23	4	137

and oils, and products that have been hydrogenated. Hydrogenation is a process which is used to change the texture and prolong the shelf-life of a product. Unfortunately, it also results in the formation of trans-fatty acids, which behave like saturated fat and raise LDL levels. Margarine and shortenings are often hydrogenated, and numerous processed foods contain oils with some degree of hydrogenation. Fortunately for nutrition conscious consumers, the amount of trans fats in foods is now required to be provided on food labels.

One additional warning about the fatty acid composition of foods is needed here. While most oils from plants are low in saturated fat, there are two notable exceptions. They are palm oil, which is 82 percent saturated, and coconut oil, which is 87 percent saturated. These two oils are harvested from plants which are grown in tropical regions, and are therefore referred to as tropical oils. Steps should be taken to minimize or avoid their consumption.

Two other types of dietary fats have interesting effects on serum cholesterol levels. Increasing the amount of polyunsaturated fat in the diet has been shown to lower cholesterol levels by lowering the LDL cholesterol without reducing the HDL. The preferred type of fat to substitute for saturated fat is monounsaturated fat. Monounsaturated fat, like polyunsaturated fat, lowers total cholesterol levels in the blood. However, this reduction in total cholesterol is the result of lowering LDLs, while the beneficial HDL levels may even be increased. One other type of fat which has received considerable attention of late is called Omega-3 fatty acids. These fats are found in fish such as lake trout, salmon, herring, and tuna and are thought to help prevent heart disease by lowering LDL and total cholesterol. The fatty acid composition of many fats and oils is shown in Figure 6.3.

Although there is certainly a difference in the three types of fatty acids and the effect they have on cholesterol levels, it is important to remember that they are all fats, and that they all contain nine calories per gram. Total fat consumption needs to be reduced to 25–30 percent of our total caloric intake, and consuming a higher percentage of calories as fat means consuming a lower percent of calories as carbohydrate or protein, and it is usually carbohydrate consumption that is compromised. And at nine calories per gram, a reduction in dietary fat intake is a major step toward reducing the total caloric consumption, which is one-half of the energy balance equation necessary for a healthy weight.

A chart with suggestions for substitutions for many high-fat food items is shown in Table 6.3. Additional tips for reducing dietary fat include:

1. Use fats and oils sparingly in cooking.
2. Use small amounts of salad dressings and spreads, such as butter, margarine and mayonnaise. One tablespoon of most of these spreads provides 10–11 grams of fat, and 90–100 calories.
3. Choose liquid vegetable oils most often because they are lower in saturated fat.
4. Become a label reader to check how much fat and saturated fat are in a serving.
5. Choose lean meat, fish, poultry, and dried beans and peas as your low-fat protein sources.

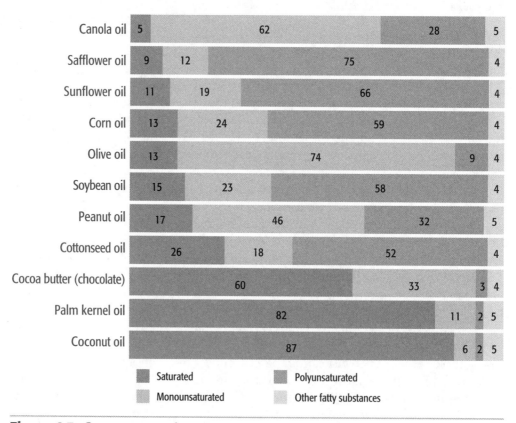

Figure 6.3 ⊙ *Percentages of saturated, polyunsaturated, and monounsaturated fats in common vegetable oils.*

Copied from *Health: The Basics* 2nd edition. Donatelle & Davis.

TABLE 6.3

Cutting the Fat

The following substitutions are helpful in reducing dietary fat.
The comparative grams of fat are shown for some items.

Instead of:	Try
Butter or margarine	Butter substitutes
Regular yogurt	Non-fat yogurt
Regular salad dressing	Non-fat salad dressing
Mayonnaise	Mustard or low fat salad dressing
Tuna in oil	Tuna in water
Fried foods	Baked or broiled foods
Dark meat poultry	Light meat poultry
Prime beef	Choice or select beef
Bacon and sausage	Lean ham
Burger and fries	Soup and salad
Pepperoni pizza	Canadian bacon pizza
Whole milk dairy products	Skim or low fat dairy products
Regular cheese	Low fat cheese, skim milk mozzarella
Pastries (38 g or more)	Hot cereals (2 g)
Muffins (5–12 g)	English muffins (1–2 g)
Croissant (12 g)	Bread (1 g)
Fried chicken (30 g)	Grilled chicken (3 g)
Fried potatoes (12 g)	Baked potato (trace)

In cooking:	Try
1 cup of oil	1 cup of applesauce
Whole eggs (6 g)	Two egg whites (trace)

When reaching for a snack:	Try
Candy bar	Fresh fruit
Ice cream bars (8–30 g)	Frozen fruit bars (0 fat)
Ice cream (11–18 g)	Sherbet, low-fat yogurt, or ice milk (2–4 g)
Doughnuts (14 g)	Bagels (2 g)
Devil's food cake	Angel food cake
High fat cookies and crackers	Fat-free cookies and crackers
Fried corn and potato chips	Baked chips or pretzels

6. Trim the fat from meat; remove the skin from poultry. (When cooking, the skin can be left on poultry without adding fat, provided it is removed before the chicken is eaten.)

7. Moderate the use of egg yolks and organ meats. While an egg contains about 215 mg of cholesterol, no fat or cholesterol is found in egg whites. Use them freely.

8. Choose skim milk or low-fat milk and fat-free or low-fat yogurt and cheese most of the time.

Carbohydrates

Carbohydrates are the body's preferred form of energy for sustaining daily activity. Many individuals believe that carbohydrates are the fattening nutrient, but they are not. Carbohydrates supply only four calories per gram and high carbohydrate foods typically provide substantial amounts of other important nutrients as well, specifically vitamins and minerals, along with dietary fiber. Most high carbohydrate foods, which include fruits, vegetables, and whole grain products, are considered nutrient dense, and should make up nearly 60 percent of one's daily caloric intake. A nutrient-dense food is one that contains relatively high levels of nutrients packed into a relatively low number of calories. A good example of a specific nutrient dense food is broccoli. One cup of the cooked vegetable provides only 46 calories and virtually no fat, yet contains 98 mg of vitamin C (the DRI is only 60–75 mg), almost half of the DRI for vitamin A, 20 percent of the DRI for calcium, ten percent for iron, as well as additional B vitamins, potassium, magnesium, and other minerals. On the other hand, a non-nutrient dense food is a typical candy bar, weighing in at 280 calories and 14 grams of fat, five of which are saturated. It is almost completely void of any valuable nutrients except for a little protein.

Carbohydrates fall into one of two categories: simple or complex. Simple carbohydrates consist of sugars, such as fructose, sucrose, dextrose, and others, and provide no significant nutritional value. Simple sugars are either monosaccharides (single sugars, like fructose and glucose) or linked combinations of monosaccharides called disaccharides (double sugars, like sucrose and lactose). Complex carbohydrates are polysaccharides which are longer chains of saccharides, the most notable of which is starch. Starchy foods like potatoes, grains, and legumes are very important for good nutrition. They are low in fat and are cholesterol free, low in calories, high in fiber, and usually nutrient dense. Complex carbohydrates should make up approximately half of the calories in our diet, while simple sugars should make up no more than ten percent of total calories.

Mention must be made here of the "low-carb craze" which has taken the American food industry by storm. Since carbohydrates should make up about 60 percent of daily caloric intake, the emphasis on lowered carbohydrate intake has clearly been misguided. It is important to note that excessive intake of any nutrient can make weight control very difficult, so carbohydrates, like all sources of calories, must be balanced with physical activity for maintenance of a healthy weight. Also, it is true that all carbohydrates are not the same. As explained above, most of the simple carbohydrates do not provide much nutritional value, so it is indeed best to minimize them in the diet, but reducing the nutrient-dense, complex carbohydrates would deprive the body of its most valuable source of low calorie, nutrient rich foods.

Proteins

Proteins are the major building blocks in the human body and are major components of nearly every human cell. They play an important role in the development of antibodies, enzymes, blood, skin, bone, and muscle. Proteins also supply the body with energy in the absence of available carbohydrates and fats. Like carbohydrates, they provide four calories per gram. Proteins are made up of amino acids. There are 20 amino acids which the human body uses, 11 of which are called non-essential because they can be manufactured by the body. The other nine are called essential amino acids because the human body cannot produce them so it is essential that they be obtained from foods. A complete protein, or high-quality protein, is one which contains all nine essential amino acids, and come from animal sources. Plant source protein does not contain all nine essential amino acids and is called incomplete protein. Incomplete protein, however, can be combined so that all essential amino acids are provided. This practice is included in the discussion of vegetarianism later in this chapter. Proteins should make up 12–15 percent of total calories.

Vitamins

Vitamins are organic compounds needed by the body in small amounts. Although they do not provide calories, they do help transform food into energy. They also promote the growth and repair of tissue, and assist in the utilization of minerals. Vitamins may be classified as fat-soluble or water-soluble. Fat soluble vitamins A, D, E, and K are stored in the body's adipose (fat) tissue and can potentially reach toxic levels if very high doses are consumed over a period of time. Water-soluble vitamins B complex and C are excreted by the body so they should be consumed on a daily basis. A guide to vitamin functions and effects of deficiencies and megadoses are found in Table 6.4.

TABLE 6.4
Facts about Vitamins

Vitamin	Major Functions	Signs of Prolonged Deficiency	Toxic Effects of Megadoses	Important Dietary Sources
Fat-Soluble Vitamin A	Maintenance of eyes, vision, skin, linings of the nose, mouth, digestive and urinary tracts, immune function	Night blindness; dry, scaling skin; increased susceptibility to infection; loss of appetite; anemia; kidney stones	Headache, vomiting and diarrhea, dryness of mucous membranes, vertigo, double vision, bone abnormalities, liver damage, miscarriage and birth defects, convulsions, coma, respiratory failure	Liver, milk, butter, cheese, and fortified margarine; carrots, spinach, cantaloupe, and other orange and deep-green vegetables and fruits contain carotenes that the body converts to vitamin A
Vitamin D	Aid in calcium and phosphorus metabolism, promotion of calcium absorption, development and maintenance of bones and teeth	Rickets (bone deformities) in children; bone softening, loss, and fractures in adults	Calcium deposits in kidneys and blood vessels, causing irreversible kidney and cardiovascular damage	Fortified milk and margarine, fish liver oils, butter, egg yolks (sunlight on skin also produces vitamin D)
Vitamin E	Protection and maintenance of cellular membranes	Red blood cell breakage and anemia, weakness, neurological problems, muscle cramps	Relatively nontoxic, but may cause excess bleeding or formation of blood clots	Vegetable oils, whole grains, nuts and seeds, green leafy vegetables, asparagus, peaches; smaller amounts widespread in other foods
Vitamin K	Production of factors essential for blood clotting	Hemorrhaging	None observed	Green leafy vegetables; smaller amounts widespread in other foods
Water-Soluble Vitamin C	Maintenance and repair of connective tissue, bones, teeth, and cartilage; promotion of healing; aid in iron absorption	Scurvy (weakening of collagenous structures resulting in widespread capillary hemorrhaging), anemia, reduced resistance to infection, bleeding gums, weakness, loosened teeth, rough skin, joint pain, poor wound healing, hair loss, poor iron absorption	Urinary stones in some people, acid stomach from ingesting supplements in pill form, nausea, diarrhea, headache, fatigue	Peppers, broccoli, spinach, brussels sprouts, citrus fruits, strawberries, tomatoes, potatoes, cabbage, other fruits and vegetables
Thiamin	Conversion of carbohydrates into usable forms of energy, maintenance of appetite and nervous system function	Beriberi (symptoms include edema or muscle wasting, mental confusion, anorexia, enlarged heart, abnormal heart rhythm, muscle degeneration and weakness, nerve changes)	None reported	Yeast, whole-grain and enriched breads and cereals, organ meats, liver, pork, lean meats, poultry, eggs, fish, beans, nuts, legumes

(continued)

		TABLE 6.4 *(continued)*		
		Facts about Vitamins		
Vitamin	*Major Functions*	*Signs of Prolonged Deficiency*	*Toxic Effects of Megadoses*	*Important Dietary Sources*
Water-Soluble				
Riboflavin	Energy metabolism; maintenance of skin, mucous membranes, and nervous system structures	Cracks at corners of mouth, sore throat, skin rash, hypersensitivity to light, purple tongue	None reported	Dairy products, whole-grain and enriched breads and cereals, lean meats, poultry, green vegetables, liver
Niacin	Conversion of carbohydrates, fats, and protein into usable forms of energy; essential for growth, synthesis of hormones	Pellagra (symptoms include weakness, diarrhea, dermatitis, inflammation of mucous membranes, mental illness)	Flushing of the skin, nausea, vomiting, diarrhea, changes in metabolism of glycogen and fatty acids	Eggs, chicken, turkey, fish, milk, whole grains, nuts, enriched breads and cereals, lean meats, legumes*
Vitamin B-6	Enzyme reactions involving amino acids and the metabolism of carbohydrates, lipids, and nucleic acids	Anemia, convulsions, cracks at corners of mouth, dermatitis, nausea, confusion	Neurological abnormalities and damage	Eggs, poultry, whole grains, nuts, legumes, liver, kidney, pork
Folate	Amino acid metabolism, synthesis of RNA and DNA, new cell synthesis	Anemia, gastrointestinal disturbances, decreased resistance to infection, depression	Diarrhea, reduction of zinc absorption, possible kidney enlargement and damage	Green leafy vegetables, yeast, oranges, whole grains, legumes, liver
Vitamin B-12	Synthesis of red and white blood cells; other metabolic reactions	Anemia, fatigue, nervous system damage, sore tongue	None reported	Eggs, milk, meat, liver
Biotin	Metabolism of fats, carbohydrates, and proteins	Rash, nausea, vomiting, weight loss, depression, fatigue, hair loss; not known under natural circumstances	None reported	Cereals, yeast, nuts, cheese, egg yolks, soy flour, liver; widespread foods
Pantothenic acid	Metabolism of fats, carbohydrates, and proteins	Fatigue, numbness and tingling of hands and feet, gastrointestinal disturbances; not known under natural circumstances	Diarrhea, water retention	Peanuts, whole grains, legumes, fish, eggs, liver, kidney; smaller amounts found in milk, vegetables, and fruits

*Niacin can be made in the body from tryptophan, so this list includes foods containing niacin and/or tryptophan.

Reprinted with permission from *Dietary Reference Intakes for Energy, Carbohydrate, Fiber, Fat, Fatty Acids, Cholesterol, Protein, and Amino Acids (Macronutrients)*. © 2005 by the National Academy of Sciences, courtesy of the National Academies Press, Washington, D.C.

Folic Acid is a B vitamin which is now widely recognized as an important nutrient for the prevention of a specific type of birth defect known as neural tube defects. Neural tube defects are conditions in which the baby's brain or spine does not form properly. The two most common of these defects are spina bifida and anencephaly, and they can result in serious disability or death. Spina bifida is the condition resulting in the incomplete closure of the spinal column. A sac of fluid comes through the babies back and part of the spinal cord in this sac is damaged. Potential problems associated with this birth defect are inability to move lower body parts, loss of bowel and bladder control, and learning disabilities. Anencephaly is the improper formation and absence of part of the brain and skull bones. Babies with this condition usually die before birth in a miscarriage or shortly after birth. About 2500 children are born each year with a neural tube defect, and the March of Dimes (2005) projects that up to 70 percent of these defects could be prevented through adequate folic acid intake by women starting before they become pregnant.

Clearly, adequate folic acid intake is important. The March of Dimes (2005) recommends a daily intake of 400 micrograms of folic acid for all women who could possibly get pregnant. Many breakfast cereals are fortified with 100 percent of the needed daily value of folic acid, and several other foods can provide folic acid as well. Women who may become pregnant may also wish to discuss taking a folic acid supplement with their physician. Foods high in folic acid are found in Table 6.5.

Vitamin C is a water soluble vitamin which must be consumed regularly for good health. It is needed for normal growth and development, in all parts of the body, and is critical in the formation of collagen, a protein used to make tendons, ligaments, blood vessels, scar tissue, and skin. Vitamin C is important in wound healing and for the maintenance and repair of teeth, bones, and cartilage. It is also known as one of the antioxidants, which are thought to block some of the damage caused by free radicals. Free radicals are by-products of the process of our bodies transforming food into energy, and may damage human cells (NIH, 2005). When one is deficient in vitamin C, several health effects become evident, including inflammation and bleeding of the gums, dry scaly skin, impaired wound healing, nosebleeds, easy bruising, weakened tooth enamel, and decreased resistance to infection. Although it has been touted by many as a way to prevent the common cold, there is currently no conclusive data that shows vitamin C to be effective in preventing the common cold. Since vitamin C cannot be manufactured or stored by the body, it must be regularly included in a healthy diet. Fortunately, vitamin C is relatively easy to attain in a healthy diet. Fruits and vegetables contain vitamin C, and the readily available source of citrus fruits and juices are quite popular in the American diet. Rich sources include broccoli, cantaloupe, tomatoes, strawberries, green and red peppers, leafy green vegetables, sweet and white potatoes, watermelon, brussels sprouts, cauliflower, cabbage, papaya, mango, pineapples, and several types of berries. Adults need 60–75 milligrams of vitamin C daily, and because smoking depletes vitamin C, smokers need an additional 35 milligrams each day. High doses (greater than 2000 milligrams per day) can lead to upset stomach and diarrhea.

Minerals

Minerals are inorganic compounds which are also needed in small amounts. They serve primarily as structural elements but also regulate a number of processes in the body such as muscle contraction, blood clotting, and protein synthesis to name a few. Some of the major minerals needed by the body include iron, calcium, phosphorus, potassium, magnesium, sodium, and chloride. A guide to the functions, sources, and effects of deficiencies and megadoses of various minerals is found in Table 6.6.

One mineral which warrants special attention is iron. Iron is a part of many enzymes and is a vital part of blood protein, hemoglobin, and the muscle protein myoglobin, both of which carry oxygen. While males, because they are bigger, require more of most vitamins and minerals, iron is an exception. Adult women require considerably more daily iron than adult men (15 mg per day for women and 10 mg per day for men) primarily due to losses of iron during menstruation. During pregnancy, iron needs increase even more, and a supplement may be recommended by a physician. If adequate amounts of iron are not consumed, the individual is at risk of anemia. Anemia is a low level of blood hemoglobin usually

TABLE 6.5
Foods High in Folic Acid

Fortified Breakfast cereals with 100 percent of daily value for folic acid

   Total
   Product 19
   Special K Plus
   Life
   Smart Start

Lentils
Spinach
Black beans
Asparagus
Orange juice from concentrate
Enriched breads and pastas
Romaine lettuce
Broccoli

TABLE 6.6

Facts about Selected Minerals

Mineral	Major Functions	Signs of Prolonged Deficiency	Toxic Effects of Megadoses	Important Dietary Sources
Calcium	Maintenance of bones and teeth, blood clotting, maintenance of cell membranes, control of nerve impulses and muscle contraction	Stunted growth in children, bone mineral loss in adults	Nausea, vomiting, hypertension, constipation, urinary stones, calcium deposits in soft tissues, inhibition of absorption of certain minerals	Milk and milk products, tofu, fortified orange juice and bread, green leafy vegetables, bones in fish
Fluoride	Maintenance of tooth (and possibly bone) structure	Higher frequency of tooth decay	Increased bone density, mottling of teeth, impaired kidney function, neurological disturbances	Fluoride-containing drinking water, tea, marine fish eaten with bones
Iron	Component of hemoglobin (carries oxygen to tissues), myoglobin (in muscle fibers), and enzymes	Iron-deficiency anemia, weakness, impaired immune function, cold hands and feet, gastrointestinal distress	Iron deposits in soft tissues, causing liver and kidney damage, joint pains, sterility, and disruption of cardiac function	Lean meats, legumes, enriched flour, green vegetables, dried fruit, liver; absorption is enhanced by the presence of vitamin C
Iodine	Essential part of thyroid hormones, regulation of body metabolism	Goiter (enlarged thyroid), cretinism (birth defect)	Depression of thyroid activity, hyperthyroidism in susceptible individuals	Iodized salt, seafood
Magnesium	Transmission of nerve impulses, bone and tooth structure, energy transfer, composition of many enzyme systems	Neurological disturbances, impaired immune function, kidney disorders, nausea, weight loss, growth failure in children	Nausea, vomiting, central nervous system depression, coma; death in people with impaired kidney function	Widespread in foods and water (except soft water); especially found in wheat bran, milk products, legumes, nuts, seeds, leafy vegetables
Phosphorus	Bone growth and maintenance (combined with calcium), energy transfer in cells	Weakness, bone loss, kidney disorders, cardiorespiratory failure	Drop in blood calcium levels	Present in nearly all foods, especially milk, cheese, cereal, legumes, meats
Potassium	Nerve function and body water balance	Muscular weakness, nausea, drowsiness, paralysis, confusion, disruption of cardiac rhythm	Cardiac arrest	Meats, milk, fruits, vegetables, grains, legumes
Sodium	Body water balance, acid-base balance, nerve function	Muscle weakness, loss of appetite, nausea, vomiting; sodium deficiency is rarely seen	Edema, hypertension in sensitive people	Salt, soy sauce, salted foods
Zinc	Enzyme reactions, including synthesis of proteins, RNA, and DNA; wound healing; immune response; ability to taste	Growth failure, reproductive failure, loss of appetite, impaired taste acuity, skin rash, impaired immune function, poor wound healing, night blindness	Vomiting, impaired immune function, decline in serum HDL levels, impaired magnesium absorption	Whole grains, meat, eggs, liver, seafood (especially oysters)

Mineral chart copied from: Fit & Well, 2nd ed. by T.D. Fahey, P.M. Insel, & W.T. Roth. Mayfield Pub. Co. Mountain View, CA, 1997.

Reprinted with permission from *Dietary Reference Intakes for Energy, Carbohydrate, Fiber, Fat, Fatty Acids, Cholesterol, Protein, and Amino Acids (Macronutrients)*. © 2005 by the National Academy of Sciences, courtesy of the National Academies Press, Washington, D.C.

caused by inadequate iron in the diet or by poor iron absorption. The low hemoglobin levels cause less oxygen to be delivered to body cells, resulting in lowered energy levels. The body's ability to absorb and use iron is affected by several factors, one of which is the type of iron consumed. Heme iron is found in animal sources and is efficiently absorbed by the body. Non-heme iron, on the other hand, is found in vegetable sources, and is less available. The iron content of several selected foods is found in Table 6.7.

Selected Sources of Dietary Iron				TABLE 6.7
1 cup cooked spinach	6.4 mg	1 baked potato	2.8 mg	
1 cup cooked lima beans	5.9 mg	3.5 oz boiled shrimp	2.2 mg	
3 oz fried liver	5.3 mg	3 oz ground beef patty	2.1 mg	
1 cup cooked navy beans	5.1 mg	1 cup spaghetti	2.0 mg	
4 oz hamburger patty	4.8 mg	1 cup cooked oatmeal	1.6 mg	
1 cup canned kidney beans	4.6 mg	1/2 roasted chicken breast	.89 mg	
1 cup cooked split peas	3.4 mg			
1 cup cooked blackeyed peas	3.3 mg	Many breakfast cereals are enriched with iron—check the label.		
1 cup cooked white rice	2.9 mg			

Another important mineral which deserves special attention is calcium. Inadequate calcium intake and poor absorption contribute to osteoporosis, or the loss of bone density. This condition, which is most prevalent in post-menopausal women, can result in bone fractures. Adequate calcium consumption, mainly from low fat dairy products, is important beginning at an early age and continuing throughout the lifespan for the prevention of osteoporosis. Osteoporosis, including additional risk factors and guidelines for prevention, is discussed thoroughly in Chapter 9.

Getting Adequate Vitamins and Minerals—The DRIs

The Food and Nutrition Board of the National Academy of Sciences has, for several years, analyzed scientific data to determine just how much of the various vitamins and minerals are needed for good health. Previously, their recommendations were published in the form of the RDAs—Recommended Dietary Allowances, and provided the levels of vitamins and minerals needed to prevent deficiency. Their recommendations are now known as the Dietary Reference Intakes (DRIs) and recommend levels that are thought to decrease the risk of chronic, diet-related diseases. While they are only estimates and are developed for healthy people, they provide an excellent guide for attainment of adequate intakes of necessary vitamins and minerals. The DRIs for several key nutrients is provided in Table 6.8.

Water

Sometimes considered the forgotten nutrient, water is every bit as important as the other nutrients. Once water enters the body, it mixes with other compounds, primarily minerals, to produce fluids critical to all life processes. These body fluids transport important nutrients and other substances to the cells, carry waste away from cells, and allow chemical reactions to take place in the body. They lubricate joints, absorb shock, and cushion the amniotic sac during pregnancy. Water also serves as a solvent for minerals, vitamins, amino acids, glucose, and other substances, regulates body temperature, and maintains blood volume. As you can see, sufficient water consumption for adequate hydration is very important to good health. The average person consumes and excretes (through the kidneys,

TABLE 6.8

Dietary Reference Intakes (DRIs): Estimated Average Requirement for Groups
Food and Nutrition Board, Institute of Medicine, National Academies

Life Stage Group	CHO (g/d)	Protein (g/d)a	Vit. A (µg/d)b	Vit. C (mg/d)	Vit. E (mg/d)c	Thiamin (mg/d)	Riboflavin (mg/d)	Niacin (mg/d)d	Vit. B6 (mg/d)	Folate (µg/d)e	Vit. B12 (µg/d)	Copper (µg/d)	Iodine (µg/d)	Iron (mg/d)	Magnesium (mg/d)	Molybdenum (µg/d)	Phosphorus (mg/d)	Selenium (µg/d)	Zinc (mg/d)
Infants																			
7–12 mo.		9*												6.9					2.5
Children																			
1–3 yr.	100	11	210	13	5	0.4	0.4	5	0.4	120	0.7	260	65	3.0	65	13	380	17	2.5
4–8 yr.	100	15	275	22	6	0.5	0.5	6	0.5	160	1.0	340	65	4.1	110	17	405	23	4.0
Males																			
9–13 yr.	100	27	445	39	9	0.7	0.8	9	0.8	250	1.5	540	73	5.9	200	26	1,055	35	7.0
14–18 yr.	100	44	630	63	12	1.0	1.1	12	1.1	330	2.0	685	95	7.7	340	33	1,055	45	8.5
19–30 yr.	100	46	625	75	12	1.0	1.1	12	1.1	320	2.0	700	95	6	330	34	580	45	9.4
31–50 yr.	100	46	625	75	12	1.0	1.1	12	1.1	320	2.0	700	95	6	350	34	580	45	9.4
51–70 yr.	100	46	625	75	12	1.0	1.1	12	1.4	320	2.0	700	95	6	350	34	580	45	9.4
>70 yr.	100	46	625	75	12	1.0	1.1	12	1.4	320	2.0	700	95	6	350	34	580	45	9.4
Females																			
9–13 yr.	100	28	420	39	9	0.7	0.8	9	0.8	250	1.5	540	73	5.7	200	26	1,055	35	7.0
14–18 yr.	100	38	485	56	12	0.9	0.9	11	1.0	330	2.0	685	95	7.9	300	33	1,055	45	7.3
19–30 yr.	100	38	500	60	12	0.9	0.9	11	1.1	320	2.0	700	95	8.1	255	34	580	45	6.8
31–50 yr.	100	38	500	60	12	0.9	0.9	11	1.1	320	2.0	700	95	8.1	265	34	580	45	6.8
51–70 yr.	100	38	500	60	12	0.9	0.9	11	1.3	320	2.0	700	95	8.5	265	34	580	45	6.8
>70 yr.	100	38	500	60	12	0.9	0.9	11	1.3	320	2.0	700	95	8.5	265	34	580	45	6.8
Pregnancy																			
14–18 yr.	135	50	530	66	12	1.2	1.2	14	1.6	520	2.2	785	160	23	335	40	1,055	49	10.5
19–30 yr.	135	50	550	70	12	1.2	1.2	14	1.6	520	2.2	800	160	22	290	40	580	49	9.5
31–50 yr.	135	50	550	70	12	1.2	1.2	14	1.6	520	2.2	800	160	22	300	40	580	49	9.5
Lactation																			
14–18 yr.	160	60	885	96	16	1.2	1.3	13	1.7	450	2.4	985	209	7	300	35	1,055	59	10.9
19–30 yr.	160	60	900	100	16	1.2	1.3	13	1.7	450	2.4	1,000	209	6.5	255	36	580	59	10.4
31–50 yr.	160	60	900	100	16	1.2	1.3	13	1.7	450	2.4	1,000	209	6.5	265	36	580	59	10.4

Note: This table presents Estimated Average Requirements (EARs), which serve two purposes: for assessing adequacy of population intakes, and as the basis for calculating Recommended Dietary Allowances (RDAs) for individuals for those nutrients. EARs have not been established for vitamin D, vitamin K, pantothenic acid, biotin, choline, calcium, chromium, fluoride, manganese, or other nutrients not yet evaluated via the DRI process.

a For individual at reference weight (Table 1.1).   *indicates change from prepublication copy due to calculation error.

b As retinol activity equivalents (RAEs). 1 RAE = 1 µg retinol, 12 µg β-carotene, 24 µg α-carotene, or 24 µg β-cryptoxanthin. The RAE for dietary provitamin A carotenoids is two-fold greater than retinol equivalents (RE), whereas the RAE for preformed vitamin A is the same as RE.

c As α-tocopherol. α-Tocopherol includes RRR-α-tocopherol, the only form of α-tocopherol that occurs naturally in foods, and the 2R-stereoismeric forms of α-tocopherol (RRR-, RSR-, RRS-, and RSS-α-tocopherol) that occur in fortified foods and supplements. It does not include the 2S-stereoisomeric forms of α-tocopherol (SRR-, SSR-, SRS-, and SSS-α-tocopherol), also found in fortified foods and supplements.

d As niacin equivalents (NE). 1 mg of niacin = 60 mg of tryptophan.

e As dietary folate equivalents (DFE). 1 DFE = 1 µg food folate = 0.6 µg of folic acid from fortified food or as a supplement consumed with food = 0.5 µg of a supplement taken on an empty stomach.

Sources: Dietary Reference Intakes for Calcium, Phosphorous, Magnesium, Vitamin D, and Fluoride (1997); Dietary Reference Intakes for Thiamin, Riboflavin, Niacin, Vitamin B6, Folate, Vitamin B12, Pantothenic Acid, Biotin, and Choline (1998); Dietary Reference Intakes for Vitamin C, Vitamin E, Selenium, and Carotenoids (2000); Dietary Reference Intakes for Vitamin A, Vitamin K, Arsenic, Boron, Chromium, Copper, Iodine, Iron, Manganese, Molybdenum, Nickel, Silicon, Vanadium, and Zinc (2001); and Dietary Reference Intakes for Energy, Carbohydrate, Fiber, Fat, Fatty Acids, Cholesterol, Protein, and Amino Acids (2002). These reports may be accessed via www.nap.edu.

lungs, and skin) about two and a half liters of water each day. To assure proper balance, and to avoid dehydration when excessive water is lost, it is important to replace this water loss. Many foods, specifically fruits and vegetables, have high water content and can help replace water loss. While information on the necessary amount of water consumption varies greatly, it is recommended that about six to eight glasses (eight ounce) of water be consumed each day. The importance of water consumption during heavy exercise for the prevention of dehydration is discussed in Chapter 9.

Fiber

Although not actually classified as a nutrient, fiber is nonetheless an important dietary element. Fiber is the indigestible part of plant foods, and is sometimes referred to as roughage or bulk. Fiber attracts water and pushes other foods through the digestive tract. There are two types of fiber: soluble and insoluble. Soluble fiber, so named because it dissolves or forms a gel in water, is thought to be helpful in lowering blood cholesterol levels. Soluble fiber is also valuable to the diabetic in that it can aid in the stabilization of blood glucose levels. It is found in citrus fruits, oats, barley, kidney beans and apples. Insoluble fiber, named because it does not dissolve in water, is found in numerous fruits, grains, and vegetables. It adds bulk to the intestinal contents and helps waste products move quickly through the digestive tract. This is thought to reduce the risk of cancers of the digestive tract as well as help prevent constipation, hemorrhoids, and diverticulosis. Diverticulosis is a condition in which a small pouch develops in the colon that bulges outward through a weak spot. About ten percent of Americans over the age of 40 have diverticulosis. When the pouch becomes inflamed, the condition is called diverticulitis, which can lead to bleeding, infections, tears, or blockages, and can result in serious illness if not properly treated. The National Institute of Health recommends a daily fiber intake of 20–35 grams. Most Americans fall short of this target, consuming less than half the recommended fiber. While including dietary fiber is important, care must be taken not to overdo it. Too much fiber can cause other valuable nutrients to be lost and can cause gastrointestinal upset, including constipation if water consumption is not increased. The fiber content of selected foods is shown in Table 6.9.

Antioxidants

One set of valuable nutrients are now widely recognized as having several beneficial qualities, and are known at the antioxidants. These antioxidants include vitamins C and E, beta carotene, selenium, and carotenoids (found in green, yellow, and orange vegetables) and appear to promote health by repairing damage done by free radicals. Free radicals are by-products of cell oxidation, and their production is increased by cigarette smoke, excessive sun exposure, stress, certain drugs, and environmental factors. They damage cells and may cause genes to mutate, and are linked to increased risk of arthritis, cancer, cardiovascular disease, and other disorders. Dietary antioxidants may reduce or pre-

TABLE 6.9
Good Sources of Dietary Fiber

Fruits	Grams
1 medium apple	4–5
1 banana	3
1 cup blueberries	5
10 dates	7
1 orange	3
1 pear	5
1 cup strawberries	3
1 watermelon slice	2–3

Vegetables	Grams
1 artichoke	4
1 raw carrot	2
1/2 cup cream style corn	6
1 cup chopped lettuce	1
1/2 cup green peas	6
1 cup cooked spinach	6
1 cup cooked squash	5–6
1 tomato	2

Legumes	Grams
1 cup cooked black beans	15
1 cup cooked green beans	3
1 cup pork and beans	18
1 cup cooked blackeyed peas	11
1 cup kidney beans	20
1 cup cooked navy beans	16
1 cup cooked pinto beans	19

Grains	Grams
1 bagel	1
1 whole grain slice of bread	1–3
4 graham crackers	3
1 bran muffin	2
hot dog/hamburger bun	1
1 cup cooked oatmeal	7–9
1/2 cup Grape Nuts cereal	3.5
1 cup Nature Valley granola	7.5
3/4 cup Shredded Wheat cereal	4
1 cup cooked macaroni	1
1 cup cooked rice	2.5–4
1 cup cooked spaghetti	1–2

Other	Grams
1 cup almonds	15
1 cup cashews	8
1 cup shredded coconut	11
1 tbsp peanut butter	1
1/4 cup sunflower seeds	2

vent the formation of free radicals, and may help remove them from the body. Antioxidants are supplied by a diet rich in fruits and vegetables.

VEGETARIANISM

An increasingly popular nutritional lifestyle is vegetarianism, with about six million Americans practicing this eating style (ADA, 2005). Individuals may choose to practice vegetarianism for a variety of reasons, including religious beliefs, personal ethical beliefs, and health concerns. Sound scientific studies show a positive relationship between vegetarianism and the reduced risk for diseases including obesity, coronary artery disease, hypertension, diabetes mellitus, and some types of cancer (ADA, 2003). However, vegetarianism should not be labeled a good or bad eating style, as the overall diet must be considered. If a vegetarian is careful and diligent in food selection and consumption, a healthy diet can be consumed with little fat and a high nutrient content. However, carelessness or lack of knowledge in the area of vegetarianism can lead to nutritional deficiencies.

One of the major concerns which vegetarians must address is the inclusion of complementary proteins into their diet. Complete proteins (those containing all of the essential amino acids) are found only in animal products. However, certain incomplete proteins which contain some of the amino acids can be combined to create complete protein intake. Legumes, or beans and peas, are good to combine with grains as well as nuts and seeds to make complete protein. Examples of these combinations are the eating of beans with rice and the consumption of peanut butter with whole wheat bread. Vegetarians who consume a wide variety of plant foods and are careful about their combinations can fulfill their protein needs on this diet. Other nutrients, specifically vitamins D and B_{12}, may also be difficult to attain through the vegetarian diet. Vegetarians must be diligent and knowledgeable to make this eating style work. It is recommended that anyone considering the practice of becoming a vegetarian consult with a registered dietitian prior to adopting this eating plan in order to discuss potential deficiencies and how to prevent them. A nutritional supplement may be recommended.

NUTRITIONAL SUPPLEMENTS

Americans spend more than $4 billion a year on vitamin and mineral supplements (Barrett, 2001). This indicates that many individuals are concerned that they are not meeting their bodies' nutritional needs through dietary measures. While there are varied opinions concerning the necessity of supplements, most nutrition scientists agree that needed vitamins and minerals are easily attainable through a balanced diet. Some individuals believe that if some nutrients are good, then more must be better, but there is no evidence that this is the case. In fact, individuals who insist on supplementing their nutrient intake should exercise caution, since there is a possibility of too high an intake of certain nutrients, especially the fat-soluble vitamins A, D, E and K. While the water-soluble vitamins B and C are not stored in fat and any excesses are readily excreted, fat-soluble vitamins are stored in the fatty tissue of the body. Continued high intake of fat-soluble vitamins can lead to a dangerous accumulation of these substances, causing a condition known as vitamin toxicity. Kidney and liver damage, as well as other health problems, can result from the consumption of these megadoses of vitamins and some minerals. High levels of some nutrients may also interfere with the absorption of other crucial nutrients. Therefore, any supplement which supplies greater than 100 percent of the DRI for any vitamin or mineral is discouraged.

Chapter 6

Furthermore, supplements may fall short in offering another valuable component to the diet. It is known that many foods contain non-nutritive chemicals which provide specific health benefits. Substances known as phytochemicals, found in plants, especially fruits and vegetables, may help prevent cancer, diabetes, hypertension, and cardiovascular disease. These potentially valuable substances are not provided through typical supplementation, but are supplied by consuming a variety of foods from plants. Phytochemicals include compounds like allyl sulfides (garlic and onions), lycopene (tomatoes and peppers), carotenoids (carrots, cilantro, celery), flavonoids and gingerols (herbs and spices), silymarin (artichokes), and phenols and ellagic acid (grapes, berries, melons), just to name a few.

The "pill mentality" is another risk of supplementation. This refers to the mind set that efforts to consume a good diet are unnecessary because nutritional needs can be met by popping a pill. Clearly, a pill is no substitute for a balanced diet, and consuming a supplement does not correct the problems found in a high-fat, high-calorie diet.

While supplements are quite popular and are available over the counter, the decision to take them is one which should not be made lightly. There are some individuals who may benefit by adding a supplement to a balanced diet. Those situations include:

⊙ iron to help some women compensate with heavy menstrual flow;

⊙ iron, folate and calcium for pregnant or nursing women;

⊙ calcium, iron, zinc and B-12 for some types of vegetarians;

⊙ a single dose of vitamin K administered by a physician for newborns; and

⊙ individuals with certain nutritional deficiencies due to a medical condition or medication.

Consult with a physician or registered dietitian before making a supplementation decision.

ALCOHOL CONSUMPTION

Alcohol is a source of calories, providing seven calories per gram, but no nutritional value. It is considered empty calories, and is an excellent place to begin cutting calories in a weight loss attempt, since calories can be eliminated without sacrificing any nutritional value. In addition, those who drink beyond moderation are at risk of alcohol related problems, including malnutrition and under-nutrition, since the drinker may rely on alcohol to provide calories and neglect the consumption of nutrient dense foods. Although controversial, there does appear to be some evidence that light drinking may bestow some health benefits, but it is not recommended that anyone begin drinking in order to attain those benefits. And for responsible adults who do choose to consume alcohol, any alcohol consumption beyond moderation of one drink per day for women and up to two drinks per day for men should be avoided.

FAST FOODS AND EATING OUT

Americans eat out one in five meals (an average of 4.2 meals per week), for a total of nearly 40 billion meals each year (National Restaurant Association, 2000). Fast food establishments are the most frequent source of outside food. When meals are selected based primarily on speed and convenience, nutrition is likely to suffer. Most fast food menu items are notoriously high in fat, saturated fat, calories and sodium, and low in fiber and other valuable nutrients. However, eating fast food and maintaining a balanced diet need not be mutually exclusive. Most fast food chains incorporate a few menu items for their more health-conscious customers. As indicated in Table 6.10, fast food selections vary greatly in fat and calorie content. Most fast food restaurants will provide information on the nutritional value of menu items upon request, and most provide nutritional data on their websites. Try these suggestions for maintaining nutritional balance while eating out at fast food restaurants:

⊙ **Think small.** Avoid "super-sized" portions and settings which encourage overeating like buffets and meal deal specials. Many fast food meals can total well over 1000 calories.

⊙ **Watch the add-ons.** Toppings like dressings, cheese, butter and sour cream can increase the fat and calorie content of the meal in a hurry while adding very little nutritional value.

⊙ **Avoid fried foods.** Frying can double, triple, or even quadruple the fat and calories of the meal.

⊙ **Beware of biscuits and croissants.** They are usually high calorie items.

⊙ **Watch the desserts and beverages.** Cookies, sundaes, shakes, and other treats can turn a low fat meal into a high fat meal, and many beverages add calories without contributing to a feeling of fullness.

⊙ **Ask for the nutritional information of menu items at fast food restaurants.** There are healthy choices out there.

TABLE 6.10		
Making Healthier Fast Food Selections		
Compare the fat and calories:	**Fat**	**Calories**
Jack In The Box Ultimate Cheeseburger	77	1090
Jack In the Box Chicken Fajita Pita	10	300
Wendy's Big Bacon Classic	29	580
Wendy's Grilled Chicken Sandwich	10	360
Burger King Triple Whopper with Cheese	82	1230
Burger King Veggie Burger	16	420
McDonald's Deluxe Breakfast	60	1220
McDonald's Egg McMuffin	11	290
Mazzio's Deep Pan Greek Pizza (1 slice)	24	406
Mazzio's Thin Crust Canadian Bacon (1 slice)	8	163
Subway 6" Meatball Marinara Sandwich	24	560
Subway 6" Turkey Breast and Ham Sandwich	5	290

When eating out at traditional style restaurants, consider these tips:

⊙ Ask your server about low fat entrees and low calorie options on their menu. Inquire about the method of preparation—just because it sounds healthy does not make it healthy.

⊙ If there are terms on the menu that you don't recognize, ask what they mean. Hints to high-fat selections include parmigiana, hollandaise, carbonara, bernaise, batter-dipped, au gratin, Alfredo and tempura.

⊙ Ask your server if certain items can be served in a healthier manner. Can skim products be substituted for whole dairy products? Can products with lots of butter be served with lower fat dips or sauces? Ask for sauces, dressing and gravies on the side.

⊙ Order a sure-fire nutrient-dense side dish with your entree, such as steamed rice or lightly stir-fried vegetables.

⊙ Ask if "heart-healthy" indicators are available to help you make healthier choices.

- Share an entrée with a friend. With today's portion sizes, you can still fill up and save money too.
- Don't feel compelled to clean your plate. If you do order too much, take a container to-go.
- Eat slowly. Fast eaters tend to eat more.

READING FOOD LABELS

One of the most valuable sources of nutrition information is found right on the food in the form of the food label, and fortunately for consumers, understanding that information is easier than ever. As shown in Box 6.1, these food labels are presented in an easy-to-read and straightforward format. Some of the most valuable information includes the number of calories per serving and the number of calories which come from fat. This can be of assistance in following the dietary guidelines, and in keeping fat consumption below 30 percent of calories consumed. The indication of the amount of saturated fat can be quite helpful, and the amount of various vitamins and minerals provided per serving can assist in the selection of more nutrient-dense foods. The amount of fiber provided can also be valuable in the effort to consume the recommended 20–35 grams of fiber per day.

HEALTHY SNACKING

Americans spend $13.4 billion per year on snack foods, and about $2.5 billion of that is poured into vending machines. Further, 86 percent of adults admit to eating between meals. We eat 23 pounds of snacks each year per person (American Dietetic Association, 2005). Unfortunately, most traditional snack foods are high-calorie, non-nutrient-dense, and draw a high percent of their calories from fat. A typical candy bar, used in an earlier example, contains about 250 to 300 calories, with approximately 40–50 percent of those calories coming from fat. Snacking and good nutrition, however, need not be mutually exclusive. Many healthy snacks are available for the choosing, and if one makes careful selections and indulges in the high-fat snacks only occasionally, snacking can be healthy. Some suggestions for healthy snacking include:

- **Consider snacks as miniature meals.** Consume meal-like snacks such as fruit, raw vegetables, bagels or yogurt, instead of traditional snack foods.
- **Designate a snack spot in the pantry and the refrigerator.** Intentionally stock it with nutrient dense foods.
- **Compensate for traditional snack foods.** When high-fat, high-calorie snacks are chosen, work in some additional exercise and keep the fat content of that day's meals to a minimum.
- **Avoid overeating in a hurry.** It is easy to reach for a snack and consume several portions or servings without giving it any thought. Think about what and how much you are eating and consume the snack slowly.
- **Have an occasional treat.** Don't feel like you must give up your favorite snack foods forever. Eating a traditional snack food is acceptable if it is occasional and moderate.

Box 6.1

Six Steps to Label Reading

Heaven Sent Frozen Mixed Vegetables

Net. Wt. 16 oz (456g)

Ingredients: Carrots, Peas, Lima Beans, Corn

- Good Source of Fiber
- Lowfat

Many factors affect cancer risk. Eating a diet low in fat and high in fiber may lower risk of this disease.

Nutrition Facts
Serving Size 1/2 cup (91g)
Servings Per Container 5

Amount Per Serving	
Calories 58	Calories from Fat 0

	% Daily Value*
Total Fat 0g	0%
Saturated Fat 0g	0%
Cholesterol 0mg	0%
Sodium 45mg	2%
Total Carbohydrate 12g	4%
Dietary Fiber 3g	12%
Sugars 3g	
Protein 3g	

Vitamin A	92%	•	Vitamin C	16%
Calcium	2%	•	Iron	5%

* Percent Daily Values are based on a 2,000 calorie diet. Your daily values may be higher or lower depending on your calorie needs:

		Calories	2,000	2,500
Total Fat	Less than		65g	85g
Sat Fat	Less than		20g	25g
Cholesterol	Less than		300mg	300mg
Sodium	Less than		2,400mg	2,400mg
Total Carbohydrate			300g	375g
Fiber			25g	30g

Calories per gram:
Fat 9 • Carbohydrates 4 • Protein 4

1. Better by Design

How to recognize the new food labels

The new food labels feature a revamped nutrition panel titled "Nutrition Facts," with nutrient listings that reflect current health concerns. Now you can more easily find information on fat, fiber and other food components fundamental to lowering your risk of cancer and other chronic diseases. Listings for nutrients like thiamin and riboflavin are no longer required, because Americans generally eat enough of them.

2. Size Up the Situation

All serving sizes are created equal

Now you can compare similar products and know that their serving sizes are basically identical. So when you realize how much fat is packed into that carton of double-dutch-chocolate-caramel-chew ice cream you're eyeing, you might opt for lowfat frozen yogurt instead. Serving sizes are also standardized, so manufacturers can't make nutrition claims for unrealistically small portions. That means a chocolate cake, for example, must be divided into 8 servings sized to satisfy the average person—not 16 servings sized to satisfy the average munchkin.

3. Look Before You Leap

Use the Daily Values

You will find the Daily Values on the bottom half of the "Nutrition Facts" panel. Some represent maximum levels of nutrients that should be consumed each day for a healthful diet (as with fat), while others refer to minimum lev-els that can be exceeded (as with carbohydrates). They are based on both a 2,000 and 2,500 calorie diet. Your own needs may be more or less, but these figures give you a point from which to compare. For example, the sample label indicates that someone with a 2,000 calorie diet should eat no more than 65 grams of fat per day. This is based on a diet getting 30% of calories as fat. If you normally eat less calories, or want to eat less than 30% of calories as fat, your daily fat consumption will be lower.

4. Rate It Right

Scan the % Daily Values

The % Daily Values make judging the nutritional quality of a food a snap. For instance, you can look at the % Daily Value column and find that a food has 25% of the Daily Value for fiber. This means the product will give you a substantial portion of the recommended amount of fiber for the day. You can also use this column to compare nutrients in similar products. The % Daily Values are based on a 2,000 calorie diet.

5. Trust Adjectives

Descriptors have legal definitions

Terms like "low," "high" and "free" have long been used on food labels. What these words actually meant, however, could vary. Thanks to the new labeling laws, such descriptions must now meet legal definitions. For example, you may be shopping for foods high in vitamin A, which has been linked to lower risks of certain cancers. Under the new label laws, a food described as "high" in a particular nutrient must contain 20% or more of the Daily Value for that nutri-ent. So if the bottle of juice you're thinking of buying says "high in vitamin A," you can now feel confident it really is a good source of the vitamin.

6. Read Health Claims with Confidence

The nutrient link to disease prevention

You can also expect to see food packages with health claims linking certain nutrients to reduced risk of cancer and other diseases. The federal government has approved three health claims dealing with cancer prevention: a low fat diet may reduce your risk for cancer; high fiber foods may reduce your risk for cancer; and fruits and vegetables may reduce your risk for cancer. A food may not make such a health claim for one nutrient if it contains other nutrients that undermine its health benefits. A high fiber, but high fat, jelly doughnut cannot carry a health claim!

NUTRITION FOR THE HIGHLY ACTIVE PERSON

Many people mistakenly believe that if they are highly active, their nutritional needs cannot be met through diet alone. Sports supplements have become a multi-billion dollar industry based on this misconception. In fact, active individuals can easily meet all of their body's needs by consuming a healthy diet. As energy expenditure increases, energy needs also increase, so the athletic individual commonly consumes a greater number of calories for fuel than the less active person. The percentage of nutrients in the total diet, however, should remain the same, with carbohydrates comprising about 60 percent of total calories. Fat should still be kept to about 25–30 percent of the total calories, with protein remaining at 10–15 percent of calories. Many individuals in training are concerned that they are not getting enough protein from their diet. However, while protein requirements may be slightly higher for highly active individuals, the increase in total caloric consumption more than compensates for any additional needs. The recommended daily protein intake is .8 gram per kilogram of body weight. This recommendation includes a margin of safety high enough to cover almost all individuals. For endurance and strength athletes in heavy training, protein requirements are slightly increased. The requirements may increase to 1.2 to 1.4 grams per kilogram per day for endurance athletes and to 1.6 to 1.7 grams per kilogram per day for strength trained athletes (American Dietetic Association, 2000). Even these levels are easily met through the increase in caloric consumption needed to meet a highly active person's energy needs (Neiman, 2003). Laboratory 6.1 is provided to help you determine your daily protein needs. A review of the protein content of selected foods in Table 6.11 demonstrates the ease with which these levels can be attained.

Protein Content of Selected Foods			TABLE 6.11
Food	**Size**	**Protein**	
Whole Milk	1 cup	=	8 g
Skim Milk	1 cup	=	10 g
1 Egg		=	6 g
Cheese	1 ounce	=	6–10 g
Ice Cream	1 cup	=	5 g
Yogurt	8 oz	=	12 g
Fish	3 oz	=	17–24 g (Tuna = 24 g)
Beef	3 oz	=	20–24 g
Pork	3 oz	=	20 g
Poultry	3 oz	=	20–25 g
Rice (cooked)	1 cup	=	4 g
Macaroni & Cheese	1 cup	=	17 g
Spaghetti/Meatballs	1 cup	=	19 g
Nuts	1 cup	=	20–35 g
Dry Beans/Peas (cooked)	1 cup	=	15–20 g
Peanut Butter	1 tbsp	=	4 g
Double Whopper w/cheese		=	51 g (61 g fat)
One slice of Pizza		=	15–20 g
Big Mac		=	25 g
Wendy Big Classic w/cheese		=	30 g
Ultimate Cheeseburger		=	47 g (69 g fat)
Fajita Pita		=	24 g (8 g fat)

The active individual does have additional fluid needs. However, the belief that these needs cannot be met with water, and that a special fluid replacement drink is needed, is erroneous. Proper hydration is important, but an increase in water consumption can assure adequate hydration.

YOUR PLAN OF ACTION

Now that you are more aware of the necessary steps for good nutrition, how will you incorporate them into your personal dietary practices? You might find the following suggestions valuable in your quest:

1. **Compare your diet to the pyramid.** By recording everything you eat over a two-day period, you can identify strengths and weaknesses in your diet and create targets for change. Calculate the number of servings from each food group you eat, and compare this information to the recommendations in the Food Guide Pyramid. If you find that your servings are too low in some groups or too high in others, commit to make those changes today.

2. **Set some goals.** Do not try to perform a total overhaul of your diet right away. From the assessment of your diet, identify two changes which could lead to more nutrient-dense food consumption. Then set goals to consume more, or less, of those food items which you identified for change. By maintaining awareness of these two changes, you are more likely to make wiser choices.

3. **Be aware of settings which create challenge.** If you typically go for a box of cookies as soon as you get home from class or work, or like to stop at a particular vending machine frequently, these are habits which could be targeted for change. Make it a point to avoid the vending machine by walking a different route so that you do not have to pass by it. Stop by the supermarket to purchase some fresh fruit on the way home so the cookies are not so tempting.

4. **Become a label reader.** Become familiar with what your favorite foods have to offer, or do not offer. Determine if certain foods make notably higher contributions to your fat intake than others, then take steps to reduce those foods in your diet. Conversely, you can identify nutrient-dense foods through label reading and try to consume those foods more often.

5. **When eating out, share an entree.** Since ordering out usually makes it a bit more difficult to eat within the goals and guidelines, and since portion sizes at many restaurants have gotten bigger, sharing an entree and ordering an extra dinner salad may help you stick with your plans for dietary changes. You may be surprised how much money it can save you too.

6. **Be a smart shopper.** Many food choices would be much easier if more preparation was made while shopping for foods in the supermarket. By going shopping with a specific goal of purchasing nutritious foods, you will find that you are setting yourself up for success when you get home. Purchasing fresh fruits, vegetables and other nutrient-dense items instead of cookies, snacks and ice creams will provide more healthful selections when mealtime rolls around. When selecting snack foods, be sure to select healthy snacks. And the old suggestion you have probably heard can actually be very helpful: "Do not go shopping while you are hungry." You may come home with a basket full of foods which do not fit with your healthy diet.

References

American Dietetic Association. (2005). *Snack attacks are OK.*

American Dietetic Association. (2005). *Vegetarian Diets.* www.eatright.org/cps/rde/xchg/ada/hs.xsl/advocacy_933_ENU_HTML.htm

Barrett, S. (2001). *Consumer health.* New York: McGraw-Hill.

National Academy of Sciences. (2004). Dietary Reference Intakes (DRIs): Recommended Intakes for Individuals, Elements. Food and Nutrition Board, Institute of Medicine.

National Academy of Sciences. (2004). Dietary Reference Intakes (DRIs): Recommended Intakes for Individuals, Vitamins. Food and Nutrition Board, Institute of Medicine.

National Heart, Lung, and Blood Institute. (2005). *The DASH Eating Plan.* www.nhlbi.nih.gov/health/public/heart/hbp/dash/new_dash.pdf

National Institute of Health. (2005). Diverticulosis and diverticulitis. www.digestive.niddk.nih.gov/ddiseases/pubs/diverticulosis

National Institute of Health. (2005). Vitamin C. www.nlm.nih.gov/medlineplus/ency/srticle/002404.htm

National Restaurant Association. (2000). *American's dining out habits.* http://www.restaurant.org/rusa/magArticle.cfm?ArticleID=138

March of Dimes. (2005). Spina bifida: Quick reference and fact sheet. www.marchofdimes.com/professinals/681_1224.asp

Thompson, J., & Manore, M. (2005). *Nutrition: An applied approach.* San Francisco: Benjamin Cummings.

U.S. Department of Agriculture. *MyPyramid.* (2005). www.mypyramid.gov

U.S. Department of Health and Human Services and U.S. Department of Agriculture. Dietary Guidelines for Americans, 2005. 6th edition, Washington, D.C.: U.S. Government Printing Office, January, 2005.

Whitney, E.N., & Rolfes, S.R. (2002). *Understanding nutrition, 9th edition.* Belmont, CA: Wadsworth/Thomson Learning.

chapter 6
LABORATORY ①

Protein Worksheet: Calculating Your Daily Protein Needs

The Recommended Dietary Allowance for protein is .8 grams of protein per kilogram of body weight per day. You can calculate your specific protein needs by using the worksheet:

1. Convert your body weight in pounds to kilograms. Since there are 2.2 pounds in a kilogram, the equation is:

   Body weight in pounds ÷ 2.2 = body weight in kilograms

   If John weighs 175 pounds, his weight in kilograms would be:

   175 ÷ 2.2 = 79.5 (or 80) kilograms

   Body weight in pounds _____ ÷ 2.2 = _____ body weight in kilograms

2. Multiply your weight in kilograms by .8. John's protein needs would be:

   80 × .8 = 64 grams of protein per day.

   Body weight in kilograms _____ × .8 = _____ grams of protein needed each day

   Sixty-four grams of protein supply 256 calories. If John is consuming approximately 12 percent (10–15 percent is the recommendation) of his calories from protein, he is consuming plenty of protein in only 2100 calories per day.

3. If John is a highly active individual who believes he requires more than the recommended .8 grams per kilogram per day, he may choose to base his protein needs on 1.2 grams per kilogram per day:

   80 – 1.2 = 96 grams of protein per day.

   Body weight in kilograms _____ × 1.2 = _____ grams of protein possibly needed for a strength or endurance athlete in heavy training

   These 96 grams of protein now provide 388 calories. If protein now comprises about 12 percent of his total calories, this would result in a daily caloric consumption of about 3200 calories per day. If he is indeed a strength or endurance athlete in heavy training, his additional energy expenditure will require at least this many calories.

© 2006 JUPITER IMAGES CORPORATION.

7 Weight Control

Key Terms

obesity
set-point
fat-cell theory
android
gynoid
resting metabolic rate
negative energy balance

positive energy balance
body fat
aerobic exercise
anaerobic exercise
behavior modification
anorexia
bulimia

Specific Objectives

1. Describe the incidence of obesity in America.

2. Describe the difference between overweigh and obese.

3. List the major health effects of obesity.

4. Understand the possible cause of obesity.

5. Explain how current theories of obesity relate to weight loss and weight control efforts.

6. Understand the difference between upper and lower body obesity.

7. Explain the role of heredity in body weight.

8. Explain the role of aerobic and anaerobic exercise in weight control.

9. Explain the role of diet in weight control.

10. Describe the changes occurring in resting metabolism as a result of diet and exercise.

11. Identify the false claims and dangers of over-the-counter diet aids.

12. Describe the proper choices for a weight loss plan.

OVERVIEW

Americans are among the heaviest people in the world, and despite wishes to the contrary, we just keep getting heavier. The number of overweight children, adolescents, and adults has risen over the past four decades, and in 2004 the Center for Disease Control reported that nearly two-thirds of U.S. adults are overweight. In addition, nearly one-third of U.S. adults are obese. The prevalence has steadily increased over the years among both genders, all ages, and all racial/ethnic groups. The prevalence of obesity has more than doubled increasing from 13 percent to over 30 percent from the year 1960 to 2000. In 1991, only four states had obesity rates of 15 percent or higher, and no state had obesity rates above 16 percent. By 2000, only Colorado had obesity rates below 15 percent, and 22 states had obesity rates of 20 percent or greater. The problem is not limited to adults. While defining obesity and overweight for children and adolescents is difficult, the prevalence of overweight is increasing for children and adolescents in the U.S. According to the Centers for Disease Control, approximately 15.3 percent of children (ages 6–11) and 15.5 percent of adolescents (ages 12–19) were overweight in 2000 (National Center for Health Statistics, 2004).

Healthy People 2010 contains the goals established by the U.S. Department of Health and Human Services to reduce the portion of the population that is overweight. The target for 6–19-year-olds is no more than five percent, and the target for adults 20 and older is 15 percent. While these goals are admirable, the trend appears to be headed in the wrong direction. Unfortunately, the tracking of progress toward goals for the year 2000 revealed more, not fewer, overweight Americans (U.S. Department of Health and Human Services, 2000).

STRIVING FOR THE LEAN IDEAL

A longing to be thin has overcome millions of Americans. Whether it be for health benefits or cosmetic purposes, a large number of people have a habit of looking at the image in the mirror or at the number on the scale and deciding whether that body size and shape is acceptable. Many are not pleased and for some, the quest for the perfect physique has become an obsession. This often leads to frustration since the image of the perfect body which has been set before us, is simply unattainable for many people. Some not only experience frustration, but also enter into eating behaviors which can be dangerous. This chapter explores the obsession

TABLE 7.1	Overweight and Obese Persons 20 Years of Age and Over According to Sex				
	Overweight				
	1960–62	*1971–74*	*1976–80*	*1988–94*	*1999–2002*
Both sexes	44.8	47.7	47.4	56.0	65.2
Male	49.5	54.7	52.9	61	68.8
Female	40.2	41.1	42.0	51.2	61.7
	Obesity				
Both sexes	13.3	14.6	15.1	23.3	31.1
Male	10.7	12.2	12.8	20.6	28.1
Female	15.7	16.8	17.1	26.0	34.0

From Center for Disease Control, National Center for Health Statistics

Chapter 7

with thinness, looking at the health benefits of achieving and maintaining a desirable body weight, as well as the pros and cons of getting trapped in the strife for the ideal. In addition, this chapter discusses proper weight control techniques.

How did we ever reach the point that we feel that our bodies have to look like movie stars and fashion models to be acceptable? Perhaps it comes from looking at too many movie stars and fashion models. The media has undoubtedly been a very powerful influence when it comes to body image. Throughout time, a current trend or style has been promoted as the perfect body. Even though the desired look has changed, there has always been a social expectation that some body parts should be more developed than others. At one time, size was in, and the bigger the better. Classic artwork depicts full-bodied women as the ideal, and as recently as the 1950s, the Marilyn Monroe look of voluptuous curves was considered everybody's dream figure. In the 1960s, thinness began to become the latest fashion. Since that time, television, movies, and print ads have consistently presented the message that if you do not have a fashion model's body, you lack in attractiveness. And most people do not have a fashion model's body.

This social phenomenon of a desire to be thin has driven millions of Americans to the task of losing weight. Oftentimes, the message of the importance of maintaining a healthy weight has been lost in the cosmetic desire to be attractive. Individuals frequently turn to fraudulent, ineffective, and sometimes dangerous methods of weight loss only to find themselves frustrated, lighter in the pocketbook, and possibly compromising their health. Too often, the media and social expectations, not the pursuit of health, drive one's actions. Dieting has become big business in the United States. About 50 million adults go on a diet each year, and those people will spend over $30 million on diet products and programs (U.S. Food and Drug Administration, 1997). The majority of that money is being wasted. Diet books, special nutrition plans, exercise gimmicks, fat farms, diet drugs and weight loss centers abound, each marketing itself to potential clients as the best way to lose weight. These approaches often take advantage of ignorance and the desire for the quick and easy fix. The truth is that most of them are unsuccessful avenues toward weight loss. In fact, less than five percent of those engaged in an effort to lose weight actually lose the weight and keep the weight off (Barrett, Jarvis, Kroger, and London, 1993).

WHAT IS OVERWEIGHT AND OBESITY?

Overweight refers to an excessive amount of body fat above that which would be considered ideal, while obesity refers to being more than 10 percent body fat above what would be considered ideal. Ideal body composition or percent body fat differs for men and women. As a rule, women have more body fat than men. Most health professionals agree that ideal body fat for men is 15 percent and for women 23 percent. Therefore for men obesity would be defined as a body fat percentage of 25 or above. For women, percent body fat to be considered obese would be 33 or above. Overweight refers to an amount of body fat above ideal but below the level of obesity. Body mass index (BMI) (defined in Chapter 3), is also used to define overweight and obesity. A BMI between 25 and 30 is considered overweight and a BMI above 30 is considered obese. As mentioned in Chapter 3, BMI does not consider the amount of lean mass a person may have, therefore BMI is not a great indicator of overweight and obesity.

BODY FAT DISTRIBUTION

Health care professionals are not only concerned with how much fat a person has, but also where the fat is located on the body. Recent information is showing that it makes a difference where the excess fat is deposited, with respect to medical complications. Health risks are greater for people who have most of their body fat in the upper body, especially the truck and abdominal areas. This is called android obesity. Gynoid obesity, which is characterized by deposition of body fat in the hips and thighs, shows less vulnerability to health risks.

HEALTH EFFECTS OF OBESITY

TABLE 7.2
Risks of Being Overweight (Increase in Risk for Disease)

	20% to 30% Overweight	40% or More Overweight	Deaths per Year
Cancer			
Male:			
Colon/rectum	26%	73%	29,100
Prostate	37%	29%	26,100
Female:			
Breast	16%	53%	39,900
Cervix	51%	139%	6,800
Endometrium	85%	442%	2,900
Gallbladder	74%	258%	5,300
Ovary	0%	63%	11,600
Diabetes			
Male	156%	419%	14,859*
Female	234%	690%	21,929*
Heart Disease			
Male	32%	95%	289,461
Female	39%	107%	251,857
Stroke			
Male	17%	127%	61,697
Female	16%	52%	92,630

*This figure does not include the many diabetics who die of heart disease.

Source: *Journal of Chronic Diseases, 32:563*, 1979; *Personal Communication,* John Lubera, American Cancer Society; Kathy Santini, National Center for Health Statistics, *Nutrition Action Healthletter,* January 1987, p. 7.

The National Institutes of Health recognizes obesity as a condition which poses significant health risks (Table 7.2). An estimated 300,000 Americans die each year as a result of poor diet and inactivity, making this combination second only to tobacco use in behavioral causes of death (McGinnis, Foege, 1993). Obesity has been linked to numerous disorders and causes of death, including high blood pressure, elevated cholesterol levels, kidney and liver disorders, diabetes, heart disease, gallbladder disease, osteoarthritis, some types of cancer and breathing problems. Obesity is also a factor in early death, with most of the increase in mortality resulting from coronary heart disease. It is estimated that if all Americans would achieve a normal body weight, life expectancy in the United States would increase by three years, there would be 35 percent less congestive heart failure and stroke, and 25 percent less heart disease (Baron, 1995). Some of the major health threats from obesity are discussed below.

Hypertension

A person's risk of developing high blood pressure is doubled if he/she is obese. This is true both in adults and children. Known as the "silent killer" because of the absence of outward warning signs, high blood pressure affects approximately 26 percent of obese men and women in America.

Hypertension is discussed in more detail in Chapter 8.

Cholesterol Levels

Overweight individuals are more prone to suffer from hypercholesterolemia, or elevated levels of serum cholesterol. Also, the risk ratio, or ratio of total cholesterol to high-density cholesterol, is higher in the obese, and this is a major indicator of risk for heart disease. On the brighter side, weight loss is an excellent way to lower the heart disease risk which is posed by elevated cholesterol. For every pound lost, there is approximately a one mg reduction in total cholesterol (Neiman, 2003).

Diabetes

The obese have a rate of diabetes which is three times the rate of the non-obese (Neiman, 2003). Nearly 80 percent of patients with non-insulin dependent diabetes are obese (National Institute of Diabetes and Kidney Disorders).

Cancers

Certain types of cancer are found in greater numbers in the obese. The American Cancer Society reports that overweight individuals increase their risk of certain types of cancer. Men who are obese are more likely than non-obese men to develop cancer of the colon, rectum, or prostate. Women who are obese are more likely than non-obese women to develop cancer of the gallbladder, uterus, cervix, or ovaries. Esophageal cancer has also been associated with obesity (American Cancer Society, 2005).

POPULAR THEORIES OF OBESITY

The Set-Point Theory

One theory of weight loss, called the set-point theory, is based on the idea that each individual has an internal control mechanism which carefully regulates body weight by adjusting metabolism. Advocates of this theory argue that each person has a specific body weight or a small weight range which is right for him/her, and that any fluctuation in this weight triggers a response in the brain's hypothalamus. The control mechanism works to maintain each person's preprogrammed "correct" weight. The theory suggests that after a certain amount of body weight is lost, the control mechanism slows down the person's rate of metabolism so that additional weight loss is blocked. In a sense, the body works to conserve its lean tissue and fat stores by reducing its need for energy to survive.

If the set-point theory is accurate, in full or in part, it is clear that attempting to lose weight strictly through caloric restriction will not be effective. This supports the importance of including exercise in any serious weight loss plan. In addition to the numerous wonderful benefits of exercise found in Chapter 2 and the benefit of calorie burning discussed in this chapter, it is also believed that exercise is one of the most effective ways to reset one's set-point. As the body responds to habitual aerobic exercise, it seems to compensate by lowering the predetermined "correct" weight. As you might expect, there is one other approach which is thought to be effective in resetting the set-point. That approach is a reduction in caloric intake. So again the message rings clear: safe and effective weight loss is accomplished through a combination of increasing caloric expenditure through exercise and decreasing caloric intake through proper diet.

Fat Cells: Too Big or Too Many

Proponents of the fat-cell theory believe that obese people have more fat cells and larger fat cells than the non-obese. Fat cell hyperplasia is when the total number of fat cells increases. Fat cell hypertrophy means that existing fat cells become filled with more lipids and are enlarged. It is believed that the number of fat cells in the body increases primarily during infancy and puberty, and that the majority of the increase in body weight during adulthood is due to fat cell hypertrophy. In other words, the fat cells which we develop early in life simply tend to enlarge

---

Box 7.1

Other Diseases and Health Problems Linked to Obesity

- Gallbladder disease and gallstones.
- Fatty liver disease (also called nonalcoholic steatohepatitis or NASH).
- Gastroesophageal reflux. This problem occurs when the lower esophageal sphincter does not close properly and stomach contents leak back or reflux into the esophagus.
- Osteoarthritis, a disease in which the joints deteriorate.
- Gout, another disease affecting the joints.
- Pulmonary problems, including sleep apnea.

with age as a result of caloric abundance and physical maturity. It is also believed that once fat cells are manufactured, they remain for life. Therefore, any weight loss involves a reduction in size of fat cells, not a reduction in number. Finally, there is evidence that fat cells do reach a hypertrophic limit, beyond which they cannot grow in size. In this case, involving the extremely obese, fat cell hyperplasia can occur during adulthood.

FACTORS AFFECTING BODY WEIGHT

A person's body weight is determined by the interaction of several complex factors. These include social, emotional, environmental, behavioral and biological determinants. While there is still much to be learned about the conditions of overweight and obesity, research has revealed some important information.

© 2006 JUPITER IMAGES CORPORATION.

Heredity

Recent evidence points to a genetic link to body fatness. Overweight biological parents appear to be a factor in an individual's experience with his/her own overweightness. In addition, it also appears that the distribution of fat in our parents is likely to determine how and where we store fat. Studies of identical twins who were separated at birth lend evidence to the theory of genetic predisposition. The sets of twins who came from obese biological parents were both likely to be obese later in life, regardless of whether they grew up in a family with fat or thin members. Also, separated twins who eat very different diets as they grow up tend to weigh about the same. These studies have led many to conclude that the role of heredity in obesity is significant. Therefore, the tendency to blame obesity on parental overfeeding during childhood or the suggestion that most people are overweight because they do not have enough self-control, is most likely inaccurate.

However, not all research points to such a strong relationship between genetics and body weight. Some large scale studies conclude that about 25 percent of the variation between people's fat mass is due to biological inheritance, with lifestyle, cultural and environmental factors being responsible for the other 75 percent of the variance.

While individuals should be aware of the importance of genetic predisposition toward body fatness, we must be careful how we utilize that information. Some may be inclined to use it as an excuse. "I come from a fat family, therefore, I can't do anything about my weight" is sometimes offered as the reason for a person having this health-compromising condition, whereas in reality, he/she has done very little to address this problem which is oftentimes preventable. There are numerous individuals who maintain a healthy weight in spite of having a "family history" of obesity. Individuals who feel as though they do have a genetic predisposition toward overweight and obesity should view their situation as an increased challenge which can effectively be addressed with a thorough understanding of the weight loss process.

Diet

The concept of weight control through diet is a very simple one. However, this simple concept is extremely difficult for most Americans to follow. Simply stated, in order for a person to maintain his/her current weight, he/she must maintain a neutral energy balance. This means that the number of calories consumed and the number of calories expended are equal; they neutralize each other. If a person consumes more calories than he/she uses, a positive energy balance exists and weight gain occurs. For example, if Johnny eats a 300-calorie ice cream cone each day and these calories are above and beyond his daily expenditure of calories, then Johnny will gain one pound of fat approximately every 12 days (3,500 calories = 1 pound). In order for a person to lose weight, a negative energy balance must exist. A negative energy balance exists when a person expends more calories than he/she consumes. If Johnny expends 300 calories each day through some type of activity, and these calories are above and beyond his daily expenditure of calories, then Johnny will lose one pound of weight approximately every 12 days. Notice that the term fat was used when referring to weight gain but the term weight was used when referring to weight loss. This is because fat is the body's storage form of energy. Every calorie that a person consumes above what is used is stored as fat. This is the case regardless of the type of food eaten. The overconsumption of calories from carbohydrates, fat, or protein is all stored as excess body fat. On the other hand, when a person loses weight, he/she may or may not lose fat.

Even though our goal in weight loss is to shed fat, we sometimes lose as much lean weight as we do fat weight. Without an appropriate exercise program, weight loss will consist of a combination of fat and lean body mass. (This topic will be covered in more detail later in this chapter.)

As we can see, in order for weight loss to occur, a negative energy balance must exist, and in order for this weight loss not to include lean tissue, an exercise program must be implemented. The question that should be addressed at this time is: What is the best way to create a negative energy balance.

A negative energy balance can be created two ways: through diet or exercise. Which would be most advantageous for weight loss? Without a doubt, a reduction in the number of calories consumed leads to weight loss more quickly than any form of reasonable exercise. If a person decides to cut back on the number of calories consumed, weight loss will be proportional to the caloric deficit created. As mentioned earlier, 3,500 calories constitutes one pound, therefore, anytime a person has a caloric deficit of 3,500 calories, one pound is lost. For someone in need of large weight loss, diet would be the fastest means to accomplish that goal. For example, if a person has a typical calorie intake of 3,000 calories daily and decides to cut back to 2,000 calories a day, then one pound could be lost every 3.5 days. For someone in need of losing 20, 30, 40, or even more weight this would seem to be the best way to achieve desired results. In a six-week period, the total weight loss would seem to be 12 pounds; in three months the loss would equal 26 pounds. Many people will look at this and say "WOW! I didn't know weight loss could be so simple or easy." In addition, people will think "WOW! If cutting back from 3,000 to 2,000 calories can result in this much loss, just think what I can lose if I only eat 1,000 calories a day, or even better, what about 500 calories?" Hopefully these people will continue to read and come to another conclusion. The above example does have flaws. In theory, going from 3,000 to 2,000 calories a day could result in the stated weight loss, but in reality this does not happen. Resting metabolism plays a significant role in body weight regulation, with a high metabolic rate causing weight loss to occur quickly and a slow metabolism causing weight loss to be slow. The resting metabolism for a 121-pound female amounts to approximately 1,190 calories per day or about 60 to 75 percent of total energy expenditure. As most individuals who have dieted know, the rate of weight loss slows during the course of dieting. This is brought about by a decreasing metabolism which occurs as a result of a reduction in calories consumed. Weight loss is most rapid during the initial days of a diet with weight loss becoming more and more difficult as the duration of the diet increases. Metabolic adjustment begins within a couple of days of caloric deficiency and will adjust to the new lower level in three to four weeks. In order for weight loss to continue, the individual will need to continue to reduce the number of calories consumed which can lead to many nutritional deficits.

In addition to the problem of reducing the caloric intake to dangerously low levels, a second major problem is created when weight is lost by diet alone. Most individuals who choose to lose weight by low-calorie diets gain the weight back in a very short time after they stop the diet. The reason for this is simple. People who are overweight, for the most part, like to eat. Their lifestyle is one that enjoys the pleasure obtained from food. If these people diet and lose weight and then go back to their previous lifestyle and eating habits, then weight gain is very rapid.

Since the resting metabolic rate decreased while dieting, the amount of food they can now eat and still maintain current weight is much less. It is true that resting metabolism increases with the increase in food intake after an individual stops dieting; however, the time for the resting metabolism to increase is much longer than it was for the RMR to decrease during weight loss. Most people will experience a gain in weight which exceeds the loss they accomplished through their diet.

A third problem associated with the reduction in calories consumed is the dedication and discipline it takes to eat less. In America, we associate food with pleasure and good times. We celebrate joyous occasions with food and drink. If we reduce our food consumption, even to a small degree, we take some of the joy out of life. (Hopefully, through the weight loss, we replace this joy loss and add more.)

Even though the weight loss equation is a very simple one, it is difficult to follow.

The following equations can be used for estimating resting metabolic rate. For females: resting metabolic rate (calories/day) = 879 + 10.2 (kg) and for males: resting metabolic rate (calories/day) = 795 + 7.18 (kg). (Kg) is the person's weight in kilograms. This can be obtained by dividing the weight in pounds by 2.2.

Exercise

Exercise is the second important component of weight control. Exercise offers a number of significant advantages to people attempting to achieve long-term weight loss. First and foremost, exercise increases energy expenditure, helping to create a negative energy balance necessary for weight loss. Unfortunately, the amount of energy expended during most exercise programs (walking, jogging, swimming, cycling, etc.) with the typical frequency and duration (three to five days per week, 20–30 minutes per session) is a modest 600–1,200 calories per week. Thus, exercise can be said to have very little effect on short-term weight control.

The importance of exercise in weight control is more clearly established in regard to long-term weight loss and weight loss

maintenance. In looking at the cumulative effect of increased energy expenditure for a year, the results are impressive (600–1,200 calories per week for 52 weeks = 9–18 pounds per year). The wonderful fact of this weight loss is that it can be permanent. Many times individuals look for the "quick fix," in other words, they want instant results!

People want to lose large amounts of weight and lose it fast. Exercise may not be the "quick fix" they want, but it is the best fix for a person. When we look at the facts concerning long-term weight loss, one conclusion is clear: exercise is a requirement for most individuals! Evidence that demonstrates the importance of exercise on weight control include data which shows that both obese children and adults exercise less than normal-weight people. Studies show that overweight children tend to be less active than lean children participating in sports. For example, while playing tennis, obese girls have been found to be inactive 77 percent of the time compared to 56 percent of the time for normal-weight girls. In general, lean children spend up to 40 percent more time in physical activity than obese children (Neiman, 1999). Obese men informally walk an average of three and seven-tenths miles per day compared to six miles per day for men of normal weight; while obese females walk two miles per day compared to four and ninth-tenths miles per day for normal-weight women. Obese individuals spend less time on their feet and stay in bed longer than normal weight people. If the obese individual is given a choice between walking up the stairs or riding the escalator, he/she is more likely to choose the escalator. Even with small children, ages four to eight, data show increased body fat levels if daytime activity is less than normal. Even though weight loss may not be rapid, the goal of weight loss should be to lose it for a lifetime. Consistent participation in aerobic activity burns substantial amounts of calories. Anaerobic exercise such as weight training does not burn as many calories during a workout, but this type exercise does enhance resting metabolism by increasing the muscle mass. This change results in an increased daily calorie expenditure for an individual. Enhancing muscle mass can be viewed as an investment in future weight control. This is one reason why both aerobic and anaerobic exercise are suggested for weight loss and weight maintenance. The energy expenditure of weight-bearing exercise (walking, jogging, games, etc.) is dependent on the body weight of the individual. If two people, one weighing 110 pounds and the other weighing 220 pounds, jog one mile together, the 220 pound person expends more calories because it requires more energy to move a heavier weight from one location to another. Table 7.3 provides an estimate of caloric expenditure for selected activities. Appendix D provides you with a caloric expenditure scale that will help you identify the ideal number of calories to be burned each week to provide optimal health.

EXERCISE AND RESTING METABOLISM

Another benefit of exercise in regard to weight control is the effect that exercise has on resting metabolism. For many years people in the fitness and wellness professions preached that exercise has a significant positive effect on resting metabolic rate (RMR), and referred to that effect as the "after burn" of exercise. One can still watch an informative commercial on television and see some "fitness expert" discussing the wonderful "after burn" of exercise. The truth of the matter is, this "after burn" of exercise is not very significant. Research indicates that additional calories are expended after the exercise bout is concluded, but the number of calories is small. For example, jogging (12 minutes per mile), walking, or cycling at a moderate intensity

TABLE 7.3

Calories Expended Per Hour in Various Physical Activities
(Performed at Recreational Level)*

Activity	Calories Used per Hour				
	100 lbs. (145.5 kgs.)	120 lbs. (54.6 kgs.)	150 lbs. (68 kgs.)	180 lbs. (82 kgs.)	200 lbs. (91 kgs.)
Archery	180	204	240	276	300
Backpacking (40-lb pack)	307	348	410	472	513
Badminton	255	289	340	391	425
Baseball	210	238	280	322	350
Basketball (half court)	225	255	300	345	375
Bicycling (normal speed)	157	178	210	242	263
Bowling	155	176	208	240	261
Canoeing (4 mph)	276	344	414	504	558
Circuit Training	247	280	330	380	413
Dance, Ballet (choreographed)	240	300	360	432	480
Dance, Exercise	315	357	420	483	525
Dance, Modern (choreographed)	240	300	360	432	480
Dance, Social	174	222	264	318	348
Fencing	225	255	300	345	375
Fitness Calisthenics	232	263	310	357	388
Football	225	255	300	345	375
Golf (walking)	187	212	250	288	313
Gymnastics	232	263	310	357	388
Handball	450	510	600	690	750
Hiking	225	255	300	345	375
Horseback Riding	180	204	240	276	300
Interval Training	487	552	650	748	833
Jogging (5½ mph)	487	552	650	748	833
Judo/Karate	232	263	310	357	388
Mountain Climbing	450	510	600	690	750
Pool; Billiards	97	110	130	150	163
Racquetball; Paddleball	450	510	600	690	750
Rope Jumping (continuous)	525	595	700	805	875
Rowing, Crew	615	697	820	943	1025
Running (10 mph)	625	765	900	1035	1125
Sailing (pleasure)	135	153	180	207	225
Skating, Ice	262	297	350	403	438
Skating, Roller	262	297	350	403	438
Skiing, Cross-Country	525	595	700	805	875
Skiing, Downhill	450	510	600	690	750
Soccer	405	459	540	621	775
Softball (fast)	210	238	280	322	350
Softball (slow)	217	246	290	334	363
Surfing	416	467	550	633	684
Swimming (slow laps)	240	272	320	368	400
Swimming (fast laps)	420	530	630	768	846
Table Tennis	180	204	240	276	300
Tennis	315	357	420	483	525
Volleyball	262	297	350	403	483
Walking	204	258	318	372	426
Waterskiing	306	390	468	564	636
Weight Training	352	399	470	541	558

*Note: Locate your weight to determine the calories expended per hour in each of the activities shown in the table based on recreational involvement. More vigorous activity, as occurs in competitive athletics, may result in greater caloric expenditures.

From *Fitness for Life* by Charles B. Corin and Ruth Lindsey. © 1990 by Scott, Foresman and Company. Used by permission.

(50–60 percent of maximum heart rate) causes the metabolic rate to stay elevated for 20 to 30 minutes after the exercise, burning an additional ten to 12 calories (Neiman, 2003). When exercise intensity is increased to 75 percent, resting metabolic rate is increased for about 30 to 45 minutes, with a caloric expenditure of an extra 15 to 30 calories. For an obese person who takes a one- or two-mile walk per day, the extra calories expended hardly seem enough to be meaningful. On the other hand, the effect exercise has on chronic metabolic rate may be a bit more attractive. Since the overwhelming majority of calories a person expends per day is a result of that person's RMR, any increase is a bonus. Research has indicated that RMR increases chronically through an exercise program (Neiman, 2003).

The amount of increase is dependent on the type, intensity and duration of the exercise program. A relationship does exist between type, intensity, duration and amount of increase in RMR. The more intense and longer a person exercises, the greater the increase. For the obese person who performs very low-intensity exercise, the increase may be minor; however, for the obese person who performs higher-intensity exercise, the increase can be very significant. Many people reading this text will say "Oh No! High intensity exercise! This doesn't sound like much fun!" Over the past few years the fitness world has been educating people on the proper exercise programs, with the trend being that low-intensity exercise is as good as higher intensities. The truth is, the higher the intensity, the greater the benefit, as long as it is aerobic. It is important that everyone realize that this does not mean that obese individuals should only perform high-intensity exercise. First, you need to know what constitutes high-intensity exercise. Aerobic exercise which requires a heart rate above 60 percent of a person's maximum heart is classified as high-intensity. This intensity is not severe to the point of great discomfort. Most people, whether lean or fat, can exercise at 60 percent of maximum heart rate (MHR) by performing a walking program. An individual should be able to conduct a normal conversation with a partner during the walk and have a pleasurable experience. While on the subject of low-intensity exercise, one other point should be made. You have probably heard that low-intensity exercise burns more fat. Although this is a true statement, it is also a very misleading statement.

When the body burns a calorie, the source of the calorie does not matter. This means that regardless of fat, protein, or carbohydrate, a calorie is a calorie in terms of weight loss. It does not matter if the calorie is a fat, protein, or carbohydrate! In fact, the major source of energy while the body is at total rest is fat. Therefore, if we buy into the low-intensity fat burning philosophy, we should become couch potatoes in order to burn the most fat.

So, this would not be wise from a weight control standpoint. From a RMR standpoint, it is clear that the higher the intensity, the greater the benefit. However, any exercise expends calories and will enhance a person's ability to lose weight.

Anaerobic exercise is also very important when programming exercise for weight control. As a person begins to diet and reduces the number of calories consumed, the natural reaction in the body is for RMR to decrease. The body always adjusts to the number of calories eaten, whether it is an increase or decrease in calories. This is demonstrated by the early weight loss or weight gain individuals experience when they eat either a very low or very high calorie diet. This weight loss or gain is large, but as the duration of the diet continues, the amount of weight lost or gained decreases, even though the individual(s) have been very faithful to their diet. Frustration is a common occurrence with people who achieve early weight loss success but experience the difficulty in losing weight after metabolism drops.

RMR will remain higher if exercise is included in the weight loss program. People who exercise aerobically and diet have more success maintaining RMR than individuals who do not exercise. Most research indicates that aerobic exercise slows the decreased RMR brought about by dieting. Slowing the decrease in RMR does not mean that aerobic exercise completely stops the decline. As much as the proponents of fitness like for everyone to believe that aerobic exercise stops RMR from decreasing, the fact is only a slowing takes place. Another benefit provided by aerobic exercise in weight control is its effect on the maintenance of lean body mass. As was mentioned earlier, a person should be concerned about his/her percentage of body fat, not scale weight. This is hard for most people. Anytime we go to the doctor, we get weighed. Most people have scales in the bathroom and it is easy to step on and look at the weight. Very few people have the opportunity to have a body fat measurement performed. However, it is the percentage of fat which is important, not weight. Weight loss through diet alone causes a much greater loss in weight than in body fat. A person using only a reduction in calorie intake, without exercise, experiences a loss not only in fat, but also in lean tissue. This is not good! Exercise is necessary to prevent the loss in lean tissue.

Data have shown that weight loss through diet alone can be as much as 50 percent fat and 50 percent lean tissue. Aerobic exercise can be useful in reducing the amount of lean tissue loss, but it cannot eliminate it. Anaerobic exercise in the form of weight training is the only way to completely stop lean body tissue loss. Most individuals think aerobic activity is most beneficial in weight control. This concept is true since more calories are burned from aerobic activity; however, preservation of lean tissue is accomplished best through weight training. For optimal body fat loss, a lower calorie diet in combination with aerobic and anaerobic exercise is needed. Weight training while dieting gives a person the dual benefit of maintaining or even increasing lean body weight and also maintaining RMR. As a result of weight training, the amount of weight loss a person achieves could decrease. For some individuals this can be discouraging. However, as mentioned, the amount of weight lost is not the significant factor, but the amount of fat lost is. When one weight-trains, lean body mass increases and fat body mass decreases. This increase in lean mass causes scale weight to stay the same or decrease at a much slower rate, but percent body fat has a significant decrease.

Again, it is body fat which needs to be lost, not necessarily the weight. Increasing the lean body weight increases the RMR by giving the person more active tissue. Lean tissue is more metabolically active than fat tissue; therefore, the more lean tissue a person possesses, the higher the RMR. It would be nice if everyone who is trying to control his/her weight had the capability of body fat testing; then he/she would not have to rely on the bathroom scale to judge his/her success, but this is just not the case. A better judge of weight than the bathroom scale method may be as simple as the fit of one's clothes. If clothing which has been too small in the past begins to fit, or clothing which is currently being worn is becoming too large, then the weight control program is working.

EXERCISE AND APPETITE

The relationship of exercise and appetite is another interesting subject in regard to weight control. Studies examining the effect of exercise on appetite have shown mixed results. These data reveal that exercise may increase, decrease, or have no effect upon food intake. Until recent years, the scientific community adopted the position that one hour of low- to moderate-intensity exercise reduces appetite. The theory was that food intake decreases during the early days of exercise and persists until the level of exercise is increased to above moderate levels. At this point, the appetite increases to be in balance with energy expenditure. Other researchers tried to duplicate the results of the earlier studies without success. Most research indicates that people eat the same amount or even increase their food consumption when they begin an exercise program.

SUCCESSFUL WEIGHT CONTROL

Obesity, even though a chronic illness, for the most part has been treated as an acute illness. Most treatment plans for obesity advertise rapid weight loss and make little attempt to involve behavior modification which is necessary for long-term success. Remember, weight control is a life long effort, and having realistic expectations about weight loss is an important consideration. Since the ultimate goal of a weight loss program is to lose weight and keep it off, a nutritionally sound, low-calorie diet that is applicable to the individual's lifestyle is most appropriate. A weight loss program that includes diet, exercise and behavior modification is more likely to lead to long-term weight control. A successful, long-term weight control program involves three elements:

1. **Diet.** The number of calories consumed should be reduced.

   ⊙ Learn to choose sensible portions of nutritious meals that are lower in fat.

   ⊙ Learn to recognize and control environmental cues (like inviting smells or a package of cookies on the counter) that make you want to eat when you are not hungry.

Box 7.2

How to Lose Weight: The NHLBI Obesity Education Initiative

In 1998, the first federal guidelines for the treatment of overweight and obesity in adults were released by the National Heart, Lung, and Blood Institute (NHLBI) as a part of their nationwide Obesity Education Initiative. With nearly 100 million overweight Americans, the NHLBI has made education about overweight and obesity a major priority. Key diet recommendations from this initiative include the following:

⊙ The initial goal of a weight-loss regimen should be to reduce body weight by about 10 percent. With success, further weight loss can be attempted, if needed.

⊙ Weight loss should be about 1–2 pounds per week for a period of 6 months, with additional plans based on the amount of weight loss. Seek to create a deficit of 500–1,000 Calories per day through a combination of decreased caloric intake and increased physical activity.

⊙ Reducing dietary fat intake is a practical way to reduce Calories. But reducing dietary fat alone without reducing Calories is not sufficient for weight loss.

Each pound of body fat represents about 3,500 Calories. To follow the NHLBI for weight loss, one must expend 500–1,000 Calories more than the amount taken in through the diet. This can be accomplished by increasing energy expenditure 200–400 Calories a day through physical activity, and reducing dietary fat intake by 300–600 Calories. Each tablespoon of fat represents about 100 Calories, so an emphasis on low-fat dairy products and lean meats, and a low intake of visible fats (oils, butter, margarine, salad dressings, sour cream, etc.) is the easiest way to reduce caloric intake without reducing the volume of food eaten.

The NHLBI recommends this diet for weight loss:

⊙ Eat 500–1,000 Calories a day below usual intake.

⊙ Keep total dietary fat intake below 30 percent of Calories, and carbohydrates at 55 percent or more of total Calories.

⊙ Emphasize a heart-healthy diet by keeping saturated fats under 10 percent of total Calories, cholesterol under 300 mg/day, and sodium less than 2,400 mg/day.

⊙ Choose foods high in dietary fiber (20–30 grams/day).

This diet starts in the grocery store. Another challenge is eating healthfully when dining out. Learn to ask for salad dressing on the side and to leave all butter, gravy, or sauces off the dish. Select foods which are steamed, garden fresh, broiled, baked, roasted, poached, or lightly sauteed or stir-fried.

National Institute of Health.

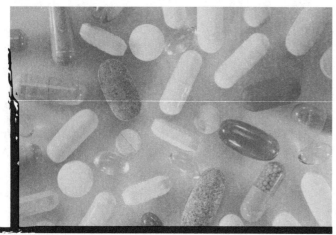

© 2006 JUPITER IMAGES CORPORATION.

2. **Exercise.** Energy expenditure should be increased at least 200 to 400 calories per day. Any form of physical activity is acceptable.

3. **Behavior Modification.** Several techniques should be used, including:

   ⊙ Self-monitoring: Keep a diet diary, with emphasis on recording food amounts and circumstances surrounding the consumption of the food.

   ⊙ Control of the events that precede eating: Identification of the circumstances that elicit eating and overeating.

   ⊙ Development of techniques to control eating: Typical behavioral modification techniques are used.

   ⊙ Reinforcement through use of rewards: Providing a system of formal rewards enhances progress.

Although obese individuals benefit from these guidelines, there are some individuals who seek additional forms of therapy in search for success. Many people choose very low calorie diets in order to achieve rapid weight loss. These diets should only be used by severely obese people under medical supervision. Very low-calorie diets contain less than 800 calories and do not contain the necessary amounts of nutrients to maintain a healthy life.

In today's world, diet aids (drinks, powders, diet bars, etc.) are widely available over the counter, and many people are tempted to rely on them for quick and easy weight loss.

However, the promises made by these products are mostly false and the overdependence on these diet aids can be dangerous. The diet aids provide far less than the needed nutritional and calorie requirements, and are not complementary to a healthy lifestyle. Although these products can help control hunger and weight in the short-term, they encourage dependence on commercial products rather than the development of healthy eating and exercise habits. The next time you see a commercial for Slim-Fast™, Dynatrim™, or Thin-Trim™, ask yourself: "Should I make this a permanent part of my life?"

Diet pills are another common diet aid. There are many brands of diet pills which can be purchased over the counter, most of which contain ineffective ingredients. Phenylpropanolamine hydrochloride (PPA), which the Food and Drug Administration has deemed safe and effective as a mild appetite-suppressant, is the most common ingredient of diet pills. However, research on the effectiveness of PPA is equivocal at best. Research indicates the PPA can cause dizziness, high blood pressure, headaches, sleeplessness and a rapid heart rate. The FDA approves the use of PPA for no longer than 12 weeks.

DANGEROUS DIETING

As mentioned earlier in this chapter, our society has created tremendous pressure for individuals to be thin. The "thin is in" look has become synonymous with attractiveness and social status, and is probably more evident in females than in males. While we have stated that about two-thirds of Americans are overweight,

Box 7.3

Habits of Those Achieving Success in Weight Loss and Management

Researchers at the University of Pittsburgh and University of Colorado have formed a national registry of people who have lost more than 30 pounds and kept it off for more than a year. Several hundred people are now in this registry, and interesting findings have emerged:

- ⊙ 94 percent of successful losers increased their physical activity level to accomplish their weight loss, with walking the most common activity reported.
- ⊙ 92 percent report that they are continuing to exercise to maintain weight loss. Those most successful in fighting back weight regain typically exercise for at least 1 hour a day, burning at least 400 Calories each day.
- ⊙ 98 percent decreased their food intake in some way.
- ⊙ 57 percent received professional help from doctors, registered dietitians, Weight Watchers, and others.

Nationwide, about 20 percent of overweight and obese individuals are able to lose 10 percent of initial body weight and keep it off for at least 1 year. Weight-loss maintenance gets easier over time. Once weight loss has been maintained for 2–5 years, the chances of longer success greatly increase.

From *Annual Review of Nutrition.* 21:323–341, 2001.

many more are dissatisfied with their body image. A recent study exemplified this as more than two-thirds of women between the ages of 12 and 23 were dissatisfied with their weight (University of California at Berkeley, 1991). Additionally, a telephone survey a few years ago indicated that most participants would change their body if given the opportunity, while only 13 percent preferred to stay the same (Princeton Survey Research Associates, 1990).

Those who have a dissatisfaction with body image sometimes feel pressured into trying to conform to the "ideal" body size and shape. Weight reduction, by whatever means they feel might work, captivates their thoughts and energies as they nurture the attitude that losing weight is a good thing, and the more they lose, the more attractive, accepted and successful they are. The relentless pursuit of thinness can result in serious and sometimes life-threatening eating disorders.

About one percent of adolescent females suffer from an eating disorder known as anorexia nervosa (Anorexia Nervosa and Related Eating Disorders, 1999). This dangerous condition is marked by suppression of appetite and intentional caloric deprivation, which results in a wasting away of body mass, or self-starvation. There also exists an intense fear of becoming overweight, and weight loss does not detensify that fear. Due to a psychological distortion of body image, the anorexic sees him/herself as fat, even if extremely underweight.

Weight loss is pursued through extremes in the limitation of caloric intake, often including fasting. Strenuous exercise, the use of laxatives and diuretics, and sometimes self-induced vomiting, are also tools of the anorexic. The onset of puberty often marks the beginning of this disorder, and it is most evident by a wasted-away, or emaciated, look.

A related disorder is bulimia nervosa. About four percent of college age women suffer from bulimia. About 50 percent of people who have been anorexic develop bulimia or bulimic patterns (Anorexia Nervosa and Related Eating Disorders, 1999). This disorder, known as the binge-purge syndrome, is marked by high amounts of food/caloric consumption followed by self-induced vomiting and the use of laxatives and diuretics. Compulsive exercise also may be a characteristic of bulimia as the person attempts to burn away as many of the recently consumed calories as possible. Although related and often coexistent, bulimia differs significantly from anorexia in that the individual may maintain a normal body weight due to the

Diagnostic Criteria for Binge Eating

Following are key diagnostic criteria for diagnosing binge eating.

1. *Characteristics of binge-eating episodes.* The binge-eating episodes are associated with at least three of the following:
   a. Eating much more rapidly than normal
   b. Eating until feeling uncomfortably full
   c. Eating large amounts of food when not feeling physically hungry
   d. Eating alone because of being embarrassed by how much one is eating

2. *Distress.* The person experiences marked distress regarding binge eating. Feelings include disgust, depression, and extreme guilt after overeating.

3. *Recurrent episodes of binge eating.* An episode of binge eating is characterized by both of the following:
   a. Eating, in a discrete period of time (e.g., within any 2-hour period), an amount of food that is definitely larger than most people would eat in a similar period of time under similar circumstances.
   b. A sense of lack of control over eating during the episode (e.g., a feeling that one cannot stop eating or control what or how much one is eating).

4. *Frequency.* The binge eating occurs, on average, at least 2 days a week for 6 months.

5. *No connection to other eating disorders.* The binge eating is not associated with the regular use of inappropriate compensatory behaviors (e.g., purging, fasting, excessive exercise) and does not occur exclusively during the course of anorexia nervosa or bulimia nervosa.

From *Diagnostic and Statistical Manual of Mental Disorders*, 4th edition, American Psychiatric Association, 1994.

binges he/she experiences. This allows the bulimic to hide his/her problem, thereby making it difficult for friends and family members to identify the bulimic.

Anorexia and bulimia nervosa are sometimes combined with episodes of crash dieting. Eventually, half of those with anorexia develop bulimia.

While manifesting themselves in dangerous dietary behaviors, eating disorders must be recognized as more than just nutritional problems. They are mental disorders, and must be treated as such. While the causes and contributing factors are complex, researchers have been able to provide some insight into the roots of these dangerous behaviors.

Causes and Contributors

A low self-esteem is often at the root of these behaviors. While the victims may appear to be very successful to others, they have become susceptible to expectations of perfection. They typically meet with success in academics, athletics and social scenarios, but success is not enough. The strife for absolute perfection leaves them feeling less than adequate, and they are driven to take total control in some area of their lives. They often share a fear of becoming fat, and choose eating habits in response to this fear. These people are determined to exhibit a control over this area of their lives. Females comprise about 90 percent of people with eating disorders.

Perhaps the pressure toward perfection comes from some outside sources. Victims of eating disorders often come from families who place unrealistically high expectations on the child members. Overemphasis on physical attractiveness and promotion of the physical ideal by the parents and other family members may be a significant contributor to the development of an eating disorder. In addition, environments which place overemphasis on physical appearance for some type of athletic or social performance may create the mind-set that control of body weight is the most important factor in the person's success. Anorexia athletica is a condition found among individuals who engage in eating disorders to control their weight in order to enhance athletic performance. Gymnasts, distance runners, dancers and others involved in performance- or appearance-related activities, in which lower weights are seen as an advantage, are more susceptible to these problems.

Eating habits may also be seen as an avenue to dealing with stress and anxiety. Mentally healthy individuals develop various resources for dealing with stressors, but the less resourceful person may turn to unhealthy coping activities. Control over one's body may temporarily provide the buffer needed to deal with these stressors, but then they become dangerous.

Finally, eating disorders do appear to run in families, but as with obesity and many other health problems, it is unclear to what degree heredity plays a role. Genetic factors may predispose a person to an eating disorder, but psychological, behavioral and environmental factors are also strong.

HEALTH THREATS FROM EATING DISORDERS

Both anorexia and bulimia pose the risk of serious medical complications. Anorexia can deprive the body of nourishment to the point that the heart and brain suffer damage. As the body slows down to conserve energy due to the absence of caloric intake, several health problems arise. Amenorrhea, or suppression of the menstrual cycle, occurs, and vital functions such as respiration, heart rate and blood pressure drop. The skin and hair become unhealthy, with nails and hair becoming brittle and dry. The risk of dehydration is also increased. Other risks include anemia, calcium loss and brittle bones, swollen joints and light-headedness. Eventually, heart failure can occur.

The specific risks associated with bulimia are related to the acts of binging and purging. Esophageal inflammation and severe tooth decay are common due to the presence of stomach acids from the vomiting. More serious complications of stomach rupture and heart failure due to mineral loss may occur.

Treatment

Treatment for an eating disorder is quite complex. The problem requires more serious intervention than simply instilling healthier eating habits or restoring a person's body mass. Certainly, medical care must be available to combat the serious physical problems brought on by this disease, but psychological assistance is crucial in addressing the underlying mental or emotional disorder which lies at the root of the problem. Treatment centers around the effort to improve a patient's self-esteem and that person's overcoming of his/her distorted body image. Struggles with depression, anxiety and inability to deal with outside pressures must be addressed. A psychiatrist is often called upon for intervention, and various types of individual, group and family therapy have been used to treat eating disorders. Medically, hospitalization may be necessary if the patient has developed certain medical complications, such as metabolic disturbances, serious depression, and suicidal tendencies, or if he/she has reached a level of being severely underweight. Certain medications have also been found effective in helping the patient deal with his/her depression and other emotional trauma. Finally, nutritional counseling can assist in the patient's development of adequate knowledge and attitudes toward new and healthier eating habits.

Helping the Person

If you suspect that someone you know is suffering from an eating disorder, your assistance could be crucial to the person's ability to overcome the problem. Anorexia Nervosa and Related Eating Disorders, Inc., provides the following suggestions for helping:

1. Be supportive. Provide information about eating disorders.
2. Be a good listener. A good repertoire of supportive comments can be valuable in helping the person find a safe zone to express his/her fears and anxieties. Comments like "I enjoy spending time with you," "That's interesting, I never thought of it like that before," or simply "Tell me more," can make the person feel more comfortable talking to you about his/her problem.
3. Encourage professional help. Counseling, medical treatment, and perhaps even hospitalization, may be needed for recovery.
4. Be prepared for denial, resistance, and even hostility.
5. Do what you can to convince the person that recovery has more advantages than the disorder.
6. Realize that the person's recovery is his/her responsibility, not yours. If you sincerely try to help, you are doing the best you can.

Several other organizations provide up-to-date resources on eating disorders. A list of those organizations is provided below:

National Association of Anorexia Nervosa and Associated Disorders (ANAD)
P.O. Box 7
Highland Park, IL 60035
(708) 831-3438

Anorexia Nervosa and Related Eating Disorders, Inc. (ANRED)
P.O. Box 5102
Eugene, OR 97405
(503) 344-1144

American Anorexia/Bulimia Association, Inc. (AABA)
425 East 61st Street, 6th Floor
New York, NY 10021
(212) 891-8686

References

American Cancer Society. (2005). Cancer Facts and Figures—2005. Atlanta.

Anorexia Nervosa and Related Eating Disorders. (1999). How many people have eating and exercise disorders?

Barrett, S., et al. (1995). *Consumer Health: A Guide to Intelligent Decisions.* Madison, WI: Brown & Benchmark Publishers.

Diabetes in America, 2nd ed. The National Institutes of Diabetes and Digestive and Kidney Disorders, 1995, NIH publication #95-1468.

Fahey, T.D., Insel, P.M., & Walton, R.T. (1994). *Fit and Well.* Mountain View, CA: Mayfield Publishing Company.

Great bodies come in many shapes. (1991). University of California at Berkeley, Wellness Letter, 7:2.

Chapter 7

Hockey, R.V. (1996). *Physical Fitness* (8th ed.). St. Louis: Mosby-Year Book, Inc.

McGinnis, J.M., & Foege, W.H. (1993). Actual causes of death in the United States. *Journal of the American Medical Association*, 270:2207–2212.

Millar, W.J., & Stephens, T. (1987). The prevalence of overweight and obesity in Britain, Canada, and the United States. *American Journal of Public Health*, 77:38–41.

National Center for Health Statistics. (2004). *Health—United States, 2004*. Hyattsville, MD: U.S. Public Health Service, p. 245.

National Institutes of Health. (1994). *Eating Disorders*. U.S. Government Printing Office, Publication #94-3477.

National Institutes of Health. (1996). *Statistics Related to Overweight and Obesity*. Publication #96-4158.

Neiman, D.C. (2003). *Exercise Testing and Prescription: A Health Related Approach* (5th ed.). New York: McGraw-Hill Publishing Company.

Princeton Survey Research Associates. (1990). *1990 Survey*. In Kobren, G. (1990). Most in survey would change their bodies if possible. SFC, B4, reprinted from Baltimore *Sun*.

Ross, J.G., et al. (1987). Changes in the body composition of children. *Journal of Physical Education, Recreation and Dance*, 9:74–77.

Rosato, F.D. (1994). *Fitness for Wellness* (3rd ed.). St. Paul, MN: West Publishing Company.

Troiano, R.P., et al. (1995). Overweight prevalence and trends for children and adolescents: The National Health and Nutrition Examination Surveys, 1963 to 1991. *Archives of Pediatrics and Adolescent Medicine*. 149: 1085–1091.

United States Department of Health and Human Services. (1991). *Healthy People 2000: A Summary Report*. Boston: Jones and Bartlett.

United States Food and Drug Administration. (1997). *The Facts About Weight Loss Products and Programs*. DHHS Publication # (FDA) 92-11-89.

U.S. Department of Health and Human Services. *Healthy People 2010*. (Conference Edition, in Two Volumes) Washington, DC: January 2000.

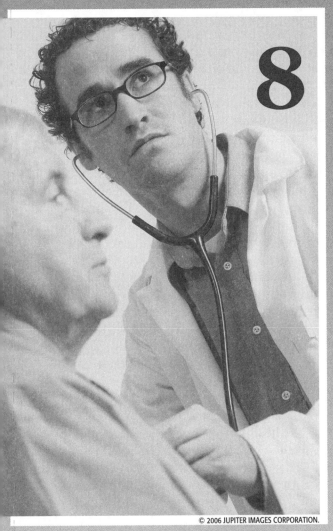

8 Cardiovascular Disease

Key Terms

cardiovascular disease
coronary heart disease
stroke
atherosclerosis
blood lipids
saturated fat
myocardium

angina
hypertension
hypercholesterolemia
triglycerides
hemoglobin
high-density cholesterol
low-density cholesterol

CVD

Specific Objectives

1. Identify the major forms of cardiovascular disease.

2. Identify the major and minor risk factors associated with cardiovascular disease.

3. Identify the warning signs of heart attack and stroke.

4. Discuss the lifestyle behaviors that contribute to the development of cardiovascular disease.

5. Explain the difference between high-density lipoprotein cholesterol and low-density lipoprotein cholesterol.

6. Identify acceptable levels for blood pressure, blood lipids, glucose and body fat.

7. Be able to assess a person's risk for cardiovascular disease.

8. Discuss the effects of exercise on reducing cardiovascular disease risk.

9. Discuss what steps an individual can take to keep his/her cardiovascular system healthy and avoid cardiovascular disease.

OVERVIEW

The lifestyle in the United States offers so many opportunities. We have the highest standard of living in the world. Transportation is for the most part both convenient and easy; entertainment is readily available; we can drive and even park our cars almost in the location to which we are going; even our food is quick and easy. However, along with the ease of living that we enjoy, there is a price to be paid. The convenience of transportation and the fast foods that we consume at an enormous rate have led to a sedentary lifestyle and high-fat diet. This in turn has led to our country having a very high rate of cardiovascular disease.

Cardiovascular disease (CVD) is the leading cause of death in the United States, accounting for roughly forty percent of the mortality rate in 2005. CVD is disease of any aspect of the cardiovascular system which includes the heart, blood and blood vessels. Major forms of CVD include high blood pressure, congenital heart disease, coronary heart disease, peripheral vascular disease, stroke, rheumatic heart disease and atherosclerosis. The most predominant form of CVD is coronary heart disease (CHD). This disease causes a narrowing of the coronary arteries which supply the heart with nutrients through its blood flow. CHD is the single largest killer of American males and females. About every 26 seconds an American will suffer a coronary event, and about every minute someone will die from one. About 41 percent of the people who experience a heart attack in a given year will die from it (American Heart Association, 2006).

The heart, like all other muscles and organs in the body, needs its own blood supply. The myocardium (muscle layer of the heart) is not nourished by the blood being pumped to other parts of the body. The heart's blood is supplied through the coronary artery system (see Figure 8.1). When a portion of the heart does not get adequate blood, it begins to die. When CHD causes the arteries to be closed by about two-thirds, chest pain called angina pectoris can occur during times of ex-

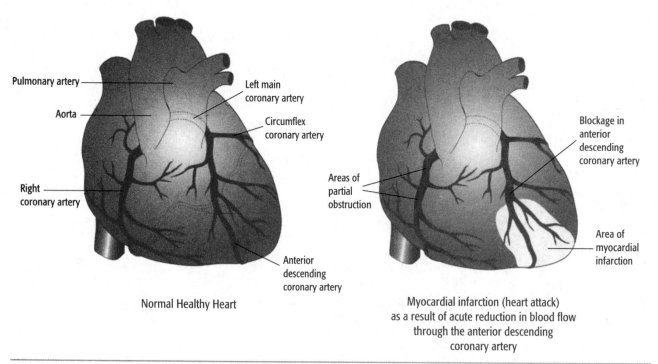

Normal Healthy Heart

Myocardial infarction (heart attack) as a result of acute reduction in blood flow through the anterior descending coronary artery

Figure 8.1 ⊙ *The heart and blood vessels.*

citement or physical exertion. A heart attack, or myocardial infarction, occurs when the blood supply to part of the heart is blocked. This is typically brought about by a blood clot forming in a narrowed coronary artery. The first indication of a heart attack may be one of several warning signals: uncomfortable pressure, fullness, squeezing, or pain in the center of the chest lasting two minutes or more; pain that spreads to the shoulders, neck, or arms; or severe pain, dizziness, fainting, sweating, nausea, or shortness of breath. Sharp, stabbing twinges of pain are usually not signals of a heart attack (see Table 8.1).

Stroke is another predominant form of CVD. Stroke affects the blood vessels that supply oxygen and nutrients to the brain. Atherosclerosis (narrowing of arteries due to build-up of deposits in arterial wall) can cause a blood clot to form inside the cerebral artery and block the blood flow to the brain. The risk factors for stroke are listed in Table 8.2. The prevalence for stroke is less than for CHD however, over 5 million people suffer from a stroke each year in America (see Figure 8.2). The most important risk factor for stroke is hypertension. As blood pressure increases, the risk for stroke increases accordingly. Some of the warning signals of stroke are: dizziness, temporary weakness or numbness on one side of the face, arm or leg, and temporary loss of speech or vision (American Heart Association, 2006).

Hypertension is considered a major risk factor for CHD and stroke; however, hypertension can also be considered a disease in itself. Blood pressure is defined as the force of the blood against the walls of the arteries and veins. This force is created by the heart as it pumps blood to every part of the body. Hypertension or high blood pressure is a condi-

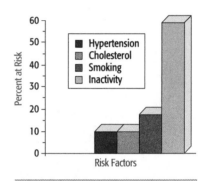

Figure 8.2 ⊙ *U.S. population at risk for physical inactivity compared with the four major risk factors.*

Adapted from Capersen, C.J.: Physical inactivity and coronary heart disease. *Physician Sportsmed.* 15:43–44,1987.

What to Do in Case of a Heart Attack	**TABLE 8.1**

When it comes to a heart attack, delay spells danger. Minutes make a difference, so it's important to know what to do.

Know the Signals of a Heart Attack

⊙ Uncomfortable pressure, fullness, squeezing, or pain in the center of the chest lasting two minutes or more.
⊙ Pain may spread to shoulders, neck, or arms.
⊙ Severe pain, dizziness, fainting, sweating, nausea, or shortness of breath may also occur. Sharp, stabbing twinges of pain are usually not signals of a heart attack.

Know What Emergency Action to Take

⊙ If you are having typical chest discomfort that lasts for two minutes or more, call the local emergency rescue service immediately.
⊙ If you can get to a hospital faster by car, have someone drive you. Find out which hospitals have 24-hour emergency cardiac care and discuss with your doctor possible choices. Plan in advance the route that's fastest from where you live and work.
⊙ Keep a list of emergency rescue service numbers by your telephone and in a prominent place in your pocket, wallet, or purse.

Know How to Help

⊙ If you are with someone who is having the signals of a heart attack, take action even if the person denies there is something wrong.
⊙ *Call* the emergency rescue service, or
⊙ *Get* to the nearest hospital emergency room that has 24-hour emergency cardiac care, and
⊙ *Give* mouth-to-mouth breathing and chest compressions (CPR) if it is necessary and if you are properly trained.

American Heart Association, 2000.

TABLE 8.2	Risk Factors for Stroke	
Risk Factors That Can Be Treated	**Risk Factors That Cannot Be Treated**	
1. High blood pressure	1. Age	
2. Personal history of heart disease	2. Male	
3. Cigarette smoking	3. Race—African-American	
4. High red blood cell count	4. Personal history of diabetes mellitus; prior stroke	
5. Transient ischemic attacks (TIA)	5. Heredity—family history	
6. Physical inactivity	6. Geographic location—Southeastern U.S.	
7. Excessive alcohol intake; intravenous drug abuse	7. Season—during periods of extreme temperatures	
8. Obesity	8. Socioeconomic—more likely among the poor	
9. Elevated blood cholesterol	9. Asymptomatic carotid bruit—atherosclerosis in carotid artery that causes a sound heard with a stethoscope	

Source: American Heart Association.

tion in which the blood pressure is chronically elevated above the normal or optimal levels.

Hypertension is diagnosed if a person has repeated measurements above the optimal levels. For example, if someone has two blood pressure measurements taken on separate occasions and the diastolic pressure is above 90 mm/Hg each time, hypertension would be determined. Many factors contribute to increased blood pressure. These factors include heredity, obesity, sodium sensitivity, alcohol consumption, age, race, caffeine and a sedentary lifestyle. Hypertension increases the workload of the heart and arteries and contributes to heart failure and atherosclerosis. Like all muscles in the body, the heart, when required to work harder than normal for a long period of time, tends to enlarge. An enlarged heart has a difficult time keeping up with the demands of the body. Statistics demonstrate that about 50 million Americans have high blood pressure (Table 8.3). Hypertension is most prevalent among the elderly, African-Americans, and the obese.

YOUR RISK FOR CARDIOVASCULAR DISEASE

Although CVD is the number one killer in the United States, the fact is that to a large degree we control our own destiny. Preventive medicine is the key to reducing the development of any form of CVD. It is evident that our lifestyle habits largely determine our susceptibility. Most physicians agree that if we ate better,

TABLE 8.3	Statistics on Heart Disease	
Prevalence	56,450,000	Cardiovascular disease
	50,000,000	Hypertension (adults)
	6,300,000	Coronary heart disease
	3,060,000	Stroke
Cardiovascular Disease Deaths	930,224	43 percent of all deaths; 20 percent occur before age 65
Heart Attack Deaths	478,530	(number one cause of death)
	6,300,000	Alive today have history of heart attack or angina pectoris
	250,000	Per year die before reaching hospital
	1,500,000	Projected heart attacks of which one-third will die
Stroke	144,070	3,060,000 victims alive today; number three cause of death
CAB Surgery	407,000	Coronary bypass operation

American Health Association, 2000.

exercised more, smoked less, and maintained proper body composition, it would do more to improve our health than anything they could do for us.

For almost 50 years, research has been conducted in an effort to determine the basic cause of CVD. Large populations have been studied over long periods with their living habits and medical records assessed in relation to the incidence of CVD. These studies have helped identify how CVD develops and what factors predispose one to CVD (Paffenbarger & Hyde, 1984). Risk factors which lead to CVD development can be classified into major and minor categories, with the major factors having much more influence on disease risk. In addition, three of the minor factors are associated with lifestyle behaviors. Although heredity plays a role in CVD, the most important determinant is personal lifestyle. A true statement could probably be made by stating that CVD is not genetically inherited, but we do tend to inherit the lifestyle of our parents. To a large degree, even though we hate to hear it, we do turn into our parents. This simply means that people typically live the type of lifestyle in which they were raised. If, as a child, you ate high-fat foods and were not encouraged to be active, then more than likely those are your habits as an adult. A CVD risk assessment can be used to evaluate the impact of an individual's lifestyle and heredity on the development of CVD (see Laboratory 1). Using this assessment can help identify individuals who may be at high risk for disease. In addition, the assessment can educate people regarding the leading risk factors for development of CVD. For example, a person who completes the assessment knows that the ideal blood pressure is 130/80 or lower, that total cholesterol should be under 200 mg/dl, and that smoking or being exposed to environmental smoke significantly increases risk (see Laboratory 1 to complete self-assessment CVD risk).

With the exception of gender, age, race, and heredity, the risk factors for CVD are preventable and reversible. A discussion of the risk factors is presented next, along with some recommendations for risk reduction.

PRIMARY OR MAJOR RISK FACTORS

Smoking

Smoking is the number one cause of CVD. Individuals who smoke have a 2.5 times greater than average risk of developing CVD. With 40 percent of all deaths being CVD related and the average risk being high, we would not like our chances if we were smokers. Cancer is the disease which typically is associated with smoking; however, smokers are much more likely to die of heart disease than cancer.

A strong relationship exists between the development of CVD and smoking. This means that the more you smoke, the greater your risk. A one-pack per day smoker is at twice the risk as a non-smoker while a two-pack per day smoker is at three times the risk (Neaton, 1992).

It is easy to understand why smoking has such an impact on the development of CVD. As smoke enters the alveoli of the lungs, carbon monoxide competes with oxygen to be carried into the blood. The hemoglobin portion of the red blood cells is the oxygen-carrying component of the blood. As you know, without adequate oxygen the body cannot function, therefore, people must depend on their hemoglobin to transport the needed oxygen. Even though hemoglobin has an affinity for oxygen, it also has an affinity for carbon monoxide. In fact, the affinity for carbon monoxide is stronger than that for oxygen, therefore, oxygen is somewhat ignored. This reduces the amount of oxygen in the blood and forces the heart to pump much more blood in order for adequate oxygen to be delivered.

TABLE 8.4

Blood Pressure Classification

Classification	*Systolic	*Diastolic	What to Do
Normal	Below 130	Below 85	Recheck in two years
High normal	130–139	85–89	Recheck in one year
Mild hypertension	140–159	90–99	Confirm within two months
Moderate hypertension	160–179	100–109	See physician within a month
Severe hypertension	180 or above	110 or above	See physician immediately

Examples

120/80	Normal	
135/85	High normal	
145/95	Mild hypertension	
160/105	Moderate hypertension	
180/115	Severe hypertension	

*Based on an average of two or more readings on two or more occasions.

Adapted from The National High Blood Pressure Education Program and the fifth report of the Joint National Committee on Detection, Evaluation, and Treatment of High Blood Pressure, *Archives of Internal Medicine*, 25 January 1993.

© 2006 JUPITER IMAGES CORPORATION.

High Blood Pressure

Although hypertension is considered a type of CVD, high blood pressure is also a major risk factor for developing CHD and stroke. As noted in Table 8.4, a systolic blood pressure consistently elevated above 140 mm Hg or a diastolic pressure above 90, constitutes hypertension. As with smoking, CHD has a strong relationship with hypertension. That is to say, the higher the blood pressure, the greater the risk for CHD.

Control of hypertension depends to a large extent on the cause. Some of the causes of hypertension include: stress, obesity and lack of exercise. Control methods may include a weight loss program, learning how to control stress and starting an exercise program.

As you may have heard on many occasions, high blood pressure is the silent killer. This statement is made to enforce the fact that individuals do not have any way of knowing their blood pressure unless they have it checked. It should be common practice for a person to monitor his/her blood pressure on a regular basis. If an individual has a family history of high blood pressure or any form of CVD, it is recommended that blood pressure be checked every six months.

For an individual with no family history of this type, one time per year may be adequate.

Hypercholesterolemia

Hypercholesterolemia is a technical name for having too much fat in the blood. Blood fats are responsible for the build-up of plaque on the walls of arteries. The higher an individual's blood lipids or fats, the greater his/her risk is for CVD.

Table 8.5 includes the normal and abnormal values for blood lipids. A person with abnormal blood lipids has double the risk of CVD as a person with normal blood lipids levels. As with smoking and blood pressure, a dose relationship exist. This means that the more abnormal a person's blood lipid levels are the greater the risk for CVD. Over the past 20 or so years cholesterol education has improved greatly in America. Many people are now aware of cholesterol and its danger. However, most people are not well informed about the different types of cholesterol. Cholesterol can be broken down to subfractions which include low-density lipoproteins (LDL-C), very low-density lipoproteins (VLDL-C), and high-density lipoproteins (HDL-C). These subfractions are very important when determining an individual's risk of CVD. In simple terms, LDL-C have a low density of protein and a high density of fat, while the opposite is true for HDL-C (high protein content, low fat). While LDL-C is harmful because of its ability to cause fatty buildup in blood vessels, HDL-C works as a scavenger, removing fatty buildup in the vessels. The higher the level of HDL-C an individual has, the lower his/her risk is for developing CVD. Evidence exists which suggests that for each 1 mg/dl increase in HDL-C there is a 2 percent reduction for men and a 3 percent reduction for women for the development of CVD. Research data also indicates that a 1 percent decrease in total cholesterol is associated with a 2 percent reduction in CVD (Robergs & Keteyian, 2003).

The NCEP guidelines given in Table 8.6 show that an LDL-C value below 130 mg/dL is desirable, between 130 and 159 mg/dL is borderline, and 160 mg/dL and above is high risk for cardiovascular disease. It is obvious that the lower one's LDL-C level, the better.

It is suggested by many authorities that the ratio between total cholesterol and HDL-C is the strongest indicator of potential CVD risk. A TC/HDL-C ratio of 3.5 or lower is excellent for men, and 3.0 or lower is excellent for women. For example, a total cholesterol value of 180 and an HDL-C value of 50 would translate into a ratio of 3.6 (180 divided by 50).

Triglycerides are also a blood lipid that, if elevated, can lead to CVD. Most people have been educated concerning blood cholesterol but not much education has been directed toward triglycerides. Readings of 200 mg/dl or below is considered to be acceptable triglyceride levels with levels above 400 considered high-risk. There is a direct relationship between body composition and triglycerides; therefore, the best control for triglycerides may be to control body composition.

TABLE 8.5

Serum Triglyceride Levels

Serum Triglyceride	mg/dl
Normal triglycerides	<200
Borderline-high triglycerides	200–399
High triglycerides	400–1,000
Very high triglycerides	>1,000

Source: From National Cholesterol Education Program. 1993. *Second Report of the Expert Panel on Detection, Evaluation, and Treatment of High Blood Cholesterol in Adults.* Bethesda, MD: U.S. Department of Health and Human Services, Public Health Service; National Institutes of Health; National Heart, Lung, and Blood Institute.

Cholesterol Guidelines — **TABLE 8.6**

	Amount	Rating
Total Cholesterol	<200 mg/dL	Desirable
	200–239 mg/dL	Borderline high
	≥240 mg/dL	High risk
LDL-Cholesterol	<130 mg/dL	Desirable
	130–159 mg/dL	Borderline high
	≥160 mg/dL	High risk

	Men	Women	Rating
HDL-Cholesterol	≥45 mg/dL	≥55 mg/dL	Desirable
	36–44 mg/dL	46–54 mg/dL	Moderate Risk
	≤35 mg/dL	≤45 mg/dL	High risk

National Institute of Health.

Blood lipids can be altered by changes made in an individual's lifestyle. Starting an aerobic exercise program is an excellent way to increase HDL-C and lower LDL-C and triglycerides. Many researchers have demonstrated the beneficial effects of aerobic exercise on blood lipids (Pronk, 1993, & Hartung, 1995). Studies suggest that an aerobic exercise program that expends 1,000 calories/week (e.g., ten miles of walking/jogging) at moderate intensity is required to produce lipoprotein changes. Greater changes occur with a greater caloric expenditure.

Exercise intensity is also an important factor in regard to lipid changes. For the past few years, exercise specialists have suggested that low-intensity exercise is as good as or even better than moderate- and high-intensity exercise. The "no pain, no gain" slogan was said to be outdated and incorrect. This does hold true in regard to total cholesterol, LDL-C and triglycerides. However, moderate- and high-intensity exercise is necessary for an increase in HDL-C to occur. For low-intensity exercise to be effective in lowering TC, LDL-C and triglycerides, weight loss must occur. This weight loss must be in the form of body fat, since the greater the amount of fat loss, the greater the decrease in these blood lipids. The independent effect of aerobic exercise on TC, LDL-C and triglycerides is limited to improving the magnitude of change in triglycerides. TC and LDL-C changes do not seem to change without body fat reduction.

HDL-C increases are directly related to the amount and intensity of the aerobic exercise performance. Exercise which is below 60 percent of maximum heart rate does not seem to have a significant impact on HDL-C. One study performed by Crouse (1995) demonstrated that an increase in exercise intensity produced gains in HDL-C. Subjects performing at 70 percent of maximum heart rate had greater increases in HDL-C than did subjects performing at 60 percent. Likewise, subjects exercising at 80 percent of maximum showed more improvement than subjects exercising at 70 percent (Table 8.7).

Dietary adjustments are another way to alter blood lipids. Total cholesterol, LDL-C, triglycerides and even HDL-C can be improved through the proper nutritional practices. The average American consumes between 400 and 600 mg of cholesterol daily; however, the body produces much more than that. The fact that a food product is cholesterol-free does not necessarily mean that cholesterol cannot be manufactured from that product. Saturated fats are the biggest concern in the diet. These fats raise cholesterol levels more than anything else in the diet. Any food product which is high in saturated fat, even though it has little or no cholesterol, raises the body's total cholesterol level.

Saturated fats are found mostly in animal sources (see Table 8.8). Fish and poultry have fewer saturated fats, therefore, they may be a better dietary choice. The American Heart Association has published dietary recommendations for the treatment of hypercholesterolemia (Table 8.9). These recommendations include a fat intake below 30 percent of total calorie consumption with not more than one-third of these calories coming from saturated fat. Since saturated fat has the greatest influence on the production of cholesterol, limiting its intake is the most important dietary control. Monounsaturated fats, such as canola or olive oil, should make up one-third or more of fat calories, since these oils may raise HDL-C levels. Polyunsaturated fats, which may help lower total cholesterol without reducing HDL-C, should account for up to one-third of the total fat calories consumed.

In addition to lowering fat consumption, the National Cholesterol Education Program (NCEP) recommends limiting dietary cholesterol to under 300 mg/day, which is about the amount of cholesterol found in one large egg.

TABLE 8.7

Conditions that Enhance the Effects of Exercise on Blood Lipids

- ⊙ Patients are currently sedentary
- ⊙ Lipoprotein levels are abnormal (especially elevated triglycerides or depressed HDL cholesterol)
- ⊙ Exercise training is long-term (>6 months)
- ⊙ Body composition changes occur (↑ lean body mass, ↓ body fat)
- ⊙ Diet is modified (e.g., ↓ saturated fat, ↑ omega-3 or omega-6 fatty acids)

		Percent Calories from Total Fat	Percent Calories from Saturated Fat	Cholesterol
Saturated Fat Sources				**TABLE 8.8**
Food	**Amount**			**(milligrams)**
Fruits		Low	Low	0
Vegetables		Low	Low	0
Grains		Low	Low	0
Nuts		High	Moderate	0
Avocado		88	17	0
Coconut, dried		88	76	0
Milk, nonfat	1 cup	—	—	5
Milk, low-fat	1 cup	30	17	22
Cottage cheese, 4% fat	1/2 cup	35	20	24
Cheese—pasteurized type	1 oz	73	40	25
Cream (half & half)	1/4 cup	79	58	26
Ice cream, regular	1/2 cup	49	27	27
Cheese, cheddar	1 oz	72	40	28
Milk, whole	1 cup	48	27	34
Butter	1 tbs	100	55	35
Margarine	1 tbs	100	18	0
Tuna, canned	3 oz	38	10	55
Chicken, cooked	3 oz	19	6	74
Pork, cooked	3 oz	73	26	76
Beef, cooked	3 oz	77	37	80
Lamb, cooked	3 oz	61	34	83
Egg yolk	1	71	43	220
Liver, fried	2 oz	43	13	250

Source: Whitney, *Understanding Nutrition*. Wadsworth Publishing, 1999.

Cholesterol testing is the first step in gaining control of this risk factor. The NCEP recommends that all adults be tested at least once every five years, beginning at age 20. If an individual has a family history of heart disease, the recommendation is for the testing to occur at least every three years.

Physical Inactivity

In 1993 the American Heart Association identified a sedentary lifestyle as a major risk factor for CVD. Lack of physical activity is on a par with smoking, high blood pressure, and high cholesterol and triglyceride levels as a major factor in determining CVD risk. When compared to the other major risk factors, lack of physical activity affects more of the population than the others combined. Roughly 60 percent of the U.S. population is at risk because of physical inactivity (Figure 8.2). This makes lack of exercise the most changeable of all the risk factors. As little as 90 minutes per week of mild exercise is reported to significantly reduce CVD risk. Exercise may include any activity which expends calories. Examples could include hiking, cycling, gardening, swimming or golf.

Most experts maintain that as long as total energy output is increased, expended through light or moderate exercise, risks of CVD are decreased. A lower risk for CVD was observed in men and women who habitually carried out light exercise (leisure-time walking, cycling and gardening) (Blair, 1995). Also, Lee (1995) reported that total energy expenditure and energy expenditure in vigorous activities (greater than 60 percent of maximum) related inversely to CVD mortality. With this information in mind, the guidelines for improving cardiovascular endur-

Cardiovascular Disease

TABLE 8.9	National Cholesterol Education Program/American Heart Association Guidelines for Dietary Prevention and Treatment of High Serum Cholesterol Levels and Coronary Heart Disease

⊙ Total fat intake should be less than 30 percent of Calories.
⊙ Saturated fat intake should be less than 10 percent of Calories (Step 2 = <7%).
⊙ Polyunsaturated fat intake should not exceed 10 percent of Calories; monounsaturated fat should not exceed 15 percent.
⊙ Cholesterol intake should not exceed 300 mg/day (Step 2 = <200 mg/day).
⊙ Carbohydrate intake should constitute 55 percent or more of Calories, with emphasis on complex carbohydrates and high fiber foods.
⊙ Protein intake should provide about 15 percent of the Calories.
⊙ Sodium intake should not exceed 2,400 mg/day.
⊙ Alcoholic consumption should be moderate (<2 drinks per day for men, <1 drink per day for women).
⊙ Total Calories should be sufficient to maintain the individual's recommended body weight.
⊙ A wide variety of foods should be consumed.

Source: National Cholesterol Education Program and the American Heart Association.

ance that were presented in Chapter 2 are appropriate to follow in order to reduce CVD risk.

Obesity

As defined in Chapter 3, obesity is considered to be 10 percent above the ideal fat percentage. In addition, some agencies use a body mass index (refer to Chapter 3, for definition) over 30 for defining obesity. Excess body fat places a strain on the cardiovascular system, creating a much less efficient engine. Although obesity is recognized as an independent risk factor for CVD, the risk attributed to obesity may actually be caused by other risk factors which are usually associated with excessive body fat. Risk factors such as high blood lipids, high blood pressure and diabetes improve with a decrease in body fat.

An increase in daily physical activity, which includes participation in both aerobic and strength-training programs, and a moderate reduction in caloric intake can lead to a significant reduction in percent body fat. See Chapter 7 for more recommendations on weight control.

SECONDARY OR MINOR RISK FACTORS

Secondary risk factors for CVD are important to control but not to the same extent as smoking, blood pressure, obesity, blood lipids and physical activity. These minor risk factors include diabetes, stress, gender, race, age and heredity. Interestingly, some of these factors are under our control while others are not. Age, race, gender and heredity cannot be altered; therefore, we are at the mercy of our biological makeup to some degree.

Diabetes

Diabetes mellitus (commonly called diabetes) is a condition in which the blood glucose (sugar) is inhibited from entering the cell. This condition is created because the pancreas either stops producing insulin, does not produce enough insulin to meet the body's needs, or the body cannot use insulin. As a result, blood glucose absorption by the cells is low, leading to high blood glucose levels. Long-term complications involving the eyes, kidneys, nerves and blood vessels re-

Box 8.1

American Heart Association Guidelines for Reducing the Risk of Cardiovascular Disease by Dietary and Other Lifestyle Practices

These guidelines are designed to assist individuals in achieving and maintaining:

1. A healthy eating pattern including foods from all major food groups
   A. Consume a variety of fruits and vegetables; choose five or more servings per day.
   B. Consume a variety of grain products, including whole grains; choose six or more servings per day.

2. A healthy body weight
   A. Match intake of total energy (calories) to overall energy needs.
   B. Achieve a level of physical activity that matches (for weight maintenance) or exceeds (for weight loss) energy intake. Walk or do other activities for at least 30 minutes on most days.

3. A desirable blood cholesterol and lipoprotein profile
   A. Limit intake of foods with high content of cholesterol-raising fatty acids.
      ○ Keep saturated fat intake at less than 10 percent of energy (<7% for those with high LDL-C). Include fat-free and low-fat milk products, fish, legumes (beans), skinless poultry, and lean meats. Choose fats with 2 grams or less saturated fat per serving, such as liquid and tub margarines, canola oil, and olive oil. Limit intake of full-fat milk products, fatty meats, and tropical oils.
      ○ Limit intake of trans-fatty acids, the major contributor of which is hydrogenated fat.
   B. Limit the intake of foods high in cholesterol.
      ○ Limit dietary cholesterol intake to less than 300 mg/day on average (<200 mg/day for individuals with elevated LDL-C, diabetes, and/or cardiovascular disease.
   C. Substitute grains and unsaturated fatty acids from fish, vegetables, legumes, and nuts.

4. A desirable blood pressure
   A. Limit salt (sodium chloride) intake to 6 grams/day (100 mmol or 2,400 mg of sodium).

B. Maintain a healthy body weight.
C. Limit alcohol intake among those who drink (no more than two drinks per day for men, and one drink per day for women).
D. Maintain a dietary pattern that emphasizes fruits, vegetables, and low-fat dairy products and is reduced in fat.

Issues That Merit Further Research

⊙ *Antioxidants.* High intake of dietary antioxidants from plant foods is recommended; insufficient evidence to support antioxidant supplements.

⊙ *B vitamins and homocysteine lowering.* The normal metabolism of homocysteine requires an adequate supply of folate, vitamin B_6, vitamin B_{12}, and riboflavin. High plasma homocysteine levels have been related to increased coronary risk in most but not all studies.

⊙ *Soy protein and isoflavones.* The consumption of soy protein in place of animal protein tends to lower blood levels of total cholesterol, LDL-C, and triglycerides without affecting HDL-C (but may require the presence of soy isoflavones which has been removed in some commercial soy products).

⊙ *ω-3 fatty acid supplements.* Consumption of one fatty fish meal per day (or alternatively, a fish oil supplement) could result in an ω-3 fatty acid intake of about 900 mg/day, an amount shown to beneficially affect mortality rates in patients with coronary heart disease.

⊙ *Stanol/sterol ester-containing foods.* Food containing stanol/sterol ester (plant sterols) have been shown to decrease blood cholesterol levels. Plant sterols (currently isolated from soybean and tall oils, esterified, and then incorporated into food products) decrease total cholesterol and LDL-C by decreasing intestinal absorption of dietary cholesterol.

⊙ *Fat substitutes.* Fat substitutes mimic one or more of the roles of fat in a food and tend to reduce fat and energy intake.

American Heart Association. *Circulation* 102:2284–2299, 2000.

sult from this condition. Diabetes kills about 75,000 Americans a year. It is the top cause of kidney failure, limb amputations, and adult-onset blindness, as well as being a contributor to CVD.

Fasting blood glucose levels above 126 mg/dl are considered to be a sign of diabetes and should be brought to the attention of a physician (Table 8.10). Values between 126–159 mg/dL are considered to be borderline high while values above 160 mg/dL are high. Other signs and symptoms of diabetes include excessive urination, excessive thirst, unsatisfied hunger, weight loss, cessation of growth among the young, irritability, and drowsiness.

Type 1, or insulin-dependent, and Type 2, non-insulin dependent, are the two major forms of diabetes. Type 1 can occur at any age but may be referred to as ju-

TABLE 8.10
Blood Glucose Guidelines

≤126	Desirable
126–159	Borderline high
≥160	High

venile diabetes because it is typically found in young people. Only about ten percent of diabetes cases are Type 1. Type 2 diabetes accounts for approximately 90 percent of all cases and more often occurs in people over 40, with the highest frequency in people over the age of 55. About 85 percent of Type 2 diabetics were obese at the time of diagnosis; therefore, the term "diabesity" has been used to describe this condition (Nieman, 2003).

The difference between Type 1 and Type 2 diabetes is that in Type 1, the pancreas produces very little or no insulin, whereas in Type 2, the insulin production of the pancreas is adequate but the body cells are unable to use the insulin correctly.

A diet high in water-soluble fiber (found in fruits, vegetables, oats and beans) and an aerobic exercise program can help prevent the onset of Type 2 diabetes.

Stress

When individuals are subjected to stressful conditions, they experience an increase in catecholamines (stress hormones), which in turn elevate heart rate, blood pressure and blood glucose levels. This is commonly referred to as the "Fight or Flight" syndrome because the body is preparing to either fight or flee. If the person takes action, either fights or flees, the higher level of catecholamines are metabolized and the body returns to its normal state. However, if a person is under constant stress due to a death of a relative or friend, loss of employment, marital troubles, or any other of a number of circumstances, the catecholamine levels stay elevated and so do blood pressure, heart rate and blood glucose.

Individuals who are unable to relax have a constant stress applied to the cardiovascular system. Eventually, this strain could lead to CVD. Developing day-to-day coping skills and the ability to deal with work and social stressors are important ingredients to a healthy life. Exercise is one of the best ways to relieve the symptoms of stress. When an individual exercises, the body metabolizes excess catecholamines and the cardiovascular system is able to return to its normal state. For more information on stress management techniques, refer to Chapter 10.

Gender

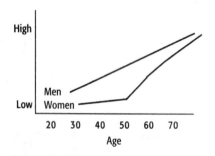

Figure 8.3 ⊙ *Cardiovascular risk by gender.*

Cardiovascular disease is the leading killer of both men and women. However, death rates are three times higher for men than for women during the early and middle decades of life (Figure 8.3). After age 55, this disparity drops dramatically. Moreover, when heart attacks occur in women, they are more deadly than for men: 39 percent of women who have heart attacks die within a year compared to 31 percent of men. After age 65 this disparity grows, with women who have heart attacks being twice as likely to die as men (American Heart Association).

Levels of HDL-C are the protective factors causing younger women to be at lower risk for CVD. As mentioned previously in this chapter, HDL-C helps clear the arteries of disease-causing plaque, thus lowering CVD risk. Women, due to high estrogen levels, naturally produce about 20 percent more HDL-C than men. After menopause estrogen levels decrease, causing a drop in HDL-C. Consequently, women experience a greater risk for CVD. Estrogen supplementation after menopause can help maintain HDL-C, however, with supplemental estrogen comes a higher risk for cancer. It is always advisable to visit with a physician concerning supplementation of estrogen.

Heredity

Even though heredity plays a role in the development of CVD, the role is much less than most people think. People with a family history of CVD are more likely to develop disease than people with no family history, but it is not clear why this is the case. Most people think that it is obvious; genetics is the reason, but as to date, no gene has been identified as a carrier of CVD. The aforementioned old saying that we turn into our parents is probably true and may be the answer why heredity plays a role. Remember that most people inherit a lifestyle from their parents. If the parents are sedentary, then more than likely the children are, too. In addition, people develop a taste for the foods which they eat as youth. If the family meals consist of high-fat, high-calorie foods, these foods are the choice of the children as they grow into adults.

Persons with a family history of CVD need to closely monitor the other risk factors. Maybe more importantly, these people need to examine the lifestyle of their family members who have suffered from CVD and make lifestyle modifications to reduce CVD risk.

Age

As we become older, our risk of CVD increases. Other factors such as less physical activity, obesity and poor nutrition may be partly responsible for this increased risk with aging. Evidence demonstrates that a fit individual at age 50, 60, or even 70 is at lower risk for CVD than unfit individuals of younger years. It is important to think physiological age instead of chronological age when determining CVD risk. Risk factor management and positive lifestyle habits are the best means for slowing down physiological aging.

Race

African-American men and women are at greater risk for CVD. African-Americans are almost one-third more likely to have high blood pressure compared to Americans of Caucasian ancestry. Mexican-Americans are also more likely to have high blood pressure and suffer from other forms of CVD. Historically, Asian-Americans have exhibited lower rates of CVD than Caucasian-Americans. However, recent data show that CVD is on the rise in this population, presumably owing to their adoption of the American lifestyle.

SUMMARY

Most major risk factors for heart disease are controllable. A person with a family history of heart disease is not doomed to develop the disease as well. Preventive medicine is the key to reducing the development of heart disease. It is evident that lifestyle habits largely determine susceptibility. Most physicians agree that eating a healthy diet low in fat and high in complex carbohydrates, exercising regularly, quitting smoking, maintaining proper body composition, and developing effective ways to handle stress does more to improve health than anything medicine could do. Heart disease is typically caused by a neglect in lifestyle, which can be reversed. What is required is a commitment to develop habits that contribute to total well-being.

References

American Heart Association. (2005). *Heart and Stroke Facts*. Statistical Supplement, Dallas, Texas, 2006.

Blair, S.N., et al. (1995). Changes in physical fitness and all-cause mortality. *Journal of the American Medical Association*, 273:1093–1098.

Crouse, S.F., et al. (1995). Changes in serum lipids and apolipoproteins after exercise in men with high cholesterol: Influence of intensity. *Journal of Applied Physiology*, 79:279–286.

Hartung, H.G. (1995). Physical activity and high density lipoprotein cholesterol. *Journal of Sports Medicine and Physical Fitness*, 35:1–5.

Lee, I.M., et al. (1995). Exercise intensity and longevity in men. *Journal of the American Medical Association*, 273:1179–1184.

Manson, J.E., et al. (1992). The primary prevention of myocardial infarction. *New England Journal of Medicine*, 326:1406–1413.

National Heart, Lung, and Blood Institute. (1993). *The Fifth Report of the Joint National Committee on Detection, Evaluation, and Treatment of High Blood Pressure*. NIH Publication No. 93-1088, Hyattsville, Maryland.

Neaton, J.D., & Wentworth, D. (1992). Serum cholesterol, blood pressure, cigarette smoking, and death from coronary heart disease. *Archives of Internal Medicine*, 152:56–64.

Nieman, D.C. (2003). *Fitness and Sports Medicine* (5th ed.). Palo Alto, CA: Bull Publishing, 1995.

Paffenbarger, R.A., & Hyde, R.T. (1984). Exercise in the prevention of coronary heart disease. *Preventive Medicine*, 13:3–22.

Pollock, M.L., & Wilmore, J.H. (1990). Exercise in Health and Disease (2nd ed.). Philadelphia: W.B. Saunders Company.

Robergs, R.A., & Keteyian, S.J. (2003). Fundamentals of Exercise Physiology. (2nd ed.). New York: McGraw Hill.

Pronk, N.P. (1993). Short term effects of exercise on plasma lipids and lipoproteins in humans. *Sports Medicine*, 16:431–489.

Scantron pencil. ch. 5-8

What will Be on the Test:

chapter 8
LABORATORY

Risk Factors for Cardiovascular Disease

Your chances of suffering an early heart attack or stroke depend on a variety of factors, many of which are under your control. To help identify your risk factors, circle the response for each risk category that best describes you.

"I'm Going To Die" LOL
do BAD.
Laugh now on paper
while I still can

1. Gender
   - 0   Female
   - (2)   Male

2. Heredity
   - 0   Neither parent suffered a heart attack or stroke before age 60.
   - 3   One parent suffered a heart attack or stroke before age 60.
   - 7   Both parents suffered a heart attack or stroke before age 60.

3. Smoking
   - 0   Never smoked
   - 1   Quit more than two years ago
   - 2   Quit less than two years ago
   - 8   Smoke less than one-half pack per day
   - (13)   Smoke more than one-half pack per day
   - 15   Smoke more than one pack per day

4. Environmental Tobacco Smoke
   - 0   Do not live or work with smokers
   - 2   Exposed to ETS at work
   - 3   Live with smoker
   - (4)   Both live and work with smokers

5. Blood Pressure
   The average of the last three readings:
   - 0   130/80 or below
   - 1   131/81 to 140/85
   - 5   141/86 to 150/90
   - 9   151/91 to 170/100
   - 13 Above 170/100

6. Total Cholesterol
   The average of the last three readings:
   - 0   Lower than 190
   - 1   190 to 210
   - 2   Don't know
   - 3   211 to 240
   - 4   241 to 270
   - 5   271 to 300
   - 6   Over 300

7. HDL Cholesterol
   The average of the last three readings:
   - 0   Over 65 mg/dL
   - 1   55 to 65
   - 2   Don't know
   - 3   45 to 54
   - 4   35 to 44
   - 5   25 to 34
   - 6   Lower than 25

8. Exercise
   - 0   Aerobic exercise three times per week
   - 1   Aerobic exercise once or twice per week
   - 2   Occasional exercise less than once per week
   - 7   Rarely exercise

9. Diabetes
   - 0   No personal or family history
   - 2   One parent with diabetes
   - 6   Two parents with diabetes
   - 9   Non-insulin-dependent diabetes (Type 2)
   - 13 Insulin-dependent diabetes (Type 1)

10. Weight
   0   Near ideal weight
   1   Six pounds or less above ideal weight
   3   Seven to 19 pounds above ideal weight
   5   Twenty to 40 pounds above ideal weight
   7   More than 40 pounds above ideal weight

11. Stress
   0   Relaxed most of the time
   1   Occasional stress and anger
   2   Frequently stressed and angry
   3   Usually stressed and angry

Scoring

Total your risk factor points. Refer to the list below to get an approximate rating of your risk of suffering an early heart attack or stroke.

Score	Estimated Risk
Less than 20	Low risk
20–29	Moderate risk
30–45	High risk
Over 45	Extremely high risk

chapter 8
LABORATORY ②

How "Heart Healthy" Is Your Diet?

MEDFICTS: Dietary Assessment Questionnaire

In each food category for both group 1 and group 2 foods check one box from the "Weekly Consumption" column (number of servings eaten per week) and then check one box from the "Serving Size" column. If you check Rarely/never, do not check a serving size box. See end of questionnaire for scoring.

Food Category	Weekly Consumption			Serving Size			Score
	Rarely/ never	3 or less	4 or more	Small < 6 oz/day	Average 6 oz/day	Large >6 oz/day	
Meats ■ ⊙ Recommended amount per day: ≤6 oz (equal in size to 2 decks of playing cards). ⊙ Base your estimate on the food you consume most often. ⊙ Beef and lamb sections are trimmed to 1/8 inch fat.				1 pt	2 pts	3 pts	_____
1. 10 gm or more total fat in 3-oz cooked portion **Beef.** Ground beef, ribs, steak (T-bone, flank, Porterhouse, tenderloin), chuck blade roast, brisket, meatloaf (w/ground beef), corned beef **Processed meats.** 1/4-lb burger or lg. sandwich, bacon, lunch meat, sausage/knockwurst, hot dogs, ham (bone-end), ground turkey **Other meats, Poultry, Seafood.** Pork chops (center loin), pork roast (Blade, Boston, sirloin), pork spareribs, ground pork, lamb chops, lamb (ribs), organ meats,* chicken w/skin, eel, mackerel, pompano	☐	☐ 3 pts	☐ 7 pts	✕ ☐ 7 pts	☐ 2 pts	☐ 3 pts	_____
2. Less than 10 g total fat in 3-oz cooked portion **Lean beef.** Round steak (eye of round, top round), sirloin,† tip & bottom round,† chuck arm pot roast,† top loin† **Low-fat processed meats.** Low-fat lunch meat, Canadian bacon, "lean" fast-food sandwich, boneless ham **Other meats, Poultry, Seafood.** Chicken, turkey (w/o skin)§ most seafood,* lamb leg shank, pork tenderloin, sirloin top loin, veal cutlets, sirloin, shoulder, ground veal, venison, veal chops and ribs,† lamb (whole leg, loin, fore-shank, sirloin)†	☐	☐	☐	✕ ☐	☐	☐‡ 6 pts	_____
Eggs ■ Weekly consumption is the number of times you eat eggs each week 1. Whole eggs, yolks	☐	☐ 3 pts	☐ 7 pts	Check the number of eggs eaten each time ≤1 ✕ ☐ 1 pt	2 ☐ 2 pts	≥3 ☐ 3 pts	_____
2. Egg whites, egg substitutes (1/2 c)	☐	☐	☐	✕ ☐	☐	☐	_____
Dairy ■ **Milk.** Average serving 1 cup 1. Whole milk, 2% milk, 2% buttermilk, yogurt (whole milk)	☐	☐ 3 pts	☐ 7 pts	✕ 1 pt	☐ 2 pts	☐ 3 pts	_____
2. Skim milk, 1% milk, skim buttermilk, yogurt (nonfat, 1% lowfat)	☐	☐	☐	✕ ☐	☐	☐	_____

Food Category	Weekly Consumption			Serving Size			Score
Cheese. Average serving 1 oz							
1. Cream cheese, cheddar, Monterey Jack, colby, swiss, American processed, blue cheese, regular cottage cheese (1/2 c), and ricotta (1/4 c)	☐	☐ 3 pts	☐ 7 pts	× ☐ 1 pt	☐ 2 pts	☐ 3 pts	_____
2. Low-fat & fat-free cheeses, skim milk mozzarella, string cheese, low-fat, skim milk & fat-free cottage cheese (1/2 c) and ricotta (1/4 c)	☐	☐	☐	× ☐	☐	☐	_____
Frozen Desserts ■ Average serving 1/2 c		1					
1. Ice cream, milk shakes	☐	☐ 3 pts	☐ 7 pts	× ☐ 1 pt	☐ 2 pts	☐ 3 pts	_____
2. Ice milk, frozen yogurt	☐	☐	☐	× ☐	☐	☐	_____
Frying Foods ■ Average servings: see below. This section refers to method of preparation for vegetables and meat.							
1. French fries, fried vegetables (1/2 c), fried chicken, fish, meat (3 oz)	☐	☐ 3 pts	☐ 7 pts	× ☐ 1 pt	☐ 2 pts	☐ 3 pts	_____
2. Vegetables, not deep fried (1/2 c), meat, poultry, or fish—prepared by baking, broiling, grilling, poaching, roasting, stewing: (3 oz)	☐	☐	☐	× ☐	☐	☐	_____
In Baked Goods ■ 1 Average serving							
1. Doughnuts, biscuits, butter rolls, muffins, croissants, sweet rolls, danish, cakes, pies, coffee cakes, cookies	☐	☐ 3 pts	☐ 7 pts	× ☐ 1 pt	☐ 2 pts	☐ 3 pts	_____
2. Fruits bars, Low-fat cookies/cakes/pastries, angel food cake, homemade baked goods with vegetable oils, breads, bagels	☐	☐	☐	× ☐	☐	☐	_____
Convenience Foods ■							
1. Canned, packaged, or frozen dinners: e.g., pizza (1 slice), macaroni & cheese (1 c), pot pie (1), cream soups (1 c), potato, rice & pasta dishes with cream/cheese sauces (1/2 c)	☐	☐ 3 pts	☐ 7 pts	× ☐ 1 pt	☐ 2 pts	☐ 3 pts	_____
2. Diet/reduced-calorie or reduced-fat dinners (1), potato, rice & pasta dishes without cream/cheese sauces (1/2 c)	☐	☐	☐	× ☐	☐	☐	_____
Table Fats ■ Average serving: 1 tbsp							
1. Butter, stick margarine, regular salad dressing, mayonnaise, sour cream (2 tbsp)	☐	☐ 3 pts	☐ 7 pts	× ☐ 1 pt	☐ 2 pts	☐ 3 pts	_____
2. Diet and tub margarine, low-fat & fat-free salad dressings, low-fat & fat-free mayonnaise	☐	☐	☐	× ☐	☐	☐	_____
Snacks ■							
1. Chips (potato, corn, taco), cheese puffs, snack mix, nuts (1 oz), regular crackers (1/2 oz), candy (milk chocolate, caramel, coconut) (about 1-1/2 oz), regular popcorn (3 c)	☐	☐ 3 pts	☐ 7 pts	× ☐ 1 pt	☐ 2 pts	☐ 3 pts	_____
2. Pretzels, fat-free chips (1 oz), low-fat crackers (1/2 oz), fruit, fruit rolls, licorice, hard candy (1 med piece), bread sticks (1–2 pc), air-popped or low-fat popcorn (3 c)	☐	☐	☐	× ☐	☐	☐	_____

*Organ meats, shrimp, abalone, and squid are low in fat but high in cholesterol.
†Only lean cuts with all visible fat trimmed. If not trimmed of all visible fat, score as if in group 1.
‡Score 6 pts if this box is checked.
§All parts not listed in group 1 have < 10 g total fat.

Total from page 1 _____
Total from page 2 _____
Final Score _____

To score: For each food category, multiply points in weekly consumption box by points in serving size box and record total in score column. If group 2 foods checked, no points are scored (except for group 2 meats, large serving = 6 pts).

Example

☐	☐	☑	× ☐	☐	☑	21
	3 pts	7 pts	1 pt	2 pts	3 pts	

Add scores on page 1 and page 2 to get final score.

Key:
≥70 Need to make some dietary changes
40–70 Very good
<40 Excellent

Source: Kris-Etherton P., Eissenstat B, Jaax S, Srinath U, Scott L, Rader J, Pearson T. Validation for MEDFICTS, a dietary assessment instrument for evaluating adherence to total and saturated fat recommendations of the National Cholesterol Education Program Step 1 and Step 2 diets. J Am Diet Assoc 101:81–86, 2001.

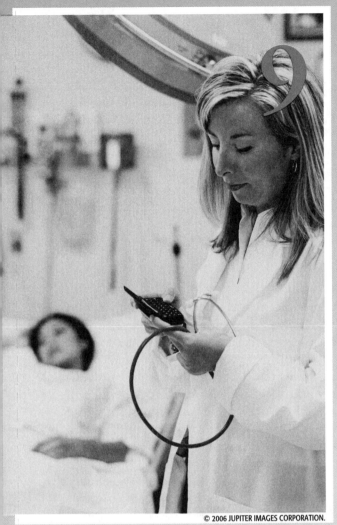
© 2006 JUPITER IMAGES CORPORATION.

Cancer, Diabetes, and Osteoporosis

Key Terms

benign tumor
malignant tumor
cancer in situ
metastasis
carcinogen
melanoma
self-examination
radiation

chemotherapy
immunotherapy
diabetes mellitus
    (Type 1 and Type 2)
hyperglycemia
insulin
osteoporosis
estrogen

Specific Objectives

1. Explain the incidence of cancer.

2. List the various theories of the causes of cancer.

3. Identify the risk factors and warning signs for the various types of cancer.

4. Present guidelines for the prevention of the various types of cancer.

5. Explain the incidence of diabetes and osteoporosis.

6. Identify the risk factors and warning signs for diabetes and osteoporosis.

7. Describe the role of proper diet and exercise in disease prevention.

CANCER

One of the most dreaded diseases known to humanity is cancer. Virtually every individual has had his/her life affected by this disease, either directly or indirectly. While cancer can strike anyone at any age, and is the leading disease killer of children, those most often affected are middle-aged or older adults. Lifetime risk is the probability that an individual will develop cancer or die from it in his/her lifetime. Women have slightly higher than a one-in-three lifetime risk of developing cancer, and in men, the lifetime risk is slightly less than one-in-two. While modern medical science provides a great deal of hope that cancer will be more preventable and curable in the future, it remains the number two killer of Americans, trailing only cardiovascular disease. It accounts for approximately 23 percent of all deaths, and cancer is now recognized as the leading cause of death for Americans under the age of 85 (American Cancer Society, 2005).

What Is Cancer?

Cancer is actually a term representing a group of diseases marked by uncontrolled growth and spread of abnormal cells. Cancer begins with one abnormal cell which has lost the mechanism of control for cell division and growth. It continues to keep dividing and forming more cells without control and order. If the growth and spread of these cells are not controlled, cancer can lead to death. As the cancer cells continue to grow, they form a group of abnormal cells called a tumor, or neoplasm. There are two types of tumors. Benign tumors are not considered cancerous because they do not have the ability to spread and invade other healthy body tissue. They are not considered a threat to health unless their location causes them to interfere with basic physiologic functioning, such as a benign tumor placing pressure on part of the brain or blocking the esophagus. Benign tumors can usually be removed if necessary and usually do not come back. A malignant tumor, or cancerous tumor, has the ability to invade nearby tissue and organs and spread to other sites in the body where secondary tumors are formed. If the cancer has not spread and remains localized, it is considered non-invasive, and is referred to as cancer in situ. If it has begun to move into surrounding tissue, it is referred to as invasive cancer. Cancerous cells can also spread through the body via the circulatory or the lymphatic system. This spreading of cancerous cells to other parts of the body is called metastasis, and occurs because cancer cells break off from one another more readily than healthy cells.

Incidence of Cancer

It is estimated that 1,373,000 new cancer cases and nearly 560,000 cancer deaths occurred in the United States in 2005. This represents about 1,500 people per day who die of cancer. One of every four deaths is due to cancer, and since 1990, there have been approximately four million cancer deaths. Over the last half of the 20th century, cancer deaths steadily rose, until a slow decline began in the 1990s (American Cancer Society, 2005).

More people are now surviving cancer than ever before. Nearly ten million Americans with a history of cancer are alive today, some cancer-free and some still undergoing treatment. While survival rates for cancer vary greatly by type and stage of diagnosis, the five year survival rate has increased to 64 percent, up from 50 percent in the early 1970s. The increased survival rate is due to advances in early detection and treatment of cancer. The number of new cases of cancer and cancer deaths are shown by site and sex in Figure 9.1.

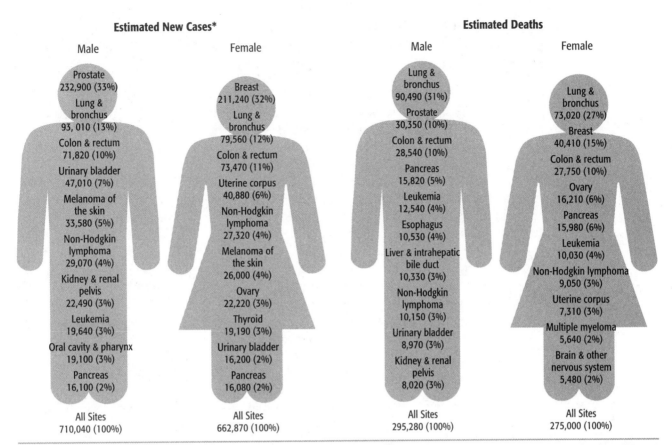

Estimated New Cases*

Male

Prostate
232,900 (33%)

Lung &
bronchus
93, 010 (13%)

Colon & rectum
71,820 (10%)

Urinary bladder
47,010 (7%)

Melanoma of
the skin
33,580 (5%)

Non-Hodgkin
lymphoma
29,070 (4%)

Kidney & renal
pelvis
22,490 (3%)

Leukemia
19,640 (3%)

Oral cavity & pharynx
19,100 (3%)

Pancreas
16,100 (2%)

All Sites
710,040 (100%)

Female

Breast
211,240 (32%)

Lung &
bronchus
79,560 (12%)

Colon & rectum
73,470 (11%)

Uterine corpus
40,880 (6%)

Non-Hodgkin
lymphoma
27,320 (4%)

Melanoma of
the skin
26,000 (4%)

Ovary
22,220 (3%)

Thyroid
19,190 (3%)

Urinary bladder
16,200 (2%)

Pancreas
16,080 (2%)

All Sites
662,870 (100%)

Estimated Deaths

Male

Lung &
bronchus
90,490 (31%)

Prostate
30,350 (10%)

Colon & rectum
28,540 (10%)

Pancreas
15,820 (5%)

Leukemia
12,540 (4%)

Esophagus
10,530 (4%)

Liver & intrahepatic
bile duct
10,330 (3%)

Non-Hodgkin
lymphoma
10,150 (3%)

Urinary bladder
8,970 (3%)

Kidney & renal
pelvis
8,020 (3%)

All Sites
295,280 (100%)

Female

Lung &
bronchus
73,020 (27%)

Breast
40,410 (15%)

Colon & rectum
27,750 (10%)

Ovary
16,210 (6%)

Pancreas
15,980 (6%)

Leukemia
10,030 (4%)

Non-Hodgkin lymphoma
9,050 (3%)

Uterine corpus
7,310 (3%)

Multiple myeloma
5,640 (2%)

Brain & other
nervous system
5,480 (2%)

All Sites
275,000 (100%)

Figure 9.1 ⊙ *Leading Sites of New Cancer Cases and Deaths—2005 Estimates**

American Cancer Society Surveillance Research, 1997. Copyright © 1997, American Cancer Society, Inc.

*Excludes basal and squamous cell skin cancers and in situ carcinoma except bladder.

Note: Percentages may not total 100% due to rounding.

Causes of Cancer

While all causes of cancer are not identified or clearly understood, research has revealed several of the major factors which cause this disease. Cancer is caused by internal factors such as genetic makeup and immune function, and external factors such as the environment and exposure to carcinogens (cancer causing agents). Internal and external factors may also interact to promote carcinogenesis, but lifestyle factors are thought to be major contributors to cancer incidence. In fact, the American Cancer Society says that 175,000 cancer deaths in 2005 were caused by tobacco use, and that one-third of the 570,280 deaths in 2005 were related to nutrition, physical inactivity, and overweight and obesity. Additionally, many of the more than one million skin cancer cases could be prevented by protection from the ultraviolet rays of the sun. Laboratory 1, at the end of this chapter, can help you determine your risk for various types of cancer.

Genetic Factors. While the exact link between genetics and cancer remains unknown, some types of cancer do run in families. A family pattern appears to exist for cancers of the colon, stomach, prostate, breast, uterus, ovaries and lungs. Whether these cancers are due to a specific genetic predisposition or due to a shared environment and lifestyle among family members is unknown. Ongoing genetic research may answer many of the questions researchers have about these biological factors.

Environmental Factors. Some products found in our environment are carcinogens, or cancer-causing agents. Certain workplaces, in which workers are exposed to materials on a regular and prolonged basis, may increase an individual's risk of cancer. Workers exposed to asbestos, for example, are known to be at risk for lung cancer. Other industrial settings which expose workers to vinyl chloride, arsenic, benzene, dyes, solvents, herbicides, pesticides, petrochemicals, and radiation may increase cancer risks. Those who work in these settings or experience frequent contact with these and other chemical compounds should take careful precautions to reduce their exposure.

Radiation is also a carcinogen. However, only high-frequency radiation, ionizing radiation, and ultraviolet radiation have been shown to cause cancer in humans. This includes x-rays, radon gas, and ultraviolet radiation, and while it is impossible to avoid all radiation, certain precautions can be taken to reduce exposure. Radon gas is a natural source of radiation found in certain geographical areas. It can increase the risk of lung cancer, and is thought to be responsible for about two percent of cancer deaths. Radon exposure is particularly dangerous when combined with cigarette smoking. Your local health department can help you determine the risk of radon exposure in your area. Medical and dental x-rays are set to deliver the lowest possible dosage levels possible without compromising image quality. These x-rays serve an important medical need, but it is a good idea to avoid unnecessary x-rays when possible.

Probably the most preventable type of cancer-causing radiation exposure is the ultraviolet rays of the sun, which are thought to cause almost all cases of basal and squamous cell carcinomas, and are a major cause of malignant melanomas. While basal and squamous cell cancers are highly curable, malignant melanomas are often deadly. The American Cancer Society estimates skin cancer to be a cause of 10,590 deaths in 2005, with about 7,770 of those deaths due to melanoma (American Cancer Society, 2005). Skin cancer is, however, one of the most preventable types of cancer, and certain precautions, shown in Box 9.1, are recommended for the prevention of skin cancer. In addition to prevention, early detection is critical to the success of skin cancer treatment. Regular skin self-examination is recommended, and is shown in Box 9.2. Laboratory 2, found at the end of this chapter, can help you determine your skin cancer risk.

Box 9.1
Protecting Your Skin from the Sun

1. Wear protective clothing—a wide-brimmed hat is most effective in protecting the head, neck and face from the sun's rays. Lightweight, long-sleeved clothing can protect the arms. Do not forget sunglasses.
2. Avoid prolonged sun exposure, especially during the peak hours of 10 a.m. to 3 p.m.
3. Seek the shade. If you are outdoors a lot, look for shelter from the sun's direct rays.
4. Wear a sunscreen. The American Academy of Dermatology recommends a broad spectrum sunscreen with a sun protection factor of 15. Apply liberally about 30 minutes prior to going out into the sun, and reapply the sunscreen often.
5. Avoid artificial tanning devices which also emit harmful ultraviolet rays.

Viral Causes. It is estimated that five percent of the cancers in the United States are caused by viruses, and 17 percent of new cancers worldwide are attributable to infection. These cancers are likely linked to immune suppression, chronic inflammation, or chronic stimulation. Some viruses may also disrupt cell cycle control, stimulating the replication of cancer cells.

Examples of virally caused cancers include cancer of the cervix and penis, which have been linked to the human papilloma virus (HPV), a sexually transmitted virus, and liver cancer, which has been linked to Hepatitis B and C. While most HPV infected women do not develop cervical cancer, nearly 100 percent of women with cervical cancer show evidence of HPV infection.

Chapter 9

Prevention of melanoma/skin cancer is obviously the most desirable weapon against this disease. But if a lesion should develop, it is almost always totally curable if caught in the early stages. To ensure that any developing lesion is caught in the early stage, a regular program of monthly self-examinations should be followed. The following is a suggested method of self-examination that will ensure that no area of the body is neglected in a regular program of self-examination.

To perform your examination you will need a full-length mirror, a hand mirror and a brightly lit room where you can study your skin in privacy. This step-by-step method, if done monthly, will provide you with an "early warning system" against melanoma/skin cancer:

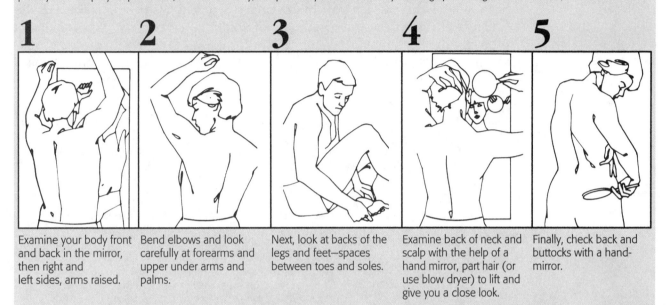

1. Examine your body front and back in the mirror, then right and left sides, arms raised.

2. Bend elbows and look carefully at forearms and upper under arms and palms.

3. Next, look at backs of the legs and feet—spaces between toes and soles.

4. Examine back of neck and scalp with the help of a hand mirror, part hair (or use blow dryer) to lift and give you a close look.

5. Finally, check back and buttocks with a hand-mirror.

Lifestyle Causes. Many of the factors which contribute to cancer are highly preventable if an individual practices a healthy lifestyle. As suggested earlier, poor dietary choices, the decision to smoke and use other tobacco products, and failure to practice protection from the sun are significant lifestyle factors contributing to cancer cases and deaths. Excessive alcohol consumption is another. Clearly, wise choices can be made which have tremendous benefits in the prevention of many types of cancers.

Of all the suspected causes of cancer, the one which is the most risky is smoking. Half of all Americans who continue to smoke will die from smoking. Tobacco use is responsible for 20 percent of all deaths in the U.S., and debilitates many others with emphysema, chronic bronchitis, and other diseases. Cigarette smoke contains at least 43 carcinogens and is responsible for 87 percent of lung cancer and about one-third of all cancer deaths in the United States. It contributes to at least 15 types of cancer, including cancer of the mouth, larynx, esophagus, kidney, bladder, pancreas, stomach, uterus and cervix. Low tar and light cigarette smokers have the same risk of lung cancer as full tar cigarette smokers. Recently, more and more people have taken up cigar smoking. According to the American Cancer Society (2005), about ten million Americans, or five percent of Americans 18 and older, smoke cigars. Cigar smoking causes increased risks for a number of lung disorders, including lung cancer. Cigar smokers are three to five times more likely to die from lung cancer than are non-smokers. Overall cancer deaths for cigar smokers are 34 percent higher than for non-smokers, coming mainly from an increase in cancer of the larynx, mouth, esophagus and lungs. Major cigar manufacturers in 2001 began

Cancer, Diabetes, and Osteoporosis

placing warning labels on cigars sold in the U.S. in order to settle a lawsuit for failure to warn users about the dangers of cigar smoking. Smokeless tobacco is also a deadly carcinogen. More than 87 percent of oral cancer cases are directly linked to smokeless tobacco and cigarette use. Smokeless does not mean harmless, and is not considered a safe substitute for smoking cigarettes or cigars. In addition to cancer deaths, tobacco use is responsible for numerous deaths due to cardiovascular disease, stroke, and other lung diseases. In all, smoking is related to nearly half a million deaths each year in the United States. It has been identified as the leading behavioral cause of death and disability in the country. Not smoking is probably the best thing a person can do for good health, so if you are a non-smoker, do not start. If you do smoke, Box 9.3 contains information on quitting.

Box 9.3

Tips for Smoking and Other Tobacco Use Cessation

If you smoke, quitting won't be easy, but it will be the greatest step that you can take toward good health. Remember, over 44 million Americans are ex-smokers, so it can be done. Hopefully, the following tips will be of assistance as you kick the habit and remain smoke free.

1. **Develop a plan.**
   - ⊙ Readiness, or the true intent and commitment to quit, is a key to smoking cessation. Spend some time thinking about the effect that smoking is having on your health (and the health of those around you), then list the benefits (physical, social, financial) that quitting would bring. Visualize yourself as a non-smoker from now on, and think of yourself only in those terms.
   - ⊙ Set a date which will be the last day that you use tobacco. It may be a significant day like a birthday, anniversary, a holiday, or the day of the Great American Smokeout. Decide if you want to quit "cold turkey," or if you want to use a period of time to taper down your smoking. Cold turkey is reportedly the easiest for most people.

2. **Have some ideas on how to avoid the temptation to use tobacco.**
   - ⊙ Substitute something for the cigarette or smokeless tobacco. Hard candy, fresh fruit or vegetables like carrot or celery sticks, chewing gum, or some other snack may help relieve the urge to use tobacco.
   - ⊙ Stay busy. Idle time may contribute to a craving.
   - ⊙ Avoid social groups, places and situations in which smoking is allowed or encouraged.
   - ⊙ Practice deep breathing or take an exercise break when the urge strikes.

3. **Enlist a support system.**
   - ⊙ Let those around you know that you are committed to quitting, and ask them to help. They can encourage and support you, and hold you accountable. Spouses, roommates, classmates, parents, co-workers and friends may all be willing to help. Ask a special friend to "adopt" you and provide special support while quitting.
   - ⊙ Consider quitting with another person who seems equally as committed as you. An accountability partner may be what you need.
   - ⊙ Talk to ex-smokers about their quitting experience. Learn from them.

4. **Stay positive and committed.**
   - ⊙ Keep a log of how long you have gone, and remember that each day that passes brings you closer to your goal.
   - ⊙ Remember to visualize yourself as a non-smoker or non-user of tobacco. Tell people you do not smoke to provide verbal self-reinforcement.
   - ⊙ Incorporate other types of healthy commitments. Learn a few healthy recipes or begin a new type of exercise program. After all, you are committed to living a healthy lifestyle now!

5. **If you need additional help, don't hesitate to ask for it.**
   - ⊙ There are many smoking cessation approaches which can help the individual quit and stay quit. The Texas Department of Health's Office of Smoking and Health can help you locate a program just for you. Call them at 1-800-345-8647.
   - ⊙ The American Cancer Society
   - ⊙ American Heart Association
   - ⊙ American Lung Association, all have programs to assist you.

Alcoholic beverages cause cancer of the mouth, esophagus and larynx, and when combined with tobacco use, the risk of these types of cancers is greatly increased. And while again inconclusive, there is some evidence of a link between alcohol consumption and breast cancer risk. As with tobacco use, if you don't drink, don't start. If you do drink, moderation is critically important to good health.

In addition to smoking and alcohol consumption, dietary factors play a role in cancer risk. A diet which consists of high portions of plant foods and limited amounts of animal products is a great step to cancer risk reduction. A high-fat diet is considered a risk for cancer of the colon, rectum, prostate and endometrium. While the evidence is not as strong, there may be a link between high-fat diets and breast cancer as well. A diet high in fiber, however, has been shown to provide protection against cancer of the gastrointestinal and respiratory tracts. Legumes, or beans and peas, may also protect against cancer. The American Cancer Society's nutrition guidelines were revised in 2001 and are consistent with the Food Guide Pyramid and the Dietary Guidelines for Americans, as well as the other nutrition information found in Chapter 6. They are found in Box 9.4.

ROLE OF EXERCISE IN CANCER PREVENTION

Another lifestyle factor which warrants attention in the discussion of cancer is exercise. Several studies have shown that exercise reduces the risks of certain forms of cancer, and there may be multiple mechanisms by which the risks are reduced. Exercise is critical in managing the amount of body fat one carries, and excess body fat increases the risk of cancer of the colon, breast, prostate, gallbladder, ovary and uterus. Exercise also speeds the movement of food through the digestive tract, reducing the amount of time that the lining of the intestine is exposed to carcinogens that may build up, thereby reducing the risk of cancer of the colon. Exercise may also decrease the exposure of breast tissue to circulating estrogen, reducing the risk for breast cancer. Colon, breast, and other cancers may also be affected by exercise as it improves energy metabolism and reduces circulating concentrations of insulin. Finally, exercise has been shown to be effective in the prevention of Type 2 diabetes, which will be discussed later in this chapter. Type 2 diabetes has been associated with increased cancers of the colon, pancreas, and possibly other sites. Several of the other chapters in this book provide excellent guidelines for developing an exercise plan, which is important not only for overall fitness, but for disease prevention as well.

Box 9.4

American Cancer Society's Nutrition Guidelines

1. Choose most of the foods you eat from plant sources.
2. Limit your intake of high-fat foods, particularly from animal sources.
3. Be physically active; achieve and maintain a healthy weight.
4. Limit consumption of alcoholic beverages, if you drink at all.

Source: American Cancer Society.

Box 9.5

American Cancer Society's 1996 Guidelines on Diet, Nutrition and Cancer Prevention

Be physically active; achieve and maintain a healthy weight:

1. Be at least moderately active for 30 minutes or more on most days each week.
   a. Physical activity does not have to be continuous to be beneficial.
   b. Thirty minutes a day can be accomplished by walking briskly (three to four miles an hour) for about two miles. Calisthenics, jogging, swimming, gardening, yard work, housework and dancing are other enjoyable activities that keep one moving.
2. Stay within your healthy weight range for your height and sex.
   a. To lose weight, restrict caloric intake and increase physical activity.
   b. To restrict caloric intake, limit serving sizes, particularly high-fat foods.
   c. Remember that many packaged, low-fat foods remain high in calories (always read the label).

MAJOR TYPES OF CANCER

Most cancers are given their name based on the location in the body where they originate. While there are too many types of cancer for all to be included in this discussion, the major types are addressed below:

Lung Cancer

Lung cancer has long been the deadliest cancer in men, and since 1987, has been the leading cancer killer for women as well. This is due to the increase in the number of women smokers. Lung cancer accounts for about 29 percent of cancer deaths (American Cancer Society, 2005). As mentioned earlier, cigarette smoking is by far the most important risk factor in the development of lung cancer, and environmental tobacco smoke (ETS) accounts for additional deaths in non-smokers. Other environmental causes include radiation exposure, radon, arsenic, benzene and asbestos, as well as other potential industrial carcinogens. Exposure to various forms of air pollution may also increase risks of lung cancer. Symptoms of lung cancer include a persistent cough, blood-streaked sputum, chest pain, and recurring pneumonia and bronchitis.

One of the reasons that lung cancer is so deadly is that early detection efforts have not yet been shown to reduce mortality. By the time a person is diagnosed with lung cancer, chances of it having spread are great, making treatment very difficult. In fact, only 15 percent of those diagnosed with lung cancer are still alive five years after diagnosis. If detected prior to spreading, the five-year survival rate is 49 percent, but few cases are discovered that early (American Cancer Society, 2005). While surgery is the treatment of choice for localized cancers, radiation, chemotherapy, and biological therapies are also often used if the cancer has spread at the time of its discovery.

Breast Cancer

Breast cancer is the most common type of cancer found in women, and is rarely detected in men. Breast cancer was the leading cancer killer in women for over 40 years, but it dropped to second behind lung cancer in 1987. It accounted for just over 40,000 deaths in 2005 (American Cancer Society, 2005). The decreasing incidence of breast cancer deaths can be attributed to increased awareness, advancing techniques in early detection, and improved treatment methods. The cause of breast cancer has yet to be pinpointed, but several risk factors have been identified.

The risk increases with age, and is greater in those with a family history of breast cancer. Other suspected risks include early menarche, late menopause, obesity after menopause, recent use of oral contraceptives, having a first child late or never having children, consumption of one or more alcoholic beverages per day, and postmenopausal hormone therapy, especially combined estrogen and progestin therapy. Several factors are thought to reduce the risk of breast cancer, including breastfeeding, physical activity, and maintaining a healthy body weight. Symptoms of breast cancer include a lump, thickening, swelling, distortion or tenderness of the breast, skin irritation or dimpling of the skin of the breast, pain or tenderness in the nipple, or nipple discharge.

Any abnormality noticed should be brought to the attention of a physician. In addition, it is important that women undergo regular exams for signs of breast cancer, as numerous studies have shown that early detection can save lives. These include monthly breast self-examinations (BSE), as well as clinical breast exams per-

TABLE 9.1

Summary of American Cancer Society Recommendations for the Early Detection of Cancer in Asymptomatic People

Test	Population Sex	Population Age	Frequency
Sigmoidoscopy, preferably flexible	M & F	50 and over	Every 3–5 years
Fecal Occult Blood Test	M & F	50 and over	Every year
Digital Rectal Exam	M & F	40 and over	Every year
Prostate Exam*	M	50 and over	Every year
Pap Test	F	All women who are, or who have been, sexually active, or have reached age 18, should have an annual Pap test and pelvic examination. After a woman has had three or more consecutive satisfactory normal annual examinations, the Pap test may be performed less frequently at the discretion of her physician.	
Breast Self-Examination	F	20 and over	Every month
Breast Clinical Examination	F	20–40 / Over 40	Every 3 years / Every year
Mammography†	F	40–49 / 50 and over	Every 1–2 years / Every year

*Annual digital rectal examination and prostate-specific antigen should be performed on men 50 years and older. If either result is abnormal, further evaluation should be considered.

†Screening mammography should begin by 40.

Copyright © 2005, American Cancer Society, Inc. Reprinted with permission.

formed by a physician, and regular mammograms. The recommended screening guidelines for several types of cancer are found in Table 9.1. As mentioned earlier, the declining death rates due to breast cancer may be attributed to better early detection methods, so these screenings should be taken seriously by all women, regardless of their risks. Many breast cancers have been detected through regular BSE, and the steps to performing this important examination are shown in Box 9.6.

Breast cancer is treated in a variety of ways, depending on the medical condition of the patient. It may include a lumpectomy (removal of the tumor from the breast) or a mastectomy (removal of the breast). These generally include removal of the lymph nodes under the arm. Radiation, chemotherapy, or hormone therapy may also be used to treat breast cancer.

Prostate Cancer

Prostate cancer is the leading type of cancer found in men, and is the second leading cancer killer of men, behind lung cancer. Aging increases the risk of prostate cancer, and black males have a greater incidence than other races, with their death rate being twice that of white men. There is possibly a family history risk, and high consumption of dietary fats is another possible risk factor. Prostate cancer is often indicated by urination abnormalities, including an increased need to urinate, painful or burning urination, inability to urinate, blood in the urine, difficulty starting or stopping urination, or interruption in the urine flow. Pain in the pelvis, thighs, or lower back may also give indication.

Studies are inconclusive concerning the efficacy of early prostate cancer testing, but tests known as the prostate specific antigen (PSA) test and a digital rectal exam

Box 9.6

Breast Self-Examination

Why you should examine your breasts every month:

Breast Self-Examination (BSE) is an important step in finding breast cancer early. When breast cancer is found early and treated promptly, women survive. That is why it is important for you to learn how to examine your breasts properly.

The Three Steps of BSE

Step One: In Front of Mirror

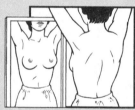

Figure 1

Let your arms hang loosely at the sides of your body. Look at your breasts from the front and from each side. You are looking for:

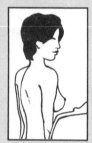

Figure 1A

- ⊙ Any change in the form and shape of the breast
- ⊙ Dimpling or puckering of the skin
- ⊙ Scaling of the skin around the nipple
- ⊙ Any change in the nipple or nipple discharge

Figure 2

Raise your arms above your head and look at each breast from the front and from each side:

Figure 3

Rest your hands on your hips and press your hands down firmly to tighten the muscles under the breast. Look at each breast from the front and from each side.

Step Two: At Bath Time

Figure 4

Figure 4A

When your skin is wet, it is easy to move your fingers over your breasts. Use the left hand to examine the right breast, and the right hand to examine the left breast. As you are examining your breasts you are feeling for:

- ⊙ A lump, a thickened area, a hardening in the breast or anything that feels different.

Imagine your breast as the face of a clock. Examine all of the breast tissue in a clockwise motion starting at 12 o'clock. Press firmly with the sensitive pads of the middle three fingers starting at the outer edge of your breast. With each clockwise motion, move your fingers in toward the nipple until you have felt all of your breast tissue.

Step Three: Lying Down

EXAMINING YOUR BREAST WHILE LYING ON YOUR BACK IS THE MOST EFFECTIVE WAY TO CHECK YOUR BREAST FOR LUMPS, THICKENING OR HARDENING.

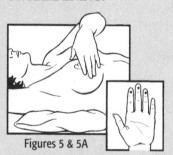

Figures 5 & 5A

Lie down on your bed. To spread the breast tissue more evenly, put a pillow or bath towel under your right shoulder and put your right hand under your head. Use the fingers of the left hand to check your breast. Use lotion or powder on the skin, which will make it easier to move your fingers over your breasts. Follow the same method as you did while you were bathing, moving your fingers in a clockwise motion, using firm pressure and feeling all of your breast tissue from the outer edge to the nipple. Examine each breast in the same way.

are recommended for men beginning at age 50, or at age 45 if there are increased risk factors. These recommendations are also found in Table 9.1. Treatment for prostate cancer may include surgery, radiation, hormonal therapy, chemotherapy, or a combination of therapies. Since many prostate cancer cases are diagnosed while localized, the five-year survival rate is very good.

Colon and Rectal Cancer

Colorectal cancer is the third most common type of cancer as well as the third most common cancer killer in both men and women, although the incidence is decreasing due to increased screening and polyp removal. The major risk factors for colorectal cancer are age, family or personal history of colorectal cancer or polyps, or a personal history of inflammatory bowel disease. Other risk factors are smoking, alcohol consumption, a diet high in saturated fat and red meat, and inadequate intake of fruits and vegetables. Polyps are small fleshy tumors that grow on the inside lining of the colon. Most are benign, but in time may become malignant. The symptoms include a change in bowel habits, rectal bleeding, blood in the stool, and cramping in the lower abdomen. Early detection methods currently available include regular rectal exams, as well as a fecal occult blood test (which tests the feces for hidden blood) or fecal immunochemical test, colonoscopy, double contrast barium enema, and sigmoidoscopy (use of a lighted tube to inspect the rectum and colon). Screening is recommended to begin at age 50. While some of these early detection tests may not sound particularly inviting, they are nonetheless critically important to maintaining good health through disease prevention. The most common treatment for colorectal cancer is surgery, often combined with radiation or chemotherapy. Again, survival rates are significantly greater if the cancer is detected and treated at an early stage.

Skin Cancer

One of the most preventable types of cancer is skin cancer. More than one million cases of basal cell and squamous cell carcinoma cancers occur each year, and most of these cases are curable, especially if caught early. The most serious type of skin cancer is melanoma, with almost 60,000 cases diagnosed in 2005, and the incidence of melanoma continues to increase, although its growth has slowed in recent years. Melanoma rates are ten times higher in whites than in blacks. Melanoma may appear as any change in the skin, such as a new growth or spot or an existing one that changes in shape, size, or color. Carcinoma signs are flat, firm pale areas or small raised red or pink, translucent, shiny, waxy areas. They may bleed following minor injury. Other signs are a sore that does not heal, a growing lump with a rough surface, or as a slowly growing reddish, flat patch. Early detection of skin cancer may be practiced through regular skin self-examination (Box 9.1), and any of the indicators should be brought to the attention of a physician. The warning signs of melanoma are known as the ABCDs. A is for asymmetry, or lack of matching between the sides of the growth. B is for border, which is jagged and irregular. C is for color, as there is no uniformity of color with shades of black, brown, or tan. D is for diameter, which is typically greater than 6 millimeters.

Risk factors for skin cancer are clear. Those who sunburn easily and have difficulty tanning as well as those with blond or red hair are at risk. Previous high levels of sun exposure including sunburns and use of tanning booths are also risky. Exposure to occupational carcinogens and past history of skin cancers also place one at risk. Finally, the risks for melanoma include prior melanoma, family tendency toward melanoma, and numerous or unusually large moles. Prevention of skin cancer is also quite clear—avoid overexposure to ultraviolet rays.

Testicular Cancer

Not a major cancer killer, testicular cancer is one of the more common types of cancer found in young adult males. It accounts for only one percent of cancer deaths in males, but it is the most common type of cancer found in males age 15–34 (National Institutes of Health, 2005).

The cause of testicular cancer is unknown but men with undescended testicles appear to be at greatest risk. Other possible risk factors include family history, HIV infection, previous testicular cancer, and race—white men have 5–10 times the risk of testicular cancer than black men. Other research has suggested multiple atypical nevi (pigmented spots or moles found on the face, abdomen, chest, and back) as a possible risk factor. Symptoms of testicular cancer include a lump or swelling in a testicle, pain or discomfort in a testicle or the scrotum, enlargement or heavy feeling of a testicle, sudden fluid collection in the scrotum, or a dull ache in the lower abdomen, back or groin. Regular testicular self-examinations, shown in Box 9.7, may identify a lump or thickening, or unusual tenderness, which should immediately be brought to a physician's attention.

WARNING SIGNS OF CANCER

Since early detection is so important to the successful treatment of cancer, it is important to know what additional signs to look for. No one knows your body better than you do, so it is a good idea for everyone to be familiar with the warning signs of the various types of cancer. In addition to knowing the warning signs of cancer, it is recommended that all persons know and practice primary and second-

---

Box 9.7

Testicular Self-Examination.

To detect testicular cancer, the American Cancer Society recommends the following self-examination:

1. The best time to perform the examination is after a warm bath or shower, when the scrotal skin is most relaxed. (*Scrotal* refers to the scrotum, the pouch in which the testicles normally lie.)

2. Roll each testicle gently between the thumb and fingers of both hands. A normal testicle is smooth, egg-shaped, and somewhat firm to the touch. At the rear of each testicle is a tube called the epididymis, which carries sperm away from the testicle; this is a normal part of your body.

3. If you find any hard lumps or nodules, or if there is any change in the shape, size, or texture of the testicles, consult a physician promptly. These signs may not indicate a malignancy, but only your physician can make a diagnosis.

   Repeat this examination every month. It is important that you know what your own testicles feel like normally so that you will recognize any changes.

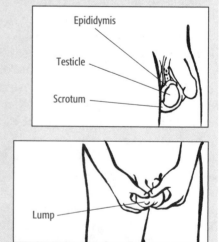

Source: American Cancer Society. 1990. *For Men Only: Testicular Cancer and How to Do TSE (a Self-Exam)*. New York: American Cancer Society.

ary prevention. Primary prevention is taking behavioral steps which are intended to prevent cancer from ever occurring. Some of the major recommendations for primary prevention include:

1. Do not smoke cigarettes or use tobacco products.
2. Protect your skin from the sun.
3. Avoid alcohol. If you drink, drink in moderation.
4. Avoid unnecessary radiation.
5. Follow prudent dietary habits.
6. Minimize your exposure to occupational and environmental carcinogens.

Secondary prevention refers to steps which diagnose a cancer as early as possible after it has developed. For many types of cancer, the earlier it is detected, the better the chances of successful treatment and recovery. Regular screenings and exams for the early warning signs of cancer are beneficial for early detection. There are nine accessible screening sites where cancer may occur: breast, tongue, mouth, colon, rectum, cervix, prostate, testicles and skin, with over half of new cancer cases occurring at these sites. Again, refer to Table 9.1 for the American Cancer Society's recommendations for early detection of cancer.

CANCER TREATMENT

Traditionally, cancer has been treated through one of three methods: chemotherapy, radiation, or surgery. Recently, several new treatments have been found to provide hope in the successful treatment of this disease.

Surgery

In cases where the cancer cells remain localized and have not spread or invaded surrounding tissue, surgical removal of the tumor is often the preferred treatment. This emphasizes the importance of early detection. If the tumor has already begun to metastasize, surgery may be unable to remove all of the cancer cells. Nearby tissue and lymph nodes may also be removed in an effort to eliminate other cancerous cells. Radiation or chemotherapy may be combined with surgery as additional precautions.

Radiation

This therapy involves targeting the cancerous cells with a stream of high-energy particles to destroy or damage cancer cells. It is very common, and is used in over half of all cancer cases. It may be administered internally, through an implant, or externally, using a machine that directs a beam of radiation. Since cancer cells grow faster than healthy cells, the goal of radiotherapy is to kill or damage them so they cannot spread. Normal cells are sometimes affected by radiotherapy, but most people fully recover from the effects of this treatment. Careful administration of the radiation is used to minimize the damage to healthy cells.

Chemotherapy

The administration of drugs and chemotherapeutic agents may be used to kill cancer cells or prevent cell division, especially when the cancer has spread to various sites in the body. Since the drugs reach all parts of the body, damage to healthy cells may also occur. More than 100 drugs have been used in chemotherapy and new agents, hopefully more effective with fewer side effects, are continually being explored.

Immunotherapy

This type of therapy, also known as biologic therapy, attempts to strengthen the body's immune system so that it becomes more efficient at eliminating cancer cells. This type of therapy is most often used along with another type of therapy. While it still plays a small role in treating most cancers, research continues to progress in this promising area of cancer treatment.

Obviously, cancer is a serious disease and a major public health concern. However, with improved education and increased public awareness, advances in early detection techniques, and continued medical advances, progress in the fight against this disease continues. Hopefully, its impact on health and well-being will be lessened in the years to come.

DIABETES MELLITUS

Diabetes mellitus is a chronic metabolic disorder characterized either by a deficiency of insulin or a decreased ability of the body to utilize insulin. Insulin, a hormone secreted by the pancreas, is necessary for efficient metabolism of carbohydrates as it allows glucose (sugar) to enter body cells and be converted to energy. In healthy people, the body produces the needed amount of insulin to enable the glucose in the bloodstream to enter the cells, but the diabetic either produces too little insulin or their body cells do not respond to the insulin that is produced. Since the body can neither store nor utilize the glucose, elevated levels build up in the blood and urine. This condition of elevated blood glucose levels is known as hyperglycemia. This can lead to several long-term complications, including damage to the body's vital organs and possible contribution to heart disease, blindness, kidney failure, and the necessity of lower-extremity amputations not related to injury.

An estimated 18.2 million diabetics live in the United States. About 13 million of these have been diagnosed, leaving 5.2 million who do not know they have the disease (American Diabetes Association, 2005). In 2002, 73,249 people died from diabetes, making it the sixth leading cause of death in the United States (Centers for Disease Control and Prevention, 2005).

Types of Diabetes

The major types of diabetes are Type 1 and Type 2. Type 1, previously known as juvenile diabetes, is the least common of the two types, accounting for five to ten percent of cases. It can occur at any stage of life but most often appears in childhood or during the teen years. In the case of Type 1 diabetes, the insulin-producing cells in the pancreas are destroyed, and the individual produces little or no insulin, and is therefore dependent on daily insulin injections to sustain life. The onset of symptoms is usually very sudden and the disease can progress very quickly. Symptoms include increased thirst and urination, weight loss, blurred vision, constant hunger and extreme tiredness. If this disease goes undiagnosed or untreated, a life-threatening coma can result.

The other 90–95 percent of diabetics suffer from Type 2 diabetes. As opposed to Type 1 diabetes, this type of diabetes is most likely to occur after the age of 40, and most frequently in those 55 and older. However, Type 2 diabetes is increasingly being diagnosed in children and adolescents. About 80 percent of people diagnosed with this disease are overweight. Type 2 diabetics usually produce enough insulin, but their body cells have become resistant to the action of the insulin, thereby causing the same problem of an unhealthy build-up of glucose in the blood. The symptoms of Type 2 diabetes are not as pronounced as those of Type 1, and typically develop more slowly. They include frequent infections, slow healing of sores, blurred vision, weight loss, unusual thirst, frequent urination and feeling tired or ill.

Type 1 diabetes is more common in whites than in non-whites. It occurs equally among males and females. Type 2, on the other hand, is more common among older people, especially older women who are overweight, and is more common among non-whites. Native Americans have the highest rates of diabetes in the world (National Institute of Diabetes and Digestive and Kidney Disorders, 2005).

Gestational diabetes is diabetes which develops or is discovered during pregnancy. It usually disappears when the pregnancy is over, but women who have had gestational diabetes have a greater risk of developing Type 2 diabetes later in their lives. It occurs more frequently in African Americans, American Indians, Hispanic Americans, and women with a family history of diabetes.

Pre-diabetes is a condition in which blood glucose levels are higher than normal but not high enough for a diabetes diagnosis. The American Diabetes Association (2005) estimates that there are 41 million people in the U.S. with pre-diabetes. Some damage to the body may be occurring during pre-diabetes. The good news is that preventive behaviors and management of blood glucose levels can delay or prevent Type 2 diabetes from occurring.

Several factors have been identified as risks for diabetes. A risk factor assessment can be found in Laboratory 3 at the end of this chapter. The National Institutes of Health (2005) list the following as risk factors:

1. A family history of diabetes
2. Low activity level
3. Poor diet
4. Excess body weight (especially around the waist)
5. Age greater than 45 years
6. High blood pressure
7. High blood levels of triglycerides
8. HDL cholesterol less than 35
9. Previously identified impaired glucose tolerance by your doctor
10. Previous diabetes during pregnancy or baby weighing more than 9 pounds
11. Certain ethnicities—African Americans, Hispanic Americans, and Native Americans

Treatment of Diabetes

People with diabetes must be treated by a doctor who assists with the control of the disease and monitors potential health complications. Several factors should be considered as the diabetic and their physician engage in diabetes management. Diet, exercise, and the use of insulin or other anti-diabetic agents are the three major strategies. While insulin is not a cure for diabetes, it is crucial to management of the severity of this disease and its complications. Daily injections of insulin are the basic therapy for Type 1 diabetes, and those individuals must closely monitor their glucose levels to properly administer their medications. Individuals with Type 2 diabetes may also require insulin injections or other medications, but careful regulation of diet and exercise habits are highly beneficial for this type.

Importance of Exercise in Diabetes Management

Research indicates that in many individuals, inactivity either precipitates diabetes or causes the condition to be made worse (Colberg, Swaim, 2000). Physical activity and exercise, on the other hand, can have positive preventive and management effects on diabetes. Exercise can increase insulin sensitivity, lower blood glucose, and even have positive psychological effects (White, Sherman, 1999). The proper combination of the lifestyle factors of proper diet and exercise can sharply lower the chances of getting diabetes for at least 10 million Americans (NIDDKD, 2001). Another benefit of exercise for the diabetic is the prevention of obesity. Since most diabetics are obese, and obesity is identified as a significant risk factor in the development of the disease, weight reduction is critical in its management. As discussed in Chapter 9, exercise is the primary factor in weight control. Also, since diabetics are at greater risk for cardiovascular disease than non-diabetics, exercise can help reduce the risk of this significant complication of diabetes. Chapter 7 discusses the role of exercise in lowering heart disease risks.

OSTEOPOROSIS

Osteoporosis is a disease marked by a decrease in bone mass that progresses painlessly until a bone breaks. As bones lose their density, they become fragile and are more likely to fracture. Osteoporosis is a major cause of bone fractures in postmenopausal women and older persons in general. These fractures may occur anywhere in the body, but the most common sites are the hip, spine, and wrist. These bone fractures may in turn interfere with the ability to maintain functional abilities, including walking, and may cause prolonged disability.

After reaching its peak at about age 35, bone mass declines throughout the lifespan. During the course of a lifetime, women lose 30–50 percent of their bone mass while men lose 20–30 percent. Women are four times as likely as men to develop osteoporosis (National Osteoporosis Foundation, 2005).

Osteoporosis threatens to affect 55 percent of Americans age 50 and over—44 million in all. Ten million already have the disease and 34 million have low bone density. It causes about 1.5 million fractures each year, including more than 300,000 hip fractures, 700,000 vertebral fractures, and 250,000 wrist fractures. In women over 50 years of age, one in two suffer an osteoporosis-related fracture during their lifetime (National Institute of Health, 2005). Some people are more susceptible to this condition and the resulting fractures. The risk factors that have been identified for osteoporosis include:

1. **Age**—Osteoporosis is clearly an age-related disease, with the risk increasing significantly with age as bones become thinner and weaker.

2. **Gender**—Women have about 30 percent less bone tissue than men, and their bone loss is accelerated, especially during the years following menopause.

3. **Race**—The greatest racial risk is for white and Asian women, but black and Hispanic women are also at significant risk for developing osteoporosis.

4. **Bone structure and body weight**—Thin, small-boned women carry a greater risk of osteoporosis.

5. **Menopause/menstrual history**—Early menopause is one of the strongest predictors for the development of osteoporosis. Women who cease menstruation prior to menopause due to anorexia, bulimia, or excessive physical activity are also at risk for osteoporosis.

6. **Cigarette smoking**—Smoking has been identified as a risk factor for osteoporosis, as well as many other diseases.

7. **Diet and exercise**—Inadequate calcium intake and getting little or no weight-bearing exercise increase the risk of osteoporosis. Immobilization and prolonged bed rest produce rapid bone loss.

8. **Family history**—Heredity may also play a role in the development of osteoporosis. Reduced bone mass may be a characteristic passed from mother to daughter.

Role of Diet and Exercise in Osteoporosis Prevention

Prevention of osteoporosis should focus on two essentials: increasing peak bone mass early in life, and reducing bone loss in later years. While several factors impact these two preventive measures, diet and exercise are certainly two of the most controllable.

After much research, it is now clear that physical activity is essential for the development and maintenance of healthy bones. People who are physically active have greater density in bone mass, and the type of activity which produces the increased bone mass is called weight-bearing exercise. Weight-bearing exercises include walking, running, and racket sports, which are better at promoting bone density than non-weight-bearing activities like cycling or swimming. Weight training, obviously a weight-bearing activity, is an excellent avenue to the development of healthy bones.

The most important dietary consideration appears to be the intake of calcium. Adequate calcium intake throughout the lifespan creates a greater peak bone mass early in life and decreases age-related bone mass. Peak bone mass is likely to be below optimal levels if calcium intake is not adequate, and many adults get only half or less of their daily calcium needs. Most adults need from 800 to 1200 milligrams of calcium per day. Pregnant and lactating women need even more. Calcium-rich foods should be incorporated into everyone's diet, especially those at risk for osteoporosis. These foods include dairy products (be sure to choose low-fat), nuts, seeds and leafy green vegetables. A list of a few calcium-rich foods is found in Table 9.2. Vitamin D is also needed so that the body can absorb the calcium consumed. The body manufactures its own vitamin D through exposure to sunlight, and several foods are enriched with vitamin D.

TABLE 9.2
Foods Rich in Calcium

3.5 oz. boiled shrimp	320 mg
1 cup nonfat milk	326 mg
1 cup yogurt	302 mg
1 cup whole milk	291 mg
1 oz. Swiss cheese	272 mg
1 cup cooked spinach	244 mg
1 cup cooked broccoli	178 mg
1 oz. almonds	75 mg
1 cup canned kidney beans	74 mg
1 tbsp. Parmesan cheese	69 mg
1 medium orange	52 mg
1 slice whole wheat bread	20 mg

Estrogen and Osteoporosis

Estrogen is another major factor in the prevention of osteoporosis, since it has a direct effect on bone by increasing its density. Estrogen is a hormone which promotes the development of female secondary sex characteristics. The lowering of estrogen levels which result from the onset of menopause creates a risk for loss of bone density, and the earlier menopause takes place, the greater the risk. This is due to a longer period of time that the protective effect of estrogen is lost. Post-menopausal women should discuss hormone replacement therapy with their physician.

References

American Cancer Society. (2005). Cancer Facts and Figures.

American Cancer Society. (2005). Can breast cancer be found early? www.cancer.org/docroot/CRI/content/CRI_2_4_3X_Can_breast_cancer_be_found_early.htm

American Cancer Society. (2005). Do I have testicular cancer? www.cancer.org/docroot/PED/content/PED_2_3X_Do_I_Have_Testicular_cancer.

American Diabetes Association. (2005). All about diabetes. www.diabetes.org/about-diabetges.jsp

American Diabetes Association. (2002). National diabetes fact sheet. www.diabetes.org/diabetes-statistics/national-diabetes-fact-sheet.jsp

Anderson, R.N., & Smith, B.L (2005). Deaths: Leading causes for 2002. Centers for Disease Control and Prevention. National Vital Statistics Report. 53(17).

Colberg, S.R., & Swaim, D.P. (2000). Exercise and diabetes control. *The Physician and Sportsmedicine.* 4(28).

Medline Encyclopedia. (2005). Diabetes risk factors. www.nlm.nih.gov/medlineplus/ency/article/002072.

McCardle, W.D., Katch, F.I., & Katch, V.L. (2001). Exercise physiology, 5th edition. Baltimore: Lippincott, Williams & Wilkins.

National Cancer Institute. (2005). Testicular cancer: Questions and answers. Cis.nci.nih.gov/fact/6_34.htm

National Institute of Diabetes and Digestive and Kidney Disorders. (2005). Diabetes overview. NIH Publication No. 05-3873.

National Institute of Diabetes and Digestive and Kidney Disorders. (2001). Diet and exercise dramatically delay type 2 diabetes: Diabetes medication metformin also effective. www.niddk.nih.gov/releases/8_8_01.

National Institute of Health. (2003). The low down on osteoporosis. www.nih.gov/news/WordonHealth/dec2003/osteo.htm

National Institute of Health. (2005). Osteoporosis overview. www.osteo.org/newfile.asp?doc=rl06i&doctitle=Osteoporosis+Overvies+%2D+HT

National Osteoporosis Foundation. (2005). Osteoporosis: A debilitating disease that can be prevented and treated.

National Osteoporosis Foundation. (2005). Fast facts: Osteoporosis.

National Osteoporosis Foundation. (2005). Prevention: Who's at risk.

National Osteoporosis Foundation. (2005). Prevention: Exercise for bone health.

White, R.D. (1999). Exercise in diabetes management. *The Physician and Sportsmedicine.* 4(27).

chapter 9
LABORATORY ①

Cancer Risk Assessment

Introduction
You can reduce your risk of getting some types of cancer, such as lung cancer, by changing your lifestyle behaviors. For other types of cancer, such as breast and colorectal cancers, your chance for cure is greatly increased if the cancer is found at an early stage through periodic screening examinations.

This questionnaire has been designed by the American Cancer Society to help you learn about (1) your risk factors for certain types of cancer and (2) the chances that cancer would be found at an early stage when a cure is possible.

Test Score Card Directions
Read each question concerning each site and its specific risk factors. Be honest in your responses. Place the number in parentheses in the correct space on your score panel to the right.

For example, Question #2 on lung cancer, above right: if you are 53-years-old (age 50–59), then enter 5 as your score.

For Women
Complete the score panel for lung, colon/rectum and breast cancer on page 180, then continue to the next page. The major cancer sites for women are included with space to enter the score totals.

For Men
Complete the score panel for lung, colon/rectum and skin cancer on pages 180–181 *only*.

About Your Answers
You may check your own risks with the answers contained in this assessment. You are advised to discuss this assessment with your physician if you are at higher risk.

Important: React to Each Statement
Individual numbers for specific questions are not to be interpreted as a precise measure of relative risk, but the totals for a given site should give a general indication of your risk.

LUNG CANCER

1. **SEX:** a. Male (2) b. Female (1) 1. _____

2. **AGE:** a. 39 or less (1) b. 40–49 (2) c. 50–59 (5) d. 60+ (7) 2. _____

3. **EXPOSURE TO ANY OF THESE:**
   a. Mining (3) b. Asbestos (7) c. Uranium & radioactive products (5) d. None (0) 3. _____

4. **HABITS** a. Smoker (10)* b. Nonsmoker (0)* 4. _____

5. **TYPES OF SMOKING:**
   a. Cigarettes or little cigars (10) b. Pipe and/or cigar, but not cigarettes (3) c. Nonsmoker (0) 5. _____

6. **NUMBER OF CIGARETTES SMOKED PER DAY:**
   a. 0 (1) b. Less than 1/2 pack per day (5) c. 1/2–1 pack (9) d. 1–2 packs (15) e. 2+ packs (20) 6. _____

7. **TYPE OF CIGARETTE:**
   a. High tar/nicotine (10)** b. Medium tar/nicotine (9)** c. Low tar/nicotine (7)** d. Nonsmoker (1) 7. _____

8. **LENGTH OF TIME SMOKING:**
   a. Nonsmoker (1) b. Up to 15 years (5) c. 15–25 years (10) d. 25+ years (20) 8. _____

SUBTOTAL _____   *Subtotal Here*

REDUCING YOUR RISK—*If you stopped smoking more than 10 years ago, count yourself as a nonsmoker. If you have stopped smoking in the past 10 years, you are an **ex-smoker**. Ex-smokers should answer questions 5 through 8 according to how they previously smoked. Then ex-smokers may **reduce** their point total on questions 5 through 8 by 10% for each year they have not smoked. Current smokers also answer questions 5 through 8.

I am stopping smoking today. (Subtract 2 points.)   TOTAL _____   *Total Here*

**High Tar/Nicotine: 20 mg. or more tar/1.3 mg. or more nicotine   Medium Tar/Nicotine: 16–19 mg. tar/1.1–1.2 mg. nicotine   Low Tar/Nicotine: 15 mg. or less tar/1.0 mg. or less nicotine

COLON RECTUM CANCER

RISK FACTORS

1. **AGE:** a. 40 or less (2) b. 40–49 (7) c. 50 and over (12) 1. _____

2. **HAS ANYONE IN YOUR FAMILY EVER HAD:**
   a. Colon cancer (18) b. Colon polyps (18) c. Neither (1) 2. _____

3. **HAVE YOU EVER HAD:**
   a. Colon cancer (25) b. Colon polyps (25) c. Ulcerative colitis for more than seven years (18)
   d. Cancer of the breast, ovary, uterus, or stomach (13) e. None of the above (1) 3. _____

TOTAL _____   *Total Here*

SYMPTOMS

1. Do you have bleeding from the rectum? Yes _____ No _____

2. Have you had a change in bowel habits (such as altered frequency, size, consistency, or color of stool)? Yes _____ No _____

REDUCING YOUR RISKS AND DETECTING CANCER EARLY

1. I have altered my diet to include less fat and more fruits, fiber, and cruciferous vegetables (broccoli, cabbage, cauliflower, Brussels sprouts). Yes _____ No _____

2. I have had a negative test for blood in my stool within the past year. Yes _____ No _____

3. I have had a negative examination for colon cancer and polyps within the past year (proctosigmoidoscopy, colonoscopy, barium enema x-rays). Yes _____ No _____

BREAST CANCER

1. **AGE GROUP:** a. under 35 (10) b. 35–39 (20) c. 40–49 (50) d. 50 and over (90) 1. _____

2. **RACE:** a. Oriental (10) b. Hispanic (10) c. Black (20) d. White (25) 2. _____

3. **FAMILY HISTORY:** a. None (10) b. Mother, sister, daughter with breast cancer (30) 3. _____

4. **YOUR HISTORY:**
   a. No breast disease (10) b. Previous lumps or cysts (15) c. Previous breast cancer (100) 4. _____

5. **MATERNITY:**
   a. 1st pregnancy before 30 (10) b. 1st pregnancy at 30 or older (15) c. No pregnancies (20) 5. _____

SUBTOTAL _____   *Subtotal Here*

REDUCING YOUR RISK

6. I practice breast self-examination monthly. (Subtract 10 points.)

7. **I have had a negative mammogram and examination by a physician within the past year. (Subtract 25 points.)**

TOTAL _____   *Total Here*

SKIN CANCER SKIN

1. Live in the southern part of the U.S.:   Yes _____ No _____   1. _____
2. Frequent work or play in the sun: Yes _____ No _____   2. _____
3. Fair complexion or freckles; (natural hair color of blonde, red, or light brown, or eye color of grey, green, blue, or hazel):   Yes _____ No _____   3. _____
4. Work in mines, around coal tars, or radioactivity: Yes _____ No _____   4. _____
5. Experienced a severe, blistering sunburn before the age of 18:   Yes _____ No _____   5. _____
6. Have any family members with skin cancer or history of melanoma: Yes _____ No _____   6. _____
7. Had skin cancer or melanoma in the past: Yes _____ No _____   7. _____
8. Use or have used tanning beds or sun lamps: Yes _____ No _____   8. _____
9. Have large, many, or changing moles: Yes _____ No _____   9. _____

REDUCING YOUR RISK

10. I cover up with a wide-brimmed hat and wear long-sleeved shirts and pants.   Yes _____ No _____   10. _____
11. **I use sun screens with an SPF rating of 15 or higher when going out in the sun.**   Yes _____ No _____   11. _____
12. I examine my skin once a month for changes in warts or moles.   Yes _____ No _____   12. _____

CERVICAL CANCER CERV

(Lower Portion of Uterus)—These questions do not apply to a woman who has had a total hysterectomy.

1. **AGE GROUP:**
   a. Less than 25 (10)   b. 25–39 (20)   c. 40–54 (30)   d. 55 and over (30)   1. _____
2. **RACE:**   a. Oriental or white (10)   b. Black (20)   c. Hispanic (20)   2. _____
3. **NUMBER OF PREGNANCIES:**   a. 0 (10)   b. 1 to 3 (20)   c. 4 and over (30)   3. _____
4. **VIRAL INFECTIONS:**
   a. Viral infections of the vagina such as veneral warts, herpes or ulcer formations (10)
   b. Never (1)   4. _____
5. **AGE AT FIRST INTERCOURSE:**   a. Before 15 (10)   b. 16–19 (30)   c. 20–24 (20)
   d. 25 and over (10)   e. Never had intercourse (5)   5. _____
6. **BLEEDING BETWEEN PERIODS OR AFTER INTERCOURSE:**   a. Yes (40)   b. No (1)   6. _____
7. **SMOKER:**   a. Non-smoker (2)   b. Smoker (3)   7. _____

SUBTOTAL _____   *Subtotal Here*

REDUCING YOUR RISK

8. I have had a negative Pap smear and pelvic examination within the past year. (Subtract 50 points.)   8. _____

TOTAL _____   *Total Here*

ENDOMETRIAL CANCER ENDO

(Body of Uterus)—These questions do not apply to a woman who has had a total hysterectomy.

1. **AGE GROUP:**   a. 39 or less (5)   b. 40–49 (20)   c. 50 and over (60)   1. _____
2. **RACE:**   a. Oriental (10)   b. Black (10)   c. Hispanic (10)   d. White (20)   2. _____
3. **BIRTHS:**   a. None (15)   b. 1 to 4 (7)   c. 4 or more (5)   3. _____
4. **WEIGHT:**
   a. 50 or more pounds overweight (50)   b. 20–49 pounds overweight (15)   c. Normal or underweight for height (10)   4. _____
5. **DIABETES** (elevated blood sugar):   a. Yes (3)   b. No (1)   5. _____
6. **ESTROGEN HORMONE INTAKE*:**   a. Yes, regularly (15)   b. Yes, occasionally (12)   c. None (10)   6. _____
7. **ABNORMAL UTERINE BLEEDING:**   a. Yes (40)   b. No (1)   7. _____
8. **HYPERTENSION** (high blood pressure):   a. Yes (3)   b. No (1)   8. _____

SUBTOTAL _____   *Subtotal Here*

REDUCING YOUR RISK

9. I have had a negative pelvic examination and Pap smear or endometrial tissue sampling (endometrial biopsy) performed within the past year. (Subtract 50 points.)   9. _____

*Note: This excludes birth control pills.

TOTAL _____   *Total Here*

ANSWERS AND TEST ANALYSIS

LUNG — Answers

1. Men have a higher risk of lung cancer than women. Since more women may also be smoking more, their incidence of lung and upper respiratory tract (mouth, tongue and voice box) cancer is increasing.
2. The occurrence of lung and upper respiratory tract cancer increases with age.
3. Cigarette smokers may have 20 times or even greater risk than nonsmokers. However, **the rates of ex-smokers who have not smoked for ten years approach those of nonsmokers.**
4. Pipe and cigar smokers are at a higher risk for lung cancer than nonsmokers. Cigarette smokers are also at a much higher risk for lung cancer than nonsmokers or than pipe and cigar smokers. All forms of tobacco, including chewing or dipping, markedly increase the user's risk of developing cancer of the mouth.
5. Male smokers of less than 1/2 pack per day have a five times higher lung cancer rate than nonsmokers. Male smokers of 1–2 packs per day have a 15 times higher lung cancer rate than nonsmokers. Smokers of more than 2 packs per day are 20 times more likely to develop lung cancer than nonsmokers.
6. Smokers of low tar/nicotine cigarettes have slightly lower lung cancer rates. Please note, however, that smokers of low tar/nicotine cigarettes may unconsciously smoke in a manner that **increases** their exposure to these chemicals.
7. The frequency of lung and upper respiratory tract cancer increases with the duration of smoking.
8. Exposures to materials used in these and other industries have been shown to be associated with lung cancer, especially in smokers.

If your total is:

24 or less	You have a low risk for lung cancer.
25–49	You may be a light smoker and would have a good chance of kicking the habit.
50–74	As a moderate smoker, your risks of lung and upper respiratory tract cancer are increased. The time to stop is now!
75–over	As a heavy cigarette smoker, your chances of getting lung cancer and cancer of the upper respiratory or digestive tract are greatly increased.

REDUCING YOUR RISK—Make a decision to quit today. Join a smoking cessation program. If you are a heavy drinker of alcohol, your risks for cancer of the head and neck and esophagus are further increased. Use of "smokeless" tobacco increases your risks of cancer of the mouth. Your best bet is not to use tobacco in any form. See your doctor if you have a nagging cough, hoarseness, persistent pain or sore in the mouth or throat or lumps in the neck.

COLON RECTUM — Answers

1. Colon cancer occurs more often after the age of 50.
2. Colon cancer is more common in families with a previous history of this disease.
3. Polyps and bowel diseases are associated with colon cancer. Cancer of the breast, ovaries or stomach may also be associated with an increased risk of colon cancer.
4. Rectal bleeding may be a sign of colon/rectum cancer.

I. **RISK FACTORS*—If your total is:**

5 or less	You are currently at low risk for colon and rectum cancer. Eat a diet high in fiber and low in fat and follow cancer checkup guidelines.
6–15	You are currently at moderate risk for colon and rectum cancer. Follow the American Cancer Society guidelines for early detection of colorectal cancer. These are: (1) a digital rectal exam** every year after 40 and (2) a stool blood test every year and a sigmoidoscopic exam every 3–5 years after age 50.
16 or greater	You are in the high risk group for colon and rectum cancer. This rating requires a lifetime, on-going screening program that includes periodic evaluation of your entire colon. See your doctor for more information.

*If your answers to any of these questions change, you should REASSESS YOUR RISK.

II. **SYMPTOMS**—The presence of rectal bleeding or a change in bowel habits may indicate colon/rectum cancer. See your physician right away if you have either of these symptoms.

**This test has an additional advantage in that it is also an early detection method for cancer of the prostate in men.

BREAST — Answers

If your total is:

Under 100	Low risk women (and all others). You should practice monthly Breast Self-Examination, have your breasts examined by a doctor as part of a regular cancer-related checkup, and have mammography in accordance with ACS guidelines.
100–199	Moderate risk women. You should practice monthly BSE and have your breasts examined by a doctor as part of a cancer-related checkup, and have periodic mammography in accordance with American Cancer Society guidelines, or more frequently as your physician advises.
200 or higher	High risk. You should practice monthly BSE and have your breasts examined by a doctor, and have mammography more often. See your doctor for the recommended frequency of breast physical examinations and mammography.

REDUCING YOUR RISK—One in 10 American women will get breast cancer in her lifetime. Being a woman is a risk factor! Most women (75%) who get breast cancer don't have other risk factors. BSE and mammography may diagnose a breast cancer in its earliest stage with a greatly increased chance of cure. When detected at this stage, cure is more likely and breast-saving surgery may be an option.

ANSWERS AND TEST ANALYSIS

SKIN   Answers

1. The sun's rays are more intense the closer one lives to the equator.
2. Excessive ultraviolet light from the sun causes cancer of the skin.
3. These materials can cause cancer of the skin.
4. Persons with light complexions are at greater risk for skin cancer.
5. A severe sunburn while growing up may increase one's risk for melanoma.
6. A tendency to have pre-cancerous moles or melanomas may occur in certain families.
7. Persons with a previous skin cancer or melanoma are at increased risk for developing a skin cancer or melanoma.
8. Tanning beds use a type of ultraviolet ray which adds to the skin damage caused by the sun, contributing to skin cancer formation.
9. Any change in a mole may be a sign of melanoma.

The key is if you answered "yes" to any of the first nine questions, you need to use protective clothing and use a sun screen with an SPF rating of 15 or greater whenever you are out in the sun and check yourself monthly for any changes in warts or moles. An answer of "yes" to questions 10, 11, and 12 can help reduce your risk of skin cancer.

REDUCING YOUR RISK—Numerical risks for skin cancer are difficult to state. For instance, a person with dark complexion can work longer in the sun and be less likely to develop cancer than a person with a light complexion. Furthermore, a person wearing a long-sleeved shirt and wide-brimmed hat may work in the sun and be at less risk than a person who wears a bathing suit for only a short time. The risk for skin cancer goes up greatly with age.

Melanoma, the most serious type of skin cancer, can be cured when it is detected and treated at a very early stage. Changes in warts or moles are important and should be checked by your doctor. For more information, ask for the American Cancer Society pamphlet, "Melanoma/Skin Cancer, You Can Recognize the Signs."

CERVICAL   Answers

1. The numbers represent the relative risks for invasive cancer in different age groups. The highest incidence of invasive cancer is among women over 40 years of age. However, abnormal changes and early noninvasive cancers occur more commonly in the 20's and 30's age groups. These early changes can be found with the Pap test.
2. Puerto Ricans, Blacks, and Mexican Americans have higher rates of cervical cancer.
3. Women who have delivered more children have a higher occurrence.
4. Viral infections of the cervix and vagina are associated with cervical cancer.
5. Women with earlier age at first intercourse and with more sexual partners are at a higher risk.
6. Irregular bleeding may be a sign of uterine cancer.

If your total is:

40–69	This is a low risk group. Ask your doctor for a Pap test and advice about frequency of subsequent testing.
70–99	In this moderate risk group, more frequent Pap tests may be required.
100 or more	You are in a high risk group and should have a Pap test (and pelvic exam) as advised by your doctor.

REDUCING YOUR RISK—Early detection of this cancer by the Pap test has markedly improved the chance of cure. When this cancer is found at an early stage, the cure rate is extremely high and uterus-saving surgery and child-bearing potential may be preserved.

ENDOMETRIAL   Answers

1. Endometrial cancer is seen among women in older age groups. Numbers in parentheses by the age groups represent approximate relative rates of endometrial cancer at different ages.
2. Caucasians have a higher occurrence.
3. The fewer children one has delivered the greater the risk of endometrial cancer.
4. Women who are overweight are at greater risk.
5. Cancer of the endometrium is associated with diabetes.
6. Cancer of the endometrium may be associated with prolonged continuous estrogen hormone intake which occurs in only a small number of women. You should consult your physician before starting or stopping any estrogen medication. The medical use of estrogen in combination with progesterone does not appear to increase risk and may have other health benefits in this case.
7. Women who do not have cyclic regular menstrual periods are at greater risk. Any bleeding after menopause may be a sign of this cancer.
8. Cancer of the endometrium is associated with high blood pressure.

If your total is:

45–59	You are at very low risk for developing endometrial cancer.
60–99	Your risks are slightly higher. Report any abnormal bleeding immediately to your doctor. Tissue sampling at menopause is recommended.
100 and over	Your risks are much greater. See your doctor for tests as appropriate.

REDUCING YOUR RISK—Once again, early detection is a key to your chance of a cure for this cancer. Regular pelvic examinations may find other female cancers such as cancer of the ovary.

Your Test Scores

Check your own risks with the answers contained in this assessment. Individual numbers for specific questions are not to be interpreted as a precise measure of relative risk, but the totals for a given site should give you a general indication of your risk.

Additional educational information is available from your American Cancer Society.

1-800-ACS-2345

You are advised to discuss the results of this assessment with your physician if you are at high risk.

chapter 9
LABORATORY ②

Skin Cancer Risk Assessment

Risk factors are those characteristics that are more frequently found in persons with a specific cancer than in persons without that cancer. The following items are risk factors for SKIN CANCER. Answer "yes" or "no" to each question to assess your personal risk factors for skin cancer.

	YES	NO
1. Did you experience a severe, blistering sunburn before the age of 18?	☐	☐
2. Does your job require frequent sun exposure?	☐	☐
3. Do you live in the southern United States?	☐	☐
4. Do you or have you used tanning beds or sunlamps?	☐	☐
5. Do you sunbathe?	☐	☐
6. Do you have outdoor recreational hobbies?	☐	☐
7. Is your natural hair color blond, red, or light brown?	☐	☐
8. Is your natural eye color green, hazel, gray or blue?	☐	☐
9. Is your skin freckled and/or fair?	☐	☐
10. Do you sunburn easily?	☐	☐
11. Have you been exposed to creosote, coal pitch tar, arsenic, lubricating or cutting oils on your job?	☐	☐
12. Have you had x-ray treatment to the skin for acne or another skin condition?	☐	☐
13. Have you had a skin cancer in the past?	☐	☐
14. Have you ever had a precancerous skin lesion removed or treated?	☐	☐
15. Have any of your family members had a skin cancer?	☐	☐
16. Have you had a severe burn to the skin that resulted in scar formation?	☐	☐

Source: American Cancer Society, Texas Division, Inc.

	YES	NO
17. Were you born with a birthmark larger than 7 inches?	☐	☐
18. Do you wear sunscreen less than half the time when outdoors?	☐	☐

All "yes" answers are considered to be risk factors for skin cancer. You can change many of your risk factors! The explanations below provide more information.

Risk Factors For Skin Cancer

Heavy Lifetime Sun Exposure (Questions 1–6): Repeated overexposure to the ultraviolet rays of the sun is the principal cause of most skin cancers. Risk increases for those who are heavily exposed to the sun in their occupations, including farmers, sailors, and road and construction workers. Risk also increases for those whose recreational activities involve heavy sun exposure, such as swimming, skiing, golfing and jogging. Tanning salons emit ultraviolet radiation which add to the skin damage caused by the sun, contributing to skin cancer formation. People who have experienced a severe, blistering burn before the age of 18 are at increased risk for developing melanoma, the most serious form of skin cancer.

Skin Pigmentation (Questions 7–10): Fair-skinned people are at increased risk, especially those with blond, red or light brown hair and light-colored eyes (blue, gray, hazel or green). Those of Celtic (Scottish, Irish) descent are at higher risk. Fair-skinned persons are at greatest risk, although it is important to remember that anyone can develop skin cancer.

Exposure to Chemical Carcinogens (Question 11): Those with occupational exposure to paraffin waxes, anthracin soot, lubricating or cutting oils, mineral oils, creosotes, coal pitch tar, or previous exposure to arsenic are at increased risk. Examples of workers at occupational risk may include roofers, road repair workers, insecticide makers or sprayers, coal miners, tar distillers, or machine operators exposed to lubricating oils.

History of Superficial X-Ray Treatment (Question 12): A history of x-ray treatments for acne, psoriasis, fungal conditions, or to remove unwanted hair, particularly when in combination with heavy sun exposure, may increase one's risk of developing skin cancer.

Personal or Family History of Skin Cancer (Questions 13–15): People who have had a previous skin cancer or precancerous lesion are at increased risk for developing skin cancer. People who have a family member with melanoma are at increased risk for developing melanoma themselves.

Birthmarks and Burn Scars (Questions 16 & 17): Persons born with a birthmark larger than seven inches ("giant congenital nevus") are at increased risk for melanoma formation later in life. A severe burn to the skin due to fire or chemicals increases risk for developing skin cancer in the scarred skin.

Reducing Your Risk for Skin Cancer

Cover Up with a wide-brimmed hat, and a bandana for your neck; wear long-sleeved shirts and pants the sun can't penetrate.

Use Sunscreens with a Sun Protective Factor (SPF) rating of 15 or higher. Apply sunscreen at least an hour before going into the sun and again after swimming or perspiring. Avoid indoor sunlamps or tanning booths.

Know the Ways of the Rays you *may* get burned on a cloudy day. And the sun's rays can reach down into three feet of water. Avoid the direct sun at midday, as the sun's rays are strongest between 11 a.m. and 2 p.m. And beware of high altitudes—there is less atmosphere to filter out the ultraviolet rays. Snow reflects the sun's rays, too.

Know Your Skin

Whatever your skin type, do a monthly self-exam of your skin to note any moles, blemishes or birthmarks. Check them once a month and if you notice any changes in size, shape or color or if a sore does not heal, see your physician without delay.

chapter 9
LABORATORY ③

Diabetes Risk Assessment

Find out if you are at risk for having diabetes now. Write in the points next to each statement that is **true** for you. If a statement is **not true**, put a zero. Then, add your total score.

At-Risk Weight Chart		
Height	**Weight**	
feet/inches without shoes	pounds without clothing	
	Women	*Men*
4'9"	134	
4'10"	137	
4'11"	140	
5'0"	143	
5'1"	146	157
5'2"	150	160
5'3"	154	162
5'4"	157	165
5'5"	161	168
5'6"	164	172
5'7"	168	175
5'8"	172	179
5'9"	175	182
5'10"	178	186
5'11"	182	190
6'0"		194
6'1"		199
6'2"		203
6'3"		209

⊙ My weight is equal to or above that listed in the chart   Yes   5 _____

⊙ I am under 65 years of age and I get little or no exercise during a usual day   Yes   5 _____

⊙ I am between 45 and 64 years of age   Yes   5 _____

⊙ I am 65-years-old or older   Yes   9 _____

⊙ I am a woman who has had a baby weighing more than nine pounds at birth   Yes   1 _____

⊙ I have a sister or brother with diabetes   Yes   1 _____

⊙ I have a parent with diabetes   Yes   1 _____

Total _____

This chart shows weights that are 20% heavier than what is recommended for men and women with a medium frame. If you weigh the same or more than the amount listed for your height, you may be at risk for diabetes.

The Mission of the American Diabetes Association is to prevent and cure diabetes and to improve the lives of all people affected by diabetes.

If you scored 3–9 points:
You are probably at low risk for having diabetes now. But don't just forget about it—especially if you are Hispanic, African American, Native American, Asian American or Pacific Islander. You may be at higher risk in the future.

If you scored 10 or more points:
You are at high risk for having diabetes. Only a doctor can determine if you have diabetes. See a doctor and find out for sure.

10 Stress Management

© 2006 JUPITER IMAGES CORPORATION.

Key Terms

stress
stressor
general adaptation syndrome
homeostasis
fight or flight
allostatic load
hardiness

social connectedness
Type A/Type B personality
coping
progressive muscle
    relaxation
biofeedback

Specific Objectives

1. Define stress.
2. Explain how the body responds to stress.
3. Describe Selye's General Adaptation Syndrome.
4. Identify real and potential sources of stress.
5. Describe how various traits and personality characteristics can buffer the impact of stress.
6. Understand interventions for stress and how to use them.

College students speak often about being under stress. Academic pressures, finances, relationships, new freedoms and responsibilities, and apprehension about their futures are but a few of the major issues that the typical college student may "stress over." But what, exactly, is stress? Do we really want a stress free life? Why do some individuals seem to hold up well in the face of intense stress, while others have difficulty dealing with seemingly minor issues in their lives? And perhaps most importantly, what are the best ways to deal with the stressors of life in a way that they do not have a deteriorating effect on life and health? These are the questions that this chapter will address.

Stress is the body's response to any demand placed upon it. Those demands can come from a wide variety of sources (called stressors), and although there are certainly universal causes of stress, the major sources of stress in an individuals life at any given time vary from person to person. Stress can actually be a pleasant experience, serving as a motivational tool and leading to improved performance. (If you know that an exam is important to your overall success in a course, you are more apt to study and come to class prepared.) This type of stress is positive and is called eustress. Most of the time, however, stress is perceived as having harmful consequences. This type of stress is negative and is called distress. Stress, both good and bad, is normal, and it follows the same general process in all people.

Dr. Hans Selye, a physician and endocrinologist, was one of the early pioneers in the research of stress and its impact on humans. His many works, including his books *The Stress of Life* and *Stress without Distress*, documented his detailed work in the field of how stress influences individual health. Through his research he observed that individuals go through three stages in response to stress, which he called the General Adaptation Syndrome (GAS):

1. **Alarm.** In this stage, the body is first confronted with a stressor and exhibits a predictable physiological response in preparation for dealing with the immediate threat. The organs that are most important for responding to threats (the brain, heart, and skeletal muscles) receive greater amounts of glycogen and oxygen as a result of increased amounts of epinephrine (adrenaline) produced by the adrenal glands. The less important organs and systems for defense, like the digestive system and reproductive organs, receive less oxygen and glycogen. The heart rate and breathing rate increase, and muscles tense in preparation to provide defense against the stressor. This physical reaction to a stressor had previously been identified as the "fight or flight" syndrome by Harvard physiologist Walter Cannon. Cannon saw the body's physical changes in the face of stress as our initial preparation to "fight" against the stressor or to "flee" the perceived harm of the stressor.

2. **Resistance.** After the initial defenses are engaged, the body now prepares for the continued presence of the stressor. It attempts to return to normal functioning while remaining prepared to resist the stressor. Blood pressure increases, alertness is heightened, and remaining energy reserves are mobilized as the stressor continues to take its toll. During the resistance stage, the person either successfully copes with the stressor and returns to homeostasis (the constant, healthy, and natural state of balance in the body) or suffers the consequence of long-term negative stress. The resistance stage cannot go on forever. If the stressor is not dealt with successfully, the third stage of the GAS is encountered.

3. **Exhaustion.** If adaptation tools are not present or not successful in managing the stressor, the organism will eventually reach a state of exhaustion. The heart, adrenal glands, blood vessels, and other systems are unable to meet the de-

mands placed upon them in the resistance stage, and begin to fail. Illness, and possibly even death may result from exhaustion.

THE ALLOSTATIC LOAD

The allostatic load is the term used to summarize the response of various systems of the human body when under stress. It is a complex phenomenon, but is represented by the load of stress that each individual carries over time—the "wear and tear" from whatever is bothering you—large or small, long-term or short-term. The allostatic systems include the cardiovascular, metabolic, immune and parts of the nervous system. If one carries a heavy allostatic load, damage to these systems can occur. If adequate coping skills are not learned and applied to stressful situations, the allostatic load remains chronically high, and is strongly suspected as a cause of illness.

Ill Health Effects of Stress

For years, most people have acknowledged that stress can make you sick. Studies on civil servants in stressful jobs, individuals who experience a family crisis like divorce or death in the family, and soldiers in war zones all give evidence that stressful events make us more prone to illness. However, breakthroughs in medical research have only recently begun to explain the physiological mechanism whereby stress actually produces illness. When a person is experiencing stress, the body mounts a chemical response. Through the autonomic (involuntary) nervous system, the brain sends a signal to the adrenal glands (located near the kidneys) and they increase their production of hormones including epinephrine (adrenalin), catecholamines, and most notably a hormone called cortisol. These hormones help us function by keeping us alert, increasing our heart rate and blood pressure, and preparing our energy reserves. But they are also known as stress hormones because they are preparing the body to deal with the stressor in one of two ways—to fight against it or to run from it (the "fight or flight" syndrome). Now the muscles are tensed, alertness is heightened, blood pressure rises, and the heart rate and breathing rate speeds up. As these systems are heightened in preparation to deal with the stressor, other systems, including the immune system, are suppressed because they are not vital at the time. These stress hormones remain in the bloodstream after the stressful situation has passed (explaining why it takes some time to calm down from a highly stressful experience) and can have negative effects on our health. Cortisol is known to speed the conversion of fats and proteins into carbohydrates so that they can be readily used as fuel as the body deals with the stressor, and while cortisol helps us get through the stressful situation, chronic stress can lead to continued production of cortisol and the other stress hormones. Abnormally high levels can lead to metabolic disturbances in the body, including suppression of the immune system, and can increase the susceptibility to a wide variety of ill health effects.

These ill health effects are still being identified, but research clearly points to a relationship between stress and heart disease, cancer, and stroke, the three leading killers of Americans. Additionally, migraine headaches, skin disorders, ulcers, vulnerability to infections, metabolic disorders, and several other physical ailments can be caused or worsened by stress. Anxiety, paranoia, depression, suicide, and other emotional disorders may also be stress related. In fact, some estimate that 75 to 90 percent of physician visits and 80 percent of all major illness are related to stress.

Too Many Stressors?

The relationship between specific life events and the resulting health effects was significantly advanced in the 1960s by medical doctors Thomas Holmes and Richard Rahe, researchers at the University of Washington School of Medicine. They observed that many of their patients had experienced a set of life events likely to be viewed as distressful just prior to their illness. From that observation, they conducted research which resulted in the "Social Readjustment Rating Scale." The conclusion of their research was that individuals who experience certain life events carry a higher likelihood of illness than their counterparts who do not experience as many of these life events. A Major Life Events and Stress Survey is available as Laboratory 1 at the end of this chapter for you to determine your likelihood of stress-related illness.

PERSONALITY AND STRESS

While the experience of the General Adaptation Syndrome is common to all, and a heavy allostatic load can negatively impact anyone, not everyone responds to stressors with the same intensity and reaction. Some individuals tend to withstand the storm of stressors quite well, while others cave in to even the smallest of stressors. Personality traits can make one more or less vulnerable to the ill health effects of stress.

Hardiness

A personality trait that can mediate the effects of stress in our lives is called hardiness. Hardiness may explain why some individuals tend to tolerate stress better than others. Hardiness has three central characteristics—commitment, challenge, and control—called the three Cs of hardiness.

- ⊙ **Commitment**—a sense of dedication to your life goals and aspirations. Hardy people understand that in life, there will be troubles, but a deep sense of involvement and commitment can help them keep their major goal in focus and withstand stress.
- ⊙ **Challenge**—a view of new events and demands which sees them not as a threat, but as an opportunity. New situations and new responsibilities are welcomed as changes in life as we grow, and personal improvement can result from these situations. Hardy people see challenging situations not as threats of failure, but as opportunities for growth.
- ⊙ **Control**—the belief that an individual has influence over the course of life events. Hardy people look for ways to gain control over seemingly out of control situations, being proactive instead of reactive. It is not a strife for total control over every life event, but a feeling of the power to influence outcomes.

People with these characteristics are capable of sizing up stressful events and responding in more favorable ways than those with a low level of hardiness. They do not suffer the ill health consequences of stress as often. To assess your degree of hardiness, take the Hardiness Scale in Laboratory 2 at the end of the chapter.

SOCIAL CONNECTEDNESS

Paffenbarger and Olsen (1996) pointed out what is quite obvious to many—social contact is a highly important aspect of our lives. Social connectedness refers to the relationships that people have with others. Various research studies on diverse populations have shown social support to be related to less depression, lower serum cholesterol levels, less reoccurrence of heart disease among Type A personalities, less melanoma recurrences, healthier pregnancies, and improved academic performance. Involvement in campus activities and the social network of friends each play a significant role in the student's college experience. While the existence of social connections is critical, the style and degree of the connections is also important. To evaluate the value of your social connections, see Laboratory 3—Social Support at the end of the chapter.

HUMOR AND STRESS

Learning to laugh at situations can bring a whole new outlook upon an event initially perceived as stressful—in fact, laughter has been called "inner jogging" because it creates a physical response that some believe to be therapeutic in the management of stress. Laughter actually stimulates respiratory activity, increases heart rate and muscular activity, promotes oxygen exchange, and perhaps most importantly stimulates the production of endorphins and decreases the level of catecholamines, the stress hormones. Endorphins are chemicals produced in the brain which act on the central and peripheral nervous systems to reduce pain. Following an episode of laughter, the relaxation response is experienced, in which blood pressure, heart rate, respiration rate, and muscular tension return to normal levels and below. Psychologically, laughter has been shown to buffer negative events and prevent them from becoming mood disturbances. Laughter is good, and anyone seeking to manage their stress in a productive way should seek wholesome opportunities for a good laugh.

In addition to humor and laughter, other personality characteristics can be beneficial as well. Looking out for the needs and interests of others (called altruism), volunteerism, expressing gratitude for the good things in one's life, seeking spiritual growth, and discussing problems with a caring friend can also bring a new perspective on some of our challenges.

TYPE A PERSONALITY

Not all personality traits help buffer stress—some make us more vulnerable. About 40–50 years ago, two cardiologists, Meyer Friedman and Ray Rosenman, identified a set of personality traits that they believed predisposed a person toward heart disease. Their research identified these characteristics as aggressiveness, impatience, time urgency, being highly competitive, overbearing and controlling, and having free-floating hostility and deep-seated insecurity. On the other hand, Type B personalities exhibit different characteristics and experience far less heart disease. Their characteristics include a contemplative nature, greater relaxation, and less extreme competitiveness, aggressiveness, and time urgency. These differences are found in both men and women. Considerable subsequent research reinforces the findings that Type A individuals experience greater coronary vessel obstruction and more coronary heart disease and that they are also more likely to have a second heart attack than Type B persons. Interestingly, however, Type A persons are more likely to survive a heart attack than Type B persons. There is, on the other hand, some research that downplays the relationship between Type A personality and mortality and the duration of stay in coronary care hospital units. This illustrates how complex the study of stress, personality, and health really is. Some studies have separated out certain components of the Type A personality to determine if they alone increased disease risk. Those characteristics which have been found to be consistent in their association with heart disease include hostility, anger, and impatience and irritability. While the research may not be conclusive at this time, the recognition of these potentially dangerous personality traits and their modification certainly appears to be a significant issue in stress management for good health. To determine if you tend toward Type A or Type B personality, see Laboratory 4—The Type A Personality Quiz—at the end of this chapter. If you are a Type A individual, Box 10.1 provides suggestions for some helpful attitude changes.

Box 10.1

Attitude Changes for the Type A Personality

Focus on one thing at a time, and perform that task to your greatest ability.

Listen quietly, be patient with others, and learn from them.

Allow others to perform tasks their way.

Identify a relaxation technique that you can use daily.

Try to work some flex time into your schedule.

Take a little time to be alone and reflect on your thoughts.

Prioritize your activities. Consider eliminating some of the less important and less valuable commitments that you have made with your life.

See life as a journey, not a destination or a task to be accomplished.

Place yourself in situations where you must wait. You may learn that it is not that bad.

© 2006 JUPITER IMAGES CORPORATION.

SOURCES OF STRESS FOR COLLEGE STUDENTS

While college students are susceptible to any life event that they may find stressful, studies have identified the major sources of stress for the college student. One study identified the major sources of stress for college students as change in sleeping habits, vacations/breaks, change in eating habits, increased work load, and new responsibilities. It also identified that daily hassles were reported more often than major life events, with intrapersonal sources of stress being the most frequently reported source (Ross, S.E., et al., 1999). Another similar study, however, reports that the main stressors for college students are many responsibilities, struggling to meet academic standards, time and money management worries, and concern over grades. They report that as the number and intensity of these hassles go up, so do stress levels. (faculty.weber.edu/molpin/dissabstract.html)

College stressors generally fall into four broad categories:

1. **Environmental stressors.** These include your living conditions and surroundings including traffic, the weather, the condition/location of your dorm or apartment, and the noise levels that you may be exposed to.

2. **Physiological stressors.** These are primarily lifestyle related sources of stress such as a sedentary lifestyle and poor nutritional habits, inadequate sleep, and physical illness or injury.

3. **Social stressors.** These stressors include difficult relationships with friends, roommates, and family, problems at work, financial difficulties, and academic challenges.

4. **Psychological stressors.** These are thoughts and perceptions that can cause stress including feelings of inferiority, fears of rejection, negative thinking, and allowing a minor stressor to balloon out of control (called catastrophizing).

INTERNAL VS. EXTERNAL STRESSORS

Stress can be internal or external. External stress includes the life events that one identifies as stressful, as well as physical and environmental conditions. For example, temperature extremes, an abusive relationship, or a death in the family would be considered external stressors. Internal stressors can come in the form of a physical illness or injury, but is quite often a negative view or mindset regarding a situation or circumstance. Intense worry about life situations are internal stressors. While control over all external events may not be possible, each person does get to decide what mindset they will take toward external stressors. The avenues for coping with external and internal stressors are different, and are discussed in the section on Developing a Plan for Coping with Stress.

MINORITIES AND STRESS

One group of students may be particularly vulnerable to stress. Minority students may experience unique stressors. Armstead and colleagues (1989) found that perceived racist feelings toward minorities were related to higher resting blood pressure. This prompted the researchers to suggest that racism in our society may be a serious health concern for all minority classes, and has led to considerable additional research on race and stress. It is now widely recognized that minority status can significantly shape how students experience campus life. Black and Hispanic students tend to experience higher levels of school stressors, external stressors, and minority student stressors than non-minority students, and the stressors resulted in fewer campus and social ties and worse outcomes. Minority stressors had the greatest negative impact on satisfaction with campus social life and psychological health, and have the potential to undermine the health and wellness of minority students. In and out of the classroom, the lack of role models and mentors as well as cultural differences in how we respond to others can contribute to minority student stress. Everyone should be sensitive to individual differences and how our treatment of one another contributes to the overall campus environment for all students. All students should be encouraged to seek out campus support services, and minority student services can play a crucial role in making the campus life and educational experience a positive one for minority students.

SIGNS OF STRESS

When we are stressed, our bodies begin emitting signs that homeostasis is being disrupted. If we are alert and aware of these symptoms, it is very likely that we can identify the source of the stress and address it in its early stages instead of letting it grow and create additional problems. The initial signs of stress generally fall into one of two categories:

Physiological Signs of Stress

Headaches and muscle aches
Neck and back pain
Increased heart rate or heart palpitations
Increased blood pressure
Chest pains
Butterflies/upset stomach

Dry mouth
Loss of appetite
Increased urination
Rash or acne
Insomnia or disrupted sleep

Psychological Signs of Stress

Inability to concentrate
Irritability
Restlessness

Depressed mood
Impulsivity
Difficulty remembering things

These physical, mental, and emotional signs of stress often manifest themselves as changes in the person's general behavior. Some behavioral changes that may result from stress include:

Emotional outbursts
Frequent crying
Angry outbursts
Lashing out at others

Isolation and withdrawal
Sexual dysfunction
Communication difficulties
Use of escape substances (alcohol and drugs)

DEVELOPING A PLAN FOR COPING WITH STRESS

When the signs of stress appear, immediate intervention is paramount in the process of returning to homeostasis. Numerous approaches to stress management are available, and while each individual has to discover what works for them, there are some basic principles that are highly effective for overall stress management.

1. Alter or Eliminate

This is the most direct approach to stress management—changing the situation that is causing the majority of your stress. It involves attacking the stressor itself and eliminating or moderating the source of the stress. If the heavy traffic and wasted time of a commute is creating a difficult transition to school, one might consider a physical move to be closer to campus and social activities. If finances are the major source of stress, getting a part time job that does not impede progress toward academic goals could help. For the student who constantly feels as they are in a state of disarray, organizational skills can be helpful. And for the large majority of college students who can never find time to get everything accomplished that they desire, implementing some time management skills may solve much of the problem. Box 10.2—Time Management Tips provides some practical suggestions for time management and the college student.

Sometimes, we are confronted with a decision that we know is in our best interest, yet difficult to make. A specific life event may need to be changed in order to prevent the stress of the event from taking a negative toll. For example, if our best efforts to get along with a difficult roommate have not resulted in a peaceful living arrangement, then a new roommate might be in order. If employment is contributing to academic failures, then cutting back on work hours might be necessary. Over-involvement in a campus organization may be stealing time away from academics, and one might be faced with restricting participation in an organization that has great value to them. While each person must decide for themselves what actions are in their best interest, try not to lose sight of the big-picture and keep your most important goals as the highest priority in your activities and lifestyles.

2. Change Your Perception

As hard as it may be to admit, sometimes the best solution to handling stress is to change our mental approach to life's situations. The old approach of counting to ten and taking some deep breaths may in fact be useful in today's stressful and fast

---

Box 10.2

Time Management Tips

Many college students are poor time managers, and poor time management can lead to increased stress and poor academic performance. The following suggestions are designed to get you started on making the most of the hours in your day.

Set long-term and short-term goals. Each student should take inventory at the beginning of each semester to determine their long range objective. Is the degree track that you are on adequately preparing you for that end? If you are unsure about your future aspirations, speak to an academic advisor or career counselor at your school. Once a goal is determined, realize that you are in a very important stage of life in the pursuit of that goal, and resolve not to waver from your quest. Then, break the long-term goal into shorter goals. They may include a specific grade point average, or a target grade in a difficult course, or a good grade on a term paper. Visit with your teachers to determine a reasonable goal for their class and projects. Put your goals in writing and share them with your support group—you will be more committed to managing your time and following through with your efforts. Reward yourself for accomplishing the goal.

Get organized. Get rid of unneeded clutter. Clean out and organize your study space. Put everything in its proper place instead of leaving it sprawled out across the dorm room or apartment. Designate a spot for items that are easily misplaced—keys, glasses, purses or wallets, cell phones—and keep those things in the same place all the time. Lots of time is wasted looking for that special item, and often it occurs when we are in a hurry, causing us to be even more time crunched. Also, many people find that making and working from a list of things to do helps them stay focused on using time wisely.

Prioritize. Simply put, some tasks are more important than others, and knowing the difference can help us manage our time. Make lists of things that need to be done, and number them in order of importance. Due dates for projects and the grade value of assignments make a great place to begin prioritizing your academic tasks. Focus on the highest priority activities one at a time, and stay intent on them until they are complete.

Don't procrastinate. Often, assignments are given at the beginning of a semester only to be due at the end. Weeks pass with no progress, creating time urgency at the end ("crunch time"), resulting in inferior work. Set progress dates for major projects, and stick to them. Use "crunch time" for fine tuning the project. Also, learning to say no to distracting commitments, especially when trying to meet deadlines, can help you stay on task.

Eliminate interruptions. When studying, get away from the phone or the flow of traffic where you are likely to be interrupted. Turn off the television and cell phone, and close the door and ask others not to interrupt you when you are working. Libraries still make great places to read, write, and study.

Maximize your time for productivity. Most of us know when we are most productive. Are you a morning or an evening person? Schedule your most important tasks for times that you know are your most industrious. Most of us also have small pockets of spare time in our day that we could use to do simple tasks like make your daily list, return short phone calls, balance the checkbook, or clean out a wallet or purse, or maybe even review a reading assignment.

Identify time wasters. Most people also know when they are least productive, and have activities in their lives that waste time. Television and video games are good sources of entertainment, but too much time in these activities results in lost productivity. Engage in these activities on a limited basis, and set a time limit for them. Set a timer when you start, allowing a reasonable time for them, and when the timer goes off, put them away.

paced life. Slowing down and viewing life's challenges in a new perspective can often help us see that our situation is not nearly as bad as we have perceived it. An individual's general outlook on life may influence a person toward suffering from stress-related effects. Catastrophizing is the practice of allowing your mind to exaggerate the intensity of a perceived stressor, sometimes referred to as making a mountain out of a mole hill. It creates a negative outlook which allows the stressor to have a more negative impact on one's health

While it may be easier said than done, turning to the characteristics of humor, altruism, and optimism can help change perspectives. How many times have you experienced an unpleasant event, only to be able to have a good laugh about it later? Altruism is the characteristic of serving and doing good deeds in the interest of another person. Optimism is the ability to keep the positive attitude that all things will eventually work for the good, even in the face of difficult times. Some people can find the silver lining in every cloud. Each of these attitudes toward stress has been shown to be valuable in developing a productive stress management plan.

3. Relax

A number of relaxation techniques have been identified as effective ways to help the body return to homeostasis. Again, while each person must find what helps them relax, some may be interested in developing a new, specific relaxation technique. Relaxation techniques do not address the source of the stress, but do assist the individual in dealing with gaining control over the physical symptoms of stress.

Positive imagery. Using mental imagery to deal with stressful situations is a simple method for creating a positive as opposed to a negative mindset. If you have ever had to give a speech in a class and had negative thoughts of the speech being poorly delivered, positive imagery might be helpful for you. Used often in the field of sports and athletics, this technique teaches the individual to create a mental picture of a highly successful outcome of a specific task or event. Prior to making the speech, envision yourself having exactly the right words, being highly articulate, and delivering a speech with a convincing method. (And don't forget to practice the speech as well.) Getting rid of negative, self-limiting thoughts can free you to perform at a higher level.

Progressive Muscle Relaxation (PMR). Pioneered in the 1930s by physiologist and psychologist Edmund Jacobsen, this technique uses a precise method to teach individuals to achieve muscular relaxation. Some psychologists consider this to be one of the most reliable and effective procedures for achieving relaxation. It works on the concept that emotional tension brings about physical, muscular tension and can result in headaches and muscle aches. As the individual is trained to relax the muscles, much of the emotional tension is relaxed as well—in other words, physical relaxation brings a mental calmness. Focusing on a specific muscle or muscle group, the muscle is intentionally tensed for a few seconds, followed by a release of the tension and focus on the deep relaxed state of the muscle. Each muscle of the body is in turn tensed and relaxed, until the individual learns to experience total physical relaxation. Anyone interested in PMR can practice the technique until they find it helpful in alleviating muscular stress. This technique, combined with deep breathing, is encouraged by the American Lung Association for those who are trying to quit smoking in dealing with the stress of their behavior change. A guideline for practicing Progressive Muscle Relaxation is provided in Laboratory 5 at the end of this chapter.

Deep breathing. Since stressful experiences can result in shallow, labored breathing, one approach to battling the symptoms of stress is to regain a deeper and more efficient breathing pattern. With deep breathing, like PMR, the individual learns to breathe using a slow and deep pattern of inhalation, breathing in through the nose and out through the mouth. Many find deep breathing a welcome respite from the stress of the day.

Biofeedback. Biofeedback uses various devices to measure the reaction of certain body processes while under stress. The individual can observe their body's physiological responses to stress, and can be taught to use specific techniques to exercise control over those responses. Common biofeedback indicators include measures of muscular tension, heart rate, skin temperature, and perspiration rate. The person can watch a screen or meter which shows the response, then practice their relaxation techniques and watch the relief of the stress as they relax. This process is typically used in a clinical setting, and teaches the stressed person how to induce the relaxation response. The subject then practices using the same relaxation techniques in their daily living situation that they find to be stressful.

Social support systems. Benefiting from the understanding and support of others is the basis behind the numerous support groups that exists for various life situations. Establishing a meaningful connection with other people has been shown to help people deal with the stressors of everyday life as well as the catastrophic types of stressors that some people face during difficult times. Disease support groups are quite popular and many participants report that these groups are critical in sustaining their efforts and energies during stressful times. Additionally, studies reveal that married people tend to live longer than single people, and while there are several possible reasons for this, many researchers believe the presence of social support from a significant other is the most important factor. For college students, establishing meaningful connections with peers can help in dealing with life changes. Making new friends, sharing common interests with classmates in your academic department, and getting involved in campus organizations are not only socially fulfilling, they can help with stress management as well.

4. Maintain Healthy Lifestyles

One's overall level of health is probably the most important component of a total stress management program. Many of the other chapters of this text, while focusing on physical fitness, also serve as stress management approaches. Maintaining a regular exercise routine, eating a balanced diet, and getting plenty of rest and sleep are three habits that develop the physical foundation to manage stress. If you have trouble sleeping, see Box 10.3 for some helpful suggestions. Additionally, avoiding tobacco products, responsible use of alcohol, having regular physical exams and check-ups, and seeking appropriate medical care when needed can contribute to a high level of physical well-being that makes a person more stress resistant.

5. Get Outside Support or Help

If your best attempts at stress management don't seem to resolve your feelings, seeking professional assistance is in order. Contact your division of student services or campus counseling center to get help. A trained professional who deals with stress and the college student on a regular basis is likely to have some valuable plans for you.

Box 10.3

Trouble Sleeping? Try these . . .

Over 90 percent of people experience some degree of insomnia at some point in their lives, and studies indicate that insomnia affects one in three adults every year in the United States. Lack of sleep can result in irritability, loss of attention, poor academic performance, and increased incidence of accidents. The "correct" amount of sleep is still unknown, and most likely varies from person to person, but the seven to nine hour rule is still a good one to follow. If you feel well rested, you are getting enough sleep. If you are tired and drowsy a lot, it is highly possible that you are not getting enough sleep. If you are having trouble sleeping, try some of these suggestions:

Establish a regular sleep schedule. Set a regular bedtime and wake up time and don't change it on the weekends. This pattern tends to set the body's clock and promote a more restful sleep.

Avoid daytime napping. This disrupts the regular sleep schedule.

Avoid tobacco, caffeine, and alcohol. Nicotine and caffeine are stimulant drugs which can disturb sleep, and tobacco also interferes with sleep due to its effects on the lungs, heart, sinuses, and cardiovascular circulation. Alcohol may cause some people to fall asleep quicker, but it tends to result in fragmented and un-refreshing sleep.

Use your established stress management techniques. Three out of four people who suffer significant insomnia are experiencing a specific stressful event in their lives.

Get daily exercise, but time it right. Exercise too close to bedtime may cause some people to not feel tired and ready for sleep due to increased metabolism.

Designate your bed for sleep only. Don't use it for reading, watching television, or studying.

If noise from distracting sources bothers you, consider using some form of "white noise" such as the hum of the motor of a small fan.

Try relaxing with a warm bath at least one hour before bedtime, and perform low key activities (reading, listening to music, or relaxation routines) just prior to bedtime.

Don't over-focus on watching the clock, but if you don't fall asleep in 15–30 minutes, get out of bed and don't return until you are feeling drowsy.

Finally, don't panic about a poor night's sleep. Occasional sleep disruptions are part of life, and getting upset or worrying about it can only make it worse.

References

Armstead, C.A., et al. (1989). Relationship of racial stressors to blood pressure responses and anger expression in black college students. *Health Psychology*, 8:554.

Cannon, W. (1932). *The Wisdom of the Body*. New York: W.W. Norton Publishers.

Girdano, M.A., Dusek, D., & Everly, G. (2005). Controlling Stress and Tension. Boston: Benjamin Cummings.

Jacobsen, E. (1938). *Progressive Relaxation* (2nd ed.). Chicago: Chicago Press.

McEwen, B.S. (1998). Protective and damaging effects of stress mediators. *New England Journal of Medicine*. 338:171–179.

Molpin, E. (2004). Perceived stress levels and sources of stress among college students. faculty.weber.edu/molpin/dissabstract.html

Paffenbarger, R., & Olsen, E. (1996). *Lifefit*. Champaign, IL: Human Kinetics Publishers.

Ross, S.E., Niebling, B.C., & Heckert, T.M. (1999). Sources of stress among college students. *College Student Journal*, 33:2.

Seaward, B.L. (2004). Managing stress: Principles and strategies for health and well-being. Sudbury, MA: Jones and Bartlett.

Selye, H. (1956). *The Stress of Life*. New York: McGraw-Hill Book Company.

Selye, H. (1974). *Stress without Distress*. Hagerstown, MD: Lippincott, Williams & Wilkins.

chapter 10
LABORATORY ①

Major Life Events and Stress

To get a feel for the possible health impact of the various recent events or changes in your life, think back over the past year and place a checkmark beside each of the events that you experienced during that time.

Health

- ⊙ An injury or illness which:
  - ○ kept you in bed a week or more, or sent you to the hospital _____
  - ○ was less serious than that _____
- ⊙ Major dental work _____
- ⊙ Major change in eating habits _____
- ⊙ Major change in sleeping habits _____
- ⊙ Major change in your usual type or amount of recreation _____

Work

- ⊙ Change to a new type of work _____
- ⊙ Change in your work hours or conditions _____
- ⊙ Change in your responsibilities at work:
  - ○ more responsibilities _____
  - ○ fewer responsibilities _____
  - ○ promotion _____
  - ○ demotion _____
  - ○ transfer _____
- ⊙ Troubles at work:
  - ○ with your boss _____
  - ○ with coworkers _____
  - ○ with persons under your supervision _____
  - ○ other work troubles _____
- ⊙ Major business adjustment _____
- ⊙ Retirement _____
- ⊙ Loss of job:
  - ○ laid off from work _____
  - ○ fired from work _____
- ⊙ Correspondence course to help you in your work _____

Reprinted from *Journal of Psychosomatic Research*, Vol. 43(3) by Miller and Rahe. "Life Changes Scaling for the 1990s," © 1997 Elsevier Inc. with permission.

Home and Family

- ⊙ Major change in living conditions   _____
- ⊙ Change in residence:
    - ○ move within the same town or city   _____
    - ○ move to a different town, city, or state   _____
- ⊙ Change in family get-togethers   _____
- ⊙ Major change in health or behavior of family member   _____
- ⊙ Marriage   _____
- ⊙ Pregnancy   _____
- ⊙ Miscarriage or abortion   _____
- ⊙ Gain of a new family member:
    - ○ birth of a child   _____
    - ○ adoption of a child   _____
    - ○ a relative moving in with you   _____
- ⊙ Spouse beginning or ending work   _____
- ⊙ Child leaving home:
    - ○ to attend college   _____
    - ○ due to marriage   _____
    - ○ for other reasons   _____
- ⊙ Change in arguments with spouse   _____
- ⊙ In-law problems   _____
- ⊙ Change in marital status of your parents:
    - ○ divorce   _____
    - ○ remarriage   _____
- ⊙ Separation from spouse:
    - ○ due to work   _____
    - ○ due to marital problems   _____
- ⊙ Divorce   _____
- ⊙ Birth of grandchild   _____
- ⊙ Death of spouse   _____
- ⊙ Death of other family member:
    - ○ child   _____
    - ○ brother or sister   _____
    - ○ parent   _____

Personal and Social

- ⊙ Change in personal habits   _____
- ⊙ Beginning or ending school or college   _____
- ⊙ Change of school or college   _____
- ⊙ Change of political beliefs   _____
- ⊙ Change in religious beliefs   _____
- ⊙ Change in social activities   _____
- ⊙ Vacation trip   _____
- ⊙ New, close, personal relationship   _____
- ⊙ Engagement to marry   _____
- ⊙ Girlfriend or boyfriend problems   _____

- ⊙ Sexual difficulties   _____
- ⊙ "Falling out" of a close personal relationship   _____
- ⊙ An accident   _____
- ⊙ Minor violation of the law   _____
- ⊙ Being held in jail   _____
- ⊙ Death of a close friend   _____
- ⊙ Major decision about your immediate future   _____
- ⊙ Major personal achievement   _____

Financial

- ⊙ Major change in finances:
  - ○ increased income   _____
  - ○ decreased income   _____
  - ○ investment or credit difficulties   _____
- ⊙ Loss or damage of personal property   _____
- ⊙ Moderate purchase   _____
- ⊙ Major purchase   _____
- ⊙ Foreclosure on a mortgage or loan   _____

Total score: _____

Scoring

If you have experienced a significant number of these events in the past year, you may face an increased risk of illness. If you have experienced only a few or none of these events, you may be at a lower risk of illness.

chapter 10
LABORATORY ②

How Hardy Are You?

Below are twelve items that appear in the hardiness questionnaire. Evaluating hardiness requires more than this quick test, but this exercise should give you some idea of how hardy you are. Write down how much you agree or disagree with the following statements.

0 = strongly disagree, 1 = mildly disagree, 2 = mildly agree, 3 = strongly agree

_____ A. Trying my best at work makes a difference.

_____ B. Trusting to fate is sometimes all I can do in a relationship.

_____ C. I often wake up eager to start on the day's project.

_____ D. Thinking of myself as a free person leads to great frustration and difficulty.

_____ E. I would be willing to sacrifice financial security in my work if something really challenging came along.

_____ F. It bothers me when I have to deviate from the routine or schedule I've set for myself.

_____ G. An average citizen can have an impact on politics.

_____ H. Without the right breaks, it is hard to be successful in my field.

_____ I. I know why I am doing what I am doing at work.

_____ J. Getting close to people puts me at risk of being obligated to them.

_____ K. Encountering new situations is an important priority in my life.

_____ L. I really don't mind when I have nothing to do.

Scoring
These questions measure control, commitment, and challenge. For half the questions a high score indicates hardiness; for the other half, a low score does. To calculate your scores, fill in the numbers of your responses as specified on the lines on the next page. Then subtract the totals in the second line from those in the first and write in the results on the bottom line. Add your scores on commitment, control and challenge together on the bottom line to get a score for total hardiness. A total score of 10–18 shows a hardy personality; 0–9, moderate hardiness; below 0, low hardiness.

From *American Health* © 1984 by Suzanne Ouellette Kobasa.

$\overline{\quad}$ $\overline{\quad}$

A + G = _____

minus:

$\overline{\quad}$ $\overline{\quad}$

B + H = _____

$\overline{\qquad\qquad}$

Control +

$\overline{\quad}$ $\overline{\quad}$

C + I = _____

minus:

$\overline{\quad}$ $\overline{\quad}$

D + J = _____

$\overline{\qquad\qquad}$

Commitment +

$\overline{\quad}$ $\overline{\quad}$

E + K = _____

minus:

$\overline{\quad}$ $\overline{\quad}$

F + L = _____

$\overline{\qquad\qquad}$

Challenge = _____

Total Hardiness Score _____

Name _____ Date _____ Course Section _____

chapter 10
LABORATORY ③

Social Support

Part I. Assessing Your Level of Social Support

To determine whether your social network measures up, select whether each of the following statements is true or false for you.

		True	False
1.	If I needed an emergency loan of $100, there is someone I could get it from.	_____	_____
2.	There is someone who takes pride in my accomplishments.	_____	_____
3.	I often meet or talk with family or friends.	_____	_____
4.	Most people I know think highly of me.	_____	_____
5.	If I needed an early morning ride to the airport, there's no one I would feel comfortable asking to take me.	_____	_____
6.	I feel there is no one with whom I can share my most private worries and fears.	_____	_____
7.	Most of my friends are more successful making changes in their lives than I am.	_____	_____
8.	I would have a hard time finding someone to go with me on a day trip to the beach or country.	_____	_____

Your Score _____

Scoring

If you marked four or more statements true, you should have enough support to protect your health. If your score is 3 or less, refer to your textbook for suggestions on how to build up your social network.

Quiz Source: Japenga, A. 1995. "A Family of Friends." *Health*, November/December.

Part II. Social Support Profile

Learn more about your network of social support by completing a social support profile. For each type of support listed below, list the people who most often provide that type of support for you. Check the category box if that person reciprocates by coming to you for the same type of support.

Type of Support	Emotional *Someone you can trust with your most intimate thoughts and fears*	Social *Someone with whom you can hang out and share life experiences*	Informational *Someone you can ask for advice on major decisions*	Practical *Someone who will help you out in a pinch*
Partner ☐				
Relative ☐				
Friend ☐				
Neighbor ☐				
Coworker or boss ☐				
Therapist or clergy ☐				

Internet Activity

The Internet can be a valuable resource for building up your social support network. Think about your hobbies and areas of interest. With the Internet, you can get in touch with organizations and people who share your interests. For example, from Yahoo's recreation and sports listings (http://dir.yahoo.com/recreation/sports), in-line skaters can learn about equipment and technique as well as local clubs and skating events. If you are interested in human rights, Amnesty International's home page (http://www.amnesty.org/) can put you in touch with a local chapter of the organization. Whatever your interests, odds are that you can find applicable Web pages, bulletin boards, chat rooms, and other Internet resources.

Choose a topic, and use a search engine to locate online resources. Describe what you find: What sites are available? What sorts of information can you obtain? Are there opportunities for you to interact online with people who share your area of interest? Did you find any organizations or groups operating in your area?

Area of interest:

Resources located:

chapter 10
LABORATORY (4)

Type A Personality Quiz

This scale, based on the one by Friedman and Rosenman, will give you an estimate of your Type A tendencies.
Directions: Answer the following questions by indicating the response that most often applies to you.

Yes	No	Statement
_____	_____	1. I always feel rushed.
_____	_____	2. I find it hard to relax.
_____	_____	3. I attempt to do more and more in less and less time.
_____	_____	4. I often find myself doing more than one thing at a time.
_____	_____	5. When people take too long to make a point, I finish the sentence for them.
_____	_____	6. Waiting in line for anything drives me crazy.
_____	_____	7. I am always on time or early.
_____	_____	8. In a conversation, I often clench my fist and pound home important points.
_____	_____	9. I often use explosive outbursts to accentuate key points.
_____	_____	10. I am competitive at everything.
_____	_____	11. I tend to evaluate my success by translating things into numbers.
_____	_____	12. Friends tell me I have more energy than most people.
_____	_____	13. I always move, walk, and eat quickly.
_____	_____	14. I bring work home often.
_____	_____	15. I tend to get bored on vacation.
_____	_____	16. I feel guilty when I am not being "productive."
_____	_____	17. I tend to refocus other people's conversations on things that interest me.
_____	_____	18. I hurry others along in their conversations.
_____	_____	19. It is agonizing to be stuck behind someone driving too slowly.
_____	_____	20. I find it intolerable to let others do something I can do faster.

Scoring
Add up the number of items for which you checked yes. The greater the number of yes items, the more likely it is that you are a Type A personality.

From: *Coping with Stress in a Changing World* by Richard Blonna, McGraw-Hill, 2005.

chapter 10
LABORATORY

Progressive Muscle Relaxation

Preparation

Generate about 70–80 percent of the total possible tension in a muscle or muscle group to avoid cramping or injury.

Spend twice as much time relaxing each muscle as you spend tensing each muscle.

Do not skip any body parts, unless that muscle or muscle group is injured.

Do not skip around in the sequence of body parts to be tensed and relaxed.

Lie supine on a comfortable mat or carpeted floor, take a few deep breaths in through your nose and out through your mouth. You may now proceed with a normal, relaxed breathing pattern throughout the rest of the exercise.

Close your eyes and prepare for a total body relaxation experience.

Relaxation

Curl your toes so your feet and calves are tense. Focus on the feeling of tension. Relax your feet and calves, quickly letting go of the tension. Concentrate on the difference between the feelings of tension and relaxation. Curl your toes and tense the calves and feet once again, this time slightly tighter. Now relax, and feel the difference.

Point your feet back toward your face this time. Study the tension. Relax and focus on the muscles of your lower legs and feet. Relax the tension in the lower legs and feet and concentrate on the difference between the feelings of relaxation and tension. Try to relax your entire body.

Push both heels against the ground. Hold them and feel the tension in the back of your hips and thighs. Relax, and feel the tension slowly diminish until you feel no more tension at all. Focus on the relaxed feeling in your calves, thighs, and hips. Feel the heaviness in your legs as you relax further. Take a nice, deep breath, in through your nose and out through you mouth.

Now tense the buttocks by raising the hips ever so slightly off the floor. Hold the tensed position for a few seconds. Relax, again focusing on the difference in the feelings. Repeat the tensing of the buttocks, and add the tensing of as many leg muscles as possible. Relax all muscles of the lower body, feeling the tension moving out of your limbs and noticing how heavy the lower body has become.

Next, suck in your stomach and tense the abdominal muscles. Remember to continue a relaxed breathing pattern. Relax the abdominal muscles. Repeat the tensing and relaxing of the abdominal muscles, concentrating on the feeling that results from the relaxation.

Take a moment to relax the entire body, breathing in through your nose and out through your mouth. Take a few of these deep, relaxing breaths. Feel the warmth of the body as it moves tension away. Feel the heaviness that comes with relaxed muscles.

Now inhale deeply, and study the resulting tension in your chest. Exhale, letting your chest collapse naturally and freely. Now continue to breathe normally and feel the relaxation grow every time you exhale. Inhale deeply once again, feeling the tightness in the chest. Exhale and relax, allowing the relaxed feeling to spread through the chest to the muscles of your back as you breathe normally.

Place your arms at your sides and tightly clench your fists. Relax. Clench your fists again, trying to keep your entire body relaxed except for your fists. Make sure you are not tensing any other body part, like the shoulders, back, or toes, or clenching your teeth. Now relax the fists, again focusing on the feeling of relaxation.

Now tense the shoulders by shrugging them upward, as high as possible. Drop your shoulders to their normal position, and feel the relaxation. Shrug the shoulders again, moving them forward and back a bit. Focus on the tensed feeling. Now relax them and concentrate on the contrast between the tensed and relaxed feelings. Allow the relaxation to move into your back and down your arms. Settle into a comfortable position and feel the relaxation taking over your entire body.

Now tend to the muscles in your neck and face. Tighten the neck muscles, clench your jaw, and scowl the muscles of the face. Relax all of those muscles. Tighten each of those muscle groups again, concentrating on the tense feeling. Relax and concentrate on the feelings in the neck, face, and jaw. Take a deep breath, in through the nose and exhale slowly out the mouth. Concentrate on the relaxed feeling of the muscles of the entire body.

The final step is to tense as many of the muscles of the entire body as possible. Tense the entire body at one time. Relax all of the muscles of the body at once, and concentrate on the total body relaxation. Repeat the total body tension and relaxation, enjoying the feeling of an entirely relaxed body. Feel the tension dissipate and the relaxation taking over. Feel the warmness, the deepest level of relaxation yet. Your desire to move should be minimal, as you enjoy the relief from all muscle tension.

Now open your eyes, and gradually adjust to your surroundings. Resist the urge to move, and if any tension creeps back into your body, allow yourself to relax it away. When you wish to get up, count backward from ten. Sit up slowly, then stand up slowly. You should feel calm, relaxed, and refreshed.

11

HIV/AIDS and Sexually Transmitted Diseases

Key Terms

human immunodeficiency
    virus (HIV)
acquired immunodeficiency
    syndrome (AIDS)
trichomoniasis
gonorrhea
syphilis

antiviral drug
chlamydia
herpes simplex virus
abstinence
monogamy
human papilloma virus

Specific Objectives

1. Identify the incidence of STDs including AIDS.

2. Describe the symptoms, complications, and treatments for sexually transmitted diseases.

3. Define human immunodeficiency virus (HIV) and acquired immunodeficiency syndrome (AIDS) and explain how it is transmitted.

4. Explain the progressive stages of AIDS.

5. Identify basic guidelines to reduce your risk for AIDS and other sexually transmitted diseases.

THE GROWING PROBLEM OF SEXUALLY TRANSMITTED DISEASES

Sexually transmitted diseases (STDs) constitute a rapidly growing public health problem in the United States, and while they strike Americans of all ages, they are especially problematic for teens and young adults. There are an estimated 19 million new STD infections in the U.S. every year, and about half of them occur in the 15 to 24 age group. More than half of all people will have a sexually transmitted disease at some point in their lifetime (Koutsky, 1997). Teenagers are especially vulnerable to contracting sexually transmitted diseases, with one in four teens contracting an STD each year (Alan Guttmacher Institute, 1994). The physical and psychological toll of these diseases is not the only way they impact our society. It is estimated that $13 billion dollars are spent every year on the direct medical costs of sexually transmitted diseases (Centers for Disease Control, 2005).

Even with these high numbers of diagnosed cases in teenagers and adults, many cases of notifiable STDs go undiagnosed and are not reported at all due to social stigmas attached to individuals with STDs (Eng and Butler, 1997). Because of the social stigma and lack of reporting, STDs are an ongoing major problem with serious economic and health consequences.

There are over 25 infectious organisms that can be transmitted sexually and most are caused by viruses or bacteria. Some are more prevalent and problematic than others. The annual report of the Centers for Disease Control (CDC) focuses on the notifiable STDs—chlamydia, gonorrhea, and syphilis—but it is important to note that many STDs go undiagnosed and many STDs are not reported at all, so highly accurate figures of their prevalence are difficult to determine. Other prominent STDs include trichomoniasis, herpes, the human papilloma virus which causes genital warts, and the human immunodeficiency virus which is discussed in detail in this chapter.

SIGNS, COMPLICATIONS, AND TREATMENT OF STDS

While each specific disease has its own symptoms, primary methods of transmission, complications, and consequences, there are some general warning signs of which every sexually active person should be aware. In males, the general warning signs include a discharge from the penis, sores on or around the penis or anus, and burning during urination. For females, common symptoms include unusual vaginal discharge, intense itching, sores on or around the vagina or anus, and abdominal cramps not associated with the menstrual cycle. It is important to note that many cases of STDs are asymptomatic, that is, they are present but do not produce noticeable symptoms. Therefore, it is important that all sexually active individuals monitor their sexual health status through regular medical exams.

In addition to the presence of the infection itself, STDs can cause serious health complications. In females, pelvic inflammatory disease (PID—an infection of the uterus, fallopian tubes, and other reproductive organs) and cervicitis (inflammation of the cervix) are potential complications, and in men, urethritis (inflammation of the urethra) and prostitis (inflammation of the prostate) may cause problems. Fertility and reproductive system problems are common in both sexes. Other complications include an increased risk of cervical and penile cancer brought on by HPV infection, and even death, most notably from HIV infection. A list of the common methods of transmission, symptoms, and treatment approaches to the major STDs is found in Table 11.1.

TABLE 11.1

Common Sexually Transmitted Diseases: Mode of Transmission, Symptoms and Treatment

STD	Transmission	Symptoms	Treatment
Acquired Immunodeficiency Syndrome (AIDS)	Primarily blood and semen through sexual contact or needle sharing	Vary based on cancer or opportunistic infection; common symptoms include fevers, night sweats, weight loss, chronic fatigue, swollen lymph nodes, diarrhea and/or bloody stools, atypical bruising or bleeding, skin rashes, headache, chronic cough, and a whitish coating on the tongue or throat	Early treatment with a combination of three or more antiretrovirial drugs plus other specific treatment(s). Specific treatment of opportunistic infections.
Trichomoniasis	Commonly through genital sexual contact; protozoan parasite *Trichomonas vaginalis*	White, yellow or greenish vaginal discharge; itching and irritation of vagina and vulva	Metronidazole (Flagyl) for men and women.
Chlamydia	Primarily through sexual contact but also from fingers from one body site to another; bacterium *Chlamydia trachomatis*	If caused by PID (pelvic inflammatory disease) in women, can cause disrupted menstrual periods, high temperature, pelvic pain, headache, nausea, vomiting, infertility and ectopic pregnancy. In men, infection of the urethra can cause discharge and burning sensation during urination.	Doxycycline, azithromycin, ofloxacin, levofloxacin.
Gonorrhea	Genital, oral-genital, or anal genital contact; bacterium *Neisseria gonorrheae*	In women, often no symptoms but may cause some green or yellowish discharge. In men, typically a cloudy discharge from penis and burning sensation during urination. If untreated, can cause inflammation of scrotal skin and swelling at base of the testicle.	Dual therapy of a single dose of ceftriaxone, cefixime, ciprofloxacin, ofloxacin or levofloxacin for seven days; single dose of azithromycin.
Herpes Simplex	Genital herpes virus (HSV-2) seems to be transmitted primarily by vaginal, anal or oral-genital intercourse; oral herpes virus (HSV-1) transmitted primarily through kissing	Small, painful red bumps (papules) in genital area (HSV-2) or mouth (HSV-1). Papules become blisters that rupture and become wet, open sores.	No known cure. Drugs that reduce symptoms include acyclovir, famciclovir or valacyclovir.
Syphilis	Transmitted from open lesions during genital, oral-genital or genital-anal contact; bacterium *Treponema pallidum*	Primary stage: painless chancre appears at site where spirochetes enter body. Secondary stage: chancre disappears followed by a generalized skin rash. Latent stage: possibly no visible symptoms. Tertiary stage: heart failure, blindness, mental disturbance and other symptoms. Death may result.	

Sources: Robert L. Crooks and Karla Baur. *Our Sexuality*, 8th edition, Pacific Grove, CA: Wadsworth, 2002; Karl Miller, et al. "Update on Prevention and Treatment of Sexually Transmitted Diseases." *American Family Physician*, Vol. 67, No. 9, May 1, 2003, p. 1915.

STDs can cause specific problems associated with pregnancy. The STD can be passed from the mother to the baby during pregnancy. Some potential complications include low birth weight, eye infections, neurological damage, blindness, deafness, and even stillbirth.

Viral STDs cannot be cured, so medical approaches focus on the treatment and management of disease symptoms. Bacterial STDs are usually curable through the administration of antibiotics. As with any disease, early diagnosis and treatment increase the chance of cure and lower the chance for serious complications. Ongoing medical exams are a must for anyone diagnosed with an STD.

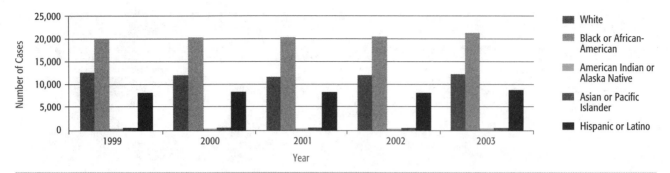

Figure 11.1 ⊙ *New AIDS cases in the United States from 2002 to 2004.*

Source: Centers for Disease Control and Prevention.

AIDS/HIV

It is important to note that all STDs are serious infections, and the prevention and treatment of all STDs is critically important to good health. However, one sexually transmitted disease has attracted amplified attention—the human immunodeficiency virus (HIV). HIV is the virus that causes acquired immunodeficiency syndrome (AIDS). This infection remains a problem worldwide even though the advent of new drug therapies have resulted in a drop in its mortality rate since 1995 (Centers for Disease Control and Prevention, 2005).

It is currently estimated that just over 40 million people worldwide are living with HIV/AIDS. Each year, however, there are an estimated 4.9 million new infections and 3.1 million deaths due to AIDS (UNAIDS/WHO, 2005). In the United States, over one million people are estimated to be living with HIV/AIDS, and approximately one-fourth of them are unaware that they are infected. Through 2004, the AIDS death total in the United States was 529,113. Worldwide, more than 25 million people have died of AIDS since 1981. Most individuals infected with HIV will likely die of AIDS within 10 years of initial infection. The sharpest increase in number of new AIDS cases (Figure 11.1) and largest percentage of cases (Figure 11.2) in the United States are in the Black or African-American population.

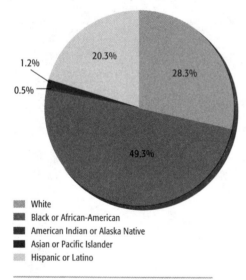

Figure 11.2 ⊙ *AIDS percent distribution by race.*

Source: Centers for Disease Control and Prevention.

HIV Progression

HIV progression is a disease process that could take over 15 years to damage the body's immune response. This damaging process makes an individual more susceptible to infections or illnesses. HIV disables the body's normal ability to destroy foreign entities such as viruses or other pathogens when they enter the body. HIV destroys CD4 T cells, monocytes and macrophages. These are vital to the body's ability to defend itself. HIV does this by entering a human cell and converting its own genetic material, RNA, into DNA. After inserting the DNA into the chromosome of the host cell, it takes over the CD4 cell and disables it. This is how HIV replicates itself and eventually destroys the CD4 cells. As the CD4 cells decline individuals begin to experience mild to moderate symptoms. A person is diagnosed with AIDS once the CD4 count drops below 200/µl. Once this stage is reached individuals are vulnerable to nu-

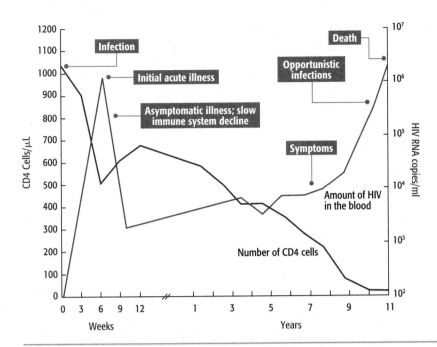

During the initial acute illness, CD4 levels fall sharply and HIV RNA levels increase; more than 50% of infected people experience flulike symptoms during this period. Antibodies to HIV usually appear 2–12 weeks after the initial infection. During the asymptomatic phase that follows, CD4 levels gradually decline, and HIV RNA levels again increase. Due to declines in immunity, infected individuals eventually begin to experience symptoms; when CD4 levels drop very low, people become vulnerable to serious opportunistic infections characteristic of full-blown AIDS. Chronic or recurrent illnesses continue until the immune system fails and death results.

Figure 11.3 ⊙ *General pattern of untreated HIV infection. The blue line represents the number of CD4 cells in the blood, a marker for the status of immune system. The gray line shows the amount of HIV RNA in the blood.*

Source: Adapted from Fauci, A. S., et al. 1996. Immunopathogenic mechanisms of HIV infection. *Annals of Internal Medicine* 124: 654–663. Reprinted with permission of the publisher.

merous opportunistic infections. Figure 11.3 illustrates the general progressive pattern of untreated HIV infection.

Treatments for HIV/AIDS

There is no known cure for HIV/AIDS. There have been significant medical advances which can significantly reduce the progress of the disease. The advent of these new drug therapies has significantly dropped the number of AIDS deaths since 1995. The four types of antiviral drugs include

⊙ Nucleoside/Nucleotide reverse transcriptase inhibitors,

⊙ Non-Nucleoside reverse transcriptase inhibitors,

⊙ Protease inhibitors, and

⊙ Fusion or Entry inhibitors.

Nucleoside/Nucleotide reverse transcriptase inhibitors make sure the DNA copy is faulty when the reverse transcriptase enzyme is used to make a DNA copy of the virus RNA (genetic material). This prevents further HIV replication. Non-Nucleoside reverse transcriptase inhibitors inhibit the action of the enzyme reverse transcriptase. Zidovudine (AZT) is a widely used reverse transcriptase inhibitor. Protease inhibitors inhibit protease, a digestive enzyme that breaks down proteins. Protease inhibitors prevent the production of mature, infectious virus particles. Highly active antiretroviral therapy, or HAART is an example of a Protease inhibitor using a combination of drugs. HAART treatment can reduce the HIV level in the blood to an undetectable level. Fusion or entry inhibitors act against HIV before it enters the cell by interfering with the proteins that allow HIV to attach itself to the cell's surface and then fuse its envelope with the cell's membrane.

HIV/AIDS and Sexually Transmitted Diseases

PREVENTION OF STDS AND AIDS

Prevention is the key to avoiding STDs and/or AIDS. Unfortunately, fewer than one in five people worldwide has access to HIV prevention services and it is estimated that 2.9 million of the 4.9 million new infections could be prevented through comprehensive prevention programs (UNAIDS, 2005). In the U.S., programs designed for the prevention of the spread of HIV and other STDs are plentiful, but many individuals, specifically young adults, do not heed the warnings presented by the programs. Key elements in comprehensive HIV prevention include:

⊙ AIDS education and awareness.

⊙ Behavior change programs especially for young people and populations at higher risk of HIV exposure, as well as for people living with HIV.

⊙ Promoting male and female condoms as a protective option along with abstinence, fidelity and reducing the number of sexual partners.

⊙ Voluntary counseling and testing.

⊙ Preventing and treating sexually transmitted diseases.

⊙ Primary prevention among pregnant women and prevention of mother-to-child transmission.

⊙ Harm reduction programs for injecting drug users.

⊙ Measures to protect blood supply safety.

⊙ Infection control in health-care settings.

⊙ Community education and changes in laws and policies to counter stigma and discrimination.

⊙ Vulnerability reduction through social legal and economic change.

Abstinence and Mutual Monogamy

There are two ways to eliminate your risk for contracting a sexually transmitted disease. One of those is to choose sexual abstinence—the avoidance of any form of sexual activity. This includes abstaining from genital, oral and anal sexual activity. The second is to engage in a mutually monogamous relationship with someone who does not have an STD. This means that sexual activity is confined to one and only one partner, and it must be a partner who also has no other sexual contacts. Monogamy is an excellent way to reduce the risk of STDs if both partners remain monogamous at all times. However, the security and protection afforded by monogamy is compromised if one partner chooses to have sexual contact outside of the relationship.

Some individuals choose to participate in some form of sexual activity and should be aware that as sexual activity increases, so does the risk of infection. Other forms of prevention, while not as effective as abstinence and mutual monogamy with an uninfected partner, can reduce the risk of contracting an STD. Laboratory 1 provides an opportunity to assess a person's risk of contracting a sexually transmitted disease.

Condoms

Latex and polyurethane condoms are another way to reduce the risk of transmitting an STD. Pores in latex condoms are small enough to prevent the transmission of most STDs. Latex condoms can be very effective if handled and stored correctly.

Latex condoms, when used consistently and correctly, are highly effective in preventing transmission of HIV. In addition, correct and consistent use of latex condoms can reduce the risk of other sexually transmitted diseases, including discharge and genital ulcer diseases (CDC's National Prevention Information Network). Some individuals are allergic to latex condoms and use polyurethane condoms. Polyurethane condoms are thinner than latex condoms and less elastic. Female condoms are also effective in reducing the risk for STDs even though male condoms are preferred.

Avoiding Drugs

Alcohol and drug abuse contributes to the spread of AIDS and STDs because these substances tend to impair reasoning and lowers one's inhibitions. Under the influence of drugs and alcohol, individuals are more likely to engage in risky sexual behavior and neglect using a condom or other protective measure. In addition, the shared use of needles to administer drugs intravenously is a common avenue for the spread of HIV and other diseases.

References

Alan Guttmacher Institute. (1994). *Sex and America's Teenagers.* New York: Alan Guttmacher Institute.

Crooks, R.L., & Baur, K. (2002). *Our Sexuality, 8th edition,* Pacific Grove, CA: Wadsworth.

Eng, T., & Butler, W., eds. (1997). *The hidden epidemic: Confronting sexually transmitted diseases.* Washington, D.C.: National Academy Press.

Koutsky, L. (1997). Epidemiology of genital human papillomavirus infection. *American Journal of Medicine, 102(5A).*

Miller, K. (2003). Update on prevention and treatment of sexually transmitted diseases. *American Family Physician, 67 (9).*

United Nations/World Health Organization. (2005). AIDS epidemic update: December 2005—Special section on HIV prevention. www.unaids.org/epi/2005/doc/EPIupdate2005_htm._en/epi05_00_en.htm

United States Department of Health and Human Services—Centers for Disease Control and Prevention. (2005). Basic Statistics. www.cdc.gov/hiv/topics/surveillance/basic.htm

United States Department of Health and Human Services—Centers for Disease Control and Prevention. (2005). Trends in reportable sexually transmitted diseases in the United States, 2004.

Weinstock, H., Berman, S., & Cates, W. (2000). Sexually transmitted diseases among American youth: incidence and prevalence estimates, 2000. *Perspectives on Sexual and Reproductive Health* 36(1).

chapter 11
LABORATORY (1)

Are You at Risk for Sexually Transmitted Diseases (STDs)?

Check all that apply:

_____ 1. I have had vaginal, anal, or oral sex. (If no, skip to #10)

_____ 2. I have had vaginal, anal, or oral sex without a barrier (condom, dental dam, female condom, etc.)

_____ 3. I have been in a sexual relationship where either I or my partner was not monogamous.

_____ 4. I have been in a sexual relationship with someone who had previous sex partners.

_____ 5. I have had a condom break or slip off during sexual intercourse.

_____ 6. I have had a sexually transmitted disease.

_____ 7. I have had sex while under the influence of drugs (alcohol, marijuana, other drugs).

_____ 8. I have had sex in exchange for drugs or money.

_____ 9. I have had sex (anal, vaginal, or oral) with someone whose sexual history was unknown to me.

_____ 10. I have injected recreational drugs or steroids.

_____ 11. I have received a tattoo, piercing, or scarification and I am not sure if new needles, ink wells, equipment were used.

*If you marked "yes" to any of the above statements, you may have been at risk for contracting HIV and other STDs. It is strongly recommended that you be tested for the presence of sexually transmitted diseases.

© 2006 JUPITER IMAGES CORPORATION.

12 Your Personal Program

Key Terms

wellness

fitness

specificity

overload

progression

reversibility

individuality

exercise prescription

longevity

safety

exercise adherence

Specific Objectives

1. Summarize the components of wellness and the components of physical fitness.

2. Understand the benefits of being a willing participant in lifetime wellness and fitness activities.

3. Explain lifestyle factors important for improving health and longevity.

4. Identify the various principles of training and conditioning.

5. Recognize the roles of warm-up and cool-down for an activity program.

6. Review the components of physical fitness.

7. Describe the characteristics of a safe and effective exercise prescription.

8. Understand how motivational techniques can assist in compliance with an activity program.

9. List safety precautions that will aid in successful initiation and maintenance of an activity program.

COMPONENTS OF WELLNESS

Recall from Chapter 1 that the overall goal of wellness is not just physical fitness, but the fulfillment of several dimensions of our lives. Wellness includes five distinct components (Figure 12.1). Social health addresses the development and maintenance of personal relationships, establishing a network of family and friends, and having feelings of comfort in social settings. The foundation of strong emotional health depends on stress management and the appropriate expression of our feelings. Although it is very normal to experience some highs and lows, the avoidance of drastic swings in emotions is important to mental health. Spiritual health means different things to different people. Regardless of religious feelings or beliefs, spiritual health is a function of personal values. Having a true sense of purpose and direction in life, understanding human nature, maintaining sensitivity and respect for others, and having appreciation for the beauty of life are all a part of sound spiritual health. Intellectual health addresses the mind and a perpetual love of learning. Reading, interacting with others, and attending lectures, are all excellent methods to maintain intellectual health. Physical health involves taking good care of the body and its systems to ensure that they remain disease free and capable of functioning at a high level of efficiency. As we have suggested throughout this text, physical health contributes significantly to total health and well-being. Physical health has perhaps the most widespread impact on overall health and can be accomplished in so many different ways. Improved quality of life and a longer life are the common end results, making it difficult to dispute the positives of physical activity.

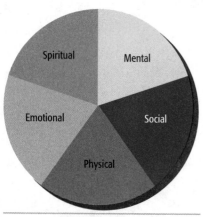

Figure 12.1 ⊙ *Components of wellness.*

HEALTH BENEFITS OF PHYSICAL ACTIVITY

The 20th century brought about tremendous strides in the understanding of health and wellness, not only through advances in the medical field, but in a more thorough understanding of how our lifestyles impact our health status. A review of the last 100 years also reveals how lifestyles have changed and how those changes have affected overall health. Certainly, the physical demands of daily life have lessened as our occupations now rely far more on automation than physical effort in the majority of professions in our country. However, just because we no longer have a need for physical activity in most occupational settings does not mean that we do not need to remain physically active to maintain our health. Risks to our society have turned from infectious diseases (polio, rubella, tuberculosis, influenza, etc.) to chronic diseases (hypertension, heart disease, stroke, cancer, emphysema, etc.). This transition took the better part of the century and only in the last few decades have we begun to recognize the relationship between physical activity and causes of death.

Being healthy and physically fit is a personal choice. It has been suggested that about two-thirds of all deaths in the United States are a result of chronic disease and 80 percent of those deaths could be prevented via lifestyle changes. In most cases, we have the ability to choose a healthy or an unhealthy diet, to be active or inactive, and to take or avoid certain risks. All of our daily choices impact our health. In 1996 the United States Surgeon General's Office released a landmark report—the first ever Surgeon General's Report on Physical Activity and Health (Appendix A). Emphasized in that report is the fact that moderate physical activity provides significant benefits to health. Among the benefits are risk reductions in diabetes, hypertension, heart disease, stroke and colon cancer. Along with reduced risk for most chronic diseases comes positive increases in bone density, reduced symptoms of depression and anxiety, and a delay of the aging process through maintenance of metabolically active muscle tissue.

FACTORS IMPORTANT FOR HEALTH AND LONGEVITY

Physical activity by itself cannot guarantee good health—other factors undoubtedly play a role in overall health. However, numerous research studies have consistently shown that higher levels of physical activity are associated with decreased risks of coronary heart disease, cerebrovascular disease, hypertension, osteoporosis, Type 2 diabetes mellitus, colon cancer, and possibly breast cancer. Research data indicate that physical activity is effective in postponing mortality and enhancing longevity (Lee, Paffenbarger, and Hennekens, 1997). In cooperation with the President's Council on Physical Fitness and Sports, the American College of Sports Medicine and the United States Centers for Disease Control and Prevention prepared a summary statement concerning physical activity and public health (Appendix A). Encouraging everyone to accumulate 30 minutes or more of moderate physical activity every day parallels the Surgeon General's Report which indicates that a minimum caloric expenditure of 1,000 weight-adjusted calories per week reduces the risk of most chronic diseases and premature death. Table 12.1 reflects the value of some fitness activities and ranges of caloric expenditures.

Naturally, other risk factors such as heredity, blood lipid profile, obesity, smoking, and excess alcohol consumption play a role in the odds for chronic disease or premature death, but no single factor has been shown to influence health more than physical activity.

TABLE 12.1
Fitness Ranking

Activity	Cardiorespiratory Endurance	Upper Body Strength	Lower Body Strength	Flexibility	Calories Burned/min
Aerobic Dance	High	Moderate	Moderate	Moderate	5–10
Basketball	Moderate	Moderate	Moderate	Moderate	5–10
Bowling	None	Low	Low	Low	2–4
Canoeing	Low	Moderate	Low	Moderate	4–10
Cycling	High	Low	High	Moderate	5–15
Golf (walking)	Low	Low	Moderate	Moderate	2–4
Jogging	High	Moderate	High	Moderate	5–15
Karate	Moderate	High	High	High	5–10
Racquet sports	Moderate	Moderate	Moderate	Moderate	5–10
Running	Very High	Moderate	Moderate	Moderate	10–15
Skating (Ice)	Moderate	Low	Moderate	Moderate	5–10
Skating (In-line)	High	Low	High	Moderate	5–15
Skiing (Alpine)	Moderate	Moderate	High	Moderate	5–10
Skiing (Nordic)	Very High	High	High	Moderate	5–15
Soccer	High	Moderate	Moderate	Moderate	5–15
Volleyball	Moderate	Moderate	Moderate	Moderate	5–10
Walking	Moderate	Low	Moderate	Low	3–4
Waterskiing	Low	Moderate	Moderate	Moderate	4–8
Weight Lifting	Low	Very High	Very High	Moderate	4–6

PRINCIPLES OF TRAINING AND CONDITIONING

Each person must take charge of planning and implementing a fitness program which best suits their personal goals. Certain principles must be understood in order to engage in the most appropriate program. At the top of anyone's list of training principles should be the overload principle. Overload refers to the intensity needed to stimulate a physiological change in the body. Whatever system we want to change for the better must be mildly stressed, or overloaded, in order for that system to be stimulated to adapt. The key is to provide an overload great enough to cause change without injury. Over time the body will adapt to the overload and a new level of intensity must be selected to cause further change. This is where the second principle, known as progression, comes in.

Progression is the principle of making gradual increments in improving each component of fitness. It is closely linked to overload, in that if no overload exists, no progression takes place. However, the principle of progression suggests that there is an optimal level of overload that is desirable. The progression must be stressful enough to place an extra demand on the system being trained, but should not be so great that it is counterproductive. Too great of a progression can lead to fatigue, injury, and muscle damage. This concept applies to aerobic activity, strength training and flexibility. For people interested in maintaining good health, progression in fitness levels becomes less important. At this point the principle of reversibility becomes the issue.

The principle of reversibility is summed up in the phrase "use it or lose it." Fitness gains do not last forever if not properly maintained. Regular and consistent exercise is the key to maintaining the benefits gained through exercise. This may be the most difficult principle for non-athletes to subscribe to in their effort to reach exercise adherence. For athletes, consistent overload and progression are commonplace. If they want to play or be competitive, they must be dedicated to practice. But many individuals claim they do not have time to be active. Once physical activity patterns are abandoned, fitness levels will begin to decline. Instead of making exercise a single task to be completed, make it an ongoing part of your lifestyle.

Specificity refers to the type of physiological change that occurs as a result of the overload an activity places on the body. To obtain optimal adaptations, one must stress the specific system. To improve flexibility of the shoulders, for example, specific stretches for the muscles crossing the shoulder joint are in order. To increase arm strength, one must complete resistance training for the arm muscles. To improve aerobic capacity, a person must engage in activities that increase breathing, heart rate, and oxygen demands at the muscle level. Muscular strength, muscular endurance, and flexibility are each considered site specific, because you must exercise the specific location (muscle or muscle group) for the intended benefit. Cardiovascular endurance and body composition are not site specific. Any aerobic activity will develop the heart and lungs, and any effective calorie burning exercise will assist in weight control.

The principle of individuality is supported by the fact that people differ in their responses to various forms of overload training. What might be an appropriate routine for one person would be excessive for another. Two individuals on identical training programs will not necessarily respond with identical advances. Both will increase fitness, but one may be able to reach a higher level of fitness that the other. This holds true for all levels of fitness. Even elite athletes cannot train alike. Therefore, guidelines for activity must always be modified to suit individual needs.

COMPONENTS OF PHYSICAL FITNESS AND AN EXERCISE PRESCRIPTION

While evidence clearly shows a strong relationship between physical fitness and wellness, experts sometimes disagree on the value and application of that relationship. To some, physical fitness is simply the ability to do daily tasks without undue fatigue. On the other end of the spectrum, some view physical fitness as the realization of maximum physical potential. Therefore, the mode and intensity of exercise should also be considered when developing your exercise prescription to reach your goal. Regardless of a person's desired application, a total fitness program should address each of the five components of fitness—body composition, muscular strength, muscular endurance, flexibility and cardiovascular endurance. From a health perspective, it is easy to identify the two most important components—cardiovascular fitness and body composition. This is because those two components offer significant disease protection, possibly helping to avoid premature death and disability. The three remaining components are very important as they protect us from injury, but not from early onset of chronic diseases. Each component may be addressed individually or in combination with the others. Whatever the method, one's program should touch on each area of fitness to be most effective.

First and foremost, the mode of exercise should incorporate some aerobic activity. This means getting sustained heart rates (HR) of 70–90 percent of maximum for 20+ minutes. For most young adults that means an exercise heart rate of at least 140 beats per minute while exercising with the large muscles of the body, usually the legs.

Intensity for aerobic activity is often an issue and it can vary according to goals. Research has shown that intensity as low as 50 percent maximum HR can have beneficial effects on sedentary individuals. As a person achieves greater levels of aerobic fitness, intensity must increase to provide adequate overload.

Duration of activity may also vary, but it is dependent on intensity and time availability. If intensity is low (<60 percent maximum HR), duration should be at least 30 minutes. If intensity is high (>75 percent maximum HR), duration can be as short as 20 minutes.

The recommendation for frequency of activity is three to five times per week. Figure 12.2 reflects the potential benefits versus risk of injury for increased fre-

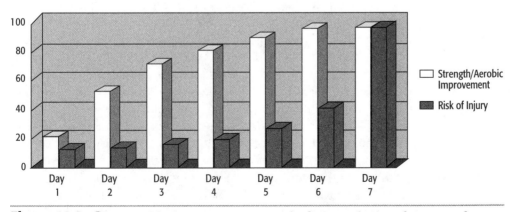

Figure 12.2 ⊙ *Potential improvements versus risk of injury relative to frequency of activity.*

quency of exercise. The greatest gains are realized by simply becoming active. Improvements in strength or aerobic fitness then diminish after five days in comparison to the increased risk of injury.

SAFETY PRECAUTIONS

Warm-up and Cool-down

In addition to applying the basic principles of exercise and considering the mode and intensity of the exercise prescription, it is critically important to take several safety issues into consideration. In an effort to reduce risk of injury, several things can be done. Warm-up should always be a precursor to activity. Warm-up serves several purposes. Although warm-up implies an increase in body temperature, its real role is to prepare the body for greater intensity activities by shunting blood to skeletal muscle and increasing range of motion of major joints. Completing 5–15 minutes of light aerobic activity to elevate the cardiorespiratory system's ability to provide energy to muscle can reduce injury, prevent delayed soreness and enhance performance in the desired activity.

After a workout, the cool-down time is very important. Cool-down activities help keep blood circulating so metabolic waste can be removed from the muscles. Continuing to move after vigorous exercise (called active recovery) hastens the body's ability to return to a pre-exercise state. Mild exercise such as a combination of walking and stretching is a common cool-down routine.

Regarding stretching, you may recall that flexibility is best improved by altering the non-elastic constituents of connective tissue, so when the muscles are warm and slightly fatigued, their elastic properties are less likely to inhibit the stretch. Therefore, if time is a constraint and you cannot stretch before and after exercise, then stretching after is best.

The adage "no pain, no gain" is inappropriate in most cases concerning involvement in physical activity. Pain is a sign that something is wrong and the source of the pain must be addressed. It is not uncommon to be sore one to two days after doing an activity for the first time. However, that soreness should diminish with continued activity. A rule to live by is "train, don't strain." It is always best to stop an activity while you still have good feelings as opposed to feelings of fatigue. After exercising you should feel slightly tired but invigorated, not drained and full of pain.

Preparing for weather conditions is also essential. Environmental conditions should always be checked before starting to exercise. Temperature, humidity, and altitude are important factors to consider. Being warm blooded, we need to keep our body temperature near 37°C (98.6°F). Increased metabolic activity from exercise generates heat. That heat is normally dispersed via the sweating response. Heat stress can occur with prolonged exposure to extreme heat and can cause cramps, heat exhaustion or heatstroke. Heat exhaustion is a result of a loss of fluid and the remedy is to ingest large quantities of cool water. Since thirst lags behind actual water needs, it is a good idea to drink water before, during, and after exercise sessions. Some experts recommend 1 pint of water just before exercising, 1 cup every 15 minutes during exercise, and another pint after exercise. Heatstroke is much more serious and can be life-threatening. The cause of heatstroke is unknown, but what is known is that heatstroke is brought about by a failure in the sweat response. Without being able to sweat to eliminate heat, body temperature can rise very rapidly. Rather than attempting to replace fluids, the treatment for heatstroke is to cool the body rapidly.

To prevent heat related problems, one should acclimate to environmental conditions. This acclimation can occur in four to seven days of gradual and continued activity combined with proper fluid intake. Another good idea for monitoring fluid loss is to record body weight before and after exercise. For every pound of body weight lost, one should consume 16 ounces of water.

Exercising in the cold presents a totally different set of conditions. Rather than heat loss, the conservation of heat becomes the issue. Hypothermia can occur with as little as a two-degree drop in body temperature. People shiver in an attempt to regain body temperature; however, as body temperature drops, shivering stops, resulting in unconsciousness. As much as 50 percent of body heat is lost through the head, hands, and feet. To conserve this heat loss, wear a hat, gloves, warm socks, and dry footwear. Dressing in layers and avoiding cotton clothing are also recommended. When wet, cotton clothing actually draws heat away from the body. Acclimating to cold is similar to heat; four to seven days of progressive activity are encouraged. In extreme cold conditions, wearing a scarf or face mask is essential.

If air temperature is too cold, the body cannot heat the air sufficiently as it enters the lungs. This can cause difficulty in breathing and a decrement in performance. Finally, it is important to check body weight before and after activity just like exercising in the heat. Because people do not feel like they have lost much fluid, they do not think about re-hydrating. In cold conditions a substantial fluid loss occurs through respiration. Combine that with sweat loss and people are at risk for dehydration even in the cold.

Women bring yet other issues to the task of exercising safely: menstruation and pregnancy. Recent medical research has confirmed that exercise has no harmful effects on menstruation. In fact, exercise may lessen the mood swings associated with hormonal fluctuations during the premenstrual period. Painful menses (dysmenorrhea) may also be reduced to some degree by moderate-intensity activity. Percent body fat less than 12 percent can cause amenorrhea (no menses). This can be a result of excessive exercise and/or restricted caloric intake. The bottom line is that moderate exercise poses no risk to women. Pregnancy is the only condition that needs special attention for women. Guidelines for exercise during pregnancy are found in Table 12.2. The key to exercising during pregnancy is to reach a moderate level of fitness prior to becoming pregnant.

MOTIVATIONAL TECHNIQUES

Regardless of the activity a person chooses to engage in, the basic principles of training and conditioning apply. First and foremost, activities should be fun. Activi-

Safe Exercise Tips for Expectant Mothers	TABLE 12.2

1. Consult your physician.
2. Do not exercise to fatigue.
3. Avoid activities that bounce, twist and jar the body.
4. Avoid high risk activities that might challenge balance.
5. Do not complete exercises while lying on your back.
6. Avoid exercise in hot, humid environments.
7. Avoid intensities that exceed 70 percent maximal heart rate.
8. Avoid starting exercise in the 1st or 3rd trimester.
9. Drink plenty of fluids before, during, and after exercise.

ties must deliver a level of enjoyment for them to be continued. Allow your exercise time to also be a social time, enjoying various activities with family and friends. Enjoyment provides the best motivation for a lifetime of activity. Box 12.1 provides a few suggestions for making physical activity a fun thing to do.

Once activity becomes a part of your lifestyle, it will be hard for you to imagine life without it. But prior to that time, you must consider activity a priority. This will help you continue a good habit. We hope that this book has encouraged you to develop or continue an active lifestyle. It's great to be fit, and the exhilarating feeling that physical activity generates can be addictive.

© 2006 JUPITER IMAGES CORPORATION.

© 2006 JUPITER IMAGES CORPORATION.

PLANNING YOUR FITNESS PROGRAM

Now that you have evaluated your overall health status through the various laboratory assessments in this textbook, it is time to create a health/fitness plan. Your plan should start with goals, followed by strategies for maintaining and/or improving your status in each health/fitness parameter. Your next step is to complete parts one and two of the Personal Program Lab and Worksheet located at the end of this chapter.

References

American College of Sports Medicine. (1993). Position stand on physical activity, physical fitness, and hypertension. *Medicine and Science in Sport and Exercise*, 10:i–x.

Arnheim, D.D., & Prentice, W.E. (1993). *Principles of Athletic Training* (8th ed.) St. Louis: Mosby-Year Book, Inc.

Blair, S., Kohl, H., Paffenbarger, R., et al. (1989). Physical fitness and all causes of mortality: A prospective study of healthy men and women. *Journal of Medical Association*, 262:2395–2401.

Centers for Disease Control and Prevention. (2004). *Leading causes of death, 1900–1998*. www.cdc.gov/nchs/statab/lead1900_1998.pdf

Centers for Disease Control and Prevention. (1996). *Physical Activity and Health: A Report of the Surgeon General*. Washington, D.C.: U.S. Government Printing Office.

Lee, I.M., Paffenbarger, R.S., & Hennekens, C.H. (1997). Physical activity, physical fitness and longevity. *Aging*, 9(1–2): 2–11.

McArdle, W.D., Katch, F.I., & Katch, V.L. (2001). *Exercise physiology: Energy, nutrition, and human performance, 5th edition*. Baltimore: Lippincott, Williams & Wilkins.

National Center for Health Statistics. (2005*). Health, United States, 2005*. Hyattsville, MD: U.S. Government Printing Office.

Neimann, D.C. Centers for Disease Control and Prevention. (2005). *The burden of chronic diseases as causes of death, United States: National and state perspectives, 2004*. www.cdc.gov/nccdphhhhp/burdenbook2004/Section01/tables

Nieman, D.C. (2003). *Exercise testing and prescription: A health-related approach*. 5th edition. New York: McGraw-Hill.

Safran, M.R. (1988). The role of warm-up in muscular injury prevention. *American Journal of Sports Medicine*, 16:123.

United States Centers for Disease Control and Prevention and the American College of Sports Medicine. (1993). Summary statement: Workshop on physical activity and public health. *Sports Medicine Bulletin*, 28:7.

U.S. Department of Health and Human Services. (2000). *Healthy People 2010: Understanding and Improving Health*. 2nd ed. Washington, D.C.: U.S. Government Printing Office, November 2000.

Wolf, L., Amey, M., & McGrath, M. *Exercise in pregnancy*. In J. Torg & R. Shepard, editors. Current therapy in sports medicine. (1995). St. Louis: Mosby-Year Book, Inc.

chapter 12
LABORATORY 1

Personal Program Lab and Worksheet

Part I—Your Lab Assessments

Health/Fitness Parameter	Lab Score	Satisfied? (Y/N)
Cardiorespiratory Endurance		
Body Composition		
Flexibility		
Muscular Strength and Endurance		
Nutrition		
Cardiovascular Disease Risk		
Smoking		
Cancer Risk		
Diabetes Risk		
Stress Inventory		

Part II—Plan of Action

For each of the health/fitness parameters, briefly describe how you plan to maintain and/or change your current status.

Cardiorespiratory Endurance _____

_____

_____

Body Composition _____

_____

_____

Flexibility _____

_____

_____

Muscular Strength and Endurance _____

_____

_____

Nutrition _____

_____

_____

Cardiovascular Disease Risk _____

_____

_____

Smoking _____

_____

_____

Cancer Risk _____

_____

_____

Diabetes Risk _____

_____

_____

Stress Inventory _____

_____

_____

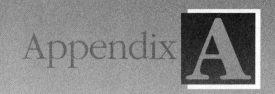
The Surgeon General's Report on Physical Activity and Health, 1996

A NEW VIEW OF PHYSICAL ACTIVITY

This report brings together, for the first time, what has been learned about physical activity and health from decades of research. Among its major findings:

⊙ People who are usually inactive can improve their health and well-being by becoming even moderately active on a regular basis.

⊙ Physical activity need not be strenuous to achieve health benefits.

⊙ Greater health benefits can be achieved by increasing the amount (duration, frequency, or intensity) of physical activity.

THE BENEFITS OF REGULAR PHYSICAL ACTIVITY

Regular physical activity that is performed on most days of the week reduces the risk of developing or dying from some of the leading causes of illness and death in the United States. Regular physical activity improves health in the following ways:

⊙ Reduces the risk of dying prematurely.

⊙ Reduces the risk of dying from heart disease.

⊙ Reduces the risk of developing diabetes.

⊙ Reduces the risk of developing high blood pressure.

⊙ Helps reduce blood pressure in people who already have high blood pressure.

⊙ Reduces the risk of developing colon cancer.

⊙ Reduces feelings of depression and anxiety.

⊙ Helps control weight.

⊙ Helps build and maintain healthy bones, muscles, and joints.

⊙ Helps older adults become stronger and better able to move about without falling.

⊙ Promotes psychological well-being.

U.S. Department of Health and Human Services
Centers for Disease Control and Prevention
National Center for Chronic Disease Prevention and Health Promotion
The President's Council on Physical Fitness and Sports

A MAJOR PUBLIC HEALTH CONCERN

Given the numerous health benefits of physical activity, the hazards of being inactive are clear. Physical inactivity is a serious, nationwide problem. Its scope poses a public health challenge for reducing the national burden of unnecessary illness and premature death.

STATUS OF THE NATION—A NEED FOR CHANGE

Adults

⊙ More than 60 percent of adults do not achieve the recommended amount of regular physical activity. In fact, 25 percent of all adults are not active at all.

⊙ Inactivity increases with age and is more common among women than men and among those with lower income and less education than among those with higher income or education.

Adolescents and Young Adults

⊙ Nearly half of young people aged 12–21 are not vigorously active on a regular basis.

⊙ Physical activity declines dramatically with age during adolescence.

⊙ Female adolescents are much less physically active than male adolescents.

High School Students

⊙ In high school, enrollment in daily physical education classes dropped from 42 percent in 1991 to 25 percent in 1995.

⊙ Only 19 percent of all high school students are physically active for 20 minutes or more in physical education classes every day during the school week.

IDEAS FOR IMPROVEMENT

This report identifies promising ways to help people include more physical activity in their daily lives.

⊙ Well-designed programs in schools to increase physical activity in physical education classes have been shown to be effective.

⊙ Carefully planned counseling by health care providers and worksite activity programs can increase individuals' physical activity levels.

⊙ Promising approaches being tried in some communities around the nation include opening school buildings and shopping malls for walking before or after regular hours, as well as building bicycle and walking paths separated from automobile traffic. Revising building codes to require accessible stairwells is another idea that has been suggested.

WHAT IS A MODERATE AMOUNT OF PHYSICAL ACTIVITY?

As the examples listed in the box show, a moderate amount of physical activity* can be achieved in a variety of ways. People can select activities that they enjoy and that fit into their daily lives. Because amount of activity is a function of dura-

Appendix A: Physical Activity and Health

tion, intensity, and frequency, the same amount of activity can be obtained in longer sessions of moderately intense activities (such as brisk walking) as in shorter sessions of more strenuous activities (such as running):†

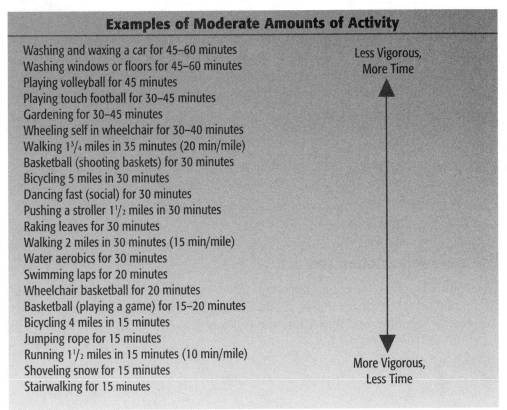

Examples of Moderate Amounts of Activity

Washing and waxing a car for 45–60 minutes
Washing windows or floors for 45–60 minutes
Playing volleyball for 45 minutes
Playing touch football for 30–45 minutes
Gardening for 30–45 minutes
Wheeling self in wheelchair for 30–40 minutes
Walking 1³/₄ miles in 35 minutes (20 min/mile)
Basketball (shooting baskets) for 30 minutes
Bicycling 5 miles in 30 minutes
Dancing fast (social) for 30 minutes
Pushing a stroller 1¹/₂ miles in 30 minutes
Raking leaves for 30 minutes
Walking 2 miles in 30 minutes (15 min/mile)
Water aerobics for 30 minutes
Swimming laps for 20 minutes
Wheelchair basketball for 20 minutes
Basketball (playing a game) for 15–20 minutes
Bicycling 4 miles in 15 minutes
Jumping rope for 15 minutes
Running 1¹/₂ miles in 15 minutes (10 min/mile)
Shoveling snow for 15 minutes
Stairwalking for 15 minutes

Less Vigorous,
More Time

More Vigorous,
Less Time

*A moderate amount of physical activity is roughly equivalent to physical activity that uses approximately 150 Calories (kcal) of energy per day, or 1,000 Calories per week.
†Some activities can be performed at various intensities; the suggested durations correspond to expected intensity of effort.

PRECAUTIONS FOR A HEALTHY START

To avoid soreness and injury, individuals contemplating an increase in physical activity should start out slowly and gradually build up to the desired amount to give the body time to adjust. People with chronic health problems, such as heart disease, diabetes, or obesity, or who are at high risk for these problems should first consult a physician before beginning a new program of physical activity. Also, men over age 40 and women over age 50 who plan to begin a new *vigorous* physical activity program should consult a physician first to be sure they do not have heart disease or other health problems.

SPECIAL MESSAGES FOR SPECIAL POPULATIONS

Older Adults. No one is too old to enjoy the benefits of regular physical activity. Of special interest to older adults is evidence that muscle-strengthening exercises can reduce the risk of falling and fracturing bones and can improve the ability to live independently.

Parents. Parents can help their children maintain a physically active lifestyle by providing encouragement and opportunities for physical activity. Family events can include opportunities for everyone in the family to be active.

Teenagers. Regular physical activity improves strength, builds lean muscle, and decreases body fat. It can build stronger bones to last a lifetime.

Dieters. Regular physical activity burns Calories and preserves lean muscle mass. It is a key component of any weight loss effort and is important for controlling weight.

People with High Blood Pressure. Regular physical activity helps lower blood pressure.

People Feeling Anxious, Depressed, or Moody. Regular physical activity improves mood, helps relieve depression, and increases feelings of well-being.

People with Arthritis. Regular physical activity can help control joint swelling and pain. Physical activity of the type and amount recommended for health has not been shown to cause arthritis.

People with Disabilities. Regular physical activity can help people with chronic, disabling conditions improve their stamina and muscle strength and can improve psychological well-being and quality of life by increasing the ability to perform activities of daily life.

For more information contact:

Centers for Disease Control and Prevention
National Center for Chronic Disease Prevention and Health Promotion
Division of Nutrition and Physical Activity, MS K-46
4770 Buford Highway, NE
Atlanta, Georgia 30341
1-888-CDC-4NRG or 1-888-232-4674 (Toll Free)
http://www.cdc.gov

The President's Council on Physical Fitness and Sports
Box SG
Suite 250
701 Pennsylvania Avenue, NW
Washington, DC

PAR-Q (A Questionnaire for People Aged 15 to 69)

YES	NO	
____	____	1. Has your doctor ever said that you have a heart condition *and* that you should only do physical activity recommended by a doctor?
____	____	2. Do you feel pain in your chest when you do physical activity?
____	____	3. In the past month, have you had chest pain when you were not doing physical activity?
____	____	4. Do you lose your balance because of dizziness or do you ever lose consciousness?
____	____	5. Do you have a bone or joint problem that could be made worse by a change in your physical activity?
____	____	6. Is your doctor currently prescribing drugs (for example, water pills) for your blood pressure or heart condition?
____	____	7. Do you know of any other reason why you should not do physical activity?

If you answered:

YES to one or more questions:

Talk with your doctor by phone or in person BEFORE you start becoming much more physically active or BEFORE you have a fitness appraisal. Tell your doctor about the PAR-Q and which questions you answered YES.

⊙ You may be able to do any activity you want—as long as you start slow and build up gradually. Or, you may need to restrict your activities to those which are safe for you. Talk with your doctor about the kinds of activities you wish to participate in and follow his/her advice.

⊙ Find out which community programs are safe and helpful for you.

Referenced from *ACSM's Guidelines for Exercise Testing and Prescription, Fifth Edition.*

NO to all questions:

If you answered NO honestly to all PAR-Q questions, you can be reasonably sure that you can:

- start becoming much more physically active—begin slowly and build up gradually. This is the safest and easiest way to go.
- take part in a fitness appraisal—this is an excellent way to determine your basic fitness so that you can plan the best way for you to live actively.

DELAY BECOMING MUCH MORE ACTIVE:

- if you are not feeling well because of temporary illness such as a cold or a fever—wait until you feel better; or
- if you are or may be pregnant—talk to your doctor before you start becoming active.

I have read, understood and completed this questionnaire. Any questions I had were answered to my full satisfaction.

_____ _____

Signature   Date

Nutrition Information for Selected Fast Foods

Baskin-Robbins® Ice Cream (serving size = ½ cup)									
	Calories	Carbo-hydrate (gm)	Protein (gm)	Total Fat (gm)	Saturated Fat (gm)	Choles-terol (mg)	Sodium (mg)	Dietary Fiber (gm)	Total Carb Exchange	Suggested Exchange Value
Banana Strawberry	130	17	2	7	5	25	40	0	1	1 other carb. 1 fat
Baseball Nut	160	16	2	9	5	30	55	0	1	1 other carb. 2 fat
Black Walnut	160	13	3	11	5	30	45	1	1	1 other carb. 2 fat
Cherries Jubilee	140	16	2	7	5	30	40	0	1	1 other carb. 1 fat
Chocolate	150	16	2	9	6	30	60	0	1	1 other carb. 2 fat
Chocolate Almond	180	17	3	11	5	30	55	1	1	1 other carb. 2 fat
Chocolate Chip	150	15	2	10	6	35	45	0	1	1 other carb. 2 fat
Chocolate Chip Cookie Dough	170	20	2	9	6	35	70	0	1	1 other carb. 2 fat
Chocolate Raspberry Truffle	180	23	3	9	6	30	60	0	1½	1½ other carb. 2 fat
Cookies 'N Cream	170	16	2	11	7	30	80	0	1	1 other carb. 2 fat
French Vanilla	160	14	2	10	6	70	45	0	1	1 other carb. 2 fat
Fudge Brownie	170	19	3	11	6	25	75	1	1	1 other carb. 2 fat
German Chocolate Cake	160	20	3	10	6	25	75	0	1	1 other carb. 2 fat
Jamoca	140	14	2	9	5	35	45	0	1	1 other carb. 2 fat
Jamoca Almond Fudge	160	17	3	9	5	25	40	0	1	1 other carb. 2 fat
Mint Chocolate Chip	150	15	3	10	6	35	45	0	1	1 other carb. 2 fat
Old-Fashioned Butter Pecan	160	13	2	11	6	35	50	0	1	1 other carb. 2 fat

From *Nutrition in the Fast Lane*, Franklin Publishing, Inc.

	Calories	Carbo-hydrate (gm)	Protein (gm)	Total Fat (gm)	Saturated Fat (gm)	Choles-terol (mg)	Sodium (mg)	Dietary Fiber (gm)	Total Carb Exchange	Suggested Exchange Value
Oregon Blackberry	140	16	2	8	5	30	50	0	1	1 other carb. 2 fat
Peanut Butter 'N Chocolate	180	16	3	12	6	30	95	1	1	1 other carb. 2 fat
Pistachio Almond	170	13	3	12	5	30	45	1	1	1 other carb. 2 fat
Prailines 'N Cream	160	19	2	9	5	30	85	0	1	1 other carb. 2 fat
Quarterback Crunch	160	18	2	10	7	30	75	0	1	1 other carb. 2 fat
Reeses® Peanut Butter Cup	160	17	3	11	6	30	70	0	1	1 other carb. 2 fat
Rocky Road	170	19	3	10	5	30	60	0	1	1 other carb. 2 fat
Vanilla	140	14	3	8	5	40	40	0	1	1 other carb. 2 fat
Very Berry Strawberry	130	16	1	7	4	25	40	0	1	1 other carb. 2 fat
Winter White Chocolate	150	16	2	9	6	25	50	0	1	1 other carb. 2 fat
Low Fat Ice Cream										
Caramel Apple ala Mode	100	20	3	2	1	5	75	0	1	1 other carb.
Devine Cherry Cheesecake	110	20	3	3	2	5	70	0	1	1 other carb. 1 fat
Espresso 'N Cream	100	18	3	3	1	5	60	1	1	1 other carb. 1 fat
Non-Fat Ice Cream										
Berry Innocent Cheesecake	110	24	3	0	0	0	100	0	1½	1½ other carb.
Check-It-Out Cherry	100	22	3	0	0	0	90	0	1½	1½ other carb.
Chocolate Vanilla Twist	100	21	4	0	0	5	100	0	1	1 other carb.
Jamoca Swirl	110	23	3	0	0	5	105	0	1½	1½ other carb.
Non-Fat Frozen Yogurt										
Chocolate	100	23	4	0	0	0	60	1	1½	1½ other carb.
Vanilla	80	16	4	0	0	5	80	1	1	1 other carb.
Other Assorted Flavors	100	22	3	0	0	0	55	0	1½	1½ other carb.
Truly Free™ Frozen Yogurt (Fat Free/Reduced Sugar)										
Chocolate	80	15	5	0	0	0	80	1	1	1 other carb.
Vanilla	90	18	4	0	0	5	80	1	1	1 other carb.
Other Assorted Flavors	90	17	4	0	0	5	80	1	1	1 other carb.
Ices										
Assorted Flavors	110	28	0	0	0	0	10	0	2	2 other carb.
Sherbet										
Assorted Flavors	120	26	1	2	1	5	25	0	2	2 other carb.
Sorbet										
Mixed Berry Lemonade	110	28	0	0	0	0	10	0	2	2 other carb.
Pink Raspberry Lemonade	120	29	0	0	0	0	10	0	2	2 other carb.
Red Rasberry	120	30	0	0	0	0	10	0	2	2 other carb.

Appendix C: Nutrition Information for Selected Fast Foods

Wendy's®

	Calories	Carbo-hydrate (gm)	Protein (gm)	Total Fat (gm)	Saturated Fat (gm)	Choles-terol (mg)	Sodium (mg)	Dietary Fiber (gm)	Total Carb Exchange	Suggested Exchange Value
Sandwiches (serving size = 1)										
Plain Single	360	31	24	16	6	65	580	2	2	2 starch 3 med. fat meat
Single w/Everything	420	37	25	20	7	70	920	3	2	2 starch 3 med. fat meat 1 fat
Big Bacon Classic	580	46	34	30	12	100	1460	3	3	3 starch 4 med. fat meat 2 fat
Jr. Hamburger	270	34	15	10	4	30	610	2	2	2 starch 1 med. fat meat 1 fat
Jr. Cheeseburger	320	34	17	13	6	45	830	2	2	2 starch 2 med. fat meat
Jr. Bacon Cheeseburger	380	34	20	19	7	60	850	2	2	2 starch 2 med. fat meat 2 fat
Jr. Cheeseburger Deluxe	360	36	18	17	6	50	890	3	2	2 starch 2 med. fat meat 1 fat
Hamburger (Kid's Meal)	270	33	15	10	4	30	610	2	2	2 starch 1 med. fat meat 1 fat
Cheeseburger (Kid's Meal)	320	33	17	13	6	45	830	2	2	2 starch 2 med. fat meat
Grilled Chicken Sandwich	310	35	27	8	2	65	790	2	2	2 starch 3 very lean meat 1 fat
Breaded Chicken Sandwich	440	44	28	18	4	60	840	2	3	3 starch 3 med. fat meat 1 fat
Chicken Club Sandwich	470	44	31	20	4	70	970	2	3	3 starch 3 med. fat meat 1 fat
Spicy Chicken Sandwich	410	43	28	15	3	65	1280	2	3	3 starch 3 med. fat meat
Baked Potatoes										
Plain Serving: 1	310	71	7	0	0	0	25	7	5	5 starch
Bacon & Cheese Serving: 1	530	78	17	18	4	20	1390	7	5	5 starch 1 high fat meat 2 fat
Broccoli & Cheese Serving: 1	470	80	9	14	3	5	470	9	5	5 starch 1 vegetable 3 fat
Cheese Serving: 1	570	78	14	23	8	30	640	7	5	5 starch 1 high fat meat 3 fat
Chili & Cheese Serving: 1	630	83	20	24	9	40	770	9	5½	5½ starch 1 med. fat meat 4 fat
Sour Cream & Chives Serving: 1	380	74	8	6	4	15	40	8	5	5 starch 1 fat
Sour Cream Serving: 1 oz. pkt.	60	1	1	6	4	10	15	0	0	1 fat

Appendix C: Nutrition Information for Selected Fast Foods

Wendy's® (continued)

	Calories	Carbo-hydrate (gm)	Protein (gm)	Total Fat (gm)	Saturated Fat (gm)	Choles-terol (mg)	Sodium (mg)	Dietary Fiber (gm)	Total Carb Exchange	Suggested Exchange Value
Baked Potatoes (continued)										
Whipped Margarine Serving: ½ oz. pkt.	60	0	0	7	2	0	115	0	0	1 fat
French Fries/Chili/Nuggets										
French Fries Serving: small	270	35	4	13	2	0	85	3	2	2 starch 3 fat
Biggie Fries Serving: 1 order	470	61	7	23	4	0	150	6	4	4 starch 5 fat
Great Biggie Fries Serving: 1 order	570	73	8	27	4	0	180	7	5	5 starch 5 fat
Chicken Nuggets Serving: 5-piece	230	11	11	16	3	30	470	0	1	1 starch 1 med. fat meat 2 fat
Chicken Nugget's Child's Portion Serving: 4-piece	190	9	9	13	3	25	380	0	½	½ starch 1 med. fat meat 2 fat
Barbecue Sauce Serving: 1 oz. pkt.	45	10	1	0	0	0	160	0	½	½ other carb.
Honey Mustard Serving: 1 oz. pkt.	130	6	0	12	2	10	220	0	½	½ other carb. 2 fat
Sweet & Sour Sauce Serving: 1 oz. pkt.	50	12	0	0	0	0	120	0	1	1 other carb.
Small Chili Serving: 8 oz.	210	21	15	7	3	30	800	5	1½	1½ starch 2 med. fat meat
Large Chili Serving: 12 oz.	310	32	23	10	4	45	1190	7	2	2 starch 2 med. fat meat
Cheddar Cheese Serving: 2 tbsp.	70	1	4	6	4	15	110	0	0	1 high fat meat

KFC®

	Calories	Carbo-hydrate (gm)	Protein (gm)	Total Fat (gm)	Saturated Fat (gm)	Choles-terol (mg)	Sodium (mg)	Dietary Fiber (gm)	Total Carb Exchange	Suggested Exchange Value
Tender Roast® Chicken (serving size = 1)										
Breast w/skin	251	1	37	11	3	151	830	0	0	5 lean meat
Breast w/o skin	169	1	31	4	1	112	797	0	0	4 very lean meat
Leg w/skin	97	<1	15	4	1	85	271	0	0	2 med. fat meat
Leg w/o skin	67	<1	11	2	<1	63	259	0	0	2 very lean meat
Thigh w/skin	207	2	18	12	4	120	504	0	0	3 med. fat meat
Thigh w/o skin	106	<1	13	6	2	84	312	0	0	2 lean meat
Wing w/skin	121	1	12	8	2	74	331	0	0	2 med. fat meat
Original Recipe® Chicken (serving size = 1)										
Breast	400	16	29	24	6	135	1116	1	1	1 starch 4 med. fat meat 1 fat
Leg	140	4	13	9	2	75	422	0	0	2 med. fat meat
Thigh	250	6	16	18	5	95	747	1	½	½ starch 2 med. fat meat 2 fat
Whole Wing	140	5	9	10	3	55	414	0	0	1 med. fat meat 1 fat

Appendix C: Nutrition Information for Selected Fast Foods

	Calories	Carbo-hydrate (gm)	Protein (gm)	Total Fat (gm)	Saturated Fat (gm)	Choles-terol (mg)	Sodium (mg)	Dietary Fiber (gm)	Total Carb Exchange	Suggested Exchange Value
Extra Crispy™ Chicken (serving size = 1)										
Breast	470	25	31	28	7	80	930	1	1½	1½ starch 4 med. fat meat 2 fat
Leg	190	8	13	11	3	60	260	<1	½	½ starch 2 med. fat meat
Thigh	370	18	19	25	6	70	540	2	1	1 starch 2 med. fat meat 3 fat
Whole Wing	200	10	10	13	4	45	290	<1	½	½ starch 1 med. fat meat 2 fat
Hot & Spicy Chicken (serving size = 1)										
Breast	530	23	32	35	8	110	1110	2	1½	1½ starch 4 med. fat meat 3 fat
Leg	190	10	13	11	3	50	300	<1	½	½ starch 2 med. fat meat
Thigh	370	13	18	27	7	90	570	1	1	1 starch 2 med. fat meat 3 fat
Whole Wing	210	9	10	15	4	50	340	<1	½	½ starch 1 med. fat meat 2 fat
Other Entrees										
Crispy Strips® Serving: 3-piece	261	10	20	16	4	40	658	3	½	½ starch 3 med. fat meat
Spicy Buffalo Crispy Strips™ Serving: 3-piece	350	22	22	19	4	35	1110	2	1½	1½ starch 3 med. fat meat 1 fat
Chunky Chicken Pot Pie Serving: 1	770	69	29	42	13	70	2160	5	4½	4½ starch 2 med. fat meat 6 fat
Hot Wings™ Serving: 6-piece	471	18	27	33	8	150	1230	2	1	1 starch 3 med. fat meat 4 fat
Original Recipe® Chicken Sandwich Serving: 1	497	46	29	22	5	52	1213	3	3	3 starch 3 med. fat meat 1 fat
Value BBQ Flavored Chicken Sandwich Serving: 1	256	28	17	8	1	57	782	2	2	2 starch 2 med. fat meat
Kentucky Nuggets® Serving: 6-piece	284	15	16	18	4	66	865	<1	1	1 starch 2 med. fat meat 2 fat
Side Choices (serving size = 1)										
BBQ Baked Beans	190	33	6	3	1	5	760	6	2	2 starch 1 fat
Biscuit	180	20	4	10	3	0	560	<1	1	1 starch 2 fat
Cole Slaw	180	21	2	9	2	5	280	3	1	1 other carb. 1 vegetable 2 fat

KFC® (continued)

	Calories	Carbo-hydrate (gm)	Protein (gm)	Total Fat (gm)	Saturated Fat (gm)	Choles-terol (mg)	Sodium (mg)	Dietary Fiber (gm)	Total Carb Exchange	Suggested Exchange Value
Side Choices (serving size = 1) (continued)										
Corn on the Cob	150	35	5	2	0	0	20	2	2	2 starch
Cornbread	228	25	3	13	2	42	194	1	1¹/₂	1¹/₂ starch 3 fat
Green Beans	45	7	1	2	<1	5	730	3	0	1 vegetable
Macaroni & Cheese	180	21	7	8	3	10	860	2	1¹/₂	1¹/₂ starch 2 fat
Mean Greens™	70	11	4	3	1	10	650	5	0	2 vegetable 1 fat
Potato Salad	230	23	4	14	2	15	540	3	1¹/₂	1¹/₂ starch 3 fat
Potatoes w/Gravy	120	17	1	6	1	<1	440	2	1	1 starch 1 fat
Potato Wedges	280	28	5	13	4	5	750	5	2	2 starch 3 fat

McDonald's®

	Calories	Carbo-hydrate (gm)	Protein (gm)	Total Fat (gm)	Saturated Fat (gm)	Choles-terol (mg)	Sodium (mg)	Dietary Fiber (gm)	Total Carb Exchange	Suggested Exchange Value
Sandwiches (serving size = 1)										
Hamburger	260	34	13	9	4	30	580	2	2	2 starch 1 med. fat meat 1 fat
Cheeseburger	320	35	15	13	6	40	820	2	2	2 starch 1 med. fat meat 2 fat
Quarter Pounder®	420	37	23	21	8	70	820	2	2¹/₂	2¹/₂ starch 2 med. fat meat 2 fat
Quarter Pounder® w/Cheese	530	38	28	30	13	95	1290	2	2¹/₂	2¹/₂ starch 3 med. fat meat 3 fat
Big Mac®	560	45	26	31	10	85	1070	3	3	3 starch 2 med. fat meat 4 fat
Arch Deluxe®	550	39	28	31	11	90	1010	4	2¹/₂	2¹/₂ starch 3 med. fat meat 3 fat
Arch Deluxe® w/Bacon	590	39	32	34	12	100	1150	4	2¹/₂	2¹/₂ starch 4 med. fat meat 3 fat
Crispy Chicken Deluxe™	500	43	26	25	4	55	1100	4	3	3 starch 2 med. fat meat 3 fat
Fish Filet Deluxe™	560	54	23	28	6	60	1060	4	3¹/₂	3¹/₂ starch 2 med. fat meat 4 fat
Filet-O-Fish®	450	42	16	25	5	50	870	2	3	3 starch 1 med. fat meat 4 fat
Grilled Chicken Deluxe™	440	38	27	20	3	60	1040	4	2¹/₂	2¹/₂ starch 3 lean meat 3 fat

Appendix C: Nutrition Information for Selected Fast Foods

	Calories	Carbo-hydrate (gm)	Protein (gm)	Total Fat (gm)	Saturated Fat (gm)	Choles-terol (mg)	Sodium (mg)	Dietary Fiber (gm)	Total Carb Exchange	Suggested Exchange Value
Sandwiches (serving size = 1) (continued)										
Grilled Chicken Deluxe™ w/o mayonnaise	300	38	27	5	1	50	930	4	2½	2½ starch 3 lean meat
French Fries										
French Fries Serving: small	210	26	3	10	2	0	135	2	2	2 starch 2 fat
French Fries Serving: large	450	57	6	22	4	0	290	5	4	4 starch 4 fat
French Fries Serving: super size®	540	68	8	26	5	0	350	6	4½	4½ starch 5 fat
Chicken McNuggets®/Sauces										
Chicken McNuggets® Serving: 4-piece	190	10	12	11	3	40	340	0	½	½ starch 2 med. fat meat
Chicken McNuggets® Serving: 6-piece	290	15	18	17	4	60	510	0	1	1 starch 2 med. fat meat 1 fat
Chicken McNuggets® Serving: 9-piece	430	23	27	26	5	90	770	0	1½	1½ starch 3 med. fat meat 2 fat
Hot Mustard Sauce Serving: 1 oz. pkt.	60	7	1	4	0	5	240	<1	½	½ other carb. 1 fat
Barbeque Sauce Serving: 1 oz. pkt.	45	10	0	0	0	0	250	0	½	½ other carb.
Sweet 'N Sour Sauce Serving: 1 oz. pkt.	50	11	0	0	0	0	140	0	1	1 other carb.
Honey Serving: 1 oz. pkt.	45	12	0	0	0	0	0	0	1	1 other carb.
Honey Mustard Serving: 1 oz. pkt.	50	3	0	5	<1	10	85	0	0	1 fat
Light Mayonnaise	40	1	0	4	<1	5	85	0	0	1 fat
Salads/Salad Dressings										
Garden Salad+ Serving: 1	35	7	2	0	0	0	20	3	0	1 vegetable
Grilled Chicken Salad Deluxe+ Serving: 1	120	7	21	2	0	45	240	3	0	1 vegetable 3 very lean meat
Ceasar Serving: 2 oz. pkt.	160	7	2	14	3	20	450	0	½	½ other carb. 3 fat
Red French (Red. Cal.) Serving: 2 oz. pkt.	160	23	0	8	1	0	490	0	1½	1½ other carb. 2 fat
Ranch Serving: 2 oz. pkt.	230	10	1	21	3	20	550	0	½	½ other carb. 4 fat
Herb Vinaigrette Serving: 2 oz. pkt.	50	11	0	0	0	0	330	0	1	1 other carb.
Breakfast (serving size = 1)										
English Muffin	140	25	4	2	0	0	210	1	2	2 starch
Egg McMuffin®	290	27	17	12	5	235	790	1	2	2 starch 2 med. fat meat
Sausage McMuffin®	360	26	13	23	8	45	740	1	2	2 starch 1 high fat meat 3 fat

	Calories	Carbo-hydrate (gm)	Protein (gm)	Total Fat (gm)	Saturated Fat (gm)	Choles-terol (mg)	Sodium (mg)	Dietary Fiber (gm)	Total Carb Exchange	Suggested Exchange Value
Breakfast (serving size = 1) (continued)										
Sausage McMuffin® w/Egg	440	27	19	28	10	255	890	1	2	2 starch 2 med. fat meat 4 fat
Biscuit	290	34	5	15	3	0	780	1	2	2 starch 3 fat
Sausage Biscuit	470	35	11	31	9	35	1080	1	2	2 starch 1 high fat meat 5 fat
Sausage Biscuit w/Egg	550	35	18	37	10	245	1160	1	2	2 starch 2 med. fat meat 5 fat
Bacon, Egg & Cheese Biscuit	470	36	18	28	8	235	1250	1	2	2 starch 2 med. fat meat 4 fat
Sausage	170	0	6	16	5	35	290	0	0	1 high fat meat 2 fat
Scrambled Eggs	160	1	13	11	4	425	170	0	0	2 med. fat meat
Hash Browns	130	14	1	8	2	0	330	1	1	1 starch 2 fat
Hot Cakes (plain)	340	58	9	9	2	25	540	2	4	4 starch 2 fat
Hot Cakes w/syrup & margarine	610	104	9	18	4	25	680	2	7	4 starch 3 other carb. 3 fat
Breakfast Burrito	320	23	13	20	7	195	600	2	1½	1½ starch 1 med. fat meat 3 fat
Desserts/Shakes										
Vanilla Cone Serving: 1	150	23	4	5	3	20	75	0	1½	1½ other carb. 1 fat
Strawberry Sundae Serving: 1	290	50	7	7	5	30	95	<1	3	3 other carb. 1 fat
Hot Caramel Sundae Serving: 1	360	61	7	10	6	35	180	0	4	4 other carb. 2 fat
Hot Fudge Sundae Serving: 1	340	52	8	12	9	30	170	1	3½	3½ other carb. 2 fat
Nut Topping Serving: ¼ oz.	40	2	2	4	0	0	55	<1	0	1 fat
Butterfinger® McFlurry™ Serving: 1	620	90	16	22	14	70	260	<1	6	6 other carb. 4 fat
M&M® McFlurry™ Serving: 1	630	90	16	23	15	75	210	1	6	6 other carb. 5 fat
Nestle Crunch® McFlurry™ Serving: 1	630	89	16	24	16	75	230	<1	6	6 other carb. 5 fat
Oreo® McFlurry™ Serving: 1	570	82	15	20	12	70	280	<1	5	5 other carb. 4 fat
Baked Apple Pie Serving: 1 slice	260	34	3	13	4	0	200	<1	2	2 other carb. 3 fat
Chocolate Chip Cookie Serving: 1	170	22	2	10	6	20	120	1	1½	1½ other carb. 2 fat

McDonald's® (continued)

	Calories	Carbo-hydrate (gm)	Protein (gm)	Total Fat (gm)	Saturated Fat (gm)	Choles-terol (mg)	Sodium (mg)	Dietary Fiber (gm)	Total Carb Exchange	Suggested Exchange Value
Desserts/Shakes (continued)										
McDonaldland® Cookies Serving: 1 pkg.	180	32	3	5	1	0	190	1	2	2 other carb. 1 fat
Chocolate Shake Serving: small	360	60	11	9	6	40	250	1	4	4 other carb. 2 fat
Strawberry Shake Serving: small	360	60	11	9	6	40	180	0	4	4 other carb. 2 fat
Vanilla Shake Serving: small	360	59	11	9	6	40	250	0	4	4 other carb. 2 fat

Burger King®

	Calories	Carbo-hydrate (gm)	Protein (gm)	Total Fat (gm)	Saturated Fat (gm)	Choles-terol (mg)	Sodium (mg)	Dietary Fiber (gm)	Total Carb Exchange	Suggested Exchange Value
Breakfast										
Croissan'wich® w/Sausage, Egg & Cheese Serving: 1	530	23	18	41	13	185	1120	1	1¹/₂	1¹/₂ starch 2 med. fat meat 6 fat
Croissan'wich® w/Sausage & Cheese Serving: 1	450	21	13	35	12	45	940	1	1¹/₂	1¹/₂ starch 2 high fat meat 4 fat
Biscuit Serving: 1	300	35	6	15	3	0	830	1	2	2 starch 3 fat
Biscuit w/Egg Serving: 1	380	37	11	21	5	140	1010	1	2	2 starch 1 med. fat meat 3 fat
Biscuit w/Sausage Serving: 1	490	36	13	33	10	35	1240	1	2	2 starch 1 high fat meat 5 fat
Biscuit w/Sausage, Egg & Cheese Serving: 1	620	37	20	43	14	185	1650	1	2	2 starch 2 med. fat meat 7 fat
French Toast Sticks Serving: order of 5	440	51	7	23	5	2	490	3	3	3 starch 5 fat
Cini-Minis w/o Icing Serving: order of 4	440	51	6	23	6	25	710	1	3	3 other carb. 4 fat
Vanilla Icing Serving: 1 oz. pkt.	110	20	0	3	<1	0	40	0	1	1 other carb.
Hash Brown Rounds Serving: small	240	25	2	15	6	0	440	2	1¹/₂	1¹/₂ starch 3 fat
Hash Brown Rounds Serving: large	410	42	3	26	10	0	750	4	3	3 starch 5 fat
Bacon Serving: 3-piece	40	0	3	3	1	10	170	0	0	1 fat
Ham Serving: 1 slice	35	0	6	1	0	15	770	0	0	1 lean meat
A.M. Express® Dip Serving: 1 oz. pkt.	80	21	0	0	0	0	20	0	1¹/₂	1¹/₂ other carb.
A.M. Express® Grape Jam Serving: ¹/₂ oz. pkt.	30	7	0	0	0	0	0	0	¹/₂	¹/₂ other carb.
A. M. Express® Strawberry Jam Serving: ¹/₂ oz. pkt.	30	8	0	0	0	0	0	0	¹/₂	¹/₂ other carb.
Land O'Lakes® Classic Blend Serving: ¹/₃ oz. pkt.	65	0	0	7	1	0	75	0	0	1 fat

	Calories	Carbo-hydrate (gm)	Protein (gm)	Total Fat (gm)	Saturated Fat (gm)	Choles-terol (mg)	Sodium (mg)	Dietary Fiber (gm)	Total Carb Exchange	Suggested Exchange Value
Burgers (serving size = 1)										
Whopper® Sandwich	660	47	29	40	12	85	900	3	3	3 starch 3 med. fat meat 5 fat
Whopper® w/Cheese	760	47	35	48	17	110	1380	3	3	3 starch 4 med. fat meat 5 fat
Double Whopper®	920	47	49	59	21	155	980	3	3	3 starch 6 med. fat meat 6 fat
Double Whopper® w/Cheese	1010	47	55	67	26	180	1460	3	3	3 starch 7 med. fat meat 6 fat
Whopper Jr.® Sandwich	400	28	19	24	8	55	530	2	2	2 starch 2 med. fat meat 3 fat
Whopper Jr.® w/Cheese	450	28	22	28	10	65	770	2	2	2 starch 2 med. fat meat 4 fat
Big King™ Sandwich	640	28	38	42	18	125	980	1	2	2 starch 5 med. fat meat 3 fat
Hamburger	320	27	19	15	6	50	520	1	2	2 starch 2 med. fat meat 1 fat
Cheeseburger	360	27	21	19	9	60	760	1	2	2 starch 2 med. fat meat 2 fat
Bacon Cheeseburger	400	27	24	22	10	70	940	1	2	2 starch 3 med. fat meat 1 fat
Double Cheeseburger	580	27	38	36	17	120	1060	1	2	2 starch 4 med. fat meat 3 fat
Bacon Double Cheeseburger	620	28	41	38	18	125	1230	1	2	2 starch 5 med. fat meat 3 fat
Sandwiches/Side Items										
BK Big Fish® Sandwich Serving: 1	720	59	23	43	9	80	1180	3	4	4 starch 2 med. fat meat 6 fat
BK Broiler® Chicken Sandwich Serving: 1	530	45	29	26	5	105	1060	2	3	3 starch 3 very lean meat 4 fat
Chicken Sandwich Serving: 1	710	54	26	43	9	60	1400	2	3	3 starch 2 med. fat meat 7 fat
Chick 'N Crisp Serving: 1	460	37	16	27	6	35	890	3	2¹/₂	2¹/₂ starch 1 med. fat meat 4 fat
Chicken Tenders® Serving: 4-piece	180	9	11	11	3	30	470	0	¹/₂	¹/₂ starch 1 med. fat meat 1 fat

Appendix C: Nutrition Information for Selected Fast Foods

	Calories	Carbo-hydrate (gm)	Protein (gm)	Total Fat (gm)	Saturated Fat (gm)	Choles-terol (mg)	Sodium (mg)	Dietary Fiber (gm)	Total Carb Exchange	Suggested Exchange Value
Sandwiches/Side Items (continued)										
Chicken Tenders® Serving: 5-piece	230	11	14	14	4	40	590	<1	½	½ starch 2 med. fat meat 1 fat
Chicken Tenders® Serving: 8-piece	350	17	22	22	7	65	940	1	1	1 starch 3 med. fat meat 1 fat
French Fries (salted) Serving: small	250	32	2	13	5	0	550	2	2	2 starch 3 fat
French Fries (salted) Serving: medium	400	50	3	21	8	0	820	4	3	3 starch 4 fat
French Fries (salted) Serving: king-size	590	74	5	30	12	0	1180	5	5	5 starch 6 fat
Onion Rings Serving: medium	380	46	5	19	4	2	550	4	3	3 starch 4 fat
Onion Rings Serving: king-size	600	74	8	30	7	4	880	6	5	5 starch 6 fat
Dutch Apple Pie Serving: 1	300	39	3	15	3	0	230	2	2½	2½ other carb. 3 fat
Shakes										
Chocolate Shake Serving: 14 fl. oz.	440	75	12	10	6	30	330	4	5	5 other carb. 2 fat
Chocolate Shake w/syrup added Serving: 16 fl. oz.	570	105	14	10	6	30	520	3	7	7 other carb. 2 fat
Strawberry Shake w/syrup added Serving: 16 fl. oz.	550	104	13	9	5	30	350	2	7	7 other carb. 2 fat
Vanilla Shake	430	73	13	9	5	30	330	2	5	5 other carb. 2 fat
Dipping Sauces/Condiment Sauces										
Barbecue Serving: 1 oz. pkt.	35	9	0	0	0	0	400	0	½	½ other carb.
Honey Flavored Serving: 1 oz. pkt.	90	23	0	0	0	0	10	0	1½	1½ other carb.
Honey Mustard Serving: 1 oz. pkt.	90	10	0	6	1	10	150	0	½	½ other carb. 1 fat
Ranch Serving: 1 oz. pkt.	170	2	0	17	3	0	200	0	0	3 fat
Sweet & Sour Serving: 1 oz. pkt.	45	11	0	0	0	0	50	0	1	1 other carb.
Bull's Eye® BBQ Serving: ½ oz. pkt.	20	5	0	0	0	0	140	0	0	Free
King Sauce Serving: ½ oz. pkt.	70	2	0	7	1	4	70	0	0	1 fat
Tartar Sauce Serving: 1½ oz. pkt.	260	0	0	29	4	20	330	0	0	6 fat

Pizza Hut®

	Calories	Carbo-hydrate (gm)	Protein (gm)	Total Fat (gm)	Saturated Fat (gm)	Choles-terol (mg)	Sodium (mg)	Dietary Fiber (gm)	Total Carb Exchange	Suggested Exchange Value
Stuffed Crust Pizza (Medium) (serving size = 1 of 8 slices)										
Cheese	445	46	22	19	10	24	1090	3	3	3 starch 2 med. fat meat 2 fat
Beef Topping	466	46	23	22	10	30	1137	3	3	3 starch 2 med. fat meat 2 fat
Ham	404	27	24	22	12	39	1190	2	2	2 starch 3 med. fat meat 1 fat
Pepperoni	438	45	21	19	9	27	1116	3	3	3 starch 2 med. fat meat 2 fat
Italian Sausage	478	46	22	23	10	35	1164	3	3	3 starch 2 med. fat meat 3 fat
Pork Topping	461	46	22	21	10	29	1176	3	3	3 starch 2 med. fat meat 2 fat
Meat Lover's®	543	46	26	29	13	48	1427	3	3	3 starch 2 med. fat meat 4 fat
Veggie Lover's®	421	48	20	17	8	19	1039	3	3	3 starch 1 med. fat meat 2 fat
Pepperoni Lover's®	525	46	26	26	13	40	1413	3	3	3 starch 2 med. fat meat 3 fat
Supreme	487	47	24	23	11	33	1227	3	3	3 starch 2 med. fat meat 3 fat
Super Supreme	505	46	25	25	11	44	1371	3	3	3 starch 2 med. fat meat 3 fat
Chicken Supreme	432	47	24	17	8	32	1111	3	3	3 starch 2 med. fat meat 1 fat
Thin 'N Crispy® Pizza (Medium) (serving size = 1 of 8 slices)										
Cheese	243	27	11	10	5	11	653	2	2	2 starch 1 med. fat meat 1 fat
Beef Topping	305	28	14	15	7	24	814	3	2	2 starch 1 med. fat meat 2 fat
Ham	212	27	10	7	3	15	662	2	2	2 starch 1 med. fat meat
Pepperoni	235	27	10	10	4	14	672	2	2	2 starch 1 med. fat meat 1 fat
Italian Sausage	325	28	14	18	7	32	865	3	2	2 starch 1 med. fat meat 2 fat

Appendix C: Nutrition Information for Selected Fast Foods

	Calories	Carbo-hydrate (gm)	Protein (gm)	Total Fat (gm)	Saturated Fat (gm)	Choles-terol (mg)	Sodium (mg)	Dietary Fiber (gm)	Total Carb Exchange	Suggested Exchange Value
Thin 'N Crispy® Pizza (Medium) (serving size = 1 of 8 slices) (continued)										
Pork Topping	298	28	14	15	6	23	875	3	2	2 starch 1 med. fat meat 2 fat
Meat Lover's®	339	28	15	19	8	35	970	3	2	2 starch 1 med. fat meat 3 fat
Veggie Lover's®	222	30	9	8	3	7	621	3	2	2 starch 1 med. fat meat 1 fat
Pepperoni Lover's®	289	28	13	14	6	22	859	2	2	2 starch 1 med. fat meat 2 fat
Supreme	284	29	13	13	6	20	784	3	2	2 starch 1 med. fat meat 2 fat
Super Supreme	304	29	14	15	6	26	902	3	2	2 starch 1 med. fat meat 2 fat
Chicken Supreme	232	29	13	7	3	19	681	3	2	2 starch 1 med. fat meat
Taco Pizza	260	27	12	11	5	20	860	2	2	2 starch 1 med. fat meat 1 fat
Meatless Taco Pizza	230	27	9	9	4	10	700	2	2	2 starch 1 med. fat meat 1 fat
Beef Taco Pizza	260	29	13	10	5	20	850	2	2	2 starch 1 med. fat meat 1 fat
Chicken Taco Pizza	260	26	11	12	5	20	850	2	2	2 starch 1 med. fat meat 1 fat
Pan Pizza (Medium) (serving size = 1 of 8 slices)										
Cheese	361	44	13	15	6	11	678	3	3	3 starch 1 med. fat meat 2 fat
Beef Topping	399	45	15	18	7	20	773	4	3	3 starch 1 med. fat meat 3 fat
Ham	331	44	12	12	4	15	687	3	3	3 starch 1 med. fat meat 1 fat
Pepperoni	353	44	12	14	5	14	697	3	3	3 starch 1 med. fat meat 2 fat
Italian Sausage	415	45	15	20	7	26	805	3	3	3 starch 1 med. fat meat 3 fat
Pork Topping	394	45	15	18	6	20	820	4	3	3 starch 1 med. fat meat 3 fat
Meat Lover's®	428	45	16	21	7	29	607	3	3	3 starch 1 med. fat meat 3 fat

Pizza Hut® *(continued)*

	Calories	Carbo-hydrate (gm)	Protein (gm)	Total Fat (gm)	Saturated Fat (gm)	Choles-terol (mg)	Sodium (mg)	Dietary Fiber (gm)	Total Carb Exchange	Suggested Exchange Value
Pan Pizza (Medium) (serving size = 1 of 8 slices) (continued)										
Veggie Lover's®	333	46	11	12	4	7	601	4	3	3 starch 1 med. fat meat 1 fat
Pepperoni Lover's®	370	44	13	16	5	18	767	3	3	3 starch 1 med. fat meat 2 fat
Supreme	385	45	14	17	6	18	757	4	3	3 starch 1 med. fat meat 2 fat
Super Supreme	401	46	15	18	6	22	854	4	3	3 starch 1 med. fat meat 3 fat
Chicken Supreme	343	45	15	12	4	16	671	3	3	3 starch 1 med. fat meat 1 fat
Taco Pizza	310	36	12	13	5	15	800	3	2	2 starch 1 med. fat meat 2 fat
Meatless Taco Pizza	290	36	10	12	4	10	680	3	2	2 starch 1 med. fat meat 1 fat
Beef Taco Pizza	300	36	12	12	5	15	770	3	2	2 starch 1 med. fat meat 1 fat
Chicken Taco Pizza	320	36	12	15	5	15	830	3	2	2 starch 1 med. fat meat 2 fat
Personal Pan Pizza® (serving size = 1 pizza)										
Cheese	813	110	31	27	12	24	1581	8	7	7 starch 2 med. fat meat 3 fat
Pepperoni	810	111	30	28	11	32	1661	8	7	7 starch 2 med. fat meat 3 fat
Supreme	808	111	30	27	10	28	1579	8	7	7 starch 2 med. fat meat 3 fat
Taco Pizza	780	90	27	35	10	30	1900	7	6	6 starch 2 med. fat meat 5 fat

Subway®

	Calories	Carbo-hydrate (gm)	Protein (gm)	Total Fat (gm)	Saturated Fat (gm)	Choles-terol (mg)	Sodium (mg)	Dietary Fiber (gm)	Total Carb Exchange	Suggested Exchange Value
Subs (serving size = 6-inch sub)										
Classic Italian B.M.T.® on Italian Roll	445	39	21	21	8	56	1652	3	3	3 starch 1 vegetable 2 med. fat meat 2 fat
Cold Cut Trio on Italian Roll	362	39	19	13	4	64	1401	3	3	3 starch 1 vegetable 2 med. fat meat 1 fat

	Calories	Carbo-hydrate (gm)	Protein (gm)	Total Fat (gm)	Saturated Fat (gm)	Choles-terol (mg)	Sodium (mg)	Dietary Fiber (gm)	Total Carb Exchange	Suggested Exchange Value
Subs (serving size = 6-inch sub) (continued)										
Ham on Italian Roll	287	39	18	5	1	28	1308	3	3	3 starch 1 vegetable 1 lean meat 1 fat
Pizza Sub on Italian Roll	448	41	19	22	9	50	1609	3	3	3 starch 1 vegetable 2 med. fat meat 2 fat
Meatball on Italian Roll	404	44	18	16	6	33	1035	3	3	3 starch 1 vegetable 1 med. fat meat 2 fat
Roast Beef on Italian Roll	288	39	19	5	1	20	928	3	3	3 starch 1 vegetable 2 lean meat
Roasted Chicken Breast on Italian Roll	332	41	26	6	1	48	967	3	3	3 starch 1 vegetable 3 very lean meat 1 fat
Subway Seafood & Crab® on Italian Roll w/light mayonnaise (processed seafood & crab blend)	332	39	19	10	2	32	873	3	3	3 starch 1 vegetable 2 very lean meat 2 fat
Steak & Cheese on Italian Roll	383	41	29	10	6	70	1106	3	3	3 starch 1 vegetable 3 med. fat meat
Subway Club® on Italian Roll	297	40	21	5	1	26	1341	3	3	3 starch 1 vegetable 2 lean meat
Subway Melt™ on Italian Roll	366	40	22	12	5	42	1735	3	3	3 starch 1 vegetable 2 med. fat meat
Tuna on Italian Roll w/light mayonnaise	376	39	18	15	2	32	928	3	3	3 starch 1 vegetable 1 very lean meat 3 fat
Turkey Breast on Italian Roll	273	40	17	4	1	19	1391	3	3	3 starch 1 vegetable 1 very lean meat 1 fat
Turkey Breast & Ham on Italian Roll	280	39	18	5	1	24	1350	3	2½	2½ starch 1 vegetable 1 lean meat 1 fat
Veggie Delight on Italian Roll	222	38	9	3	0	0	582	3	2½	2½ starch 1 vegetable
Salads (serving size = 1)										
Classic Italian B.M.T.® Salad+	274	11	14	20	7	56	1379	1	0	2 vegetable 2 med. fat meat 2 fat
Cold Cut Trio Salad+	191	11	13	11	3	64	1127	1	0	2 vegetable 2 med. fat meat
Ham Salad+	116	11	12	3	1	28	1034	1	0	2 vegetable 1 lean meat

Subway® (continued)

	Calories	Carbo-hydrate (gm)	Protein (gm)	Total Fat (gm)	Saturated Fat (gm)	Choles-terol (mg)	Sodium (mg)	Dietary Fiber (gm)	Total Carb Exchange	Suggested Exchange Value
Salads (serving size = 1) (continued)										
Meatball Salad+	223	16	12	14	5	33	761	2	1	1 starch 2 vegetable 1 med. fat meat 2 fat
Pizza Salad+	277	13	12	20	8	50	1336	2	0	2 vegetable 1 med. fat meat 3 fat
Roast Beef Salad+	117	11	12	3	1	20	654	1	0	2 vegetable 1 lean meat
Roasted Chicken Breast Salad+	162	13	20	4	1	48	693	1	0	2 vegetable 3 very lean meat
Steak & Cheese Salad+	212	13	22	8	5	70	832	1	0	2 vegetable 3 lean meat
Subway Melt™ Salad	195	12	16	10	4	42	1461	1	0	2 vegetable 2 med. fat meat
Subway Seafood & Crab® w/ light mayonnaise (processed seafood & crab blend)	161	11	13	8	1	32	599	2	0	2 vegetable 2 very lean meat 1 fat
Subway Club® Salad+	126	12	14	3	1	26	1067	1	0	2 vegetable 2 lean meat
Tuna Salad w/light mayonnaise	205	11	12	13	2	32	654	1	0	2 vegetable 1 very lean meat 2 fat
Turkey Breast Salad+	102	12	11	2	1	19	1117	1	0	2 vegetable 1 very lean meat
Turkey Breast & Ham Salad+	109	11	11	3	1	24	1076	1	0	2 vegetable 1 lean meat
Veggie Delight™ Salad+	51	10	2	1	0	0	308	1	0	2 vegetable
Salad Dressings (serving size = 1 tbsp.)										
French	70	5	0	6	1	0	100	0	0	1 fat
Fat Free French	18	4	0	0	0	0	98	0	0	Free
Creamy Italian	65	3	0	7	1	4	133	0	0	1 fat
Fat Free Italian	5	1	0	0	0	0	153	0	0	Free
Ranch	88	2	0	10	2	6	118	0	0	2 fat
Fat Free Ranch	15	4	0	0	0	0	178	0	0	Free
1000 Island	65	3	0	7	1	8	155	0	0	1 fat

Long John Silver's®

	Calories	Carbo-hydrate (gm)	Protein (gm)	Total Fat (gm)	Saturated Fat (gm)	Choles-terol (mg)	Sodium (mg)	Dietary Fiber (gm)	Total Carb Exchange	Suggested Exchange Value
Specialties										
Regular Battered Fish Serving: 1 piece	230	15	12	14	5	30	560	N/A	1	1 starch 1 med. fat meat 2 fat
Junior Battered Fish Serving: 1 piece	140	10	6	9	3	15	360	N/A	1	1 starch 1 med. fat meat 1 fat
Battered Chicken Plank Serving: 1 piece	130	10	7	7	3	15	380	N/A	1	1 starch 1 med. fat meat

Appendix C: Nutrition Information for Selected Fast Foods

	Calories	Carbo-hydrate (gm)	Protein (gm)	Total Fat (gm)	Saturated Fat (gm)	Choles-terol (mg)	Sodium (mg)	Dietary Fiber (gm)	Total Carb Exchange	Suggested Exchange Value
Specialties *(continued)*										
Battered Shrimp Serving: 1 piece	35	2	1	2	<1	10	75	N/A	0	1 fat
Breaded Clams Serving: 1 piece	250	26	9	14	4	35	560	N/A	2	2 starch 1 med. fat meat 2 fat
Lemon Crumb Fish Serving: 2 piece	240	10	23	12	4	55	790	N/A	1	1 starch 3 med. fat meat
Lemon Crumb Fish a-la-carte Serving: 2 piece w/ rice	480	52	27	17	5	55	1490	N/A	4	4 starch 2 med. fat meat 1 fat
Lemon Crumb Fish Add-A-Piece Serving: 1 piece w/rice	150	9	12	7	2	30	460	N/A	¹/₂	¹/₂ starch 1 med. fat meat
Meals *(serving size = 1 meal)*										
2 Junior Fish w/Fries	620	57	15	37	9	30	1380	N/A	4	4 starch 1 med. fat meat 6 fat
2 Chicken Planks w/Fries	600	57	18	33	9	35	1420	N/A	4	4 starch 1 med. fat meat 6 fat
5 Shrimp w/Fries	500	47	10	30	7	50	1030	N/A	3	3 starch 6 fat
1 Chicken Plank/ 3 Shrimp w/Fries	550	51	14	32	8	45	1230	N/A	3	3 starch 1 med. fat meat 5 fat
1 Junior Fish/1 Chicken Plank w/Fries	610	57	17	35	9	30	1400	N/A	4	4 starch 1 med. fat meat 6 fat
1 Junior Fish/1 Chicken Plank w/Fries	610	57	17	35	9	30	1400	N/A	4	4 starch 1 med. fat meat 6 fat
1 Junior Fish/3 Shrimp w/Fries	560	52	13	34	8	45	1210	N/A	3¹/₂	3¹/₂ starch 7 fat
Lemon Crumb Fish Meal	730	89	31	29	6	60	1720	N/A	6	6 starch 2 med. fat meat 4 fat
Sandwiches *(serving size = 1)*										
Ultimate Fish™	430	44	18	21	7	35	1340	N/A	3	3 starch 1 med. fat meat 3 fat
Fish Grab 'n Go	340	40	11	15	4	20	800	N/A	2¹/₂	2¹/₂ starch 1 med. fat meat 2 fat
Fish Grab 'n Go w/Cheese	390	40	14	20	9	35	1050	N/A	2¹/₂	2¹/₂ starch 1 med. fat meat 3 fat
Chicken Grab 'n Go	330	40	13	13	4	20	820	N/A	2¹/₂	2¹/₂ starch 1 med. fat meat 2 fat
Chicken Grab 'n Go w/Cheese	380	40	16	18	9	35	1070	N/A	2¹/₂	2¹/₂ starch 1 med. fat meat 3 fat

Appendix C: Nutrition Information for Selected Fast Foods

	Calories	Carbo-hydrate (gm)	Protein (gm)	Total Fat (gm)	Saturated Fat (gm)	Choles-terol (mg)	Sodium (mg)	Dietary Fiber (gm)	Total Carb Exchange	Suggested Exchange Value
Sandwiches (serving size = 1) (continued)										
Wraps	840	99	20	41	10	50	2180	N/A	6^1/$_2$	6^1/$_2$ starch 8 fat
Side Items										
Cheese Sticks Serving: 5-piece	160	12	6	9	4	10	360	N/A	1	1 starch 2 fat
Cole Slaw Serving: 4 oz.	170	23	2	7	0	0	310	N/A	1	1 other carb. 1 vegetable 1 fat
Corn Cobbette Serving: 1	80	19	3	<1	0	0	0	0	1	1 starch
Corn Cobbette (w/butter) Serving: 1	140	19	3	8	2	0	0	0	1	1 starch 2 fat
Fries Serving: regular	250	28	3	15	3	0	500	3	2	2 starch 3 fat
Fries Serving: large	420	46	5	24	4	0	830	4	3	3 starch 5 fat
Hushpuppy Serving: 1	60	0	1	3	0	0	25	0	^{1}/$_2$	1 fat
Rice Serving: 4 oz.	180	34	3	4	<1	0	560	N/A	2	2 starch 1 fat
Salads (serving size = 1)										
Ocean Chef Salad+	130	15	14	2	0	60	540	N/A	1	3 vegetable
Grilled Chicken Salad+	140	10	20	3	<1	45	260	N/A	0	2 vegetable 2 very lean meat
Garden Salad+	45	9	3	0	0	0	25	N/A	0	2 vegetable
Side Salad+	20	3	1	0	0	0	10	N/A	0	1 vegetable
Salad Dressings (serving size = 1 oz.)										
Fat-Free French	40	10	0	0	0	0	240	N/A	^{1}/$_2$	^{1}/$_2$ other carb.
Italian	90	2	0	9	2	0	290	N/A	0	2 fat
Ranch	170	1	0	18	3	10	260	N/A	0	4 fat
Fat-Free Ranch	40	9	0	0	0	0	290	N/A	^{1}/$_2$	^{1}/$_2$ other carb.
1000 Island	120	5	0	10	2	15	290	N/A	0	2 fat
Desserts (serving size = 1 slice)										
Pineapple Creme Cheesecake Pie	310	36	4	17	9	5	105	N/A	2	2 other carb. 3 fat
Chocolate Creme Pie	260	29	4	17	8	15	125	N/A	2	2 other carb. 3 fat
Double Lemon Pie	350	41	6	18	10	40	180	N/A	3	3 other carb. 4 fat
Strawberries 'n Creme Pie	260	32	4	15	8	15	130	N/A	2	2 other carb. 3 fat
Key Lime Creme Cheese Pie	310	33	4	19	11	20	140	N/A	2	2 other carb. 4 fat
Pecan Pie	390	53	3	19	4	40	250	N/A	3^1/$_2$	3^1/$_2$ other carb. 4 fat

Healthy People 2010
Selected Goals and Objectives

AREA 5—DIABETES

Goal:

Through prevention programs, reduce the disease and economic burden of diabetes, and improve the quality of life for all persons who have or are at risk for diabetes.

Objectives:

5-1. Increase the proportion of persons with diabetes who receive formal diabetes education.

5-2. Prevent diabetes.

5-3. Reduce the overall rate of diabetes that is clinically diagnosed.

5-4. Increase the proportion of adults with diabetes whose condition has been diagnosed.

5-5. Reduce the diabetes death rate.

5-6. Reduce diabetes-related deaths among persons with diabetes.

5-7. Reduce deaths from cardiovascular disease in persons with diabetes.

5-8. (Developmental) Decrease the proportion of pregnant women with gestational diabetes.

AREA 12—HEART DISEASE AND STROKE

Goal:

Improve cardiovascular health and quality of life through the prevention, detection, and treatment of risk factors; early identification and treatment of heart attacks and strokes; and prevention of recurrent cardiovascular events.

Objectives:

Heart Disease

12-1. Reduce coronary heart disease deaths.

12-2. (Developmental) Increase the proportion of adults aged 20 years and older who are aware of the early warning symptoms and signs of a heart attack and the importance of accessing rapid emergency care by calling 911.

12-4.   (Developmental) Increase the proportion of adults aged 20 years and older who call 911 and administer cardiopulmonary resuscitation (CPR) when they witness an out-of-hospital cardiac arrest.

Stroke

12-7.   Reduce stroke deaths.

12-8.   (Developmental) Increase the proportion of adults who are aware of the early warning symptoms and signs of a stroke.

Blood Pressure

12-9.   Reduce the proportion of adults with high blood pressure.

12-10. Increase the proportion of adults with high blood pressure whose blood pressure is under control.

12-11. Increase the proportion of adults with high blood pressure who are taking action (for example, losing weight, increasing physical activity, or reducing sodium intake) to help control their blood pressure.

12-12. Increase the proportion of adults who have had their blood pressure measured within the preceding 2 years and can state whether their blood pressure was normal or high.

Cholesterol

12-13. Reduce the mean total blood cholesterol levels among adults.

12-14. Reduce the proportion of adults with high total blood cholesterol levels.

12-15. Increase the proportion of adults who have had their blood cholesterol checked within the preceding 5 years.

12-16. (Developmental) Increase the proportion of persons with coronary heart disease who have their LDL-cholesterol level treated to a goal of less than or equal to 100 mg/dL.

AREA 13—HIV

Goal:

Prevent human immunodeficiency virus (HIV) infection and its related illness and death.

Objectives:

AIDS

13-1.   Reduce AIDS among adolescents and adults.

13-2.   Reduce the number of new AIDS cases among adolescent and adult men who have sex with men.

13-3.   Reduce the number of new AIDS cases among females and males who inject drugs.

13-4.   Reduce the number of new AIDS cases among adolescent and adult men who have sex with men and inject drugs.

13-5.   (Developmental) Reduce the number of cases of HIV infection among adolescents and adults.

13-6.   Increase the proportion of sexually active persons who use condoms.

13-13. Increase the proportion of HIV-infected adolescents and adults who receive testing, treatment, and prophylaxis consistent with current Public Health Service treatment guidelines.

13-14. Reduce deaths from HIV infection.

13-15. (Developmental) Extend the interval of time between an initial diagnosis of HIV infection and AIDS diagnosis in order to increase years of life of an individual infected with HIV.

13-16. (Developmental) Increase years of life of an HIV-infected person by extending the interval of time between an AIDS diagnosis and death.

AREA 19—NUTRITION AND OVERWEIGHT

Goal:
Promote health and reduce chronic disease associated with diet and weight.

Objectives:

Weight Status and Growth
19-1.   Increase the proportion of adults who are at a healthy weight.

19-2.   Reduce the proportion of adults who are obese.

19-3.   Reduce the proportion of children and adolescents who are overweight or obese.

Food and Nutrient Consumption
19-5.   Increase the proportion of persons aged 2 years and older who consume at least two daily servings of fruit.

19-6.   Increase the proportion of persons aged 2 years and older who consume at least three daily servings of vegetables, with at least one-third being dark green or orange vegetables.

19-7.   Increase the proportion of persons aged 2 years and older who consume at least six daily servings of grain products, with at least three being whole grains.

19-8.   Increase the proportion of persons aged 2 years and older who consume less than 10 percent of calories from saturated fat.

19-9.   Increase the proportion of persons aged 2 years and older who consume no more than 30 percent of calories from total fat.

19-10. Increase the proportion of persons aged 2 years and older who consume 2,400 mg or less of sodium daily.

19-11. Increase the proportion of persons aged 2 years and older who meet dietary recommendations for calcium.

Iron Deficiency and Anemia
19-12. Reduce iron deficiency among young children and females of childbearing age.

19-14. (Developmental) Reduce iron deficiency among pregnant females.

AREA 22—PHYSICAL ACTIVITY AND FITNESS

Goal:
Improve health, fitness, and quality of life through daily physical activity.

Objectives:

Physical Activity in Adults

22-1. Reduce the proportion of adults who engage in no leisure-time physical activity.

22-2. Increase the proportion of adults who engage regularly, preferably daily, in moderate physical activity for at least 30 minutes per day.

22-3. Increase the proportion of adults who engage in vigorous physical activity that promotes the development and maintenance of cardiorespiratory fitness 3 or more days per week for 20 or more minutes per occasion.

Muscular Strength/Endurance and Flexibility

22-4. Increase the proportion of adults who perform physical activities that enhance and maintain muscular strength and endurance.

22-5. Increase the proportion of adults who perform physical activities that enhance and maintain flexibility.

AREA 25—SEXUALLY TRANSMITTED DISEASES

Goal:

Promote responsible sexual behaviors, strengthen community capacity, and increase access to quality services to prevent sexually transmitted diseases (STDs) and their complications.

Objectives:

Bacterial STD Illness and Disability

25-1. Reduce the proportion of adolescents and young adults with Chlamydia trachomatis infections.

25-2. Reduce gonorrhea.

25-3. Eliminate sustained domestic transmission of primary and secondary syphilis.

Viral STD Illness and Disability

25-4. Reduce the proportion of adults with genital herpes infection.

25-5. (Developmental) Reduce the proportion of persons with human papillomavirus (HPV) infection.

STD Complications Affecting Females

25-6. Reduce the proportion of females who have ever required treatment for pelvic inflammatory disease (PID).

25-7. Reduce the proportion of childless females with fertility problems who have had a sexually transmitted disease or who have required treatment for pelvic inflammatory disease (PID).

25-8. (Developmental) Reduce HIV infections in adolescent and young adult females aged 13 to 24 years that are associated with heterosexual contact.

Personal Behaviors

25-11. Increase the proportion of adolescents who abstain from sexual intercourse or use condoms if currently sexually active.

AREA 27—TOBACCO USE

Goal:
Reduce illness, disability, and death related to tobacco use and exposed to second hand smoke.

Objectives:

Tobacco Use in Population Groups
27-1.   Reduce tobacco use by adults.
27-2.   Reduce tobacco use by adolescents.

Cessation and Treatment
27-5.   Increase smoking cessation attempts by adult smokers.
27-6.   Increase smoking cessation during pregnancy.

Exposure to Secondhand Smoke
27-9.   Reduce the proportion of children who are regularly exposed to tobacco smoke at home.
27-10. Reduce the proportion of nonsmokers exposed to environmental tobacco smoke.

To view the entire Healthy People 2010 document, visit www.healthypeople.gov.

U.S. Department of Health and Human Services. *Healthy People 2010: Understanding and Improving Health*. 2nd ed. Washington, DC: U.S. Government Printing Office, November 2000.

Healthy People 2010 Fact Sheet

All Americans have the opportunity to help build the nation's health agenda for the 21st Century. Developing the objectives for Healthy People 2010 offers individuals, private and voluntary organizations, businesses, and the public health community the opportunity to help define the critical measures the United States must undertake to promote healthy behaviors, achieve improved health outcomes, reduce risk factors, and assure access to preventive strategies and health services that can improve the health of all Americans.

The first set of national health targets was published in 1979 in *Healthy People: The Surgeon General's Report on Health Promotion and Disease Prevention*. Healthy People 2000, the second and current national prevention initiative, is the product of unprecedented collaboration among government, voluntary and professional organizations, businesses, and individuals. Healthy People's national targets have served as the basis for monitoring and tracking health status, health risks, and use of preventive services. Many states and localities have used the same process to guide local public health policy and program development.

Healthy People Homepage. More information about Healthy People 2010 developments and Healthy People 2000 activities are posted on the Internet at **http:// odphp.osophs.dhhs.gov/pubs/hp2000**. Also at this website is the guide *Developing Objectives for Healthy People 2010*, which describes the who, what, when and how of the 2010 development process. Included in this publication are the names of people in Federal and State agencies who coordinate Healthy People activities, as well as contact information for organizations that are members of the Healthy People Consortium.

Development of Objectives. There will be two separate public comment periods on Healthy People 2010. Comments will be accepted electronically at: **http:// web.health.gov/healthypeople**. Once the comment period closes, HHS work groups will develop the 2010 draft.

A second public comment on the draft Healthy People 2010 document is scheduled for fall of 1998. Publication of *Healthy People 2010* is slated for early in 2000.

For more information about Healthy People 2010, contact the Office of Disease Prevention and Health Promotion, Room 738G, Hubert Humphrey Building, 200 Independence Avenue, S.W., Washington, DC 20201 at (202) 205-8583.

Proposed Healthy People 2010 Framework

Vision of 2010: Healthy People in Healthy Communities

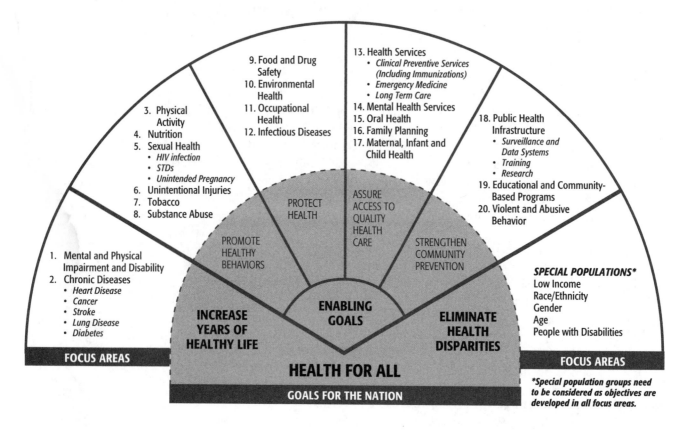

Appendix E: Healthy People 2010 Fact Sheet

Index